Margaret Kornfeld
Cultivating Wholeness

A Guide to Care and Counseling in Faith Communities

A comprehensive and innovative approach to pastoral care and counseling

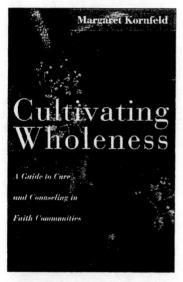

400pp 0-8264-1064-2 $29.50 hbd
Continuum August
Religion

Commissioned by the Blanton-Peale Institute, *Cultivating Wholeness* is a practical, comprehensive, and contemporary guide to community care and counseling. Its aim is to prepare those who would help all who suffer emotionally. Its emphases on the dynamics of change, on wholeness, and on community as not only the context for healing but the means by which healing happens, on an inclusive understanding of spirituality, and on the caregiver/counselor who these days is as likely to be a lay person as a member of the clergy — all place the book on the leading edge of its field.

> *"The best book on pastoral care and counseling in scope and specifics with which I am acquainted."* — DR. JAMES ASHBROOK, Professor Emeritus, Garrett-Evangelical Seminary

> *"At once psychiatrically sound, methodologically useful, spiritual, poetic, and philosophical. Well-referenced sources range from the classics in human development to the latest resources for theory and practice. The reader receives instruction through concrete examples, informed by pastoral care and brief therapy techniques."* — JANE SIMON, M.D., Medical Director Blanton-Peale Counseling Center

Margaret Kornfeld is a faculty member of Blanton-Peale Institute of Religion and Health's graduate residency program. She is a diplomate of the American Association of Pastoral Counselors and a certified marriage and family therapist. She is a minister of the Baptist Churches of the U.S.A. and has been a pastoral psychotherapist for almost 30 years.

KEY FEATURES

- A text for pastoral care specialists and seminary pastoral counseling courses.

- A resource for all clergy and lay readers in community and all professionals, whether therapists, social workers, or medical practitioners.

- Foreword by Ruth Stafford Peale and James C. Wyrtzen.

Cultivating
Wholeness

Cultivating Wholeness

*A Guide to Care and
Counseling in
Faith Communities*

Margaret Zipse Kornfeld

for Blanton–Peale Institutes

*A Giniger Book
published in association with*
Continuum   •   New York

1998

The Continuum Publishing Company
370 Lexington Avenue, New York, NY 10017

Published in association with the K. S. Giniger Company, Inc.
250 West 57th Street, New York, NY 10107

Printed in the United States of America

Library of Congress Cataloging-in-Publication Data
ISBN 0-8264-????-?

Scripture quotations unless otherwise noted are from the New Revised Standard Version Bible, copyright 1989 by the Division of Christian Education of the National Council of the Churches of Christ in the United States.

In the interest of protecting confidentiality, all clinical vignettes have been created by Margaret Zipse Kornfeld. In making this synthesis, she has drawn upon her experience as a member of healing communities, a teacher of seminarians at Union Theological Seminary (NYC), a teacher and supervisor of pastoral counselors at Blanton-Peale and thirty years of clinical experience with lay and ordained community caregivers. The only "real people" in the book are her friend Pamela Chamberlain Dollarhide — who is "Pam and Elizabeth" in the stories about death and dying and the members of the Judson AIDS Support Group — to which she belonged. The vignette about the cancer care group is largely based on the work of the Rev. Lee Hancock and the Cancer Care Group that she developed at Judson Memorial Church and that later was led by the Rev. Regina Harding.

To the Blanton-Peale community
who invited this book to emerge
and to my family — Larry, Sarah, and Scott —
whose love and support have grounded me

Contents

Prefaces

Norman Vincent Peale, my husband, became pastor of a Fifth Avenue Church in New York City at the time of the Great Depression in the 1930s. People were losing their jobs, their homes, their savings, and they were distraught. Many of them came to him with their troubles.

He soon wondered if his advice was adequate and correct. Did he always get to the root of the trouble in his counseling? In his seminary training there had been no mention of psychiatry. But wasn't knowledge of the psyche desperately needed?

He went to the head of the New York Medical Society and asked if there was a psychiatrist who would be willing to work with a pastor in helping people. The doctor was skeptical. Finally, he brought Dr. Smiley Blanton to Norman.

Dr. Blanton's first question was, "Do you believe in prayer?" And he continued, "I have been praying for years that some pastor would believe that a pastor and a psychiatrist could work together to get people well."

Thus, in 1937 the Blanton-Peale Institute was founded. Today, though those two great men are no longer with us, the impact of their partnership lives on at Blanton-Peale, a vibrant, growing community focused on teaching clergy and lay caregivers of all denominations — priests, rabbis, nuns, ministers and laymen — to help people reach their potential of psyche and soul.

It was at Blanton-Peale that author Margaret Kornfeld studied and developed her great sensitivity, and even greater insight, into ways of helping all people make the most of their lives. This book, *Cultivating Wholeness,* is the distillation of all she has learned spiritually and intellectually. Her reason for writing such a valuable book is quite simple: to help everyone, both professional caregivers and interested laymen, to develop the skills to be healthy and whole themselves and to share that wholeness with their communities.

Anyone can benefit from this book, for it touches, in simple, straightforward words, the very roots of our being, and proves how we can heal ourselves — and others — using the skills and wisdom of spirituality and psychology. It's truly a book for everyone who cares about caring — on whatever level!

Ruth Stafford Peale

A Pastoral Psychotherapist's Perspective

Ever since Dr. Norman Vincent Peale and Dr. Smiley Blanton joined forces to develop pastoral care, counseling, and psychotherapy services provided through the religious community, we have been dedicated to training ministers, priests, nuns, rabbis, and religious and lay ministers to lead congregations as healing communities. Margaret Kornfeld has now given us a book to guide us through this important ministry.

But *Cultivating Wholeness* is more than that: it will assist everyone interested in helping human beings who suffer. People today are hungry for spiritual and emotional growth. They do not separate these into neat divisions, but rather expect a psychologically healthy spiritual experience in their faith community.

This is a book about change: how it happens — for individuals, families and communities — what creates the possibilities for it, what impedes it, the environment in which it happens, and the different types of change we can experience. It also gives us a clear model for the kind of counseling that a clergyperson or lay minister is called upon to do and how to apply this model to the different life-cycle experiences the reader encounters. At the same time, the reader is not locked into one school of thought, but is introduced to different approaches applied to different situations.

Dr. Kornfeld's metaphor of the garden is a beautiful way to look at the community as a force for health. It opens us up to today's paradigmatic shift toward holistic approaches to life and community. Her book is an interesting and edifying "read" as well as a reference source that clergy and laypeople can refer to again and again as they approach the concerns, frustrations, and pain of those with whom they minister. It is not limited to individual healing but shows how our communities can be healthy places. She helps us to see how each of us can use ourselves as healer, knowing our limitations, and joining where God is healing.

I am deeply grateful that Margaret has shared the depth of her person, her wide knowledge and understanding with all of us who believe that, with proper care and guidance, the human spirit can reach its God-given potential.

James C. Wyrtzen, D. Min.
Director, Blanton-Peale Graduate Institute
Former President, American Association of Pastoral Counselors

A Psychiatrist's Perspective

Drs. Blanton and Peale already knew what today's neurologists, molecular biologists, geneticists, psychiatrists, and others are discovering: body, mind, and spirit are united, even in our cells. Research is documenting the physiological benefits of positive thinking. This knowledge base is permeating our belief systems. It is in the context of this paradigm shift that *Cultivating Whole-*

ness is written. It is also written out of the principles of holism that are the foundation of Blanton-Peale's programs. Margaret Kornfeld draws on Norman Vincent Peale's revolutionary idea: the science of psychiatry and the faith of religion, *together,* can ease human suffering.

It was a revolutionary concept because at that time in the history of psychotherapy, most therapists were highly suspicious of religion and most clergy believed that psychiatrists were in cahoots with the devil. But Dr. Peale, honest enough to admit his own counseling need and courageous enough to reach for the best answers, brought his idea to fruition in 1937. Through medical contacts, he was introduced to Dr. Smiley Blanton, a psychiatrist trained by Freud, who was known for his high professional standards and his deep appreciation of the spiritual dimension. Peale and Blanton became close personal friends. Together, at Marble Collegiate Church, they offered counseling, informally at first, then added training for others to carry on their work, and gradually adopted a strong structure that endures to this day.

Dr. Blanton was a unique person: short of stature, pugnacious, a Tennessee mountain boy, an amateur boxer, a teacher of Shakespeare at Vassar. Educated at Vanderbilt, Harvard, and Cornell University Medical School, he documented his experience with Freud in *Diary of My Analysis with Sigmund Freud.* A core of wisdom was evident early in his life.

When he was only eight years old, he found a church that did not meet his family's approval, and he experienced the pain of their rejection. He could not understand their feelings or their thinking, they seemed so set in their narrow beliefs, setting one church against another. From that experience, Smiley maintained a healthy skepticism toward such "man-made disciplines." Although spiritual concerns motivated him, he did not join a formal church until he was sixty years old.

Smiley Blanton's appreciation of the pain and struggle of his patients, so deeply shared by Dr. Peale, plus his healthy iconoclasm and constant curiosity, set the stage for our current work. At Blanton-Peale, individuals can explore all aspects of their lives, including their philosophical, religious, and spiritual beliefs, with the aim of meeting their fullest human potential.

Blanton-Peale has grown to meet the changes of our "global village." Students come from all over the world, from heterogeneous religiospiritual backgrounds and traditions. Many return to their countries of origin where they, in turn, train others.

Positive change comes from the therapeutic relationship. Care is a key component of this relationship. Everyone who comes to Blanton-Peale, be it as student or as patient in one of our counseling centers, leaves with the sense of having been profoundly affected and positively changed by the caring experience.

Margaret Kornfeld has given us a lucidly written learning tool. It is at once psychiatrically sound, methodologically useful, spiritual, poetic, and philosophical. Well-referenced sources range from the classics in human development and psychotherapy to the latest resources for theory and practice. The reader receives instruction through concrete examples, informed by pastoral care and brief therapy techniques. Thorough and comprehensive, *Cultivating Wholeness* includes advice to counselors in congregations on how to attend to their own emotional needs as they engage in the intricate tasks of pastoral ministry. The author's years of teaching, experience, and wisdom shine through every chapter.

Jane Simon, M.D.
Medical Director Blanton-Peale Counseling Center

A Pastor's Perspective

Cultivating Wholeness is a beautifully articulated statement on mental health and healing. It recognizes the remarkable insights by the French scientist and mystic Teilhard de Chardin: that we are not human beings having a spiritual experience but spiritual beings having a human experience. Teilhard reframes reality for us; Margaret Kornfeld draws upon his understanding and helps clergy and laity apply these insights in practical ministry.

After college, because of my own interest in healing and religion, I was drawn to New York's Union Theological Seminary. Part of the excitement was that Union was the first seminary anywhere to have a psychiatrist on its faculty. There was, of course, criticism among students — and some of the faculty — that a mental health expert should have a place beside experts in the mysteries of the spirit. To this novice, who was as fascinated with my own psychology as with the appeal of the spirit, a psychiatrist next to a theologian made sense. It was a right next step.

The psychiatrist was Dr. Earl Loomis. During the question and answer period following a well-attended opening lecture, a student raised a question about Norman Vincent Peale, phrasing it in a way that he hoped would bring criticism of the famous minister. Dr. Loomis refused the bait and said that were it not for Norman Vincent Peale and his collaboration with Dr. Smiley Blanton, he, Earl Loomis, would not be at this prestigious seminary. He added that these two men were the first to bring religion and psychiatry not only into dialogue but into a close working relationship.

Several years later I took a course for pastors at Blanton-Peale Institute, then known as the American Foundation for Religion and Psychiatry. At the height of popular criticism of Norman Vincent Peale for not preaching enough about sin, Dr. Peale expounded to me, a young and impressionable minister-to-be, what he thought of the criticism. He said, "It hurts to be criticized like this. Maybe they are right, but the way I look at it, everybody who comes through the door of my church is broken, and most are broken by sin. And I don't need to remind them."

I understand his use of the word "sin" to be like that of Jesus — that sin really is missing the mark. Dr. Peale then added, "My task is to help them out of their sin and up to their potential." That was his philosophy of ministry, which was demonstrated in his preaching and writing, and in the work of the institute he cofounded.

I have since learned, in my ministry and most particularly in my own journey and struggle to be whole, that spiritual growth and freedom depend in large part on psychological health. Unless we deal with the internal forces that compel and drive us toward self-destructive and self-defeating behavior, we will stay stuck and continue in troubled living, which doesn't have to be.

If this is so, and I believe it is, then the God who created the universe and the wonderfully complex human being did so in order for the soul to have a growth experience in the mode we know as human. It is therefore imperative that the persons who are called to care for the soul also know how to care for the mind and the emotions.

Cultivating Wholeness not only shows how to help the mind and the emotions function more fully, it also shows clergy, and *all* who are counseling in congregations and communities, how best to deal with those who suffer emotionally. Every minister, of whatever persuasion, should read and internalize this book in order to serve the Lord by serving the human family.

And every human being could benefit from this book. It gives the reader deep insight and practical guidance on how to untie those internal knots that constrict and prevent us from becoming the people God dreamed us to be.

Arthur Caliandro, D. Min.
Senior Minister Marble Collegiate Church

Acknowledgments

I am grateful to Kenneth Giniger, great friend and editor of Norman Vincent Peale, who challenged the Blanton-Peale faculty to tell its story. I thank Ken — on behalf of Blanton-Peale — for his seasoned ability to "know a good story" and for bringing this work to fruition.

In response to this challenge and through an extensive communal process, I was asked to give voice to a book that would be helpful to religious communities and that would reflect Blanton-Peale's philosophy. I was to speak as an individual — but to write the book *for* the community: both on behalf of Blanton-Peale and for its pastoral care students. In order to write on behalf of Blanton-Peale I have shared the manuscript with faculty who then have been in dialogue with me about its content. They, in turn, tested it for clarity and usefulness, using portions of it in teaching. I have also tested material with Blanton-Peale Residents and Union Theological Seminary students. This manuscript is an outgrowth of lectures I have given over the years in the Introduction to Pastoral Counseling course at Union Theological Seminary. I am grateful to my Union students who have taught me much by their openness to the Spirit and their insistence on honesty.

I have been enriched by this writing project. This book has been written, and revised and reshaped, by many conversations and Faxes. I hope I have done a "good enough" job of telling the Blanton-Peale story — not in narrative form, but by showing what we do as we teach pastoral ministry through our holistic point of view. Although I have had "a lot of help from my friends," I take responsibility for the final product — hoping that I have been faithful.

I have been given great support and encouragement by Blanton-Peale's Chief Executive Officer, Anne Impellizzeri; Director of Training James Wyrtzen, and Board of Trustees Chairman John Allen. Not only did they give me loving encouragement, but they took the time to read the manuscript reflectively, giving insight and editorial comments. The supportive voice of the Blanton-Peale Community was also heard in the Introduction, for which I want to thank Ruth Stafford Peale, Jim Wyrtzen, Jane Simon, M.D., and

Arthur Caliandro. As an alumna of Blanton-Peale, I am grateful that the vision of Normal Vincent Peale and Smiley Blanton is continuing to be lived out under their leadership.

I thank Blanton-Peale graduates Mary Cattan and Regina Fredrickson for their contribution to the solution-focused material. I am grateful to the Pastoral Care Program, directed by Paul Hamilton, and faculty members David Assomanig, Marta Green, Gretchen Janssen, Charles Mayer, Catherine Morrisett, Beverly Musgrave, Rebecca Radillo, and David Wells for this collegial experience. I have also benefited from the response of Blanton-Peale Graduate Institute faculty — Drs. Jean Bailey, Thelma Dixon Murphy and Jim Murphy, M.D.

I am indebted to friends who have critiqued the material through their eyes as spiritually wise teachers. I give particular thanks to Lee Hancock, Marie McCarthy, Sarah Rieth, and Charles Mayer.

Because I wanted this book to be truly useful to religious communities, I have also asked friends in ministry to read the manuscript and to give me feedback. I am grateful to my friends The Reverends Louise Green, Ronald Harris, Ann Halstein, Lee Hancock, Peter Laarman, Sue Maybeck, and Dan Shenk, Rabbi Ellen Lewis and theological educator Maureen Weeks, and to the staff of the Samaritan Counseling Center in Ambler, PA. I am grateful to the staff of Calvary St. George Episcopal Parish in New York City — where I am a member of its "healing team." I am very indebted to Calvary's Vicar, Stephen Garmey, for his critical editorial eye, his wisdom, and his loving friendship.

I thank my colleagues with whom I practice in pastoral counseling ministry, David Robb, pastoral psychotherapist, and Renee Gorin, movement therapist, who read the manuscript, listening for authenticity. I am grateful to Renee who has taught me the meaning of "embodiment": of a spirituality that isn't fancy — but is rooted in movement and centeredness.

I also relied on the perspectives of pastoral psychotherapist friends who read versions of the manuscript and helped me think about pastoral ministry, using a wide lens. I thank Reginald Burgess, Larry Graham, Charles Lindner, Mary Ragan, Chris Schlauch, and Mike Woodruff, AAPC's legal counsel. I give heartfelt thanks to Han van den Blink and the Eastern Region of the American Association of Pastoral Counselors who have taught me much about collegial leadership in community.

Dan Gallagher is given special thanks for his patience in helping me move toward a more solution-building approach. I have learned about the solution-focused method from him in his workshop and from his careful reading and helpful suggestions for this manuscript.

I want to acknowledge particularly the contribution of James Ashbrook to this work. In reading it you have noticed how seminal some of his ideas have been to the text. Dr. Ashbrook, Blanton-Peale's first graduate, has committed himself to more completely understanding the unity of the body, mind, and soul — both as metaphor and physical reality. His ideas and person have enriched the pastoral counseling and theology field. I am personally grateful to him.

I have also been blessed with other smart and honest friends who have critically and lovingly read the manuscript and who have helped it grow. Thanks to Bob Parkin, M.D., and Bill Sykes, M.D., psychiatrists, mentors and friends, and to Jane Ciabattari, Gretchen Haight, Amy Hotch, Jane Lucas, and Micala Sidore — friends who write and are wise.

I thank my Continuum editor, Frank Oveis, for embracing this project and for including my friend and editor, Sally Arteseros. Sally has cultivated the manuscript, giving it more clarity. Her loving faith has kept me going.

John McNeill and Charles Chiarrelli are given my most loving gratitude. This book was written at their cottage on Starlight Lake. There, John and Charlie, my husband, Larry, and I spent many Sundays eating, laughing, and then reading this manuscript and John's *Freedom Glorious Freedom.* Larry's and Charlie's responses were wise and to the point. John and I learned from them and from each other. Because John McNeill had been writing his book out of a profound spiritual place, my spirit was touched as well. John McNeill's influence is now in the book. I also want to thank my generous friends, Jack and Judy McMahon, whose frequent hospitality at the Inn at Starlight Lake renewed me.

For much of the content of the book I have drawn on my own good fortune — I have had rich experience in community. My family in Colorado has been strong. I am grateful to my late parents, Evelyn and Clarence Zipse, and my sister, Kathy Forsman, as well as a loving extended family, for giving me a secure base. I have been a member of vital religious communities — The First Baptist Churches of Grand Junction, Colorado, and Ottawa, Kansas. Roger Fredrickson, minister of the Ottawa church was particularly concerned about the development of intentional communities and our midwestern church came in contact with the church universal. For five years I served on the staff of Mariners Temple Baptist Church in New York City — where I served my true apprenticeship in ministry. Senior Minister George Younger, the team ministry and the congregation were my teachers. For over thirty years I have been a member of Judson Memorial Church, a community that struggles authentically to serve God and the world. It was in Judson Church that I was ordained an American Baptist minister. Through my husband's membership, I have been a sojourner in the Fifteenth Street meeting of The Religious Society of Friends (Quakers). I have also been a part of the supportive community of those living and dying with AIDS. It is to those community experiences — and all my teachers in them — that I am deeply grateful. It is out of those experiences that I write.

And leaving the best to the last. It is to my daughter, Sarah, and my husband, Larry, that I now turn to say "thank you." Sarah's gentle question, "Mom, why don't you write a book?" and my reflection on it, made me open to saying "yes" when asked to do this project. Without Larry this book would

not have happened! He made it possible in ways only he and I will know —
and through the editing, cooking, cheerleading, and organizing that others
saw him do. To him I give my deepest thanks.

Margaret Zipse Kornfeld, D. Min.
Starlight Lake, Pennsylvania

PART I

Support Change:
Be a Gardener

Be a gardener.
Dig a ditch
toil and sweat,
and turn the earth upside down
and seek the deepness
and water the plants in time.
Continue this labor
And make sweet floods to run
and noble and abundant fruits to spring.
Take this food and drink
and carry it to God
as your true worship.

—Julian of Norwich[1]

In a Time of Change

Ice mountain melted
ages ago
*   and made this ridge,*
this place of changes.

Now we are rooted in it,
*   we of the old ones*
*   we of the new ones from afar;*
oatgrass meadow, douglas fir thicket,
we are rooted in the ridge of changes in the time of
*   changes.*
The winds carry strange smells; this is a day of change.

Chinook Psalter[1]

"This is a day of change." Change is all around us. Some of it feels good: we are living longer, healthier lives because of the gifts of science and technology.

Some changes make us anxious: the shape of work is being transformed by new technologies and enormous shifts in the global economy. We are unsure about our future: will social security be there for us? How are the alterations in medical insurance and health-care delivery going to affect us? Other changes challenge us to *think* in new ways.

There are those of us who are uprooted in this time of change. Some are uprooted as we move to look for different work, others are spiritually uprooted. We yearn for the spiritual security spoken of in the Chinook Psalter: "We are rooted in the ridge of changes in the time of changes." We are looking for God in the midst of change itself.

Others of us are yearning for change that transforms: we are stuck in ourselves. We wish to be moved, to feel alive, to be whole.

Many of us are drawn to churches, synagogues, and other religious communities because we are seeking a place where we can put down our roots and be supported, even as we are changing. We are seeking personal transformation and nurture for our souls.

Today we have an opportunity to become more available to deep religious experience because of a significant change that is happening in our culture. A reflection of this change, but not in itself the cause, is the growing number of people who are becoming *conscious of soul and emerging community*.

In our time, more and more people are becoming actively engaged with their spiritual lives. Several years ago this interest in spirituality was seen by some as "new age" and was criticized as narcissistic self-absorption. However, it is now apparent that interest in matters of the soul is shared by active members of faith groups, by people whose religious practice has lapsed, by those who have no formal religious training or belief.

All kinds of people are being drawn to their inner lives and are finding God there. Some speak of this as inner work, or soul work; others speak of being on a spiritual journey. Some meditate, some write in journals, some pray. The practice of soul work takes many forms. For some it is private and isolated, or it may take place in workshops, retreats, or with spiritual directors. For some it is with groups studying the Bible or other sacred texts. For some, it is in the company of traditional Christian, Jewish, or Islamic congregations; for others it is through the teaching and practice of other ancient religious or spiritual traditions.

Another sign of an underlying change is the emergence of new kinds of community. Although many religious, neighborhood, and work communities are changing and often disappearing, in the last fifty years an enormous number of *communities of care* have been formed. Some, like Twelve Step and other recovery and growth groups, are based on the principles of non-hierarchical, mutual helpfulness. Other communities of care are found in neighborhood action and outreach groups, services for the homeless, AIDS groups, etc. In these groups millions have experienced love in action.

Computer technology is contributing to the strength of human communities. Many families, friends, and associations stay in contact and their bonds are strengthened through using E-mail and Fax. However, this technology is more than a facilitator of community. It has *become* a community.

The cyberspace community has millions of members gathered in enclaves of interest groups, technologies, and associations. Through this technology, relationships are formed, information is freely exchanged and services are obtained. Its users experience a sense of connection both to its cerebral resources and to other users. Those using the Net often feel empowered through the information they obtain and the connections they make.

While the possibility of Internet addiction might be a cause for concern, its widespread use points to the needs it fulfills: people want direct access to information, empowerment, connection, and networking. Because the Net moves beyond the boundaries of race, age, geography, and gender, the world is larger for those who use it.

People are engaged in their spiritual lives or are drawn to communities of cyberspace and human interaction because of their *felt needs*. They are also open to them because of the very way they view the world.

A New Way of Seeing

In our lifetime, scientists, philosophers, theologians, and other adventurous minds have been making startling new discoveries, occasioning a new way of seeing. Their discoveries of the unity of body-mind-soul and of our connection to each other and the universe have not merely given us new facts, ideas, and theories, but are transforming our consciousness. Our perception is changing.

Because we are living in the midst of it, it is hard for us to comprehend that this is a time in history just as momentous as that time when Copernicus promulgated his theory that the Earth was not the center of the universe.

To see these changes better, we need to remember that in the time of the Scientific Era which has just preceded us, people believed (and many still do) that mind, body, and soul were separate. Indeed, dualism, that intellectual system that separates spirit and matter, is still at the core of most contemporary scientific thinking. Because of this dualistic belief there developed a division of labor and power in which physicists investigated matter while psychologists looked at the mind, doctors treated the body, and clergy watched over the soul.

In the process of this fragmentation, religious practice was moved to the periphery of ordinary life. Clergy's most important role became that of preparing others for the hereafter. By the eighteenth century educated people in the West thought that God, too, had gone away from the world he created. Sharing the view of science, they believed that the orderly universe was like a complex, well-oiled machine that ran perfectly by itself according to immutable laws. The machine no longer needed God's supervision.[2]

Before the birth of this scientific revolution — which ushered in the modern era — it was religious views that had the upper hand in the Western world. The world was very much understood through the eyes of theology. Theology had already created its own dualism: The soul was supreme; the body was inferior; they were separate. The dualistic ideas of the scientific revolution were simply added on to these earlier distortions of our wholeness.

There has been a profound downside to the belief that when God created the world, he made a Perfect Machine and then went off and let it run by itself. However, we have also been blessed by many of the fruits of the Scientific Era. Because scientists have studied in depth the particularity of matter, we know more about the parts that make up the whole. It was while going into the depths of the smallest particles of matter that scientists also explored the mysteries of the expanding universe. Specializing has been necessary. Because of it we can know ourselves and our world in more depth.

Specialized ministries have also contributed to the movement away from dualism. While scientists were investigating the particularity of matter, many in ministry were clinically studying the relationship of the soul to mind and body. Often this was done in hospital settings. Since the middle nineteen thirties, ministers, priests, rabbis, and lay ministers have participated in Clinical Pastoral Education (CPE) in the course of their theological studies. Through this training, they learned the art of hospital chaplaincy and also contributed to the movement that has done much to humanize hospital care and to help lay the foundation for a new understanding of integration and wholeness.

The American pastoral counseling movement has also contributed to an understanding of holism. Sixty years ago, pastoral counseling training was organized to train clergy to counsel more effectively in their congregations. Over the course of time, pastoral counseling has evolved into an adjunctive profession based on the theoretical premise that body, mind, and soul are indeed united and that psychological healing is rooted in spiritual principles. Pastoral counselors have been accumulating clinical data that supports the growing awareness of holism.

At the time when scientists and mathematicians were discovering new mysteries of time and space, Martin Buber, Jewish mystic and scholar, was inquiring about the relationship of God to man. Just as scientists were sensing the interrelatedness of matter and being, Buber, through his spiritual investigation, also was asking about time and space and was seeking to understand people's relationship to God and to each other. In his classic work, *I and Thou*, Buber writes that people can live together in time and space because of our relationship to God who is at our Center. Through this relationship, community is formed. Buber says that because of our relationship to God at the Center, we are connected to each other. However, it is not the community members' connection to each other that comes first, but the quality of relation with the Center. He writes, "This alone guarantees the authentic existence of the community."[3]

Scientists have been opening our eyes to our place in an expanding universe. They have also discovered, through studying the smallest cells of our bodies, how our brains and neurochemical systems allow us not only to think but to feel. As our very bodies strive to understand and make meaning of our lives, these systems also allow us to experience soul. Mystics like Martin Buber have taught us that through our relationship to God, we are connected to each other, and that we need community that supports us as we dwell in time and space.

Change and Transformation

Today there is growing popular acceptance of the reality of mind-body-soul unity. Although dualistic thinking remains and righteous battles are still being fought over professional and other power turfs (doctors are still body experts; theologians still speak with religious expertise), there is growing public acknowledgment, supported by research, that the body and the inner experiences of mind, emotion, and spirit are inextricably related. An example of this is a research report of a group monitoring a managed health-care company that found that 70 percent of all medical visits were related to a psychological concern.[4]

Many ordinary people are now consciously aware of their own mind-body connections. They know that when they have the flu, not just their bodies, but their very selves are affected. They also know that when under a lot of stress, they are more susceptible to the flu; that when they've been exercising, not only do their muscles feel stretched, but their mood is better. They know that when they are experiencing spiritual hopelessness, they have feelings of clinical depression.[5]

Our growing acceptance of the unity of body-mind-soul is a paradigmatic shift. The term "paradigmatic shift" was coined by Thomas S. Kuhn, who defines paradigm as "an entire constellation of beliefs, values, techniques, and so on shared by the members of a given community."[6]

The idea of a paradigm shift is not new to us. Christians know it to be at the heart of Jesus' teaching. Jews know it from Moses, and Moslems from Mohammed. Jesus' teaching provoked a change in an entire belief system. His good news was like new wine. People could not accept his message without their actions and feelings changing as well. Seeing life through Jesus' eyes caused *everything* to look new. This is what Jesus meant when he said:

> And no one puts new wine into old wine skins; otherwise, the wine
> will burst the skins, and the wine is lost, and so are the skins; but one
> puts new wine into fresh wineskins. Mark 2:22.

Jesus taught that there can be no significant change in the human spirit without changing the world around us: a radical paradigm shift.

Paul Watzlawick and his colleagues John Weakland and Richard Fisch of the Mental Research Institute in Palo Alto, California, have studied how people change. They discovered that people make two types of changes: *first order change, and second order change.* In first order change, people adjust to their present situation. They learn to function better, *but their basic situation does not change.* A second order change is a paradigmatic shift in which a whole constellation of beliefs, attitudes, and actions are altered because of a new perception of reality. In second order change, *a whole system is changed.*[7]

Most of us have experienced second order change. If we are parents we certainly have. When a first child is born into a family, parents experience a complete change. It is not simply that where there were two there are now three. With the presence of the child, *everything* seems different. The space of the house is seen differently. The relationship of the parents to each other —

and to their own parents — shifts. Suddenly there seem to be more babies in the world because the parents are *seeing babies.*

Second order change can occur when one falls in love, or when a minister is ordained, or when one changes professions or receives a diagnosis of serious illness. Second order change occurs in religious conversion: St. Paul's experience on the Damascus road was a second order change. Second order change is transformation.

Second order change can also come through insight. For example, through counseling, a wife becomes aware of her contribution to a spouse's alcoholism. She sees her part in it. Through her awareness, she experiences a complete change. It is as if she has gone into another room. She is in a new place. She has become conscious of her habit of collusion. She thinks before she acts. Her behavior changes. She begins to pay attention to herself rather than to become preoccupied with her husband. She treats her children differently. She has her own life. She experiences *second order* change. Before opening to this awareness, she had made *first order* changes. She had been busy rearranging the situation. She nagged her husband, she made excuses for him, she paid his credit card bills. She made changes within the system of his alcoholism and her collusion. Sometimes her activity caused her husband to drink less for a while, producing a modification within the system. However, the system itself was fundamentally altered when she changed.

Today, as in the time of Jesus, people yearn for profound change and they look to the traditional healers for help: doctors for their bodies, clergy for their souls. Because doctors, clergy, psychologists, and medical and biological researchers are beginning to share information and to network with each other, their perceptions and assumptions are changing. The healing professions are on the brink of beginning to respond to people's need in a new, nondualistic manner.

Through sharing experience with others in the healing arts, many of us who are paying attention have been learning that there is more to being well than just the removal of symptoms. We are learning that to be healthy does not mean to be symptom-free. We are learning that health is not just the opposite of illness: health is the consciousness of one's wholeness — and that means accepting one's limitations as well as one's strengths. We are also learning that we can become aware of our wholeness and still die. We can experience "health" and well-being even though our bodies might have conditions labeled "terminal illness."

This understanding of wholeness accepts death as a part of life. When viewed through this understanding, people are not made to feel guilty because they are sick or dying. If those who are terminally ill believe that death is "acceptable," they will be able to relax, to let go of tension, and to truly live until they die. This new understanding can make it possible for us not to split off our negative experience of the fear of death and project it onto others — whether the "others" are individuals or groups or nations.

Now, to be sure, *change in itself* will not make individuals experience their wholeness. However, cultural acceptance of the reality of integration of mind, body, and soul will support the journey to wholeness and help us move away from the old dualism that reinforces fragmentation.

Many of the people seeking care and counseling are, in some way, aware of this new consciousness and are hungry for deep healing. Some are emotionally or physically ill, others do not experience themselves as ill, but suffer from a sense of emptiness, loneliness, or confusion. Some know their fragmentation, and they experience the pull of conflict. Some feel life to be meaningless. Others are driven by compulsions or are controlled by phobias or addictions.

These people are not looking merely for first order change. They do not want simply to adjust or accommodate to the status quo. They want to be whole. They want awareness of second order change.

New Wine for New Wineskins

The truth of the many discoveries of the interconnection of mind-body-soul has been filtering into the culture, unsettling it, freeing it, healing it. This paradigmatic shift is not actually about a new fact or theory or idea, it is about the *transformation* of consciousness. Although we see something new, we are really discerning a transforming unity that has always been possible for humankind.

This unity was once actually known. The ancient near-eastern people knew it. Those who have studied the Hebrew Bible have learned about the Hebrew concept of the *corporate personality:* the properties of mind and soul are encoded in the Hebrew names of body parts. So *ruah,* "breath." also meant "spirit" — including the Spirit of Yahweh. And *leb,* "heart," also meant "understanding." One thought with one's heart. In ancient stories of the Hebrew people we learn how the children of Jacob, who went down to Egypt to beseech their brother, Joseph, were not individuals, but were the tribes of Israel. Just as body-mind-soul were one, so were people experienced as being one with each other. Ancient far-eastern people also shared this understanding. Like the Hebrew, the Chinese word for breath, *chi,* means "spirit."

Our growing awareness of holism is causing us to reassess our attitude toward beliefs we have dismissed as "primitive." We are now appreciating that the people of Africa, for instance, intuited the Life Force in all of creation in a manner that was a precursor of modern physics. As African-Americans are rediscovering their roots, they have the possibility of embracing a more holistic approach to living. We can also find this wisdom in Native American beliefs.

Because modern Western culture has trained us to think dualistically, theologians of all faiths have interpreted their religious beliefs from this fragmented perspective. But with the paradigmatic shift, we can begin to see with new insight. Each faith community can rediscover its tradition's basic religious truths, truths that were originally perceived from a more holistic position.

For example, through this awakened perspective Christians can look at the message of Jesus in a fresh way and see how clearly he understood our integrated selves. Jesus recognized that inner experience could create physical illness. Much of his healing involved casting out "unclean spirits" so that those who had been ill could be filled with new life (Mark 1:23). He also recognized that sinful behavior and illness can go together: he first forgave a paralyzed man's sins, then healed him (Mark 2:5–12). Jesus affirmed the power of prayer and religious belief — people were made well through their faith (Mark 5:34).

Jesus' message was the good news that the Kingdom of God has come near — *now*. Although he called people to repent, all people were loved by God. The new wine that Jesus spoke of was life lived in a fresh way in the present; the new wineskin was the *new context* in which life was lived.

Jesus spoke about the need to put new wine into new wineskins in response to the criticism that he sat down to eat with tax collectors and sinners. Jesus responded that he had come to be the physician not to righteous people, but to those who were sick. He was creating a new community — new wineskin — made up of *diverse* people. This new community was to be a "new family" composed of anyone who does the will of God (Mark 3:35).

Becoming aware of our wholeness is good news, and it leads us to community. Just as God holds the wholeness of Creation, our connections to each other hold and sustain us. Our healthy communities can hold us, nurture us and change us. And dysfunctional communities can harm us. In this time of change, faith communities are being challenged to become authentic places where members can experience their wholeness. Because religious communities and their members are functioning in the natural transitions of life, they can use their experiences for healing past wounds as well as for supporting growth. Communities also can be the holding ground where they can help their members discover their own solutions to problems and conflicts.

Be a Gardener

The medieval mystic Julian of Norwich understood the metaphor of "gardener" as an expression of ministry. We would like to suggest this image for ourselves today.

A gardener, like a community's counselor and caregiver, has a twofold task. Gardeners must tend to the ground as well as cultivate the plants growing in the ground. The gardener does not make the plants grow, God does. The gardener attends to their growth as the plants become what they are meant to be.

We are like gardeners when, as we continue to tend to ourselves, we tend to others in all of the seasons of life. Our care and counseling grow out of *our participation* with others in the natural events of life: marriage, birth, coming of age, death, illness, and all the normal life crises. Our care and counseling also occur when life goes awry. Then we must find ways to help people deal with the extraordinary.

Sometimes, also like gardeners, there is nothing much we can do to "fix" a situation. Often when counseling people who are experiencing grave loss, we can only be with them. We have to learn to accept our limitations and to develop patience. Often we cannot know the effect our accepting attitude or simply our presence has. We may feel ineffective, only to learn that in a caring session a seed was planted that much later bore fruit.

"Gardener," like any metaphor, has its limitations. We do not "tend" people as though they are objects to be acted upon. Counseling is always the healing *interaction* between counselee and counselor. Both we and counselees are rooted in the same ground because we are sustained by the same community. We both draw upon the spiritual resources of the community.

Much pastoral theory and technique involves one-to-one, and sometimes couple or family situations. However, in faith communities it is not only the religious or lay professional who supports change. The community itself heals, or, if it is dysfunctional, harms. Caregivers, counselors, and all who are mindful of concern need to understand the characteristics of a healing community and have skills to help the community develop its potential for supporting life.

Principles to Guide Us

God has been ahead of us, preparing individuals *and* the culture for healing. Our work is lightened by these guiding principles:

- People are whole: mind, body, psyche, and spirit are integrated in that whole.
- Because of a paradigm shift, we are becoming more aware of our wholeness.
- People need each other. We live in systems; we're connected to one another, to the environment and to the universe.
- We are always changing. Life is in flux; chaos is an understandable aspect of creativity.
- Our wholeness contains both the negative and the positive, health and illness. Death is a part of life.
- We become aware of our wholeness in relationship; we stay aware in relationship. Some relationships can harm us.
- We are moving away from mostly hierarchical relationships towards those of collegiality. A new balance is being achieved as we appreciate the interrelationships of the masculine and feminine and as we respect and utilize our unique gifts.

- We are integrating and synthesizing insights of science, human behavior, and religion.
- As we develop more flexible ways of thinking we are also learning to live with ambiguity.
- Individuals are to be respected, with all their uniqueness and diversity. They need community but they are not to be swallowed up by community.

You may ask: "How can you say 'people want to be healed'? Isn't that a generalization? So many people who come for counseling seem to want only a Band-Aid. They only want support or a chance to ventilate and complain. They *say* they want to feel better, but they seem to resist any real change. I don't see a great clamoring for 'second order change'!"

This is a fair question. We are living in a time of a new understanding of wholeness, but many people have not had time to catch up. They are not aware of the good news. They do not yet have a sense of a new extension of belief that could give them hope. For you, the concept of body-mind-soul integration may not be new. However, many people do not know that they can experience wholeness. Why should they know? They are still treated as objects by most medical people. Many religious institutions still shy away from talking about the resources for wholeness that are possible through faith and spiritual practice. Even when people "get" the basic *idea* of wholeness, they may not have experienced it.

Our first job as "gardeners" is to speak of the revolutionary concept of mind-body-soul integration in our communities. As this new concept is absorbed, people then can begin to hope for wholeness. Our first task is educational. Through sermons, study groups, lectures, and workshops we can begin to challenge the belief that says "It is '*natural*' to be fragmented" or "I can't do anything about feeling well unless a doctor gives me medicine to feel better" or "I've learned from TV programs that I come from a 'dysfunctional' family. I guess I'm stuck being this way."

❧

This book is constructed like a practical gardener's manual to help all of you who counsel and care for souls. It contains both theory and suggestions for practice, bibliography for further reading, and the names and addresses of additional resources for referral and networking. It will draw upon many diverse resources to support healthy changes people can make. Each chapter is designed for personal reference as well as to help you create courses and workshops.

We will be addressing caring for the self and the soil of community, the use of yourself as cultivator and gardener (caregiver and counselor), basic counseling skills and theory, and particular issues that arise in counseling others in all the seasons of life. We will introduce the basics of the solution-focused therapy method that we recommend for brief therapy. We will also address the need for self care to protect you from personal and professional burnout.

Clergy as well as nonordained ministers and leaders are vulnerable to professional burnout. The old system of fragmentation is dangerous. Many of us *think* we believe in integration and wholeness, yet we accept being treated as "cases" or "symptoms" or "body parts" by medical and other specialists. We resemble those who, when in the hospital, are referred to as "the gall bladder in room 202." We do not complain because we do not notice. We have become used to being thought of as objects.

In addition to unconsciously accepting this fragmentation, religious leaders are often subjected to a unique form of dehumanization that comes from "acting" the role of religious leader. The old system of fragmentation reinforces this. In chapters 3 and 10 we will be investigating the dangers leaders face in ministry that can affect our well-being, and also the resources we have for living out, not acting out, our ministry in effective, creative ways.

Traditionally, counseling and care in religious communities is referred to as "pastoral care and counseling." This name pointed to the person — the pastor — who was doing the counseling. In this text we call this work *community care and counseling.* In this name change we are pointing to both the context of care (the community) and to the persons cared for (the members of the community).

We refer to those who are caregivers and counselors by the more abbreviated name, *counselors in community.* This broad title includes ordained and nonordained people: clergy, lay ministers, and leaders, religious professionals, and other members who counsel and give care in community. The assumption is that many lay counselors in community have had some special training. Some may have had ministry courses for lay people. Others may be helping professionals — counselors, social workers, educators, and others — who volunteer their time in the ministry of their religious communities.

Let us now turn to our next task, helping our communities to become rooted in change.

Chapter One
Reading and Resources
Publishing information is found in the Bibliography.

• The *paradigm shift toward wholeness* is a foundation of Howard Clinebell's classic *Basic Types of Pastoral Care and Counseling* (rev.) and *Counseling for Spiritually Empowered Wholeness.* Larry Graham's *Care of Persons, Care of Worlds* is a thoughtful *application of the new paradigm shift to pastoral counseling.* He has important things to say about community and our relationship to the environment.

• For an understanding of the ideas that have shaped the modern age, and of the paradigm shift, read Richard Tarnas's *The Passion of the Western Mind.*

• To grasp the *scientific insights that have contributed to the paradigm shift* (written for the nontechnician) see Heinz R. Pagels, *The Cosmic Code;* Thomas Kuhn, *The Structure of Scientific Revolutions;* Fritjof Capra, *The Turning Point.*

• The literature on *mind-body-soul connection* is growing. See Gerald M. Edelman's *The Remembered Present: A Biological Theory of Consciousness,* which integrates findings in neuroscience with current knowledge of anatomy, cell biology, and psychology; and Herbert Benson's *Timeless Healing: The Power and Biology of Belief,* which reports research and explores the relationship of religious belief to physical well-being.

• We see evidence of *holism in the writings of contemporary theologians.* James Ashbrook understands the Spirit dwelling in our very cells. See his *Brain, Culture, and the Human Spirit; Brain and Belief; Faith and Ministry in Light of the Double Brain;* and *Minding the Soul.* James Nelson writes of integration, paying particular attention to the body, sexuality, and spirituality in *Embodiment: An Approach to Sexuality and Christian Theology; Body Theology,* and *The Intimate Connection: Male Sexuality and Masculine Spirituality.* John J. McNeill celebrates holism in *Freedom, Glorious Freedom.* Virginia Ramey Mollenkott writes of it in *Sensuous Spirituality* as does Matthew Fox in *Creation Spirituality.*

• To understand more about *theory of change,* see Paul Watzlawick et al., *Change: Principles of Problem Formation and Problem Resolution.*

• To return to the *roots of the pastoral care and counseling movement,* read Anton Boisen's autobiographies *Out of the Depths* and *The Exploration of the Inner World.* Also see Leroy Aden and J. Harold Ellen, *Turning Points in Pastoral Care: The Legacy of Anton Boisen and Seward Hiltner,* and Glenn Asquith, *Vision from a Little Known Country.*

• We have used "gardener" as a metaphor for healer. Other *formative images for pastoral counselors* are: "shepherd" in Seward Hiltner's *Preface to Pastoral Theology;* "wounded healer" in Henri Nouwen's *The Wounded Healer;* "wise fool" in Donald Capps's *Reframing: A New Method in Pastoral Care* and Alistair Campbell's *Rediscovering Pastoral Care.*

• The more *holistic understanding of medical practitioners* can be found in Bernie Siegel, *Love, Medicine and Miracles* and *How to Live between Office Visits;* Larry Dossey, *Space, Time, and Medicine;* Bill Moyers, *Healing and the Mind;* Daniel Goleman and Joel Gurin's *Mind Body Medicine;* and Andrew Weil, *Spontaneous Healing.*

• For an understanding of the *meaning of soul and spirit* in light of scientific and medical discoveries about human life, see *The Treasure of Earthen Vessels: Explorations in Theological Anthropology,* edited by Brian Childs and David Waanders.

• We would like to recommend two pastoral counseling works of an encyclopedic nature to be used as companions to this "gardener's manual." These are written for lay and professional readers. The *Dictionary of Pastoral Care and Counseling,* edited by Rodney Hunter, is written out of both the Jewish and Christian tradition. The *Clinical Handbook of Pastoral Counseling,* Vols. 1 and 2, edited by Robert Wicks, Richard Parsons, and Donald Capps, expand clinical concerns we explore.

⁓ 2 ⁓

The Ground of Community

God stir the soil,
Run the ploughshare deep,
Cut the furrows round and round,
Overturn the hard, dry ground,
Spare no strength nor toil,
Even though I weep.
In the loose, fresh mangled earth
Sow new seed.
Free of withered vine and weed
Bring fair flower to birth.

Prayer from Singapore,
Church Missionary Society[1]

Gardeners know that before they plant, they must consider the composition, condition, and needs of the soil. After understanding the nature of the soil, they will know which plants thrive in it. They will know what nutrients will be needed to supplement the soil, and will understand how the ground holds water. After knowing the soil, they proceed.

That is why, as gardeners who care for souls, we must first consider the community in which we do our work. The community of your church or synagogue is the ground that supports and nurtures both you in your work, and the individuals who are members of the community.

Rather than acknowledging our groundedness in community, most psychological counseling theory reflects an individualistic medical model. The primacy of a confidential doctor-patient relationship is assumed where the doctor rarely deals with the patient's whole family. The doctor usually has little direct knowledge of the patient's lifestyle, support systems, or religious experience and values. The doctor limits his or her actions to understanding what is wrong with the patient and then, if possible, curing what is "wrong."

Most counselors, too, work in private with the counselee without direct input from the counselee's family or friends. The counselor is taught to diagnose the illness, help the counselee solve problems, and if possible, help provide a cure.

Those who minister in community do not work in such an individualistic, compartmentalized way. You have *multiple relationships* with those who come to you for counseling. Because most of those whom you counsel are known to you through your leadership in their religious or civic community, you are never simply an objective, neutral counselor. Unlike other mental health professionals who first meet their clients in consultation and draw out case studies from strangers, you often know those who come to you for help. In fact, sometimes you feel you know too much! Because you know the counselee's extended family and friends, you may have heard other versions of the problem that a counselee comes to discuss. In listening, you have to bracket off what you have heard from others so you may hear the counselee's story in a fresh way.

Counseling methods that are based solely on the illness model are not particularly helpful to those of us who counsel in community. Because of our understanding of mind-body-soul integration, we of course need to be able to identify the physical and psychological symptoms that often accompany spiritual distress. We also need to know how to make appropriate referrals so that those suffering from them can be helped. But we cannot be limited to illness-based knowledge. We also need to know how to care for the soul and to learn how spiritual *dis-ease* can create imbalance. We need counseling theory and technique that will help train our eyes to see wholeness.

By focusing first on community, you are starting where you are. You are not in an office protected by neutrality and anonymity. Because you work *within* community, your job as counselor and caregiver is both harder and easier than that of other mental-health professionals. It is hard to be both *connected* to your counselees due to your personal and/or clerical relationships to them, and yet also be *separate* enough to see them clearly. You need to understand how the complexity of your relationship affects the counseling process. You also need to learn techniques for managing limit setting and for organizing life-history information.

It takes special skill to be a counselor and caregiver in community. However, your work is made easier because you have the resource of community itself to support you and to be a place of healing for those whom you counsel. Community is not only the *place* where healing takes place, it is a *means* through which it happens.

Community: Our Great Resource

Authentic community is the "medicine" our society needs. We and other mental health professionals know that loneliness, isolation, emptiness, and a sense of meaninglessness are the frequent complaints of those coming for help. Often, these complaints are accompanied by symptoms of psychological disorder hat can be treated by medication. However, even when the symptoms are relieved by medication, often the spiritual malaise is still there. Medication alone cannot quiet this pain, which comes from the depths of the spirit. This is the pain of souls who have been traumatized through internal fragmentation and ruptured relationships.

We know that people can find healing in community because we have witnessed such healing. We also have known those who through spiritual discernment listen deeply to themselves and to God and have begun to know themselves. We have seen them come alive. We have watched them make close friendships in the community in which they experienced their wholeness.

The assertion: "religious communities can be healing places" gives rise to essential questions. You might ask: "Do all communities heal? Some people seem to be healed more through their Alcoholics Anonymous group than through their church," or "Isn't a person's faith in God enough for healing? Why do people need a group?" Answers to these questions can be found through more thorough study of community.

To understand community, we must return to our consideration of "ground." The ground in which we plant is composed of many different types and compositions of soil. Our religious gardens are complex and beautiful. They each thrive in the soil of our varied religious traditions. Even though the soils — the religious traditions — differ, the *function* of the ground is the same in all our gardens, where the ground nurtures, supports, and holds the plants, regardless of the composition of the soil. As we understand more about how community functions, we are able both to work with the "soil" and to rest and be supported by the "ground."

Religious communities do not exist as an end in themselves, they are created in response to a call. Faithfulness to the call comes first. Community follows. Religious communities share a common vision or goal that is supported by theological understanding and nurtured by religious observance and spiritual practice. Secular communities, too, bond through shared missions that are reinforced through ritual.

While religious communities differ in their theological expression and religious practice, Christians and Jews believe that their communal experience is intrinsically rooted in their faith experience. Both groups study the Hebrew scriptures and their own sacred writings to be guided in their communal life. Both Christians and Jews acknowledge that those in their communities are able to love and accept each other and to care for the world *because God first loved them.*

Jewish religious communities are bound together through their experience of God's covenanted relationship with them and their promise to respond through faithfulness. Holy days, festivals, and related religious practices celebrate God's saving works and nourish a sense of communal identity and historical continuity. These practices also provide an opportunity for members of the community to care for each other and to express their commitment to social justice.

Christian communities have differing understandings of what it means to be "the body of Christ" and to "go into all the world and preach the Gospel." Some religious communities emphasize individual personal salvation; others believe that members are brought into the church and redeemed in community. Although theological understanding of sacraments and religious practice differ, Christians are drawn together in communities to discern what it means to be modern-day faithful disciples. They are challenged to be like Christians of the early church who were signaled out as "those who loved each other," and by Jesus' admonition to reach out to "the least of these," and to the "sick not the well" — to embody God's love for the world. The New Testament is filled with instructions for life in community.

All communities, whether religious or public, have a spiritual basis. Communities organize themselves for the common good. They are rooted in care. In an essay on the spirituality of public life, teacher and activist Parker J. Palmer says that even secular communities that view themselves as external social structures have an interior reality. He quotes Annie Dillard who reminds us that before community can be built as a social and political reality, it must be received as a spiritual fact. Dillard believes that if we are to retrieve a sense of a common life, our "hidden wholeness," we must begin not with activity, but with contemplation.[2]

Communities have a spiritual center; they are lived out in human fashion. For communities to function — to hold and support — they must be places where their members are able to:

- Communicate with each other honestly and without fear.
- Resolve conflicts with each other individually and within the group.
- Learn to love themselves so they can love each other and reach out to strangers.

Such communities are *safe, inclusive and just.*

The concept of religious community as a living organism is not new. The early Christian church was described as a body whose head was Christ, in which individual members were "one with another" (Romans 12:3–8). As members of faith communities today are recovering from their dualistic perceptions, they are becoming increasingly aware of the ways in which their own religious community is actually a living organism within the living organism of the larger community, which is itself in the world.

Because of our interconnectedness, the vitality of our religious communities contributes to the strength and energy of the larger community. And when there is toxicity in our communities' bodies, it adversely affects the whole.

Through the corrective vision of holism, we no longer see the religious requirement to "act justly" as something privileged ones do "for those *other* people." Because we are one body, our community and all those in it are made sick by the poison created by racism, economic greed, homophobia, and other expressions of hardheartedness and hatred.

As we begin to sense the implications of our interconnectedness to each other, we can become overwhelmed. But we are helped by the observations of meteorologists who note the "Butterfly Effect" — the flutter of butterfly wings in one part of the world can create vibrations that in turn cause massive weather changes in another part of the world. One small movement can create great change. Communities need to be reminded that small *just* actions can contribute to big changes in the entire organism.

Communities: Pseudo and Real

Undoubtedly you have had the experience of belonging to a group at school, church, synagogue, or in your neighborhood in which you were supposed to feel a communal spirit — but you did not. You were not able to tell anyone you were frightened, alienated, or feeling unaccepted. *You could not be yourself.* You did not trust that the group could accept your real, vulnerable self. In all likelihood, you were in a pseudocommunity.

Pseudocommunities hold themselves out as genuine communities. Often they seem friendly with an emphasis on "group identity" and "involvement"; often their members feel pressure to reflect the group and its values. But pseudocommunities are not places where members are safe to be different, to disagree, to question the program or the leadership of the group. Members who do not reflect the group are in fact shunned, sometimes in subtle ways. Conflict is either not allowed or there is no effective mechanism for resolving it. People are not valued for their differences or uniqueness. The group is exclusive rather than inclusive. In such a group, you were wise to go into hiding. You were not safe.

Now, in contrast, there are communities where you feel *at home,* in which you can be yourself, warts and all. What is there about that group that makes it possible for you to be you, and to be there for others? In all probability, in that group you feel safe. You can risk being angry or disagreeing. You are able to get to know members who at first you felt were different from you. You felt listened to. You really care about other members of the group. You listen openly to them because you are interested. You don't feel *pressured* to be in the group, you feel free to be there, and free when you are there. In that community you experience grace.

※

All true communities are the gift of grace. Some come about spontaneously, others are intentionally formed. Some communities have a long life, others are short-lived. Some grow out of the work place, some from involvement with a cause. Some are consciously religious; others are not. Although the explicit purpose of communities may differ, people in them experience something similar. They experience grace.

Grace was experienced by those in a spontaneous community that grew out of support of a friend, Pam, who had cancer. At first, Pam's friends spent time with her, one at a time. Eventually each met other friends who were caring for her as well. In time, they were telephoning each other to schedule visits to Pam, and to plan for her home care. Eventually, they were together at the hospital. They began to go out for meals together. They were working as a team to tend to their friend's business as well as her hospice care. By the time Pam died, this friendship group had become a community. At first it was their mutual love for Pam that drew them together. As they spent time together, they began to reveal themselves to each other.

Becoming friends was not completely easy. Sometimes they jockeyed for place — some needed to feel more special to Pam. There was anger — anger caused by Pam's approaching death. This anger sometimes got displaced onto one another. There was fear. None had yet lost a close friend their own age. And yet, they were able to deal with these conflicts, able to accept each other's idiosyncrasies. Their connection to each other was deep. They were able to laugh and to mourn. After Pam died, the group, which was no longer in daily contact, was not intact as a community. However, all felt changed because of it. Each person had become more whole. Members of the group retained an emotional connection to one another and when they remember that time they are grateful. The group experienced grace. It was like being in love.

Communities are fluid. They are made of networks of caring clusters, not unlike the group that was called into being as it responded to Pam, their dying friend. In the course of ministry you have probably observed groups such as the one just described. You are struck by the love that unites the group members. You have observed them becoming a living organism — a cell — in the community.

The gift of community comes through grace, as does the gift of love. We cannot *will* someone to love us. However, when we are loved, there are ways to support that love. Marriage is one way to support love; it, after all, is a building block of community. Just as we learn principles to help people have rich marriages, we also learn similar principles about community. Often falling in love occurs unintentionally, just as do those unplanned community experiences. But once in love, people become committed. Love then becomes intentional.

In true communities members can communicate authentically, resolve conflicts, learn to love and accept themselves and each other, and reach out to strangers. True communities are works in progress reflecting the New Testament understanding of perfection. Perfection — (*teleiosis*) — means being on the right road and progressing nicely. Communities are always changing; they never fully "arrive." True communities are always "becoming." For example, such a community might be an inclusive group in which members trust each other enough to be themselves even though they have difficulty resolving some conflicts. But the group is *aware* of this difficulty and struggles with it. The community is "on the right road."

Community: Where Members Can Communicate Honestly and without Fear

"I can be myself here!" People who can say that are probably speaking of genuine community. I am using the experience of "being myself" as synonymous with "open communication." The ability to talk is a primary aspect of communicating; through talking we reveal ourselves to others. And for many of us, it is through talking that we reveal ourselves to ourselves, as well. Some of us do not know what we are thinking, or what we really mean, until we hear ourselves saying it aloud. In community, we can tell our story. We can become more experienced in saying what we really mean. By being listened to, we can know more fully who we are. The words "communicate," "community," and "communion" have similar meanings. When we communicate, we are in deep relationship, communion, with others. We give. We receive. We do this with our total being — body, mind, soul. We think and we feel. We are whole. We are ourselves.

Religious communities can be greatly helped by our understanding of *effective* communication, which comes from the study of communication in the family. It is also through our study of marriage and the family that we have learned about *ineffectual communication*. Each person sees the world differently, through lenses shaped by gender, race, sexual orientation, age, class, culture, language, birth order. To be known in our intimate relationships, we must constantly be explaining who we are. When we sense that our partner really wants to know us, we risk revealing ourselves. When we feel that our partner is not much interested, we feel vulnerable, unaccepted, lonely. Couples need to be very rooted in their love and care for each other to commit themselves to trying to understand the other.

The ineffective communication that we often see in religious communities is similar to the communication problems of couples. However, because of the large number of people trying to understand each other in community, the problems are more complex. Still, communication can be helped by applying the principles used to help couples:

- focus on understanding the other, rather than first being understood;
- pay attention to each others' differences; appreciate uniqueness;
- do not be judgmental.

In communities where these rules are practiced, people feel safe enough to reveal themselves. Because they feel accepted, they are more relaxed and they, too, are more accepting.

In religious communities it is easy to make false assumptions about others because of shared religious tradition and in some cases, ethnic or cultural backgrounds. In our diverse and mobile modern culture, religious tradition is a place of stability. Often, families who are transferred from place to place because of their work seek out the religious group of their childhood for familiarity. Even though the family has moved to a new neighborhood, the Holy Days are celebrated in the known way!

We all tend to look for the ways in which we are similar to others; it makes us feel at home, less anxious. We feel sympatico with those of our cultural and religious "tribe." However, in our attempt to find people like ourselves, we often do not see others as they really are. We screen out the ways in which they are different.

It is in acting upon these perceptions of "alikeness" — rather than listening for "differences" — that misunderstandings arise in community. Communication would be helped if, rather than making assumptions about another person, one asked: "What meaning does she make of our religious tradition? How is it different from the way I see and experience it? Even though her theological position is different from mine, can I understand what she means?" We do not really know each other until we can see and appreciate our differences. Religious congregations that do not tolerate the anxiety that arises when members acknowledge their differences develop severe communication problems. And when these problems become chronic, the community begins to experience a sense of failure, not unlike the sense of despair and disappointment that causes couples to make an appointment for counseling.

Those of us who are counselors in community have a great deal of experience in observing troubled marriages. We know the disappointment of those who, before they married, felt that they loved enough to be married well. Some of these disappointed couples made the assumption that having fallen in love they would stay in love. When we listen to them, we often find that a significant part of their problem is the inability to communicate to each other *who they are.* They have been unable to move beyond the "being in love" state in which each had idealized his or her view of the other. Through counseling, they must learn that their marriage has not failed. Rather, their love has not yet grown up. Love in marriage must mature. In the course of the maturation of love, couples will learn to communicate.

Religious communities often share a similar disappointment. They *intend* to be loving places but like these "failed" marriages, they experience themselves as "dysfunctional." They have moved from a state of being "in love" to one of being burned-out, cynical, and unloving. Unloving communities can be cold and unfriendly, they can be judgmental and nonaccepting, they can be friendly but superficial, or busy but lacking intimacy. The complaints of these communities are very similar to those of couples who are disappointed in their marriage and who accuse themselves and each other of failure.

Communities in which people *can* communicate — reveal — are those in which love is maturing. It is not commonly understood that religious communities, like couples or families, can obtain counsel to discover what they can do to help love mature in the community. In fact, the very act of beginning a process whose goal is to help members understand each other — rather than problem solving or taking action — can begin the healing.

When a community is troubled, in conflict, or has experienced "falling out of love," many members are not truly interested in understanding others. *They* want to be understood. In fact, their very need to be understood keeps them from understanding others. We all have had experiences in group meetings when we knew that real understanding was not happening. People were not listening to one another. They were rehearsing in their heads as they awaited their turn to speak. Each was making a speech. No one was responding to what others were saying. But it is necessary for us to know that even such troubled religious communities can learn to listen and understand.

Communities can choose to become more loving and to facilitate understanding and cooperation. Just as parents, many from unhappy families, can learn parenting skills, so can communities learn to listen with understanding and acceptance. They can learn to be safe places.

Community: Where Members Are Able to Resolve Conflicts

It might seem strange that the healthier the community, the more potential there is for conflict. Conflict, as we are defining it, means "to differ." Conflict often has a negative meaning: "to clash," "to be at odds with," "to fight." But conflict need not be seen in this negative way. It can be seen as part of the creative process. Perhaps you have been part of discussion groups in which ideas and opinions seemed to be at odds; those holding conflicting opinions were not, however, fighting even though their ideas differed. Although verbal sparks were flying, you were not frightened; you felt alive and stimulated. The group was struggling to come to grips with a complex issue. Without healthy conflict — differing ideas — they could not have reached a full understanding of the issue.

Groups that have a friendly attitude toward conflict are more able to live cooperatively. Conflict does not lead to war if it is understood to be "differing" rather than "fighting." When members are invited to differ and to express these differences for the common good, there will be less anger. A great deal of the anger that arises in community comes when people feel that their opinions are misunderstood or bypassed: that they don't count.

Communities that do well with conflict have these characteristics. They:

- have a positive understanding of conflict. Conflict is part of the creative process.
- have agreed to differ and resolved to love.
- work to understand each other's differences.
- see conflict as a difficult process to be worked through, not as a problem in and of itself.
- accept anger when it does arise. Paradoxically, the accepting attitude of the community reduces occasions for anger.
- are able to tolerate ambiguity. Because differing positions are allowed, there is less need for a rigid approach.
- are intentional about learning to listen to each other and to God. They have formal and informal ways to work through differences and to affirm each other.

Communities that have difficulties with conflict have the following characteristics. They:

- have a negative attitude toward conflict. They believe "conflict" and "fight" are the same.
- do not understand the role of conflict, or differing, in the creative process.
- are frightened by differences. Value is placed on people being similar, not different. Change is threatening.
- see conflict as a problem: The potential for conflict needs to be eliminated whenever possible.
- cannot accept anger. Because anger cannot be fully expressed, it becomes resentment, which gets expressed in many covert, hidden ways.
- cannot accept ambiguity. Because there is only one acceptable way of understanding the mission and life of the community, the community is more comfortable with "right" versus "wrong"; or "our way" versus "their way."
- believe they are listening to each other although they often are simply making assumptions based on the belief that they are alike. Although they are serious in their devotion to God, they rely on their religious leaders for the interpretation of God's will. Conflicts tend to get settled by authorities *outside* the immediate community.

Most religious communities fall somewhere between these two groups. In fact, most communities can get confused about their response to conflict. It would be useful for religious communities to spend some time reflecting on these two scenarios. The very process of discussing conflict in an objective way is helpful. It is impossible to have a reasonable discussion about your position on communal conflict when you are in the middle of a fight! Some communities would find it difficult to have forums or workshops on conflict resolution. They are phobic about talking about conflict and avoid discussion of it. They are similar to children who believe that when their parents fight they are on their way to divorce. However, when communities discuss their attitudes and make plans for conflict resolution, the fear felt by those who are phobic about communal conflict can be reduced.

It can be useful for you to look at the areas in which your community has had conflict. If you are not in the midst of struggling over these issues, you can consider how the community dealt with them in the past. You can also see how much unfinished business has been left or who might still be hurting. Below are some of the common areas of conflict found in religious communities:

- Personal disagreements: misunderstandings, hurt feelings among individuals.
- Disagreements around leadership and maintenance of the group (issues around power, money, building and community assets).
- Mission — what the community believes it is, or should be, doing.
- Doctrine, practice of faith and religious life, communal ecclesiastical policies.
- Social practices and issues: today many issues are sexual — e.g., family planning, premarital sex, abortion, sexual orientation, celibate clergy, role of women. A few years ago, the most prominent issues were war and civil rights.
- Change: Institutions fear change, and change is experienced as threatening. Change that is the result of a changing world or that the community initiates, will be experienced as threatening by some in the community who remember the "good old days."
- Problems in the group process caused when two members (or groups) manage their anxiety by bringing another member into the middle, when leaders do not function in their roles, or when interpersonal boundaries are not respected.

It is probable that at this time your community is dealing with some of the conflicts on this list. Perhaps some are acknowledged, some not. It is important for communities to claim their conflicts. Conflicts that are unacknowledged become *problems* that lead to overt fights or go underground to be fought indirectly. When a conflict is faced directly, it becomes redefined. And although it becomes an issue that is difficult to deal with, it is not a fearful conflict because the community agrees *together* to tackle it.

※

Many communities intend to be safe places where conflicts can be resolved, but they find it difficult to do because so many of their members have difficulty appropriately expressing anger. Some members are afraid of their anger and cope with it by pushing it down or denying it. Others are what science writer Daniel Goleman calls *hijacked* by it. People then feel picked up by rage and out of control. They lose their ability to think reasonably or act appropriately. They behave as if they were fighting for their lives. And in fact, their brain has sent neurochemical signals that are telling them to fight for their lives. They have difficulty appropriately expressing their anger because they are neurochemically off balance.

The religious community is one of the few places where adults go for education. Because of their educational programs, communities can be of great service to their many members who have difficulty with anger. Many angry and impulsive people drink to self-medicate; they act out their anger by striking their spouses and children and they have a high risk for heart disease. And most are ashamed to talk about it. Programs of the community can address these problems effectively.

In recent years there has been much investigation of anger: the expression of anger is learned in families and it also has a neurochemical basis. Members of your community who have difficulty with anger can be helped by reading, workshops, and behavioral training, which can help them diffuse and de-escalate it. They can also be helped by learning communication skills to express anger more effectively.

Often community conflict comes from the unfinished business of unresolved, or poorly resolved, conflicts. Serious disruptions in congregations have been caused by conflict over leadership changes. This is usually true when beloved, charismatic clerics leave. Those leaders who follow are then found wanting. When revered leaders leave, many members feel abandoned, angry, and in pain. Anger at the person who leaves sometimes goes underground and the hostility is taken out on the new leader. Often communities go through several leadership changes before this unfinished business is lived — or worked — out.

Another example of conflict is that of a congregation's divided loyalties toward a controversial leader who has been found guilty of a serious trespass of ethics. When a leader is asked to leave a community because of incompetence, professional or personal impropriety, or criminal offense, the community always takes sides. Some members go to the leader's defense; they feel he or she has been victimized or falsely accused. Some feel the leader is guilty, others are filled with denial or disbelief. But always, the community is torn and will need special attention. Because of the increased incidents of clergy misconduct, there are hundreds of congregations that are torn by conflict. Most religious bodies are now developing methods for helping distressed congregations air conflicts so that corporate wounds can be healed.

Another source of communal wounding comes from community "family secrets" about unacknowledged or hidden pain in the congregation. As in families, when a community member has been sworn to secrecy by someone who has been seriously mistreated by another member of the community, the pain goes underground. Since secrets are rarely perfectly kept, others know that something is amiss. Often suspicion and gossip arise, but neither the person injured nor the one who has abused their trust can be addressed. Often the secret is about sexual activity — of the clergy or other community leaders. Sex, of course, is not the only topic of communal "family secrets." Sometimes, these secrets are protecting personal privacy, but most often they are hiding sexual misconduct or abuse. Sometimes these secrets are about present activity, sometimes about past events that are still being lived out in the pain of those whose trust has been violated. Communities struggling with "family secrets" need special help. It is useful to know that many religious bodies have consultants and resources available that congregations can engage to help heal these wounds.

Psychotherapeutic theory teaches us the importance of helping people look at their conscious — and eventually, their unconscious — conflicts so that they can be resolved. The therapist does not turn on a third-degree spotlight as the client tries to articulate and work through these conflicts. Instead, the therapist is a supportive, accepting presence who "keeps the client company" while the conflict becomes clear. It takes time to understand what a conflict truly is about. And it is only after the client can *feel* the trouble that resolution can take place. The client has to know what it is about the conflict that is troubling. Very often the conflict is resolved when its meaning is understood. In order to reach this understanding, both the client and the therapist must learn patience. The Tao Te Ching asks:

> *Do you have the patience to wait*
> *till your mud settles and your water becomes clear?*
> *Can you remain unmoving*
> *till the right action arises by itself?*
>
> Tao Te Ching 15[3]

Hundreds of years before psychotherapeutic methods were developed, the Religious Society of Friends (Quakers) created effective processes for resolving conflict. Their methods are very similar to the psychotherapeutic process we have just described. When a Quaker community is in conflict, leaders will call the community together for a "threshing" (as in "threshing wheat") session in which:

- The leader, or convener, like the therapist, "keeps the community company" as a *nonanxious* presence who helps the group become clear about what the problem really is.
- The first purpose of the meeting (s) is not to solve the conflict, but to name and understand it. Acting before there is agreement about the conflict is to "stir up the water" before it has time to settle.
- All of the members need to be able to speak about their view of the conflict — how they think and feel about it. If what they have said is unclear

to others, they will be asked to clarify their meaning, but at this point there is no debate or discussion.

- Everyone has a chance to speak, giving members assurance that they have been heard. Time is given for silence between speakers so that the group has time to reflect on what has just been said.
- This process takes time and patience. However, in the long run, it saves time because when the group is ready to solve the conflict, there is agreement about what the nature of the problem is. Everyone feels consulted and everyone's viewpoint is a part of the group's corporate understanding.
- In the process of listening, the problem "sorts itself out." The group knows when an understanding about the trouble is reached when it has a felt sense of "Oh, that's it!" *The group senses clarity. The water is clear.*
- Almost always, the conflict has been redefined in this process. While there is often a further task to be done, it is more manageable.

Buddhists, like Quakers, are peacemakers who have developed creative methods for resolving conflicts that have ecumenical applications. Buddha gave his followers these seven practices for resolving the conflicts that arose in communal living:

Face to Face Sitting Practice: "According to this practice, the dispute must be stated before the entire convocation, with both sides of the conflict present. This is to avoid private conversations about the conflict that inevitably influence people against one side or the other, creating further discord and tension."

Remembrance Practice: "In the convocation, both parties involved try to remember from the beginning everything that led up to the conflict. Details should be presented with as much clarity as possible. Witnesses and evidence should be provided, if available. The community listens quietly and patiently to both sides in order to obtain adequate information to examine the dispute."

Nonstubbornness Practice: "The people in question are expected to resolve the conflict. The community expects both parties to demonstrate their willingness to reach reconciliation. Stubbornness is to be considered negative and counterproductive. In case a party claims he violated a precept because of ignorance or an unsettled state of mind, without actually intending to violate it, the community should take that into account in order to find a solution that is agreeable to both sides."

Voluntary Confession Practice: "Each party is encouraged to admit his own transgressions and shortcomings without having to be prodded by the other party or the community. The community should allow each party ample time to confess his own failings, no matter how minor they may seem. Admitting one's faults begins a process of reconciliation and encourages the other party to do likewise, This leads to the possibility of full reconciliation."

Decision by Consensus Practice: "After hearing both sides and being assured of the wholehearted efforts by both sides to reach a settlement, the community reaches a verdict by consensus."

Covering Mud with Straw Practice: "During the convocation, a venerable elder...is appointed to represent each side in the conflict. These are [elders] who are deeply respected and listened to by others in the [community]. They sit and listen intently, saying little. But when they do speak, their words carry special weight. Their words have the capacity to soothe and heal wounds, to call forth reconciliation and forgiveness, just as straw covers mud, enabling someone to cross it without dirtying his clothes. Thanks to the presence of these elders.... The disputing parties find it easier to release petty concerns. Bitterness is eased and the community is able to reach a verdict agreeable to both sides."

Accepting the Verdict Practice: "When the verdict is reached...it will be read aloud three times. If no one in the community voices disagreement with it, it is considered final. Neither party in dispute has the right to challenge the verdict. They have agreed to place their trust in the community's decision and carry out whatever verdict the community reaches."[4]

Members of modern congregations would do well to adapt these ancient methods to their own conflicted situations.

While acknowledging that it is essential for communities to have processes through which they can settle conflicts, family therapist Rabbi Edwin Friedman believes that congregational conflicts can be avoided through the clear leadership of the rabbi or minister. In his book *From Generation to Generation* Rabbi Friedman argues that religious leaders who have successfully differentiated from their own parental families — who have been able to leave home, without being cut off from their families — are able to help the families *in* their congregations and the family *of* their congregations communicate more clearly and function more effectively. Rabbi Friedman believes that religious leaders must look at their own marriages, families, and bonded relationships to make certain that they are healthy. The health of the minister or rabbi's family affects the family of the congregation.

Community: Where Members Who Are Able
to Love Themselves Can Love Others

It is profoundly true that *those who do not love themselves cannot love others*. We see this every day: The bully who feels inadequate takes it out on little children; the parent who was beaten as a child is now abusing his own child; the successful executive who never really feels successful is always preoccupied with his own situation and is therefore unable to care for others.

It must be stated firmly that children are not born hating themselves. As the song from the musical *South Pacific* says, "You've got to be taught to fear and to hate." Children are taught not only to hate others; *children are also taught to hate themselves.*

Most parents want to love their children. How are we to understand some of these very parents who teach their children to hate themselves?

At least two sad parental ingredients are necessary for children to learn to hate themselves: *fear* and the *experience of not being seen as they truly are*. It is said that "the sins of the fathers (and mothers) go down to the third generation." It is also true that the *fears* of the parents go down from generation to generation as well. Parents who teach their children to hate are themselves frightened people who cannot love.

Parents are frightened for many reasons and their fear takes many forms. Some are frightened because their own parents scared them into obedience and submission through harsh treatment and shame. Their parents worshiped a frightening God and believed that it was their duty to punish children harshly to keep them from going to Hell. Often this fear was reinforced by Scripture:

> You shall not bow down to them or worship them; for I, the Lord your God, am a jealous God, punishing the children for the sin of the fathers to the third and fourth generation of those who hate me.
> Exodus 20:5

They had not been touched by another passage from the Hebrew Bible:

> *For thus says the Lord:*
> *I will extend prosperity to her like a river,*
> *and the wealth of the nations like an overflowing stream;*
> *and you shall nurse and be carried on her arm,*
> *and dandled on her knees*
> *As a mother comforts her child, so I will comfort you;*
> *you shall be comforted in Jerusalem. Isaiah 66:12–13*

Other parents are not so much frightened that their children will be bad as that they will be lively. Parents who have grown up in family systems of fear have had liveliness squelched. They were not supposed to be sexy, or spunky, or opinionated. They were taught to push down their own assertiveness, sexuality, and creativity. Children, however, are innately assertive, sexual, and creative. Frightened parents, who have been trained to think that these traits are bad, are scared when their children act in these "unacceptable" ways. Frightened parents then "straighten" their children out. They squash this liveliness. The children learn that *to be themselves is BAD*.

The process by which children learn "I'm BAD" is called *internalization*. It is an unconscious process. Children take in the messages of their parents' words and actions. They can sense, even before they can understand language, that their anxious parents experience them as bad.

Children have *introjected*, taken in, not only what their parents have told them, they have taken in their parents' fears, as well. "Introjection" is another process of the unconscious. Children are not aware that they are absorbing their parents' — and their grandparents' — fears. Parents are not aware that they are *projecting* their fears onto their children. "Projection" is an unconscious process. Parents consciously think that they are simply trying to make their kids behave. They are unaware that when they were children, their own parents could not tolerate their liveliness and because of their own parents' censure, they became afraid of the liveliness in themselves. Parents see in their children, through the mechanism of projection, their own potential liveliness that they have been taught to fear and hate. When they censor their lively children, they are perpetuating an unconscious cycle.

Children who grow up in this family system of fear are not really seen. They are underdeveloped. They are unknown to themselves. People who grow up in fear do not know who they are meant to be. They have learned either to hate or not to see the *best* in themselves: their lively assertiveness, sexuality, and creativity.

Not everyone in our religious communities is filled with self-hate, but all of us need to learn to love ourselves better. None of us has been loved unconditionally in our families, although some families love and see their children in "good enough" ways. It is God who loves us unconditionally.

Religious communities that worship the God of Love are places where those who do not love themselves are able to learn to love themselves. In these communities, the God of Love replaces the God of Fear: "Perfect love casts out fear" 1 John 4:18. Persons who have grown up to hate or not even know themselves, first need to know about God's unconditional love, which they can experience in communities that try to accept their members *as they are*. Accepting communities remember the instruction, "Love others as God has loved you."

All people "take in" their parents and other important people in their lives. In fact, it is through taking in and finally identifying with others that we can grow to be sturdy and loving people. In religious communities children learn to "be like Jesus" or to identify with other religious and moral leaders. They also "take in" adults who love and mentor them. We learn moral values through relationship and experience. At first children introject important people "whole" — they think their parents' thoughts and reflect their attitudes. In time they "digest" their experience. They learn to claim their own thoughts. While in many ways they may become like their parents, eventually they also become their own unique selves.

People also commonly experience "placing on" (projection). Anyone who has had an enemy knows this phenomenon. New Testament theologian Walter Wink says: "My enemy is my mirror. I project onto my enemy everything in myself that I cannot stand, tolerate, acknowledge, or accept. My enemy returns the compliment. My enemy also stirs up in me those very aspects of myself that I cannot stand, tolerate, acknowledge, or accept. We are locked into a very tight embrace, my enemy and I."[5]

Jesus' instruction to "love your enemies" requires that we discover those parts of ourselves that we dislike and disown. It is by looking at what we do not like in our enemy that we can discover a denied, disliked part of ourselves. It is through accepting those parts of ourselves that we had once found unacceptable that we can love those who have frightened us or whom we have dismissed.

The community heals by being itself. Religious communities do not have to rely only on special programs or special activities to be healing places. By being authentic, the community helps the people in them become more whole. The properties that characterize community — open communication, effective means of conflict resolution, and the love and acceptance of members who can then reach out to others — are the conditions under which healing can happen. We have seen that those who have been hurt by growing up in families in which they were frightened and unseen are particularly in need of becoming whole in community. Experiencing the unconditional love of God and the acceptance of friends in the community gives people a possibility for rebirth. Persons in a loving community are supported as they get to know themselves and as they claim their own liveliness. Many are able to accept their assertiveness, their sexuality and their creativity for the first time. As they wake up and become alive, they begin to really see and love other people — even those who are different from themselves.

Community: The Place Between "I" and "Thou"

Both Judaism and Christianity affirm the importance of an individual's *becoming* and believe that we are called by God to become ourselves. In his work *Hasidim and Modern Man*, Martin Buber quotes Rabbi Yechiel Michal of Zloczov:

> It is the duty of every man in Israel to know and consider that in his nature he is unique in the world and that there has never been another like him. For had there been another like him, he would not need to

be in the world. Each individual is a new thing in the world and must perfect his own nature in this world.[6]

According to Hasidic teaching, all men and women "perfect their own nature" in the world by serving God in their own way, in their own situation.

Martin Buber writes that living community occurs when those in it know and are known as "you" rather than "it." Buber speaks to our time of isolation and loneliness. He recognizes that when people are alienated they reach out for something to relieve their loneliness. If they reach out and do not find God, perhaps they might reach *into* themselves. Many in this process do not find themselves but become *individualists* who are self-absorbed and increasingly lonely. Others try overcoming isolation by becoming absorbed in groups. They participate in political or social *collectivism* that places emphasis on society and ignores individuals. Buber understood that both individualism and collectivism derive from fear of the world and fear of life.[7] Some religious institutions function as collectives that become worlds unto themselves to protect members from their fear of the world and life. These become pseudocommunities.

We are indebted to Buber for his spiritual insights about true community. He understood the need to attend to individuals in community, to the community itself, and to recognize connections between them. Both individuals and the feelings they have for each other, and organizational context (with its ever-changing form) are necessary for the creation of community. But Buber reminds us that a third presence, God — Thou — is at the Center and makes the human life of community possible. Buber visualized community as the periphery of a circle created through our relationship to God. He says:

> Only when these two arise — the binding up of time in a relational life of salvation and the binding up of space in the community that is made one by its Center — and only so long as they exist, does there arise and exist, round about the invisible altar, a human cosmos with bounds and form, grasped with the spirit out of the universal stuff of the aeon, a world that is house and home, a dwelling for man in the universe.[8]

Those who are drawn to religious community because they are looking for wholeness come to the right place when the community is open to God who is at the Center. It is through their relationship to the "Thou" of God that they are in relationship to others. They will learn to know "I" through becoming "You" to others. Salvation comes in relationship.

✖

We have been considering the many ways in which communities nurture growth and wholeness. Before proceeding, it is important to issue a warning: some members of the community can be unintentionally harmful *in the very act of trying to be helpful.* Perhaps you have observed community members who with the best of intentions, moved in on people who were in pain, offering them unwanted advice or solicitude. They were unaware of their intrusiveness. They confused it with caring. These members identify with the pain of others and they want to do something about it.

It is sometimes difficult to be with people who are in intense pain, who are fragmented, or who speak about feeling empty, without wanting to do something about it! Sometimes this desire "to do something" comes from care and empathy. But often the need to be helpful can also be caused by our own need not to be anxious. Many of us are anxious when we are around people who feel hopeless and frightened. We then compulsively try to help them change. We have a *need* to cheer them up, or solve their problem, or talk them out of their worries for our sake.

Yet often it is not in another's best interest to talk them out of anxiety. Anxiety is a *signal* of distress. We need to learn to pay respectful attention to anxiety. Members of communities can be taught to become a "nonanxious presence" in order *to be with* those who are frightened and anxious.

Alleviating one's own anxiety is not the only reason for "wanting to do something about" the distress of others. Some people really do believe that they know what the other needs, even if the person being "helped" does not yet know what is truly the trouble. They give gifts — of advice, food, information, opinion — to those who have not asked for them. They try to change people.

All of us have been recipients of such unasked-for gifts. We know that when others have tried to get us to diet, to exercise more, or to be more cheerful we usually eat, vegetate, or are more grumpy — just to be in charge. An essential principle of healing is this: people change after they are first accepted as they are. People do not change when others try to change them.

People who try, anxiously, to change others do not trust that we are each on our own path. They do not trust that God is working in us to draw us into our own soul. When we believe truly that those in our community are learning to listen to themselves and to God, we can relax our need to be in charge of their life plan. Our first role in the healing of others is *to be with them* as they discover their wholeness, to learn to practice the art of being accepting. As we learn to accept those aspects of ourselves that we still don't like, acceptance of others will be easier. This takes practice. It is "practicing the presence of God."

True community is given to us by grace but at the same time communities require upkeep. Healing skills can be learned by the entire community. So as not to interfere with the nurture and growth of others, members of the community need to learn to:

- Trust that each person in the community is responsible to listen to and be led by God to find wholeness.
- Overcome any compulsive *need* to be helpful.
- Not "read minds," try to change others, or give unasked-for "presents."

Caring for the Soil

The community is the *ground* of our work: the community supports and upholds us. Now we will begin to consider what we, as gardeners, must do for the ground.

I have made a distinction between "ground" and "soil." In this metaphor, the "ground" is the community itself, with all the properties that make it a safe, healing place. The "soil" is our religious tradition and our expression of it. We know that there are many types of soil that differ in appearance, chemical composition, and use. We have only to observe the rocky New England soil, the rich soil of the Mississippi Delta, and dark midwestern farmland soil to appreciate this variety.

And so it is with the "soil" of our religious communities. Our religious traditions are composed of a variety of gifts. Some communities have rich and complex liturgies, some meet in silent contemplation. Some experience healing energy of the Holy Spirit through singing and dancing, others meet for serious, quiet Biblical or Talmudic study. Some communities meet in homes; others in cathedrals. Our soils (traditions) differ but it is our communities that serve as the *common* ground. It is understood that even those traditions that are sacramental and liturgical and that place less emphasis on congregational life are supported in an essential way by the presence and communal activity of the congregation.

As a leader in a religious community it is necessary that you make certain the *community itself* stays "healthy." Sometimes the congregation understands this "health" to mean growing in numbers, meeting the budget, maintaining the building, and getting along with each other. Certainly communities have such practical needs that must be met for survival, and you are under pressure to make certain that these survival needs are met. We know, however, that "survival" is not synonymous with "health" any more than the "absence of symptoms" is the same as "wholeness." There is something else.

Our consideration of the community's care emphasizes wholeness. We are looking at the community as a living organism, as the gardener looks at the garden. When the gardener analyzes the needs of the soil, he asks, "Does it need to lie fallow? Does it need nutrients? Is it getting enough water? Is there infection from fungi or environmental waste?"

When we pay attention to the community, we ask these gardeners' questions: Does the community need to be fed? What ingredients are needed in a nutritional program? Does the community need support for spiritual growth, or workshops to learn skills for listening, or conflict resolution? Does the community need to rest or play? Shall we plant new crops, change an emphasis or program? Have we been infected by the toxins of resentment or unfinished business? Have we become insular or too self-serving? How can we be more whole?

Are you asking about the *quality* of life in your community? We will look for answers to these questions using the same kind of discernment process by which members of the community can learn to know themselves. This is the process of prayerful listening. As members ask, "What does our community need to be?" we will find answers through careful listening — listening to God and to each other.

After you know more about the *condition* of the community, you can make a plan in response. You are helped in this response if you understand two fundamental principles known to gardeners: paying attention to balance, and expecting change.

Gardeners seek balance. In one season, the ground needs to rest; in another, it needs to be intensely fertilized so a bumper crop can grow. Gardeners understand the balance of the garden to be a bit like that of a gymnast on the balance beam who is always slightly *in motion* — and focused both inwardly and outwardly. Gardeners know that although they prepare, they must always expect the change that nature brings.

When you apply these principles to community you may well ask how your community can become balanced — flexible, focused, and in movement. How can you be more comfortable with change and in harmony with nature?

To answer these questions, you have to be very specific about your community. What is the tradition of your religious group? What are its resources — spiritual, cultural, programmatic? Some religious traditions place an emphasis upon the sacraments and use these rich spiritual resources for healing the community; others emphasize study and preaching of the tradition. These groups use the mind and understanding for healing. Some groups, such as African-American churches, use the gifts of relationship and music to heal. You need to discover — and, in some cases, to uncover and recover — the healing gifts in your tradition.

Look at your tradition the way a gardener looks at the soil. What mixture is your soil?

Rather than separating religious traditions along doctrinal or sectarian lines, look at the *components* of your religious life and observances: sacrament, worship, scripture, personal religious experience, community life, social-justice activity, spiritual contemplation and prayer. These components are found in both Jewish and Christian traditions. The emphasis placed on them differs within the various denominations and divisions of both Judaism and Christianity.

If you understand the composition of your community's religious life, you can learn how to make it more balanced and lively.

Gifts Found in Religious Traditions

As you look at the following list, determine in which areas your community devotes its time and energy. Which components give your community nurture? With which does your community *traditionally* identify? Which components seem unfamiliar or insignificant to your community's life? Rank the eight components in the order of importance to your community, beginning with most to least important.

- *Sacraments:* emphasis on Eucharist and other sacramental rites; affinity to the "mysteries."
- *Liturgy, worship, music, holy days, festivals:* emphasis on Sunday morning, Sabbath, or other services, holy days; worship central to community experience; services conducted at home or at houses of worship.
- *Word:* preaching, Bible, Talmud and other religious study; religious education; lectures; importance of intellectual understanding of belief and its everyday application; strong tradition of scholarship.
- *Mission:* living out the calling of the community.
- *Personal religious experience (relational):* emphasis on direct experience with God.
- *Congregation:* emphasis on community life; pastoral care, fellowship. (Some Christian groups believe the "body of Christ" is found in the community of believers rather than primarily in sacraments. In Judaism, God is known through the "Chosen People," therefore the corporate experience is essential.)
- *Social justice, charity, service:* belief that God is in the world and the activity of the community should focus on the needs of the world; Jewish value of *Zedekah:* appreciative charity and cooperative social justice.
- *Contemplative meditation, prayer life, spiritual direction, personal devotions:* emphasis on individual religious practice and religious growth, supervised by spiritual director, or led through discernment of God's leading.

Now factor in the time that is spent on *community maintenance:* fundraising, membership development, board and committee activity, staff supervision, etc. Where does community maintenance rank? How much time is spent on maintaining the building of the church, synagogue, or educational facilities? How does this affect the balance?

Almost all religious communities are blessed with a mixture of religious gifts — their "soil." Some communities have stayed close to their tradition and reflect its primary gifts; others have become more ecumenical and their soil has a greater variety of elements. What gifts are found in your community? What nutrients does your community need and where will you find them? For nurture and renewal of your religious community, we suggest the following:

Draw more deeply from your own religious roots: Perhaps you need to tap more deeply into the primary emphasis of your community's religious traditions. For example, if Roman Catholic, you might plan spiritual retreats that feed on an understanding of the sacraments. A Protestant community that has grown overly dependent on the leadership of the pastor might benefit from studying the Free Church doctrine of the "priesthood of all believers," which asserts that all are ordained to ministry through baptism. Such study might free members to find their own expression in ministry.

Adjust your balance: To find better balance within your present community life, you may need to *let go* of customs or programs that have outlived their usefulness. For example, the Community Fair, which involves many members for months at a time, may take far more energy than it is worth either as a fund-raiser or as an occasion for fellowship. If the Fair has become a duty dance, perhaps your community could benefit more by a restful weekend retreat in the country. Balance is achieved by letting go of activities and concerns that are no longer useful and taking hold of new activities that are needed. Examples of "letting go" and "taking hold":

- If your tradition is congregational with an emphasis on study, your community might decide it also needs the nurture of a more richly liturgical worship.
- If your congregation has been overly preoccupied with its own community maintenance, it may need to become more involved in service to the neighborhood.
- If your community is becoming worn out by serving the homeless, it may also need to find means for its own renewal.

Like the gymnast on the balance beam, communities need to become flexible and in motion — letting go, holding on. Communities that are in motion do not become insular, they freely look out to the world, see it and respond to its need.

Learn from other religious traditions: More and more religious communities are learning from the traditions of others. Roman Catholics sing Protestant hymns and are engaged in Bible study. Free Church Protestants are using the liturgies of more High Church Protestant groups. Many Protestant congregations are being enriched through the traditions of Catholic and Eastern Orthodox spiritual direction. Within the Jewish tradition, Reformed congregations are recovering the richness of the tradition that characterizes Hasidic and Orthodox groups.

The Ground as Gardener

Our metaphor continues. You are the "gardener"; the people in your community are the "plants" whose souls you tend.

But in the fluid ecological system of wholeness, you, the "gardener," are sometimes also the "plant," ministered to by the community. Sometimes members of the community who have been a part of the "ground" assume the "gardener's" role by being responsible for specific healing activities.

Previously we observed that communities heal when they are truly themselves. Even without conducting special programs, communities can heal because of their properties of honest communication, effective conflict resolution and the loving acceptance of their members. Religious communities heal intentionally through their unique spiritual gifts and traditions.

Historically, religious institutions "healed the sick" through hospitals, hospices, medical clinics, and nursing homes. While some religious institutions still sponsor medical and nursing facilities, most religious healing activity, involving many members, is now found in the life of congregations. Such activities are:

- *Religious life:* sacraments, prayers, sermons, healing services, anointing the sick, last rites and final blessings.
- *Groups: prayer and fellowship groups* for spiritual nurture; *support groups* for those who are grieving, recovering from abuse, or addiction; *educational groups* for parenting, personal growth, preparation for aging, life crises; *healing groups* for those with life-threatening illnesses, Twelve Step groups.
- *Educational programs:* religious education for children and adults, lectures, workshops, forums, retreats that in some way address concerns about wholeness.
- *Calling:* on the ill in hospitals, hospices, nursing homes, shut-ins; Eucharistic ministry; preparation for dying.
- *Counseling* (formal and informal) by clerics and lay persons.
- *Seeking guidance, spiritual direction, religious retreats.*
- *Outreach:* evangelism and social outreach — soup kitchens, shelters for the homeless, child care centers.

As you look at the scope of your healing activities, you will become aware of the many people who are involved. You are not alone, and it is necessary for you to grasp this truth. Counselors and caregivers become susceptible to burnout when they believe they must do the work alone. You will be a more effective religious leader if you are able to recognize the healing gifts of other members.

Many times those who work in religious education programs, or who sponsor youth groups, or call on shut-ins, are not aware that they are functioning members of a wholeness network. You can help them discover their identity as people who are helping others become more whole. These "gardeners" should also have an ongoing education about the principles of healing in community, training in listening skills and other skills that are specific or unique to their task. For example, those calling on shut-ins should know very basic counseling skills; they need to be comfortable praying with others, and to be aware of problems in the congregation that may require attention from you or another on your ministry team.

※

A community that is aware and intentional about being a resource for wholeness must create new structures in which members will share responsibility for healing activities in a more inclusive and participatory way. At the same time, religious leaders must help the congregation set up clear lines of accountability so that there can be appropriate follow-up for community care.

In the old way, the religious leader was responsible as the shepherd of the flock. He felt the burden of all of the community care and counseling. There was always more need than could possibly be met. However, there was a certain freedom; often clergy could do as much or as little as they wished with little accountability. Now as more members become involved in the activities of care and nurture, the entire community will benefit and the leader will feel supported. However, he or she will need to make certain that there is a communication system that works. The person in charge of community care and counseling must know what is going on.

It is useful to have regular meetings with those with whom you are working. Those in the ministry of wholeness will need ongoing education, supervision, and systems that will facilitate communication. As members who are involved in this ministry become aware of their identity, there will be an increase in both the amount of information known about other members of the community and the quality of it.

As teachers, youth workers, and parish callers begin to assume more responsibility as members of the wholeness network, the community needs to have a process for sharing concerns about the welfare of members and for making certain that there are follow-up calls by clergy and others where this is appropriate. By having a mechanism in place for sharing vital information, everyone in the community will be able to receive better community care.

For some of you, the model of community that we have been describing might seem to be a radical departure from your own experience. You might well be asking, "Where do we begin?" "How do we create such a new organization?" "How can we change?" "Is such a community really possible and if so, how does it *remain* healthy?"

It is comforting to realize that this process of change has already begun. God is ahead of us. God has already been active in our midst. Our primary task is to open our eyes to see in a new way and *to be open to God's activity.* Clergy and lay leaders have only to ask: "How is our community — and how are the members in it — becoming more aware of our wholeness?" Clergy usually ask, "What work do we have to do?" or "How can

I keep this organization going?" or "How can I finesse this potential Board of Trustees squabble?"

When we ask "How are we becoming more aware of our wholeness?" we have *reframed* the situation. God gets into the equation. God prepares our work for us. There is no way we can become aware of our wholeness without God's grace. This reframing also helps to avoid taking an excessive personal responsibility for maintaining our religious organization. It helps us understand that community maintenance is a part of the community's function as "ground."

We suggest that you begin by getting a group of your perceptive community members together. Spend time listening to each other's insights as you ask the questions: "How is God working in our midst? How are we becoming more whole? How is God unsettling us and causing us to look beyond ourselves?"

One way to begin is with the list of healing activities present in most religious communities — religious life, groups, educational programs, calling, counseling, spiritual direction, and retreats. You may ask:

"Is our community experiencing healing in these expected places?"
"Does our healing come in unexpected forms?"
"What activities in our communal life heal?"
"Who in our community are drawn to healing ministry?"

As you raise these questions you might wish to take an inventory. List the names of all members who are involved in these activities. Become aware of the real extent of your healing system. We have prepared a sample information form for the *Wholeness Network* that may help you. You will find it in *Appendix B*.

In addition, we suggest that you carefully identify all of the individuals who are working with you in this ministry. Many of these are "natural" counselors to whom others are drawn to seek support and nurture. Some are persons who themselves have experienced healing through their recovery from addictions or other serious illness. Others have cared for sick friends or have experienced grief. People who have been healed or who have learned about healing from the care of others need to be identified. In all probability, they are even now quietly supporting others.

In using the *Wholeness Network Form* we suggest that you identify members who work in the helping and healing professions or who are connected *in any way* to health care institutions. This group should be identified because those in it can become resources for you as you make referrals and have other needs for professional consultation. These persons also may need the community's special support because of the drain *they* experience daily.

In the *Wholeness Network Form* we also suggest that you keep your eyes open for unexpected healing. God surprises us with grace. However, we often miss God's presence. We have trained ourselves to look for God's healing in *predictable* places, when people are in hospital, for example. But God leads us to wholeness in surprising ways.

Return to the ground of community. It holds and supports you. When you help your community to be open and responsive — a place where members can be known, where they learn that conflict is not dangerous, and where they can learn to love themselves so that they can love others — you are supporting wholeness.

Chapter Two
Reading and Resources
Publishing Information is found in the Bibliography.

• *The Need for Community: Habits of the Heart,* edited by Robert Bellah, explores the trend in American society toward individualism and isolation, and documents a need for community. In *The Good Society,* Robert Bellah et al., make a convincing argument that religious communities need to be intentionally involved in caring for society's common good. He and the research team document churches' "loss of moral vision and sense of social mission" and ask: "The question is whether organized religion can offer a genuine alternative to tendencies that we have argued are deeply destructive in our current pattern of institutions, or whether religious institutions are simply one more instance of the problem" (p. 184).

• *Understanding and Nurturing Community:* M. Scott Peck explores the nature of community in *The Different Drum: Community Making and Peace* and *A World Waiting to Be Born,* stressing the importance of communication, conflict resolution, and acceptance as principles of community.

The Alban Institute has literature and training opportunities for understanding and nurturing community. Included in their rich literature are: George Parsons and Speed Leas, *Understanding Your Congregation as a System,* and Martin Saarinen, *The Life Cycle of a Congregation.*

Ronald Richardson's *Creating a Healthier Church: Family Systems Theory, Leadership and Congregational Life* is addressed to laypeople to help them understand the emotional life of congregations, to help them manage group conflict and to become effective leaders. Gary Gunderson's *Deeply Woven Roots: Improving the Quality of Life in Your Community* suggests practical ways congregations can improve the health of their communities.

• *Training for Lay Care Giving:* Most faith groups have their own resources for developing the ministry gifts of the laity. We recommend these additional resources: Howard Stone, *The Caring Church: A Guide for Lay Pastoral Care;* and Diane Detwiler-Zapp and William Dixon, *Lay Caregiving,* and team-building materials developed by Stephen Ministries for clergy and laity.

• *Community's Resistance to Change:* John C. Harris's book *Stress, Power, and Ministry,* addresses the difficulties leaders have in helping communities change.

• *Resolving Conflict in Community:* The Alban Institute publishes excellent books on the creative use of conflict. We recommend Speed B. Leas, *Discover Your Conflict Manage-*

ment Style; Leadership and Conflict; Moving Your Church through Conflict; How to Deal Constructively with Clergy-Lay Conflict; A Lay Person's Guide to Conflict Management.

• *Resolving Conflict through Spiritual Discernment:* Quakers offer their rich tradition of peacekeeping and creative listening to all religious communities. Among these resources are Tova Green, Fran Peavy, and Peter Woodrow, *Insight and Action,* which teaches Friends' methods of support groups, clearness process and strategic questioning. Quaker methods for conflict resolution and decision-making processes are explored in: Michael Sheeran, *Beyond Majority Rule: Voteless Decision Making in the Religious Society of Friends;* Patricia Loring, *Spiritual Discernment: The Context and Goal of Clearness Committees* and *Quaker Dialogue "Creative Listening."*

Edward P. Wimberly applies the principles from the tradition of spiritual discernment to the practice of pastoral counseling in *Prayer in Pastoral Counseling: Suffering, Healing and Discernment.*

• *Ministering to Angry People:* Carroll Saussy's *The Gift of Anger: A Call to Faithful Action* helps people assess their anger and find ways to express it. It raises the question, "How can people of faith find ways to understand their anger as a gift of God and avoid expressions of anger that are sinful or destructive?" Daniel Goleman's *Emotional Intelligence* provides useful information about the neurochemistry of anger and has suggestions for dealing with emotional hijacking. Redford Williams's *The Trusting Heart* reports on research about hostility and heart disease and has a program for anger control. Also see Carol Tavris, *Anger: The Misunderstood Emotion.*

• *Diversity in Community:* We have noted that the richness of diversity can also lead to conflict (difference). For help in using difference creatively, see Stephen Kliewer's *How to Live with Diversity in the Local Church,* which offers helpful strategies for living creatively with pluralism. David W. Augsburger's *Conflict Mediation across Cultures: Pathways and Patterns* addresses such questions as: Can mediation, negotiation, and transformation of conflict occur? It also explores reconciliation: the many faces of forgiveness. *Human Diversity: Perspectives on People in Context,* edited by Edison Trickett et al., examines the similarities as well as the differences among diverse groups, highlighting crosscutting themes of oppression, intergroup dynamics, culture, and identify.

• *Workshops for Healing Racism:* Contact Charles Young at Healing Racism, P.O. Box 110, Evanston, IL 60204.

• *Internalizing the God of Fear or the God of Love:* John J. McNeill clearly describes this process in his book *Taking a Chance on God.* While his book is addressed to gay Christians, Dr. McNeill's understanding of the processes by which self-hate and fear are internalized — but can be transformed through loving community — is applicable to everyone.

Carroll Saussy's *God Images and Self-Esteem: Empowering Women in a Patriarchal Society* shows the process through which women internalize a god of oppression. She also demonstrates how the wounds created by the idolatry of worshiping the god of fear can be healed and women's self-esteem can emerge. She draws upon Anna Marie Rizzuto's *Birth of the Living God,* which studies the ways in which images of God are internalized.

See Gerald G. May, M.D.'s profound book, *Will and Spirit,* for his understanding of the ways in which love casts out fear. Dr. May writes from an experience of holism that grows out of spiritual practice.

• *Rediscover Your Tradition's Richness:* See Langdon Gilkey in an essay, "Forgotten Traditions in the Clergy's Self-Understanding," in *Clergy Ethics in a Changing Society,* edited by James P. Wind, Russell Burck, Paul F. Camenisch, and Dennis P. McCann.

• *Community Outreach:* Although in this chapter we focus on the life of the community itself, there is the underlying assumption that religious communities are called to love those outside their own group: they are gifts to the world. For stimulation and practical guidance see: George M. Furniss, *The Social Context of Pastoral Care: Defining the Life Situation;* A. David Boss, *A Practical Guide to Community Ministry;* Carl S. Dudley, *Basic Steps toward Community Ministry: Guidelines and Models in Action;* and Pamela D. Couture and Redney J. Hunter, eds., *Pastoral Care and Social Conflict.*

Resources for Nurturing the Community

The following groups have publications, training programs, and consultants for community building and conflict resolution:

• *Alban Institute,* 4125 Nebraska Avenue N.W., Washington, DC 20016 Tel. (202) 244-7320. This is an ecumenical institution.

• *Foundation for Community Encouragement,* P.O. Box 17210, Seattle, WA 98107-0910 Tel. (206) 784-9000 Fax: (206) 784-9010 *E-mail...FCEonline@aol.com.* M. Scott Peck, M.D., founder.

• *Quaker materials* can be ordered through: Friends General Conference (publications catalog) 1216 Arch Street 2B, Philadelphia, PA 19107 Tel. (215) 561-1700. You can learn about Quaker consultants, training, and other resources through the *Quaker Information Center,* 1501 Cherry Street, Philadelphia, PA 19102 Tel. (215) 241-7024. Peggy Morscheck, Director.

• *Stephen Ministries,* 1325 Boland, St. Louis, MO 63117 Tel. (314) 428-2600. Kenneth Haugk, founder. Offers training in team ministry that includes ongoing support and supervision.

• *Blanton-Peale Institutes* 3 W. 29th Street, New York, NY 10001-4597 Tel. (212) 725-7850 Fax: (212) 689-3212. *Clergy Consultation Service* offers telephone resourcing to members, and its *Wholeness Resources* program offers services to individuals, families, congregations, and other communities.

Caregiver, Counselor:
Yourself as Gardener

*Can you coax your mind from its wandering
and keep to the original oneness?
Can you let your body become
supple as a newborn child's?
Can you cleanse your inner vision
until you see nothing but the light?
Can you love people and lead them
without imposing your will?
Can you deal with the most vital matters
by letting events take their course?
Can you step back from your own mind
and thus understand all things?*

*Giving birth and nourishing,
having without possessing,
acting with no expectations,
leading and not trying to control:
this is the supreme virtue.*

Tao Te Ching 10[1]

Whether you are a *generalist* — a cleric or lay person who counsels as well as performs other healing tasks; or a *specialist* — one who has had additional training and is a certified pastoral counselor or other mental-health professional, you use yourself as a tool for healing. In this chapter we will seek answers to two basic questions: "What do *you* need to do this job?" and "How can you support and nourish wholeness in the lives of individuals and in the life of the community?"

The gardener metaphor can still be helpful. Traditionally, gardeners trained through apprenticeships, where they learned practical skills and obtained horticultural knowledge from a master with an affinity for nature. The master gardener knows the plants, loves the earth, and is connected to nature. The apprentice gardener learns to garden from *the being* of the master.

Like a gardener, it is important for you to become a counseling apprentice. At one time clergy learned community caregiving skills through being closely supervised in seminary and then beginning their ministry as cleric's assistants. Today, many new clergy begin their ministry "on their own." They have not had the necessary apprenticeships in ministry in which they can learn "from the being" of experienced clergy who give counsel and care. Perhaps you are one of those. However, all clergy can still become apprentices. They can hone their skills through pastoral supervision.

Of course, counselors in community who are clinical social workers, certified counselors, and other health professionals have been clinically supervised. They, as well as those who have been supervised in Clinical Pastoral Education, have served apprenticeships and know their value. They have learned *to do* from the *being* of a master.

One's self is the tool that the community counselor uses in the work. It is one's self that listens, empathizes, thinks, and connects. You use your own experience, and your imagination. You use your woundedness, your strength, your faith. You use your doubts. You listen with your whole self, not just your mind. You understand with your heart while, at the same time, you apply counseling technique and theory. You must know yourself, while continuing to learn about yourself.

When working with a healing community, counselors need to help counselees learn to:

- communicate their authentic selves,
- resolve conflicts and accept differences,
- accept themselves and through that, love others.

Counselors need to be able to use themselves in ways that facilitate healing through interaction with counselees.

Although in the following chapters we make a distinction between the functions of community care and counseling, in this chapter, for the sake of brevity, we will include the role of caregiver in the word "counselor." While the goals of community care and counseling differ, you use yourself in similar ways in both roles. We will use the word "counselee" with the same broad meaning as we refer to one whom you care for in ministry.

In community, people learn to know themselves when they are perceived by others who really want to know them. Through their experience of being known, people often become greater than they thought it possible to be. Counselors, like the community itself, help counselees know their wholeness through *listening*, through *being with*, through *understanding*. As the counselor, you must learn to listen with your whole self. Listening is the heart of the process.

Static-Free Listening

Can you picture a counseling session in which the counselee is comfortably talking about himself or herself to a counselor who is listening with lively attentiveness? In this picture, the counselor seems to be a "real" person who listens in such a way that the counselee feels safe. Perhaps you can create this picture because of a personal experience with such a counselor or counselee. However, perhaps you, like many of us, have conducted counseling sessions in which you did not feel like the counselor in this picture. You felt scattered and anxious. Your counseling space did not seem like a "safe place," even to you.

When we are filled with anxiety, it is analogous to a radio emitting static that interferes with reception. When we are filled with the static of unspoken anxiety, the counselee experiences us as lacking in receptivity. It is very difficult to create a safe place in which your counselees can know themselves if you are filled with inner tension fueled by anxiety. It is therefore necessary for you to identify your own anxiety and to acknowledge it to yourself. That way you can decide whether it is useful or useless anxiety.

Useful anxiety is a signal from yourself that there is imminent danger to yourself or another. In listening to a counselee's distressful story, you might send yourself an anxiety signal that allows you to go into emergency mode. In this mode you are then able to make a necessary intervention.

But often the anxiety we feel in our counseling sessions is not useful. This useless anxiety comes from a *misperception* of danger. For example, we feel that we are in danger of "messing up" in the counseling session because we are not doing it well enough or someone else could do it better. The degree of danger we feel is inappropriate. Our bodies are geared up for a life or death situation. If we were to breathe and center ourselves, we would discover that although we are uncertain, we know enough to get our bearings. Our sense of danger was based on the mistaken belief that we must have a complete plan for counseling.

Anxiety does not come from nowhere. It is often connected to the activation of an idea. We can deal with anxiety by discovering the scary things we say to ourselves. An idea that often stirs anxiety in a counselor is: *"I'm not enough to do this.* My supervisor, Bill, my therapist, Susan, my friend, John, could do this better. They'd know what to do." The belief — and fear — of "not being enough" can plague even the most experienced therapist. The great therapist and theoretician, Dr. Carl Rogers, regularly worked to change a thought pattern that triggered his anxiety. It is said that even in his later years, Dr. Rogers would center himself before beginning a master class, and would remind himself: "I am enough." He just had to be himself.[2]

When we think that some wiser counselor should be in the counseling room because "I am not enough," we disconnect from ourselves. We focus on the "expert" who is not in the room. We leave ourselves and in leaving, create anxiety. We abandon ourselves. If we were to breathe and use Dr. Roger's mantra: "I am enough," we would return to ourselves and find the truth. *If we are truly ourselves, we have enough.*

Our work as counselors is to be with those who are finding their path. To be with them we are not required to be geniuses. We are required to be as authentically ourselves as we are capable of being at that time. When we are connected to ourselves, we can use our experiences and gifts. For some, it might be the experience of growing up with an alcoholic father or a critically ill mother or it might be a sense of humor or the ability to reframe experience. For others, it might be the painful experience of feeling like an outcast because of racism, sexism, ageism, homophobia, etc. For yet others, it might be a gift of the spirit. In counseling, experiences that we have thought of as weaknesses can be transformed and used to help others. Perhaps you have been ashamed of your learning difficulties or your divorce or your child's struggle with addiction. These painful experiences, when seen in a new light, can be gifts that help you to be more understanding and less judgmental. As you become more whole yourself, you are able to use all of your experience. You discover that you have within you what you need. As you relax into this truth, you can listen to others without creating static.

Listening to Yourself

We cannot listen to others unless we know, first, how to listen to ourselves.

It is necessary for counselors to have consciousness of what helps them lessen and utilize their anxiety. Relaxation techniques, running and other forms of exercise are practices by which many have learned to lower anxiety and to become more centered. While the intention of prayer and meditation is spiritual, we know that we become deeply centered and less anxious through these experiences.

We also recommend that counselors learn to *breathe*. When you are anxious, you hold your breath. When you hold your breath, you do not think well. By simply becoming conscious of your breathing pattern, you can become more centered, more present. The significance of breath is found in many religious traditions. In the Hebrew Bible, God inspirited humanity with *ruach*, breath, life; in the New Testament, the Holy Spirit was breathed on the people. Intentional breathing is essential in many Buddhist meditation practices. Being conscious of your breath can help you be aware of your life.

Intentional breathing helps us listen to ourselves. Try the simple experiment of focusing on your breathing for just five minutes. Notice *where* the breath moves in your body when you breathe in. Follow your breath as it moves out. Do not try to breathe in any special way. As you do this, you will probably find your mind wandering. Your attention will probably be distracted by thoughts that move in and out. As you continue to focus, you may begin to become one with your breathing. As this happens, your mind feels clearer. You may begin to feel other parts of your body. A tight muscle in your back may become noticeable. Or you may become aware of sadness or anger, or tiredness. Don't try to suppress these thoughts or feelings. As you focus on your breathing, you begin to get a new kind of information about yourself.

Some people find it more helpful to *see* the results of breathing rather than to *feel* the process. If you like to see what is happening, you might be helped through using biofeedback techniques.

Many of us have been taught that "listening to ourselves" means to listen to our thoughts. But through doing the experiment with intentional breathing, we become aware that we can experience much more than words when we truly listen to ourselves. In order to know through listening, we need *silence*. Many of us do not allow ourselves silence. Because of our frantic pace, restful quiet has become a luxury. Even those of us who know better find it hard to have times of quiet contemplation in which we listen to ourselves and to God.

Although we are often unaware of it, those of us who spend so much time tending to others can become lonely for ourselves. When we do not spend time with ourselves, we can unconsciously become resentful of those who come for counseling and community care. Contrary to what we often believe, spending time with ourselves is not a luxury. It is a necessity.

Creating a Space for Others

We use the expression "creating a space for others" to mean that the counselor is ready to be hospitable to the person coming for counseling. Many counselors do not consider the question of their readiness to meet their counselees because of the radical idea that lies behind it: *You* are also in the picture. Many counselors believe that they must give themselves away, must meet the needs of others, and must always be available. They do not ask: "Am I ready?" Their needs are not factored into the equation.

However, if you do not pay attention to your own readiness, it is hard to pay attention — to be present — to those whom you are counseling. Those of us who counsel often have experienced being in a session before we were ready. As we were trying to listen to our counselee we remembered an urgent phone call we needed to make, or we felt physical tension that would have been eased by stretching, or we were preoccupied with some other unfinished business. Because our own needs kept interrupting us, we were unable to be present to the other person.

It is helpful to learn to practice readiness. A simple readiness practice is this: Before beginning your day of counseling or other ministering activity, sit in silence and center yourself through intentional breathing. Ask yourself, "Is there anything that is keeping me from being present to myself right now?" Don't rush the process. Listen for the answer. You might hear yourself saying, "I'm tired," or "I'm concerned about how my son will do with his college board exam," or "I'm worried about my parishioner's cancer diagnosis," or "I forgot to pay the phone bill, or cancel the meeting, or turn on the answering machine." In identifying what is keeping you from being present to yourself, you can then decide what tasks you must attend to before you begin your day and what concerns must be bracketed for another time when you can give them serious attention.

Readiness practice is a form of prayer. If we are to be able to listen to others with lively attentiveness, we must be centered and mentally uncluttered. Our own anxieties need to be acknowledged and dealt with. As we quietly breathe, we can pray to be given the gift of "leading and not trying to control."[3] It is only through grace that we are given these virtues that are necessary if we are to create a welcoming space within ourselves so that we can welcome others into our counseling rooms.

When beginning a counseling session, it is useful to wait to begin to speak until you feel ready. As you are breathing, listen to yourself. Make certain that you feel "in" your body. If you are experiencing a cluttered mind or are anxious, you might not be aware of your self. Because you are taking time, your counselee will also have time to become composed. You both have time to breathe. Now, as you are becoming connected to yourself, you are able to get the counselee into focus. You have become "all there and accounted for." You have given both yourself and your counselee "space" in which either of you feels free to speak.

As you go through this readiness process, you will perhaps begin to notice subtle changes within your own body. Because you have been breathing intentionally, your hands have become comfortably warm. You may notice that your stomach muscles are relaxing and your abdomen is experiencing the sensation of "melting." You begin to return to your center. As this happens, you are feeling more at home in your self. Because you are "at home," you can open the door of your self to your counselee. If you had started the session before you caught up with yourself, you might have seemed distracted or preoccupied. Now you are available.

Using Your Emotional Response and Imagination

When you have created a hospitable place through your availability, your counselee will be more able to tell his or her story and to risk being understood. *The counseling process requires bravery.* When counselees open their hearts to you, they experience vulnerability and they often silently wonder "Will I be accepted? Do I dare say what is really on my mind? Will this religious person — or God — condemn me for being myself?" But you, the counselor, are also taking a risk. To understand your counselee, you must use all of your self and your experience, even that which you have buried or would like to disown. To be open to your counselee you, too, become vulnerable.

As counselors we are often confused about how to use ourselves in the counseling process. How do we handle our own need for love and acceptance while we are in a counseling relationship that is often emotionally charged? How "real" is it appropriate to be in the counseling relationship? Is the therapeutic relationship "real" or is it different or special?

Often the counseling relationship is described as "therapeutic" or "professional" in a way that makes it seem less "real" or personal than, say, friendship. Sometimes we feel that to be "professional" we must be distant and objective, but we find that when we are this way we feel as if we are role playing. However, when we have become more emotionally available or have shared information from our own lives, we have sometimes felt embarrassed or intrusive. We have felt that we stepped out of our role as counselor. We then experience confusion, thinking, "How can I be a *real* person and be in this *role* at the same time?"

We believe that in the counseling relationship both counselor and counselee are sometimes given the gift of grace in which they can know themselves and each other in their fullness. Although the counselor uses him or her self in this process, *the counseling relationship is not about the counselor. It exists for the healing of the counselee* although often counselors become more whole themselves because of their experience as companion. Learning to use your self — in all its reality — to do the work of counseling requires training and practice.

As you become clear about your role as counselor, you begin to know how to use yourself in the process. When you see that you are a *companion* to those on their journey toward wholeness you know not to get in the way; you must use your eyes, ears, mind, and heart to help your counselees see and understand themselves well enough to proceed on their journey. To do this well, you must not confuse your own journey toward wholeness with that of the counselee. You must claim your own life story; you must have an understanding of your hurts and wounds. You must know how you are trying to make up for your own early losses. You must have some awareness of your thinking and personality style. You must acknowledge your gifts.

We feel that it is essential that counselors be in an ongoing process of self-reflection and self-understanding. Because we are always changing, we must have practices that help us continually to be conscious of our inner lives. We must keep track of our souls. Some counselors find that personal or family therapy helps them gain self-knowledge. Others work with a spiritual director. Some use retreats and workshops to facilitate personal growth. Others record their dreams and write in journals. Some actively use their creative gifts to connect them to inner experience, others use meditation and prayer. No matter which method you use, your ongoing task is to know yourself.

Although we use our minds to understand the meaning our counselees make of their experience, we first make contact with them through our emotional responses and empathic listening. It is this contact that first makes those to whom we are listening *feel* heard. We listen both sympathetically and empathetically. We use ourselves differently in these different processes.

When you listen sympathetically, you are using your sense of *being similar* to the counselee. You feel a sense of mutuality that comes through the affinity you feel with the counselee. You have a shared emotion. You feel *with him or her*. The etymological meaning of sympathy is "feeling for." When you feel yourself responding with sympathy you need to ask: "In what ways is her or his story like mine and how are we different?" If you have had an experience that parallels that of the counselee, you *might* be able to share knowledge that could be pertinent. For example, a counselee might be coming to speak to you about the terror she feels about her recent cancer diagnosis. She is unaware of your life experience. She does not know that you have successfully recuperated from a breast cancer operation. When she speaks to you, your heart goes out to her in sympathy. You know what it is like to be in her shoes. But you are left with the questions: How do I use my experience? Do I tell her about me? If I do, will she experience it as me wanting to talk about myself perhaps to gain her sympathy? Or will she see me as a potential coach who can help her navigate through the shoals of her imminent experience?

We all use our life experience in counseling others. A rule of thumb, however, is only to tell our story about an event in our lives to counselees after we have worked the event through and feel little conflict about it. If the counselor in our example has recovered and has worked through the fear and anger that often accompany cancer, she might find it helpful to tell certain counselees who are undergoing a similar trauma that she has been there, too.

But let's go back to the counselor's question: "How do I use my experience? Do I tell her about me?"

Before sharing a story about yourself, think about it first. Will it get in the way of the experience of the counselee? How will it help? Will it be a metaphor that points to the counselee, or will it obscure, confuse, or take away? With practice, we use our feelings, but we also use our judgment. You must clearly understand how you are different from the counselee. *You must not confuse your similar experiences with his or her life story.*

However, even though you might not speak about your similar experiences, you use these for understanding. For instance, If both you and your counselee have had alcoholic fathers, you share a common experience. As he speaks to you about his childhood, you remember yours. Although your experience with your alcoholic father was not identical to his, it was similar. You feel an interrelated sense of sympathy toward him. Your heart reaches out. You might never tell the counselee about this commonality. However, your counselee will feel your sympathy. Your sympathy will be experienced by him as a finely tuned emotional response.

When we respond out of *sympathy* to a counselee, we often feel comfortable. Even when we are sharing a feeling of loss or pain, we are being moved by a familiar place in ourselves and we meet another at a similar point. When we feel sympathy, we are warmed.

Our experience of *empathy*, on the other hand, can sometimes make us feel uncomfortable because it always requires us to *journey into the unknown*. When we are sympathetic, we use similar experiences to feel with another. When we empathize, we first have to acknowledge how we are *different* from the counselee. We then use ourselves and our experiences to *feel into* their experience and to know them in their uniqueness.

Empathic listening is paradoxical. In order to make contact with another, we must acknowledge how singular, unique — *alone* — we all are. No one, even if we have an identical twin, is like us. No one can know *exactly* what we feel. It is when we accept our uniqueness and do not assume that we know the other's experience that we can be open to the aloneness of others — and then meet them. It is in this meeting, which Martin Buber called the meeting of "I" and "thou," that we can know each other — because God, "Thou," is with us.[4]

To be empathic, we must acknowledge that, initially, *we don't know* the other. Most of us become uncomfortable about not knowing. Counselors, especially religious counselors, feel pressure to know. When counselees come to us for advice, they expect us to know solutions to life's problems. They expect practical, doctrinal, and spiritual answers.

Empathic listening requires you to develop a more friendly attitude toward the experience of "not understanding." If, when counseling another, you find yourself listening and saying to yourself, "I really don't understand what she means," or "I don't know why he sees it that way," or "I don't know what she's feeling when she cries," then perhaps you have already begun listening empathically.

On the most basic level, to say "I really don't understand" indicates that you already know that you are different from the counselee. You are not able to make assumptions about the person even though you might share the same religious culture, ethnic background, etc. The acknowledgment of being different is a requirement for empathetic listening.

When we listen empathically to another, we pay attention to the content of the words and the "music" of the feelings. We form impressions on a preconscious level. Our bodies register sensations, our minds form associations. Often we *slowly* form impressions of the person we're getting to know. In this process, we know more about the other than we are consciously aware. We do not feel the other's feelings or read the other's mind but we have an approximation of his or her experience.

This sense of empathy is not in and of itself benign. After all, con men are often very skillful at "feeling out" others in order to "take" them. Being empathic, on the other hand, has a positive effect on others. Being empathic means not only to be able to *be with* the other as we sense their experience, but to *think about* the other as we try to understand what his experience means to him. When we are being empathic, we move between participating in what we believe is the other's experience (feeling into) and moving back into our own experience in which we observe the other from a more objective stance. Our understanding of his experience is informed by our own subjective experience as well as what we observe about him. We then use our empathic experience to voice comments about the person's internal state that causes the person to feel understood or soothed.[5]

Some people confuse being empathic with mind reading (which they might call "being intuitive"). But even when you are highly attuned and experiencing empathy, you never know the other's experience in its totality. You need to check with the other to see if you are "getting it." Often you have a sense that you are understanding only in part what another is experiencing. For example, after listening empathically, you might say to the counselee, "You seem weighed down, burdened." After you speak, the counselee's body relaxes and he says, "Yeah." Although you can see that you have "read" him correctly, you might sense that you still have not understood what is *truly* burdening him. He has been speaking with sadness about his marriage but you need more information. You sense that because of your comment he has felt relief, but you do not know why. And so you ask, "You seem more relaxed, can you tell me what just happened?" He then tells you that he feels he is unloading a secret.

You are not required to "get" what a person means at once. Often people feel soothed when they sense that you *want* to understand them and that you are in the *process* of understanding. You are in the process of understanding when you keep checking with the other to see if you are understanding both the words and the feelings of their communication. You may need to say, "This is what I'm sensing; is it right?" or "Help me understand what you mean when you say," or "I'm going to say this back; correct me if I'm off." You need to keep asking for this feedback because it is easy to distort or misconstrue someone else's experience as you read it through the lens of your own. Your empathic experience moves you in the direction of knowing others. But you need help from them to know them more completely.

Listening empathically and then being empathic is an art that takes practice and patience. It involves:

- Managing your own feelings, which come when you realize you don't understand the experience of others who are different from yourself.
- Understanding others, not by making assumptions but by learning the language of their experience so that you can speak to them.
- Getting information about them not only from what they tell you through their words, feelings, body language, and the language of their unconscious, but also from listening to your own response to them.
- Checking your understanding with them so that they can correct distortions and misconstructions you make because of your difference from them.

If you have found, after breathing and checking in with yourself, that you are able to be empathically present, you are often left with the awareness of that nagging first clue: "I don't know what she means about...." If is often best to bracket that question and to begin to be present to the counselee *where he is now*. Although you, the counselor, have an agenda — you want to understand the other — you must go about this in a way in which the counselee feels that the activity is about him or her, not about you. Sometimes this requires that you sit with your own questions and wait for them to be answered as the counselee reveals him or herself to you.

In the meantime, try to feel your way *into* your counselee's experience. As you listen to his story use your imagination to visualize and experience. Identify with him. For example, you might discover that even though you are very different from your counselee, you are both oldest sons. You know what he is talking about when he tells you how burdened and responsible he still feels for his mother and sisters. You also use your own body feelings to understand when he speaks of the burden he feels. You have become aware that, as he speaks, his body is beginning to look heavy, his shoulders are sagging. He is speaking to you nonverbally through his body. Your own body can identify and resonate with his experience.

When we listen empathically we become highly tuned receivers. We pay attention to all the communicating signals the counselee sends. We listen to words, associations, and feelings. We sense how the counselee is experiencing his body. We are aware of silence. We are aware of what is not being said. We receive these messages with our own complete self. We are thinking about what we hear. Our emotions and our bodies are responding. Our imagination is using our own experience to identify with what is being said. Our unconscious is processing and making meaning. Our spirit is moved. We are making "sense" of the other in a total way. We are not simply collecting data. *We are knowing.*[6]

As we move into empathic listening we usually lose the initial sense of discomfort that comes from our awareness that we do not know the other. However, over and over in the listening process we will realize that we still need to know and we will be seeking to understand what the other is meaning. Unlike sympathetic listening, we will be aware of our differences and we will feel a distance that helps us have perspective. We use this sense of perspective to help us see the counselee as clearly as we can.

We want to underscore that being empathic is not something you *do to* a counselee. Pastoral psychotherapist A. J. van den Blink reminds us that empathy is inherently a *relational* process that helps us bridge diversity not only in the counseling process, but in the religious community as well.

It is easy to think of empathy in individualistic terms as your experience with the subjective processes of another. Dr. van den Blink offers a corrective. He says that empathic relationships always occur in a *context* that is *"the total environment in which we are and which is in us."* Both you and your counselee live in a context that is not outside of yourself; you are in it and it is in you. The context of your life involves your relationships, work, class, gender, race, sexuality. It involves your history, culture, language. It involves the environment of workplace and nature and your communal and spiritual experience. It involves the impact of the world upon you.

Often counselors have erred on the side of not taking their counselee's *total environment* into the picture. Dr. van den Blink says that when he wishes to be listened to with empathy:

> What I want and need is for someone to take the time and trouble to discern the shape of my experience, the gestalt of what I have gone through or what I am struggling with, and to help me understand it better. For in participating in that kind of respectful and caring exploration of my life or my issue or my problem, no matter how difficult or painful, I feel affirmed in my humanity. I feel empowered and begin to understand myself better and am able to see and grasp things about myself that I have not seen or grasped before.[7]

Empathic relating, he says, is a form of research into the other, and inevitably, as we have stressed, into oneself. It can only be done with the permission of all involved, with respect, with a phenomenological frame of mind that brackets and suspends assumptions, diagnoses, and judgment.

The process of knowing another is complex. The experience of knowing another is one of mystery and grace.

Finding Courage to Face the Projections of Others

We now must look at the more frightening part of our work. How do we use ourselves so that others might know themselves when those people are more seriously disturbed? Is it possible to be both the religious leader of and counselor to those who are psychologically unbalanced? How can we be helpful to them and still feel safe ourselves?

Faith communities have long been the haven for psychologically disturbed people. It is not unusual for a congregation to be hospitable, or at least to adapt, to peculiar, bizarre, and sometimes "crazy" people. They, in turn, relate as best they can to the life of the community. As counselors, you have frequently ministered to these pained and often marginalized souls.

Also, you have ministered to disturbed people at cost to yourself. Allow yourself to remember your first attempt at ministering to a highly disturbed person. Your body may still remember the sense of sickening fear, or the rush of adrenalin, or the sense of panic or confusion you experienced as you tried to make sense of the situation or to make a useful intervention.

It is very upsetting to deal with people who project their fearful world upon us and who then respond to us as if we were in that world. Our upset often has a long aftereffect on our systems. Sometimes we feel it in our bodies. We may belatedly have the shakes or a tension headache or a back spasm. We may not want to answer the phone for fear that the person who has upset us will call.

Often, counselors disassociate themselves from the fear or anger or confusion they feel when they have been affected by the mental and emotional disturbance of others. They try to ignore the physical messages their bodies send because they unwisely believe that it is not loving — or professional — to be affected in such a profoundly disturbed way. Their disturbance is then internalized; it goes underground. If we adapt in this unhelpful manner, in the course of time we will be physically or emotionally sick ourselves. High blood pressure, ulcers, alcoholism, and other stress-related illnesses are created when we internalize toxic, unprocessed experience.

Ministry can be a dangerous job. You must learn to be respectful of its dangers and to protect and care for yourself while still being available to the healing process in others.

One of the ways you can protect yourself is to understand what hits you when you become the focus of the unconscious projections of others. We all project unresolved conflicts from childhood on to people in the present who symbolize those with whom we have unfinished business. This is a normal, unconscious process. As we mature, we usually become more aware of this process and begin to discover that we are treating others as stand-ins for our parents or others who have influenced our lives. As we work through early conflicts in the course of living our lives, we begin to see that it is inappropriate to treat a husband as if he were a father or a mother. Seriously disturbed people also project their frightened past onto the present. However, at times they are not able to distinguish the past traumatic events from the present reality. If they experienced their childhood as a nightmare, they often experience — -and sometimes create — a terrifying present.

I described in chapter 2 how damaged people often come from families that worshiped a God of fear. Many disturbed people are drawn to religious communities in search of the God of love. Even when they begin to experience acceptance in your community they might treat you, the person they see as the representative of God, as if you were the stand-in for the fearful God of their childhood. They then respond to you out of that place and you become the recipient of their fear, or rage, or crazy thoughts, or strange behavior. In some instances, you might be placed on a pedestal and be placated or adored. Sometimes this adoration is accompanied by a sexual fixation. In other instances, the projection takes the form of clingy, childlike behavior. In other instances, you are experienced as a harsh or judgmental authority figure who must be knocked down, destroyed or neutralized. You are treated with anger or disdain. Sometimes these projections are acted out in subtle ways; sometimes the energy they create is strong and frightening.

Most counselors are unprepared for the *force* of these unconscious projections, nor did they begin with an understanding of the *source* of the projections. When we entered our ministry we did not know that the authority of our office and our religious role would invite these unconscious projections. We did not know that when people are caught in the force of the projection they would be unable to see us as we are, that when they are living out a response to past experience there is nothing we can do, in that moment, to "change the plot of the play."

Undoubtedly you have also experienced others in your community, people you feel are usually "well put together," who, seemingly out of the blue, treat you as if you were not you. You feel as if they had placed a *mask* of another's face on your face.

How do we use ourselves to help those who are projecting their unconscious onto us? How can we be personally effective when we are trying to minister to those who because they are living out an old script, do not see us?

The most helpful act we can perform for others who are caught in the force of their unconscious projections is *to know and be ourselves.*

To illustrate the process of projection, we have just used the metaphor of the mask. When you experience another's projections, you feel you are not being seen. You sense that a mask of another's face has been put over yours. You can not see whose face it is, you can only feel that something has been put over your face that constricts it and affects you. At the moment when you sense this is happening, it is very important for you to breathe and keep track of yourself. When you are being "erased" by another, you must be real to yourself.

Then you can listen empathically to the *behavior* of the person projecting the mask on you. When you are able to "hear" this behavior as language you will know more about the way in which *that* person has been not seen. As in other instances of being empathic, you will have to wait to communicate insights from your empathic listening. When someone is caught in the force of projection they are not receptive to your reasonable interpretations of their behavior. You do not argue or try to get people to be sensible. You maintain contact with your reasonable self and set reasonable limits so that you do not get recruited into the projecting person's drama and inadvertently act like the one whose mask has been placed upon you. Sometimes you do not know that a mask has been placed upon you until you find yourself treating the person in an unreasonably angry way, or feeling "crazy," "sucked into" his or her chaos. The better you know yourself, the quicker you can catch yourself from acting out the feared response of one who has projected upon you.

Let us look at the process of recruitment in the drama of projection. In the first place, this drama is always an unconscious process. The projecting person does not consciously seek you out. You have not knowingly been auditioned for the part. If the projecting person is needing an authority person to work through old hurt, his or her unconscious found you because of your *role.*

Sometimes, paradoxically, introverted counselors are seen as angry, aggressive parents, or sometimes patient counselors are seen as highly critical parents. It is your role, more than your personal style, that gets you cast in the part. However, we sometimes find ourselves acting out the role in which we have been cast, as in this example:

John was an active layreader in his local parish and was also an occasional fishing buddy of his pastor, Father Scott. He was the child of a workaholic father who was often absent but who, when he did pay attention to John, was angry and highly critical. He treated John erratically, either spoiling or severely punishing him. John valued his relationship to Father Scott. Although they sometimes fished together, John felt that Father Scott was "above" him.

Over time, Father Scott began to feel that, when in church, John was treating him in a distant manner. He found John's behavior confusing because he was still friendly when they went on fishing trips with other men in the parish. One Sunday, John said to Father Scott, "I know you think I messed up on the reading...." This was the first that Father Scott knew something was troubling John. However, he did not yet know that he had been recruited to play the role of John's father.

During the following weeks, John became highly sensitive to every nuance of Father Scott's voice. He began to hear criticism when it was not there. He felt panic before he read. He felt shame. Although he was angry at Father Scott for "being hard on him" he at first did not admit it. Rather, he became obsessed with "reading right" and pleasing Father Scott. When speaking to Father Scott, he would say, "I know you don't like this but...," or "I'm sorry that I can't get this right...." John's anger became more generalized. When he was with Father Scott in church council meetings he was argumentative, sarcastic, and passively undercutting. Father Scott began to get annoyed. He felt unjustly accused of being highly critical, and he started to avoid John. John then experienced Father Scott to be distant like his father. John, by now, was experiencing Father Scott *as* his father. Father Scott was recruited into the part. He felt anger toward John who was openly hostile to him. At a church council meeting, Father Scott lost his temper and humiliated John. He was now acting like John's father.

Father Scott did not know he was acting out an unconscious role. John had not told Father Scott much about his childhood. Father Scott only knew that *he was not being himself;* he felt something had "taken him over."

By now, Father Scott was experiencing the disturbance caused by being the recipient of the unconscious projections of another. He felt hurt personally. Because of his anger, his body had been infused with adrenalin. He felt ashamed. His professional confidence was shaken.

Father Scott was moved by this upset to join a group of clergy who met with a pastoral psychotherapist for supervision. It was in the course of the supervision that he learned he had been playing a part in a drama of the unconscious. He realized that although he could not have stopped John's projections upon him, he could have handled them differently had he been able to hear himself better. He saw that he got recruited into the drama at the point when John experienced him as highly critical, although Father Scott knew he was not behaving that way. At that point, Father Scott did not hold on to his own sense of himself. Instead of taking a reasonable position about how he had responded to John, he became defensive. He was not able to be empathic with John and to find out what John's acute fear of criticism was about.

Because of the supervision, Father Scott was able to rework his pastoral relationship to John and in time, he was able to refer him to a therapist who helped him decode the drama that he and Father Scott had played out together.

It is particularly important for you to remain constant and to be as much your real self as possible with those who distort you. Sometimes, usually with therapeutic help, they are able eventually to "see" you and know you are not the person they feared you to be.

Father Scott's experience also illustrates that we cannot do this work alone. Just as he did not understand "what hit him" until he was in the supervisory group, many of us find that it is through the perspective of other eyes that we realize we have been playing a part in someone's drama of projection. The supervisory group also helped Father Scott discover that he had been ashamed of finding help earlier because he felt he should be able to manage this difficult matter alone. He had unrealistic expectations of himself and felt he should give without limits.

Like Father Scott, we all need supervision and continued professional education. Supervision and peer support help us get the toxic residue from our response to the projections of others out of our system. Usually, when we talk about these disturbing situations, we release stored-up emotion as well. We feel the fear, or anger, or panic that we disowned about the event. Often we realize that we had also been soaking up the unconscious feelings or experience of the other, and the tragedy and cruelty of the unconscious drama that is projected upon us. Father Scott discovered that he was the recipient of the anger that John had never been able to express toward his cruelly abusive father. John *consciously* believed that he was angry at Father Scott for "being too hard on him." Father Scott felt the force of John's anger and hostility, but In addition, he was *unconsciously* picking up the pain that John was *unconsciously* experiencing about his relationship with his father — the relationship he was reliving through the drama of projection.

When we are able to talk about and release both our pent-up experience and the pain we have absorbed we often feel relief. We are like one cleansed of demons whom Jesus described:

> When the unclean spirit has gone out of a person, it wanders through waterless regions looking for a resting place, but not finding any, it says, "I will return to my house from which I came." When it comes,

it finds it swept and put in order. Then it goes and brings seven other spirits more evil than itself, and they enter and live there; and the last state of that person is worse than the first. Luke 11:24–26.

It is as true for you as it was for that person: it is not enough to have the "evil spirits" of the toxic residue of your work released through helpful supervision and support. Like the man in the story, you are vulnerable if you have a clean but empty house. You must also be ready to have your house filled with good spirits. You must "fill your house" with the richness *of your own life*. We have said that courage — taking heart — is an appropriate response to danger. However, Jesus gives an essential corrective when he reminds us that *the presence of destructiveness, or serious disturbance, is not as dangerous as the vacuum that is created and then not filled with the goodness of life.*

Those of us engaged in the ministry of religious counseling are in greatest danger when we do not live our own lives. It is easy to be absorbed in the drama, crisis, or excitement of the lives of others. It is important for us to stay connected to our own liveliness, to become who we are meant to be and to care for our own souls.

Listening as an Act of Prayer

The work you do as a religious counselor can feed your soul, particularly when you stay connected to your own experience. Empathic listening, which Margaret Guenther, professor of ascetical theology and spiritual direction, calls *"holy listening,"* can be an act of prayer.[8]

When we are listening empathically, we are seeking to be open to *what is true* in the present moment. We are also trying to discern the truth of experiences in the past. In this deep listening process we are open to revelation. We are engaged in meaning making, an activity that many of us feel is profoundly religious.

When we are listening deeply we are waiting — waiting for the other to speak or feel or know. In this waiting, we trust that he or she is in the process in which "mud settles and the water is clear."[9] As we are waiting, we sometimes experience a sense of being in a state of silent, wordless prayer. We have been "praying without ceasing." Sometimes, at these moments, we are aware that both we and the counselee have been feeling very present to each other. And sometimes, we are aware of a Presence holding us in the hovering silence.

We are not always conscious of our counseling experience as "holy work." At the times when we are feeling discomfort we are unaware of "praying without ceasing." We are confused by not understanding or by the strong emotions directed at us. We are uncomfortable with the conflicts in the other. At these times we have the need to make it "all right," to remove the other's anxiety. At these times we are usually very focused — and sometimes lost — in the other. We are trying to "figure him out." If we are able to listening to ourselves we sometimes find, to our surprise, that we have been silently praying for guidance and clarity. We then find that we are given the grace to begin to find our breathing and to connect to our center so that we can begin again to listen empathically.

You may be asking, "How do I use my spiritual experience to help others know and accept themselves?" "Do I tell them when I'm experiencing the Presence of God? If I don't pray out loud, will they not know this is 'religious counseling?' Do I share stories of my or my tradition's faith experience to instruct them?"

Before answering these questions, let us consider another set of questions in order to simulate an experience in counseling. There are times in the course of your work when you are surprised and unsettled when, seemingly out of the blue, you are asked: "What do you believe? Do you have faith that God will help me?" or "Will you pray with me?" or "Why haven't you prayed with me?" or "Have you ever doubted God?"

When questions like these arise, what guidelines do you use in responding to them? Let us suggest some:

Before answering a direct question about yourself, it is helpful to find out what is really being asked. What does the question *mean* to the questioner? Sometimes people ask questions when they are really making statements. The question, "What do you believe? Do you believe God will help me?" might really mask the statement: "I feel helpless. Even if you believe God will help me, it won't do me any good. I'm not you." If you had not found the statement underneath the question, you might have gone on with a story from your life that would have told the counselee something about you, but you would have missed him and his profound sense of helplessness.

Sometimes the question is not the question that was really meant to be asked. The same question, "What do you believe? Do you believe God will help me?" might instead have meant: "I don't really want to know, 'Do you believe in God.' I want to know 'Do you believe in me,' but I'm afraid to ask."If you had not discovered the question behind the question, you would have told him something he did not really need to know.

It is useful to be gentle when inquiring about direct questions asked about you. You might say, "I will respond to your question, but can you help me understand it better? I hear several questions in what you say and I want to respond in a helpful way. Tell me more about what your wanting God's help is about." Take the case of a dying person who asks this same question. "What do you believe? Do you believe God will help me?" is a direct request to help him with his dying by sharing the comfort of his own religious beliefs. In this situation it would be important for you to listen to what the person's approaching death means to him and for you to share, honestly, what you believe in such a way that his experience is illuminated, not obscured.

However, often questions that begin with "What do you think?" "What do you believe?" camouflage deeper questions about where the person believes he stands with you or with God. Sometimes the questioner is wondering: "If I think enough like you, will you like me?" Or, "I need to find out what *you* believe. I know what *I don't* believe. Will you accept me if I doubt?" Often questions that sound intellectual are indirect inquiries about the basic question (which few people ask directly) "Do you like me?" This is not asked directly because it is connected to a belief, "I can't believe you like me. I don't like myself."

Through careful listening and through asking questions about questions, you can discover whether someone is intending to ask about what you think or know, or if the questions are indirect routes to learning what you think about the person himself. It is useful, when responding, that you not answer the first level of a question in such a way that you never learn about the unspoken deeper question. If you quickly respond to the question, "Do you like me?" with an "Of course I do," you might not know of the disbelief with which your words would be received. If instead you replied, "I see a tenseness in your face that makes me wonder if I said 'Of course, I like you.' what you would think?" Such a response might create an opening through which the disbelief could be voiced. If he is able to tell you why he does not like himself, you will be beginning together the journey toward his self acceptance and love.

The same guidelines apply to questions about your personal life:

- Find out what the question *means*. See if there is a statement behind it. Sometimes the question, "Why do you ask?" is helpful.
- If the question contains a request for information that is necessary for guidance and illumination, provide it, but make certain that you are answering the *real* question with the information.
- Pay attention to questions such as: "What do you think?" "What do you believe?" Often these sound like a request for information but they may camouflage questions about your relationship to the counselee.
- The counseling rule of thumb for sharing stories about yourself applies here, too:

  — Share stories from your religious life if they are conflict-free and worked through. We can share our doubt, as well as our faith, if we have worked through our conflicts about it.
  — Think before you tell stories from your life. Tell them only if they will help to illuminate the counselee's experience, not obscure it.

The "telling stories about your life" rule of thumb was made to apply to those times when we *choose* to share and use our experience. It is more diffi-cult when we are *asked* to tell our religious experience. However, we still must first consider whether in answering direct questions about our religious expe-rience we will illuminate or obscure the experience of the counselee. Rather than feeling we must immediately respond because a *religious* question is asked, it is sometimes helpful to say: "Could you help me know how my experience could be helpful to you?" The counselee can help you decide whether your story illuminates or obscures the process.

Let us now consider how you might respond to questions such as: "Will you pray with me?" or "Why haven't you prayed with me?"

Again, when a counselee asks for prayer, you must make a decision about what the question means and whether or not praying, at that moment, would be in the service of healing. We handle these questions as we do other requests for information — we create a space in which to *think* and *choose* an appropriate response.

There are times in the course of counseling that we might choose to pray with counselees, particularly in grief counseling or with persons in critical life situations. At these times we pray because we must: praying to God is what our hearts need to do. However, even if you are speaking the prayer, it is helpful to encourage the counselee to listen to his deep longings and to talk about them as you pray on his behalf.

It is necessary, though, to address "Will you pray for me," or "Why haven't you prayed with me?" in the same careful way: *Find out the meaning of the question.* By opening up the question rather than feeling the obligation immediately to offer up a prayer, you will have an opportunity to enter into your counselee's inner world. By inquiring about the question, you are inviting him to tell you about his spiritual journey.

Before praying with a counselee it is helpful to discover *who* the counselee wants you to pray to, or fears you will pray to. If you prayed, would it be to the God of love or the God of fear? What does your counselee expect from prayer? Why does he want *you* to pray? Does he feel able or want to pray himself? What does he want you to pray for?

Does the question "Why haven't you prayed with me?" indicate that your counselee had an expectation that you did not fulfill? If he feels it is your *job* to pray with him does he have other expectations that he wants you to fulfill? Does he believe his prayers will be answered if only you pray? Is his belief based on faith or magic? If he has magical beliefs associated with you, does he believe that you can see into him and know his secrets — and shame? If, in your other pastoral roles, you perform the rites of confession and absolution, are you being indirectly asked for these blessings? If so, is the counselee speaking out of shame or guilt or fear?

We can see, in just these few examples, that the request for prayer can have complex ramifications. Sometimes praying might be an "easy out" that could short circuit an inquiry that might help you discover profound pain. If you have been listening as an act of prayer, you will be able to discern if, when, and how to pray "out loud."

We have been considering the many ways in which *we use ourselves as tools* in the counseling and caregiving process. But to be effective counselors, we also need to be conscious of our connection to the *ground*. We are not alone in our work. We realize this as we center ourselves and feel grounded as we make contact with the Source of our being. We can also feel grounded when we remember that we are:

- Undergirded by the *principles of holism* — body, mind, and soul are integrated. We need not experience the world and ourselves as fragmented.
- Undergirded by *our religious and collegial communities,* in which we do our work.

Chapter Three
Reading and Resources
Publishing information is found in the Bibliography.

• Instruction for *intentional breathing meditation practice* can be found in Thich Nhat Hanh's *Peace Is Every Step*. William Johnston, in his book *The Mirror Mind,* explores the affinity of intentional breathing meditation to Christian spiritual practices. Tilden Edwards in *Living in the Presence* gives instructions for meditation practices, centering prayer and other spiritual exercises.

• Eugene Gendlin's book *Focusing* is a valuable resource for *learning to listen.* Dr. Gendlin has developed a method for helping you teach others to listen to their inner imagery so that they may gain a felt sense of themselves. He also has insights that will help you learn *readiness practice.*

• We recommend that you use Charles Taylor's *The Skilled Pastor* to complement this chapter. Dr. Taylor teaches *listening skills* needed for being an empathetic presence. Gerald Egan's *The Skilled Helper: A Systematic Approach to Effective Helping* is also an excellent learning tool.

• For further help in *ministering to difficult members* see Wayne Oates, *The Care of Troublesome People.*

• We have used "companioning" to describe the process of *"being with"* those whom you counsel. This concept, which is at the heart of many spiritual practices, is explored in Margaret Guenther's *Holy Listening.*

• Much of the work on *empathic listening* comes out of psychoanalytic insight. For a sampling of this theory see: Stanley L. Olinick, M.D.'s article, "A Critique of Empathy and Sympathy," in *Empathy,* Vol. 1 (Kohutian view); Ann Ulanov and Barry Ulanov, *The Healing Imagination: The Meeting of Psyche and Soul* (Jungian view); Alfred Margulies, *The Empathic Imagination* (Freudian Psychoanalytic view.)

For a *pastoral theological* understanding of empathy we recommend Marie McCarthy and A. J. Van den Blink, "Empathy amid Diversity," and Patricia H. Davis, "Women and the Burden of Empathy," in the *Journal of Pastoral Theology,* Summer 1993; and Marie McCarthy's "Empathy: A Bridge Between," in the *Journal of Pastoral Care,* Summer 1992. Pastoral theologian Chris R. Schlauch, in his article "Defining Pastoral Psychotherapy, II," *Journal of Pastoral Care,* December 1987, defines empathy as "the capacity to be objective in one's subjectivity."

• *Speaking with your own voice* is as essential as listening with your whole self. For the support of the voices of women caregivers we recommend: Christie Cozad Neuger, ed., *The Arts of Ministry: Feminist-Womanist Approaches;* Maxine Glaz and Jeanne Moessner, eds., *Women in Travail and Transition;* as well as Mary Belenky et al., eds., *Women's Ways of Knowing;* and Carol Gilligan, *In a Different Voice: Women's Conception of Self and Morality.*

• Because community caregivers use their whole selves in the healing process, we encourage you to explore the literature on *body-mind-soul unity.* See the collection of essays edited by James B. Nelson and Sandra Longfellow, *Sexuality and the Sacred: Sources for Theological Reflection,* which explores the belief that sexuality is fundamental to our existence and is a fully integrated dimension of spirituality.

• The gift of *spiritual direction* is discussed in Tilden Edwards, *Spiritual Friend: Reclaiming the Gift of Spiritual Direction;* Alan Jones, *Exploring Spiritual Direction: An Essay on Christian Friendship;* William Barry and William Connolly, *The Practice of Spiritual Direction;* and Gerald May, *Care of Mind/Care of Spirit: A Psychiatrist Explores Spiritual Direction. The Handbook of Spirituality for Ministers,* edited by Robert J. Wicks, is a valuable resource for caregivers of all faiths.

• *Listings of training programs for spiritual formation: The Common Boundary Graduate Education Guide,* edited by Charles Simpkinson, Douglas Wengell, and Mary Jane Casavant. Common Boundary, Inc. 5272 River Road, Suite 650, Bethesda, MD 20816 Tel. (301) 652-9495.

• *Supervision resources:* Pastoral counselors who are certified by the American Association of Pastoral Counselors (AAPC) are particularly trained to supervise your community care and counseling work. We suggest that you phone their Association office, Tel. (703) 385-6967 for referral. You may also find pastoral studies and supervisory groups connected to a pastoral counseling agency or seminary in your vicinity. Supervision of your community caregiving work is also available through the telephone service of Blanton-Peale's Clergy Consultation Service, Tel. (212) 725-7850.

~ PART II ~

Facilitating Wholeness

For as the rain and the snow come down from heaven.
   and do not return there until they have watered the earth,
making it bring forth and sprout,
   giving seed to the sower and bread to the eater,
so shall my word be that goes out from my mouth;
   it shall not return to me empty,
but it shall accomplish that which I purpose.
   and succeed in the thing for which I sent it.

For you shall go out in joy,
   and be led back in peace.

Isaiah 55:10–12

~ 4 ~

A Guide to
Facilitating Change

God, give us grace to accept with serenity the things that cannot be changed, courage to change the things that should be
changed, and the wisdom to distinguish the one from the other.
— Reinhold Niebuhr[1]

And give us grace to *see* the things that are changing and the strength to
support those changes that are good for us and others.

Counselors in community have a powerful role. You are in the position to
support others as they make crucial changes that benefit their lives. Through
your interventions, you can help them sustain these changes. Through your
leadership, your faith community can become a "holding environment" that
not only nurtures growth, but occasions it.

While in this chapter we will be discussing your role as community caregiver and counselor, we are making the assumption that many others are
sharing these tasks with you through the network of care we spoke of
in chapter 2.

You, the reader, might be the cleric or layleader of your faith community.
In that role you are not only a community caregiver and counselor but also
a leader in your religious community's *wholeness network*. This is a much
broader interpretation of your role than is commonly understood. Of course,
you are a caregiver and counselor to individuals, couples, and families. However, it is only a fraction of what you do as a *leader of a community* that helps
people become aware of their wholeness. As a leader, you are first an educator
who introduces your community to the concept of a wholeness network.

We use the term "wholeness network" to mean the interaction of:

- nurturing and healing, derived from the life of the religious community
  itself, from its worship and practice of prayer and meditation.
- healing, caregiving and supportive activities of your community and
  your ministry.
- counseling, performed by you and others on the staff and congregation,
  of individuals, couples, families, groups.

· consultants, to whom referrals are made, or who educate, facilitate, or contribute to the wholeness of those in the religious community.

This network is connected to and receives support from health care and other healing resources of the larger community.

A religious community that is accepting of and committed to wholeness makes it easy for members to ask for help in living their lives to the fullest. *The healthier your community is, the more requests you will have for counseling.* You need to be able to counsel, *but you don't have to do it all yourself.*

In the first place, because you are developing and supporting your wholeness network you do not have time to counsel over a long period of time with everyone who calls for help. In the second place, to do other than brief counseling takes a great deal of additional training and supervision; it is a completely different job. The *brief* solution-focused counseling method that we will introduce in chapter 6 will take some additional training and supervision. We do not assume that you will learn to do it simply by reading a chapter in this book. However, learning to do it is necessary because *brief counseling is part of your job!*

Faith communities that understand their own participation in healing will not expect you to do it all yourself. Through your leadership, the members of your community can become conscious of both the healing properties of community and the ways in which they as individuals can participate in activities that help them become aware of their wholeness. They can be taught to see you as one of many resources for growth and nurture. Because you do not have to do it all, you can develop more modest expectations of yourself and learn to do what you must do: be a facilitator for healing.

Facilitating Healing

We must make a distinction between being *a facilitator* and being *the healer.* It is helpful to remember that you are not, *in and of yourself,* a healer. You are a facilitator in the mysterious healing process that has already begun in those who call you for help.

People who call you are usually unaware that healing — or change — has already begun. They believe that they are calling out of sickness or fear, desperation or guilt or crisis. They sometimes feel that another — a mother, wife, or husband — is "making" them call. But, in all cases, something has already moved within them that has allowed them to reach out and ask for help. Change has happened. Often they are moved by the belief that they can be helped by you. They have hope. Sometimes, in the case of those who feel someone else is "making" them come, there is the hope that you will learn that their parent or spouse needs help and you can help their family system.

Your first task as facilitator is to discern the emergence of healing and to cooperate with it.

Your next task is to understand what the caller wants from you. Sometimes a person is asking for the caregiving resources of the congregation, sometimes for a referral. Sometimes the person has a problem that he or she wants you to *help* solve. It is not your job to solve the problem "by yourself." However, it is your job to understand what the problem is and to help the person discover — and follow through — her own solutions. In chapter 6 we will show how the solution-focused therapy method can be effectively used in the *brief* counseling of those who come to you with problems.

You are uniquely in the position to see, understand, and support people when they are in the place to make profound changes in their lives. Unlike many mental-health professionals, you are often on the scene at the time of change. People have potential for significant change when the circumstances of their lives change: when a marriage is made and they redefine their relationship to their family of origin; when a baby is born and a new family is started; when a spouse or partner dies and new independence is needed; when a serious illness requires a lifestyle adjustment.

You are often there at these times of profound change, offering comfort and encouragement. However, if you see your role only as that of comforter, you are missing an opportunity to identify and support radical — *second order* — change. More than many mental-health professionals, you have an opportunity to support radical change because you have a natural entrée to the changing system. You visit the family after the birth as you make plans for the baby's dedication, baptism, bris, etc. You visit after hospitalizations or funerals.

If you understand the nature of change, your visits can be more than routine community care. In many cases, they can be used by you to undergird — and sometimes intervene — so that those who have experienced this change can hold onto and integrate the benefits that the change brings.

As I said in chapter 1, when people make a first order change, they do so *within* their present system or circumstance. With a second order change, they *change the system,* or circumstance itself.

There is always loss in the process of radical, second order change. Even when people expect that the second order change will produce happiness, there is loss. Parents "lose" their familiar role in their children's lives when children go away to college or are married. However, this "loss" is necessary if the children are to move into a more independent place. In spite of the relief that parents feel when their children move on to college, or the happiness they feel when children marry, they also experience underlying sadness.

The feelings that accompany second order change are ambiguous. For example, death may produce second order change for those left behind. When a spouse dies, his or her partner feels grief. But the widow or widower might also feel relief or freedom. When we counsel those experiencing second order change, we must help people accept the *ambiguity* of their experience: they are mourning. They are relieved. They are frightened. They are excited. In recognizing the complexity of experience that accompanies second order change, we can both comfort the mourner and support the excitement of new possibilities — and in the process, help lessen survivor guilt.

People are often ambivalent about change itself: we want change, yet we resist it. Sometimes the more we try to make ourselves change, the less we change. For example, during the first week of a new exercise regime we are faithful to our plan. However, we begin making exceptions and within three weeks we find that we have slipped away from both the plan and our good intentions. Even when we do make a change, for instance, by getting married, we might find ourselves wishing to be pulled back into an old system. People who marry usually want to be in a new family. They want to leave home. They want to establish a new home where they can "do it their way." Even when couples have acted upon this desire for newness and have created a new home, they sometimes act as if they had not left home. New couples often have their first fights because each person wants to do a holiday, Thanksgiving for instance, in their family of origin's way — the very family from which they were eagerly trying to separate.

When systems — couples, families, other institutions — or individuals in systems change, there is often a pull to return to the former balance, back to the familiar. However, when this pull is resisted and the new change is reinforced, new growth can be experienced. When the new couple establishes its new ways, we often see a spurt of maturity in the individual lives of the husband and wife. Couples that find ways to make their own rules and customs without having to cut themselves off from their families of origin create a context where they both can thrive. Often, they do not seem to be struggling to change, but they make profound changes in a way that seems natural.

Religious communities are often the context of second order change. People who have experienced conversion or religious renewal and awakening know new life in which everything changes. Their new belief and meaning system and their heightened sense of commitment give them a new sense of themselves and the world. It is not only people of ancient times — such as Saul, who through conversion became Paul — but also people whom we know, whose lives have been turned around through their faith.

Often the second order change in people's lives does not come through the natural events of life — birth, death, or an inner spiritual conversion experience — but is dependent on change in the larger community. The experience of a homeless family illustrates this. We know that members of a homeless family are constantly striving to make first order change as they struggle to survive by moving from the home of one relative to another, or from one homeless shelter to another. They are trying to survive *within* the system of homelessness. If their community were to build permanent low-income housing that they could rent, they could make a second order change. They would move from homeless to housed, and within that new house, they could create a home. A second order change would then occur: children would attend school more regularly, parents could be employed, the physical and emotional health of the family would be improved, they would live in a neighborhood where they could be supported by its resources, they could become a part of a religious community, they could experience esteem rather than stigma.

Many religious communities are active in trying to create and support both first and second order change. Using the example of homelessness again, religious communities often have soup kitchens for the poor or shelters that are safe havens from the streets. Food and shelter support first order change. Because of them, people are able to survive within the system of poverty. Because soup kitchens and shelters do not solve the problem of homelessness, these same communities are usually involved in coalitions that try to move the political process so that permanent housing will be built. Sometimes these same congregations participate in actually building permanent housing as they work with Habitat for Humanity or other groups. And they might also be supporting legislation that addresses the complex issues contributing to homelessness and the conditions that surround it.

Urban and rural homelessness will not be changed to the second order until people and their communities change. We know this to be true as we consider social movements from the past. Even though individual prophetic leaders called for change, it was not until a groundswell moved communities that the institution of slavery was abolished, that segregation was moved to integration, that education for the elite became education for the public, or that women as well as men were able to vote.

Often it has been society's rediscovery of the ancient covenants of Israel that called forth second order change. Through the message of the prophets, the Hebrew people were instructed that, until Israel itself changed, the lives of its people would not change. This understanding of second order change can be found in the new covenant that Yahweh made with those exiled from Jerusalem:

> Therefore say: Thus says the Lord God: I will gather you from the peoples, and assemble you out of the countries where you have been scattered, and I will give you the land of Israel. When they come there, they will remove from it all its detestable things and all its abominations. I will give them one heart, and put a new spirit within them; I will remove the heart of stone from their flesh and give them a heart of flesh, so that they may follow my statutes and keep my ordinances and obey them. Then they shall be my people, and I will be their God. But as for those whose heart goes after their detestable things and their abominations, I will bring their deeds upon their own heads, says the Lord God (Ezekiel 11:17–21).

In this passage, Yahweh is saying that the hard-heartedness of the people can only be changed through a spiritual heart transplant. Through being given a new heart of flesh, they will be able to put into practice the laws and judgments of Yahweh.

Because of "softening of heart," congregations are able to choose to become a wholeness system that supports both first and second order change.

The work of social justice and healing are intertwined. Our knowledge of first and second order change helps us understand that, when we think of social justice and community care as either separate or conflicting entities, we create a false dichotomy. Justice must also be merciful. Healing requires a second order change of systems as well as first order change.

First and second order change begin in the same way: *with one small step.* Freedom Marches and the Civil Rights Movement began with the *small step* Rosa Parks took when her feet were tired and she decided not to go to the back of the bus where blacks were supposed to sit. While it was Mrs. Parks's action that precipitated the movement led by Martin Luther King, at that time many others had been taking their "small steps" in other ways. Through the small actions of many, a climate had been created that made social change possible.

Supporting Change through Community Care

There is a distinction between facilitation that occurs in the course of your *caregiving ministry,* and *brief counseling,* which is done in the more formal setting of your office. When doing community care, you are often in the midst of an action that produces change. Brief counseling, on the other hand, often occurs when people feel that they are not able to act or change. People come to you for counseling when they feel stuck in an impasse and therefore need you to help them find a solution to their problem. Occasionally, through re-framing the problem and helping people listen to their own solutions, you can help them become unstuck in the course of one counseling session. However, most people work with a counselor for more than one session in order to solidify their solutions to the problem.

When doing the work of community care, you often do not need to help people get into motion: the action has already begun. Sometimes the action was not planned or intended, such as when one is hurt in a car accident or when one is ill, but something has happened that requires response. You are there to give comfort and support and to help congregants make meaning of the event. At other times the action is intentional, such as when marriages are made or babies are blessed. Again, it is in the midst of these events that you undergird change. You do not need to help people change, you are in the midst of change.

You know from your experience that healing does not require a formal setting. It often happens not at your office or study but rather at a hospital or deathbed, a funeral home or courtroom, a coffee shop, a wedding rehearsal. In all of these places, you may have had intense conversations or have made therapeutic interventions that have helped promote healing. It was when you were in the midst of action that you had the opportunity to help people resolve a conflict, become reconciled, identify unfinished business, forgive themselves or another, or come to terms with a family secret.

An example of facilitation in the midst of community care can be found in the experience of Father Moran, who was officiating at the funeral of a middle aged man who had died of cancer:

In the midst of the wake, the man's nineteen-year-old, estranged son dramatically appeared. Father Moran swiftly moved to greet the son, and was able to take him to a private room where he could speak privately to his mother and brother and sister. Although Father Moran felt pressure from the extended family to be a part of the meeting, Father Moran was able to contain the situation and to create a safe place in which the complicated feelings of relief, anger, confusion, and contrition could at least be identified. He then was able to arrange for the son to be alone by his father's casket so that grief — which was compounded by anger, hurt and guilt — could be expressed privately. The breach between the son and his family was repaired enough so that he was able to sit with the family at the funeral. The action — the son's return, the family's response, and Father Moran's intervention and facilitation — created more change than *talking,* in and of itself, could do. In the son's return there was both closure — the son said good-bye to his father — and also an opening for further counseling work.

Often, when you are making therapeutic interventions, the action generated produces enough closure that follow-up counseling sessions are not needed. At other times, the therapeutic intervention is the prelude to more formal counseling. In the example of the son who returns for his father's funeral, both he and his family needed additional counseling although healing had already begun in the life of the son, healing that had softened his heart and given him the courage to come to his father's funeral.

Let us look at a sampling of occasions that often create the opportunity for therapeutic, community-care interventions in the midst of the event itself:

Weddings sometimes produce conflicts in families in which all sorts of unfinished business can arise. Often this occurs among family members of the bride's and groom's parents' generation. It is not unusual for the effect of old slights, buried family secrets, and sibling jealousy to erupt among aunts, uncles, and grandparents. If you have a relationship with members of the extended family, you might have a chance to help them resolve these old conflicts. Because they are intruding upon the wedding at hand, you have an opportunity to help the new couple set limits so that they do not need to incorporate the family drama and make it their own.

As the bride and groom plan the wedding, the differences in the styles of their families are experienced. You have a lively opportunity to help the couple learn to identify, accept, and negotiate differences as they arise in planning the event. Often you must deal with the complicated shapes of families that might include stepparents or parents with new partners. Sometimes these previous marriages and family constellations have unresolved conflicts and pain. Often it is in the midst of making practical arrangements — who sits with whom at the rehearsal dinner or who walks with whom — that unfinished business erupts.

Although conflicts cannot always be resolved in this setting, they can be identified in such a way that the bride and groom can contain the impact on their new family. Sometimes there is even an opportunity for renegotiation or for resolution of tension among family members. With help, parents — and any new partners — are often able to put away old grudges in order to celebrate the wedding of their children. (In chapter 7 we will discuss in more detail community care at the time of weddings.)

Caring for the dying, ministering to their loved ones, conducting funerals. When caring for those who are dying, you are privileged to be with those who are taking stock of the meaning of their lives. You often must move between the need of the dying one to let go and the needs of those whom he or she is leaving. At times, either the dying one or his or her loved ones have difficulty because of unfinished business, often guilt or anger, in their relationship. When you are able to understand these issues, you can help conflicts be resolved so that both find release; one may die and the other may mourn and be comforted.

In some instances, the death of a loved one allows family members to experience the unhealed wounds caused by another's death long ago. When you become aware of buried grief while comforting a mourner, you can help these old wounds be healed. Often wakes and funerals are times when estranged family members appear to seek reconciliation. You can help families deal with the conflict and confusion, anger and unhappiness that families experience when this occurs. Families sometimes experience hurt at funerals when wills are read or when family members rearrange themselves without the presence of the person who died. (In chapter 8 we will discuss in more detail community care for those who are dying and those who mourn them.)

Emergency rooms and the scenes of crises. You have been called to be with community members at a time when a crisis and the problems that precede it cannot be denied. Families often hide their struggles with conflict, with alcoholism and addictions, with violence or other troubles because they fear stigma or judgment. However, in a time of crisis they sometimes call upon you to give support or advice. It is in emergency rooms, jails, rehabilitation centers, and courtrooms that you learn the severity of your congregants' problems and it is in the midst of crisis that you can make an intervention that allows you to contribute resources for healing. (In chapter 9 we will discuss in detail community care and crisis counseling.)

Let us now look at guidelines for knowing if, when, and how these opportunities to facilitate healing are moved into formal, brief counseling.

First, it is necessary to learn to recognize *closure* when it occurs in the healing events of community care. If you do not recognize it, and therefore believe that a problem still exists, you can inadvertently create a worse problem.

To go back to our example of the son who returned to his father's funeral: Father Moran spoke with the son, heard his confession, and witnessed the son at the casket of his father. He was present when the son said good-bye to his father. If Father Moran had later said, "Do you want to come to talk with me about the way you didn't get to the hospital in time to say good-bye to your Dad?" he would have caused confusion and implied that what had happened had not happened. *It is not necessary to initiate talking about an action that has been completed, that has come to closure.* Sometimes those experiencing closure might eventually want to talk more about their experience. In fact, the son later said to Father Moran, "I'd like to talk with you about what happened at the wake. I can't get over how I felt when I was talking directly with Dad — and how it felt okay."

It is tempting, when making therapeutic interventions as a part of community care, to try to be helpful, to offer unwanted advice or to invite people to come for continued counseling before they are ready. When we are with people in the midst of their troubles, we are privy to much information; we see the big picture. Often we form a conclusion about which family member really needs help. We are tempted to help that person change by saying, "Wouldn't you like to talk with me?" This question really contains the statement: "I would like to talk to you. If you could change your ways, this whole family could be helped." We must remember the principle: people do not change when we try to change them. They change when they feel accepted as they are and when they are able to listen to their own solutions to problems.

The greatest gift you give when doing community care is your ability to *be with* people. It is because of your availability that you will be asked by those at the wedding, funeral, or bedside, "Could I come and talk?" It is necessary that you wait for people to *ask* for help.

If you are in the midst of counseling as part of a ministry visit and it is obvious that your conversation is unfinished, it is appropriate for you to suggest the possibility that you *extend* your counseling at another time when you can be intentional about the counseling relationship. Again, you should add, "if you wish." Sometimes people experience an invitation for extended counseling as *your need* to continue to talk. It is useful to spell out why you are making the suggestion. For example, you might say, "We seem to be understanding the problem, but it's not quite clear. Would you like to talk with me about this later?" or "You and your mother seem to be on the verge of understanding why you left home. The service is about to start now. Would you both like to talk with me about this later?" In these examples the unfinished business is identified and an open-ended invitation is extended. Even if you do not help them with this unfinished business, it has been labeled so that it can be dealt with later, when the choice is made to do so.

When you are making therapeutic interventions in the midst of community care, the conditions, time spent, and limitations are determined by the situation itself. You know that you cannot totally control your schedule. If you are with a family in family court, or at the bedside of one who is dying, you know that the action of the court schedule or the dying process will determine your stay. It is your flexibility and your ability to be present while still being aware of your own needs that enhances your effectiveness.

Your role as a community caregiver is very much defined by the expectations of your religious tradition and the culture of your congregation. Because of your role — as minister, priest, rabbi, staff member, layleader, wholeness team member, counselor — you are given authority. When you are with a family whose loved one has just died, you are looked to for leadership. The family expects you to pray, to give words of comfort and to know what to do next. They look to you to know how to make funeral arrangements and how to conduct the rituals of mourning. Because they trust that you know what to do, the family can let go and give in to their grief.

Most of us live much of our lives *between* the dramatic points of radical change. After the second order change of marriage, life settles in to "learning to be married." After children are born, they are then raised. People live their lives hoping they can do it in a "good enough" fashion. In these in-between, ordinary times, people find the resiliency to survive, cope, thrive. All people, at times, experience difficulties that will require first order change, change within their situation or circumstance.

While some people will come to you to deal with problems through brief counseling, many more will be helped through preventative programming. Sermons can give members inspiration and encouragement. However, most people also need continuing education and support to live their lives well. For example, because instruction sets do not come with newborn babies, parents need to *learn* to be parents. They can be helped if their religious communities sponsor classes, workshops, or support groups that give them information about parenting skills and knowledge of child development as well as offering emotional support.

In all probability, your community has already been asking the question: "What do our members need to help them live their lives more abundantly?" After needs are assessed, community programs are planned. We know of congregations that have classes and workshops for parenting — some address the complexities of nontraditional families, job training, and résumé writing. Some have programs for sex and health education, others have day-care or after-school programs. Some have support groups for former middle managers who have been outplaced and for those returning to the workforce. There are communities with programs for spiritual enrichment and Bible study. These programs are designed to meet the particular needs of a particular community.

We return now to the *principle of networking*. It is probable that because of budget cuts in schools and social agencies, programs that have been helping your members are now being eliminated. Religious communities are going to have to find creative ways to pick up pieces of canceled social programming. However, this does not mean that every congregation must do everything. For example, it might be that the local Methodist Church has an excellent workshop series on parenting and would welcome people from other communities. Perhaps your congregation has an unusually high number of "outplaced" workers and has a group that both supports them and helps them find solutions to their situation. Another congregation might have a support group for those with HIV or AIDS, or for recovering cancer patients. All of these groups might welcome people from other congregations.

Religious communities will need to cooperate if they are to meet the challenge of our country's grave social needs. Communities that have an active "wholeness system" task force will already know where programs and other resources exist in the wider community. Some task-force members are also on the Internet and through it have found resources for meeting community needs.

Learning Not to Create Problems

In addition to giving information and support, religious communities can help their members learn to deal with difficulties and to make them manageable. In so doing, they can be helped to avoid creating problems. We believe that people can be helped to live their lives more gracefully and that communities can learn to be less conflicted when they are taught basic theory of how problems are formed. This knowledge can be used as *preventative medicine* for communities.

Our understanding of *problem formation* comes from the work of the Mental Research Institute in Palo Alto, California, which has studied the principles of change. We have already cited their book, Watzlawick et al., *Change: Principles of Problem Formation and Problem Resolution* in our discussions of first and second order change.

The theorists at the Mental Research Institute have extensively studied the structure and formation of a wide variety of life's problems and have come to the conclusion that problems that are experienced as impasses, knots, deadlocks, *are created when difficulties are misunderstood or maintained.* They have found that problems can be eased when people understand how they are mishandling their difficulties and that problems can be prevented when difficulties are dealt with more effectively.

They have discovered that problems, in spite of their variety and complexity, are *created* through mismanagement when:

· the solution to the difficulty becomes the problem.

- a solution to the difficulty is seen where there is none.
- the difficulties, themselves, are denied.[2]

When the solution to the difficulty becomes the problem. You may have had the experience of being very tired at the beginning of a meeting that you were chairing. You thought, "I'll feel better if I just get this over." Because of your fatigue you were not thinking clearly; you allowed the meeting to run on and on. The discussion was getting muddled, but you thought, "If we stay at this, maybe we can straighten it out." The more the talk went on, the more tired you got; the longer the committee continued to meet, the less was accomplished. A problem had been created.

The original difficulty was your tiredness, which you tried to "solve" by getting through the meeting. A problem was then created when you tried to "get the meeting over" by allowing everyone to talk on and on. (You tried to solve the muddled deliberation by continuing to do what clearly was not working — more talk.) Problems that are created in this manner are often augmented when people try to do *more of the same thing* that caused the original problem.

A simple problem from gardening also makes this point. It is not uncommon, when a house plant looks droopy, for its caregiver to give it water. When it still looks droopy, more water is given. It is only later, when the caregiver picks up the pot, that she discovers that the plant had been overwatered in the first place. The solution had caused the problem. And the problem was reinforced by doing *more of the same* — giving the plant more water.

When problems are created, solution-focused therapists have a simple rule. *"Do something different!"* The problem we described would have been simply solved if the committee had been allowed to stop talking and go home.

People can be helped not to create inappropriate solutions to a difficulty, by learning to listen to themselves, particularly to messages that come from their bodies. If, for example, before beginning the meeting, you had known the depth of your fatigue, you could have attended to it more appropriately. You needed rest. Someone else could have chaired the meeting, or it could have been canceled, or you could have asked the group to help you make it brief.

Religious practices like prayer and meditation help people to be centered and to be in touch with where they are and with how things are. Through using these practices, they are able to find more realistic solutions to difficulties.

When the solution to a difficulty is seen where there is none. Reinhold Niebuhr asked: "God give us grace to accept with serenity the things that cannot be changed." Those with such serenity would not create a problem by finding a solution when none is possible. An example is the common problem created when people try to change a "difficult" person. They try but because people cannot easily change other persons, they meet with fierce resistance. A problem is created because action was not necessary or possible.

Niebuhr's prayer then went on, "Give us...courage to change the things that should be changed and the wisdom to distinguish the one from the other." This addresses the next cause of problems:

When the difficulties, themselves, are denied. People *can help change what can be changed.* They can create a hospitable place where others are accepted. However, they may not do that if they are denying that they have difficulties in accepting other people. Problems in religious communities are often created when communities deny their difficulties with acceptance and inclusion. Problems are created when difficulties are denied because people *do not take the action that is needed.* We will illustrate these various problems with a community case study:

Pastor Helen was called to the home of a young man, Steve, who was slowly dying from an excruciatingly painful cancer. Steve had recently been sent home from the hospital because the last medical treatment had not been successful. When she arrived, Steve said, "Pastor Helen, thank you for coming. I want to say good-bye to you because you've been so special." He had a plan to take his life.

When she was told, Pastor Helen was at first shocked and saddened. If she had not understood the structure of problems, she might have acted upon her feelings and begun a theological discussion about her church's position on suicide. She would have understood Steve to be having a spiritual problem that required a theological response. She might also have panicked and called an ambulance. Instead, because she knew that problems are not what they appear to be on the surface, she began to inquire about what had been going on before he made the plan. She asked, "What do you want to solve with this plan?"

Pastor Helen had the hunch that he might be trying to solve the difficulty he was having with pain. As he spoke, she learned that her hunch was wrong. "The pain control is working. I feel out of it, but I'm fairly comfortable. What I can't stand are the looks on Mom and Dad's faces. I can see this is killing them. They only way to make things better is for me to die." As they talked, Pastor Helen learned that Steve was not ready to die but he could not go on living with the guilt he felt about his parents' anguish. Steve expected Helen to condemn his plan. However, even though he was conflicted about it, it seemed to him to be the solution to his difficulty.

She began to inquire about other attempts he had made to deal with his feelings about his parents. He said, "Well, that's the real problem. They don't want to talk about what's going on." As he said this, his body shifted; he sighed, and became very sad.

It was clear to Pastor Helen that Steve did not intend to commit suicide. She helped him *reframe* his problem by saying: "Well, it looks like you have a problem — you need to talk with your folks. That would be even harder to do if you were dead." Steve responded, "Yeah. It really wasn't much of a plan anyway. I'm hooked to this I.V. but I just couldn't think of anything else to do." By reframing it, Steve's "problem" about suicide was resolved. (Counselors need to be able to assess the potentiality for suicide and know how to make appropriate interventions. We attend to this in chapter 9.)

Steve was still in a difficult situation because of the interlocking problems of his family. After leaving Steve's room, Pastor Helen went to the living room where she spoke to his mother, Nancy. She soon discovered that Nancy had a *problem that was created because no solution to the difficulty was possible.* Nancy told Pastor Helen that her problem was Steve. Nancy said, "He's not being cooperative. I know there's an experimental drug that would help him if he had a more positive attitude. It's a matter of the right outlook."

Pastor Helen began to explore with Nancy the ways in which she had tried to get Steve to change and become more cooperative. Nancy found it hard to talk about Steve himself. Instead she went back to her ideas about how "cancer can be overcome through the right attitude." She talked about the way things *should* be for Steve. It became evident that she found it difficult to talk about how he actually was. Steve was dying. By being obsessed about finding the miracle drug and by trying to get him to be different, she could remain distracted from his dying.

Pastor Helen responded, "It seems difficult for you to talk about how you feel about Steve." Nancy said, "Life isn't supposed to be this way." Nancy's frantic attempts to find miracle cures were not only to save Steve's life, but also to keep the world looking like "life's supposed to be." In the course of their conversation, the problem shifted from "Steve who won't cooperate" to Nancy and her view of the world. Pastor Helen and Nancy then talked about how Nancy's Utopian beliefs about "how life *should be*" kept her from seeing life as it *actually was.* As she sorted out these ideas, she was able to see Steve and she knew that she wanted to be close to him. *She was able to stop taking action where it was not necessary.* She had been frantically taking action to keep him alive. With this new understanding, she was able simply to be with him and keep him company in his dying.

Steve's father, George, would not have come to see Pastor Helen had his wife not insisted. Because they were there, George did not mind telling Pastor Helen that Nancy was being unreasonable about her search for drugs. He believed that Steve was going to beat this crisis and go into remission as he has done before. He intended to make reservations for a winter vacation for the family because he was certain that Steve would be able to go. George was *creating a problem by denying a difficulty.*

Because he was denying that Steve was dying, George was *not taking an action that was necessary* for Steve's well-being. Steve needed his parents to talk with him. Pastor Helen continued to explore George's understanding of the problem. At first, George felt that his problem was Nancy. Pastor Helen asked what he had done to try to solve his problem with Nancy and he replied, "I tried to get her to go out to the movies to get her mind off it."

When Pastor Helen asked, "Have you talked with her about this?" he replied: "Talking is hard. I don't like to think about this. I feel bad."

After George said, "I feel bad." Pastor Helen had a clue that she explored with him. She discovered that George had used denial to deal with his difficulty in handling his feeling of "badness." George began to see that his problem was not Nancy, but had something to do with his feelings of *being* bad. Although he did not understand everything about it, he had a hunch that he had been holding himself responsible for Steve's illness, and he began to realize that he had more work to do that would require psychotherapy. However, he was better able to talk with Steve.

Steve's parents' inability to talk with one another had created an impasse. This was dissolved because Pastor Helen did not take the situation, as presented, to be the problem. She did not believe the problem to be Steve's potential for suicide, or Nancy's search for miracle drugs, or George's plans to take a winter vacation. *Pastor Helen helped this family discover that problems were being created because of the way difficulties were handled — and not handled.* Nancy and George were finding it difficult to say good-bye to Steve. Although they were unable to talk together, their faces registered their emotions. Steve read their feelings and felt responsible for them. Because Pastor Helen understood, she was able to help them loosen the knot of the problem. Talking together became possible. Healing began to happen.

By paying careful attention to the ways in which the problems were formed, Pastor Helen helped resolve the problems without getting sidetracked by what the problems *seemed* to be. By asking, "how have you tried to solve the problem?" she opened up the possibility for a different solution.

Often problems are created by those who try to alleviate difficult situations through trying to change others. However, these helpers discover this does not work. In their book *A Brief Guide to Brief Therapy*, William O'Hanlon and Brian Cade have chronicled ineffective interventions people use when attempting to get others to change. We have included them in *Appendix D*.

Preaching and Prayer: The Bridge to Care and Counseling

Through your preaching and your participation in the prayers and religious rituals of your ministry you have been laying the groundwork for a counseling relationship. When you preach you may not consciously be intending to invite your listeners to seek counseling. However, those who hear a message of hope and liberation may feel welcomed to speak with you about their lives. People who are touched by a message of love and acceptance feel invited to come to talk to you, particularly if they are having difficulty living their lives. If they know through your sermons that you are sensitive to the struggles of daily living, they can feel hope that you will understand their problems.

Prayer is another avenue of invitation. When people experience your prayers as interceding for them, they feel especially invited to talk with you.

You speak to peoples' conditions when, in intercessory prayer or during the prayers of the people, you pray for those who struggle with the difficulties of living or who are physically or emotionally ill. When you pray for the healing of those struggling with all forms of addiction or from the trauma of family violence or physical and sexual abuse you touch those who often feel outcast. Those whose circumstances you remember in prayer will be more likely to speak with you about their pain. Members of the community are invited to use its resources not only by the prayers of the leader. Prayers offered up in small group meetings and in personal devotions also create openings that allow members to reach out for help.

For many, the healing that has begun through the mysteries of worship gives them the courage to speak about their pain, conflict, or confusion. It is because of this healing that they may be able to speak to you at the end of the service and say, "I'd like to talk." Sometimes they might add "about the sermon" because they are not quite ready to say "about myself." It is important not to hear such comments as polite chitchat or an intellectual gambit. This indirect request for your time needs to be responded to directly with: "I'd like that. I'm in the office tomorrow. Could you call me in the morning and we'll set up a time?"

Sometimes your sermon, or some aspect of worship, will disturb or unsettle a listener and shake him out of numbness or despair. It is important if, after a service, you are told: "I didn't like your sermon. It really bothered me. I'd like to talk about it," that you not take this as personal criticism. This also can be an indirect request for help. Not all counseling is initiated when people feel warm and accepted.

Most requests for counseling are not so indirect. Often these come from persons who are already predisposed to expect help and acceptance from you. They have identified you, the messenger, with the message that you preach. Some whom you do not know feel you know them because your sermons and prayers have touched them personally. They believe you *must* know their story, even though they have never told you, for how else could you have reached them?

There are both advantages and disadvantages for the clergy whose counseling sessions begin in the pulpit. You have the advantage of easily making a positive therapeutic alliance because you have already been experienced as trustworthy. People coming to see you feel they know you because they have listened to what you have to say. They can begin counseling sessions with at least a modest amount of hope and trust. But you also have a disadvantage when people you do not know think you know them. Because they are making assumptions about how much you know, they often omit parts of their story because they think you know it already. It is useful to identify these people. You will need to be particularly empathetic rather than sympathetic with them. You must not make assumptions based on their assumptions.

Faith Community: A Life-Affirming Milieu

Healthy communities are safe places where people are known because they feel free to reveal themselves to others. In community, people tell their stories. And in telling these, people become known to themselves. In this process, using pastoral theologian and counselor James Ashbrook's phrase, *they remember who they are.*

Storytelling happens both formally and informally in communities. The process of personal sharing is central to most of the community's study groups and other small groups where people speak of their religious and other personal experiences. In some religious communities, witnessing or testifying to God's action in their lives, is another way people tell their stories. And certainly in the many friendship groups that make up community, people talk to each other about their lives. They reminisce together about what has happened to them *that matters.*[3]

Telling one's story, reflecting on life's meaning and remembering one's lost memories and experiences — becoming known to one's self — is *soul work.* God has planted within us a need to make meaning out of our lives. Even on their deathbeds, people review their lives and try to understand them. People struggle to comprehend the truth of their experience. Meaning making is possible because of the physical processes of the brain that make memory possible.[4]

Just as the capacity to remember is God-given, so is our ability to forget. We know that people who have experienced great pain, abuse, or other traumas will forget — repress — memories of the event because knowledge of the event is too much to bear. We also "forget" less painful events in our lives, synthesizing and tucking them away to give our minds space to function in daily living.

However, these experiences are not permanently lost to us. They sometimes return in flashes of memory, or are encoded in our dreams. They are also remembered by the cells of our bodies. Our bodies remember through our senses. Perhaps you have had the experience of eating something, and through associations of tasting and smelling, remembered a scene from your childhood. When we remember in this way, we feel totally "back there." The emotional memories of childhood that are stored by the neurochemical processes of the brain can be retrieved and relived.

Often these pleasant memories of childhood, while unbidden, seem to come easily. It is, however, usually only when people are in a *safe place* with *dependable people* that they can remember painful experiences that they have needed to forget. They remember these when they are strong enough and have the support to make meaning of them. While these memories are usually retrieved in a therapist's office, they can also be recovered in the safety of loving religious communities. It is essential, therefore, that you understand some basics about the function of memory and its role in healing, particularly *body memory.*[5]

I have mentioned the memory of the taste buds and the olfactory senses, but *other* parts of the body can remember, too. For example, the face can remember feeling slapped or shamed. In fact, any place in the body that has been traumatized can "remember." Perhaps you have counseled someone who experienced body memory and was confused and frightened by the process. Most people believe that memory happens through having thoughts or seeing pictures in the mind. When they remember with their bodies, they fear they are having an aberrant experience. Because you know something about the complexity of memory, you can assure the counselee that his or her memory experience, while unsettling, is normal.

When buried memories resurface, the process of healing can continue. When painful events are acknowledged and reexperienced, people can mourn the effect that these have had on their lives. They can move beyond the experience in a new way. In remembering painful events, we join together with part of our lost selves. We are *re-membered.* Our lives become fuller. Because of the safety and support of our communities, we can know ourselves and we can allow others to know us.

Martin Buber has reminded us that although we become known to ourselves by being known by others in community, what we really have in common with each other is our Center — God.

God is a God who wants to be remembered and has created our bodies — with their complex neurochemical systems — so that memory is possible. Memory is necessary for our faith. Our Judeo-Christian traditions are rooted in rituals of remembering the mighty acts of God. Perhaps God not only created brains that could remember, but all of our senses were designed to remember God. God has planted into our psyches a thirst for God. As the Psalmist said:

> As a deer longs for flowing streams,
> so my soul thirsts for God, for the living God. (Psalm 42:1–2)

We *yearn* for Ultimate Meaning and Truth.

When acceptance, affirmation, support, care — love — are given to members of the community, they thrive. They are *alive.* A loving community is a natural therapeutic milieu in which people who are open to it can heal, grow, and mature.

Sometimes this love is expressed by what people *do* for each other when they support, listen, show practical acts of caring, affirm, tell the truth. And sometimes simply *by being themselves,* members help others make changes in their lives. Communities often have in them members who have significant, life-changing influence on others.

Children and young people in faith communities are surrounded by adults who often become profoundly influential in their lives. Some adults become surrogate parents, others become role models, or provide extended families. Because faith communities are multigenerational, children and teenagers have a chance to "adopt," or be "adopted by," "honorary" grandparents, aunts and uncles who substitute for missing family members or who supplement missing emotional nutrients. Sunday school teachers, youth group leaders, coaches, adult friends — all have impact on the lives of young people, not simply because of what they *do* with them, but because of how they *are* with them. Because they are able to be accepting and caring, children want to "be like" them. They influence children by example more than through religious talk.

When significant adults have a larger worldview than their families, children are introduced to more options. And these significant adults often see potential and promise in these young people who are attached to them. Children and teenagers grow with confidence and self-esteem because they have absorbed the belief that loving adults have in them.

Adults, too, are influenced by those in the community who are significant to them. As adults, we continue to grow because of the influence of others, mentors for example, whom we admire and with whom we identify. Communities have much to offer the many resilient adults in their midst. Resilient people are folks who, in the middle of their lives, have landed on their feet. The clinical definition of *resiliency* is, "The self-righting tendencies within the human organism."[6] Some resilient people have had disadvantaged childhoods, or troubled adolescence; some, when younger, were *in* trouble, some had failed first marriages — but in middle adulthood they "get it together." And many find their way to faith communities.

Students of adult development have been curious to learn why some, who in spite of unpromising, troubled, or disadvantaged childhoods, land on their feet later as adults and are then able to live productive and satisfying lives. Extensive research has revealed that a significant source of resiliency is *social support* — occurring often, in great abundance, in faith communities. Researchers have also found that resilient people are able to internalize their social supports and that they have hope and faith.[7] They are often drawn to communities that support them and reinforce their hope and their faith. And they, in turn, add to the community's renewal of faith and hope.

❧

"And in all things, give thanks!"

Thankfulness and hope go hand in hand, and each supports the other. We *learn* to give thanks. It is a point of view. In our society, faith communities — which teach families, who in turn, teach children — are the main resource for this teaching. Thanksgiving is at the heart of worship.

Consumer cultures do not reinforce thankfulness. In fact, they subliminally influence us to *want more,* to be dissatisfied. We do not remember to be grateful when we are anxious. Yet, paradoxically, a grateful heart quiets anxiety.

To live with thanksgiving is a teaching of mystics. It is also an attitude found in all people who are wide awake with a zest for life: those who are open to creation and to creativity.

It is through religious celebration of the liturgical year that most of us stay connected to the cycles of life: to birth, death, and rebirth in human life and in nature, even to our own biorhythms. In recent times there has been a radical change in our relationship to the cycles of nature and to time, itself. Many adults today had grandparents or great-grandparents who worked the land. (In 1850, 60 percent of the working population was employed in agriculture.) Today, many of us only have memories of having visited a farm — we are far from the land. (Now, less than 2.7 percent of the working population is directly engaged in farming.)[8] Today, in any modern supermarket we can buy any food, at any time, from anywhere. In being disconnected from the cycles of the seasons, we forget our creatureliness.

The relationship of the cycles of religious celebration to our experience of *time* may have even farther reaching implications to our health and well-being. Our sense of the time of the week has been changing. It used to be punctuated by the Sabbath or by Sunday. There was a break in the week for rest and renewal and this break was experienced by us and our neighbors. Now, for many, Sunday is a day almost like any other. Many stores are open for shopping. And because of shifts in work — very much created by technology — machines work full-time, therefore their operators work all the time, too. While most of us have a "day of rest," it might not correspond with that of our family or friends.

We still have bodies with biorhythms connected to another time, when we were more in contact with the rhythms of nature. Built into our bodies is a rhythm of activity, rest, renewal. James Ashbrook has noted that this cyclical rhythm, which we experience in waking and sleeping, is also the rhythm of the Sabbath. The Sabbath is a time set apart by God for rest and remembering. It is a time for a change in activity — from working and making to reflecting and synthesizing the experiences of the week. This is what Dr. Ashbrook calls "meaning-making...remembering who we are." He also sees a parallel between the rhythm of the Sabbath and the rhythm of our deepest "active" sleep, REM ("rapid eye movement") sleep. Through REM sleep we rest, dream, synthesize the experience of the day, and are thereby renewed. Through sleep we are reintegrated. Through keeping Sabbath we experience a similar integration. He says that we can keep the Sabbath by setting aside a "timeless" time to catch our breath and savor life. *Sabbathing* can be "the way in which we keep body and soul together"[9]

We are supported, as we support others in their changing lives, by remembering who we are. And as we remember, we will experience the Sabbath cycle of activity, rest, synthesis, renewal.

Within the circles of our lives
we dance the circles of the years,
the circles of the seasons
within the circles of the years.[10]

— Wendell Berry

Chapter Four
Reading and Resources
Publishing information is in the Bibliography.

• We recommend that, as companions to this chapter, you read: James Ashbrook's book, *Minding the Soul: Pastoral Counseling as Remembering.* Dr. Ashbrook describes the neurochemical processes of the brain that makes remembering — necessary for soul and soul keeping — possible.

Daniel Goleman's *Emotional Intelligence: Why It Can Matter More Than I.Q.,* which cites research supporting the relationship of hope to physical and emotional health.

• Herbert Benson, M.D.'s *Timeless Healing: The Power of Biology and Belief,* documents the ways in which faith in God and other *religious beliefs make a critical contribution to one's physical health* and well-being. His concept "remembered wellness" is similar to Dr. James Ashbrook's discussion of "remembering who we are." Like Ashbrook, he describes the brain as being "wired for God." In *Timeless Healing* Dr. Benson provides references to books and scientific research on "belief inspired healing."

• As you create your *Wholeness Network* you can learn about groups through the *Self-Help Directory,* a guide to mutual-aid self-help groups and how to form them. This can be ordered from: Self-Help Clearinghouse, St. Clare's Riverside Medical Center, Denville, NJ 07834 Tel. (201) 625-9565.

• If the concepts of "first" and "second order change" are new to you, you might be helped by Donald Capps' s clear presentation of them and other aspects of the theories of Watzlawick et al. (found in *Change: Principles of Problem Formation and Problem Resolution*) in his book, *Reframing: A New Method in Pastoral Care.*

• Paul Watzlawick has written an amusing book, *The Situation Is Hopeless, But Not Serious* to illustrate how people make themselves unhappy by applying the principles of problem formation in their daily lives.

• George Vaillant's *Wisdom of the Ego* provides research on and detailed description of the personality type of resilient people as well as other sources of their resiliency.

• There is abundant literature on religious resources for healing. A sampling:

Healing touch and ritual: Zack Thomas, *Healing Touch: The Church's Forgotten Language;* Kate Kerman, *A Friendly Touch: Therapeutic Touch among Quakers;* Elaine Ramshaw, *Ritual and Pastoral Care.*

Prayer: Edward P. Wimberly, *Prayer in Pastoral Counseling;* John Calvi, *Suffering, Healing and Discernment;* Hobart Mitchell, *The Dance between Hope and Fear; Prayer for Healing* (training for healing prayer and development of healing groups in Friends meetings); John Biersdorf, *How Prayer Shapes Ministry.*

Preaching: Donald Capps, *Pastoral Counseling and Preaching.*

Use of tradition: Willliam Oglesby, Jr., *Biblical Themes for Pastoral Care* Ralph Underwood, *Pastoral Care and the Means of Grace;* William Hulme, *Pastoral Care and Counseling: Using The Unique Resources of the Christian Tradition;* David Feldman, *Health and Medicine in the Jewish Tradition;* Richard McCormick, *Health and Medicine in the Catholic Tradition.*

Spirituality: Terence Duniho, *Wholeness Lies Within: 16 Natural Paths to Spirituality* John Ackerman, *Spiritual Awakening:A Guide to Spiritual Life in Congregations.*

• The moral context for pastoral care and counseling is explored in Donald Browning's *The Moral Context of Pastoral Care* and James Poling's "Ethics in Pastoral Care and Counseling," in *The Handbook for Basic Types of Pastoral Care and Counseling,* edited by Howard Stone and William Clements.

• Research has verified that religious practices can contribute to mental health. This is documented in *Religion and Prevention in Mental Health: Research, Vision and Action,* edited by Kenneth I. Pargament, Kenneth I. Maton, and Robert Hess.

5

Preparing for Community Care, Counseling, and Referral

I'm going to plant a heart in the earth
water it with love from a vein
I'm going to praise it with the push of muscle
and care for it in the sound of all dimensions.
I'm going to leave a heart in the earth
so it may grow and flower
a heart that throbs with longing
that adores everything green
that will be a strength and nourishment for birds
that will be the sap of plants and mountains.[1]

—Rosario Murillo

Counselors are like gardeners: they prepare before they plant. In the midst of winter, many gardeners spend hours poring over seed catalogs, dreaming. They organize the plant shed, clean and sharpen tools. They analyze and prepare their soil. Like gardeners you, too, must get ready to counsel.

To help you get organized, we have designed a check list. Unlike a gardener who begins afresh at each season, you may have been counseling for many years and have a system in place. However, if you have been doing "business as usual," you may be overlooking important aspects of the process. We invite seasoned counselors to read this chapter with the eyes of a novice so that you may discover something new. We begin with you, yourself, and move on to your counseling space.

Check List: Preparation for Care and Counseling

Self
The poet Rosario Murillo is "going to plant a heart in the earth / water it with love from a vein" — in order that the earth may flourish. Many counselors "plant" their hearts in their work, in the ground of community, nurturing others who flower and grow.

But we must not stretch the metaphor too far. To "plant" one's heart could imply the loss of self. Counselors need to give of themselves without giving themselves away. You, too, need to be nourished. You, too, are growing.

This is why we have placed "self" at the top of the check list. You need to build into your weekly calendar time for your own self care, personal and professional support, and continuing education. The importance of self nurture is discussed in chapter 10, "Tending Yourself."

Hospitable, Safe Counseling Space

You and the physical environment of your counseling room create a container, a safe place, to which people can come for healing. We have discussed the importance of *your* readiness, but It is equally important that you create a pleasant, hospitable space that feels safe and private. Your office must be soundproof. If you can hear voices of those outside your room, people can also hear you and your counselee. Get soundproofing advice from an expert. Buy a "white noise" machine or use radio music in your waiting room to mask sound.

Give some thought to the arrangement of chairs in your counseling space. Make certain that your chair is not higher than those of counselees. Although it is subtle, if you are sitting higher you send a message of higher status and power. As a counselor, your role is to help people empower themselves by finding their own path. You get in the way if you send an authoritarian message. Be aware that if you are sitting behind a desk that separates you from counselees, an appearance of your authority and distance is heightened. Some counselors are more comfortable with this arrangement because it reinforces their sense of personal boundaries. Some use an arrangement of chairs and a small sofa in which they and individuals, couples, and families can sit comfortably together. This arrangement creates a situation in which people feel more at ease.

Wholeness Network

In *Appendix B* you will find a *Wholeness Network Form,* which will help you organize information about the members of the wholeness network of your community. Compiling this information will make you aware of your resources as well as prepare you for referral counseling. It will also help make you conscious of who is in the network so that you can help people be aware of each other.

In this time of change in insurance funding and the health-care delivery system, religious communities are likely to have more opportunities to meet counseling and other social service needs. Communities that are conscious of the wholeness network in their midst can meet these needs more readily. They can also organize more easily to serve as advocates for health and other social services.

One of your functions as facilitator is to both make referrals to other professionals, and also help people find a wide variety of resources. It often takes creativity and persistence to create this network. The shape of the network will depend on the context in which you are working. If you are in a large urban area you might have many resources available but these might be difficult to use because of the impersonal and complicated bureaucracies that manage them. If you are in a rural area your local resources might be sparse, but you might have personal relationships with people in county or state agencies that give you support and perhaps efficient access to resources.

Your referral network might include:

Individuals

- Mental health professionals (including pastoral counselors) to whom you can refer those who need individual, couple, or family counseling, and with whom you can consult for assessments and supervision.
- Spiritual growth and spiritual direction practitioners; chaplains in hospitals, hospices and other institutions.
- Medical specialists who can evaluate those with physical problems; and wellness practitioners (nutritionist, massage, body, art and music therapists) whose work supports health.
- Social workers, educators, lawyers and others who can help you utilize the social welfare, education, and justice systems and who can lead workshops and educational activities.

Organizations:

- Twelve Step Groups — Alcoholics Anonymous, Adult Children of Alcoholics, Al-Anon, Overeaters Anonymous, Gamblers Anonymous and Narcotics Anonymous, Parents Anonymous (parents who have abused their children).
- Grief groups: Compassionate Friends, Alive Alone.
- Support groups for those recovering from physical and sexual abuse.
- Groups that support growth, life transitions, parenting (including nontraditional groups such as Single Mothers by Choice and P-FLAG — Parents and Friends of Lesbians and Gays).
- Support groups for those with critical illnesses and their caregivers.
- Suicide and other crisis hotlines.

Agencies:

- Community recreational, educational, and other service centers for children and adolescents.
- Shelters for homeless people and battered women and their children.
- Hospice care.

• Rehabilitation and treatment centers for those suffering addictions.

Those who become part of this group of consultants are de facto members of your religious community's wholeness network. It is helpful for you enlist people who consciously share your values and who will see themselves as working with you and other members of your community in a shared ministry. Developing such a referral network takes time because each person needs to be known personally; the network is built on relationships.

But you do not have to build this network alone. We suggested in chapter 2 that you organize a group or committee in your congregation to help you identify those in your congregation who are involved in the work of healing. This same group can help you build this referral network through their own personal and professional relationships. They can introduce you to these consultants, whom you, in turn, will get to know before you use them.

Your committee can make its research known by creating a resource center for announcements of workshops, support, and Twelve Step groups; medical, health, and self-help articles, books and newsletters; cassettes, and other resources for spiritual growth, etc. Members of the community can be encouraged to add to this information center. The more that your entire community knows about the existing resources for healing the better.

Plan For Care/Counseling Ministry

In making plans for community care and counseling, it is useful to define their function:

Community Care occurs within the changes of life itself. Faith communities are asked to be with members in their situations, in all the seasons of life. This caregiving ministry includes counsel, support, education, resourcing to meet physical, social, and spiritual needs, prayer, and liturgical acts to those who experience changes caused by life itself. (Occasions for community care at times of new beginnings, loss, and predictable life difficulties will be explored in chapters 7, 8, and 9.)

Community Care is very labor intensive and it functions both formally and informally. It is the community *being* the community. In small communities in a simpler time there was a common understanding of the rituals of care. Women "knew" intuitively that they should bring food to families at times of illness and death. Men "knew" intuitively that they should offer help to a family in crisis. Today faith communities cannot make assumptions that pastoral needs will just be taken care of by those who "always do it." Many of the women who traditionally served as volunteers and called on shut-ins now have jobs. In fact, many members have two jobs to make ends meet. Communities need to be more organized to do their work of ministry.

Sometimes in the midst of forming community care, leaders become confused about their function. People come for spiritual direction and ask for spiritual advice. In confirmation and conversion classes and in other small groups, members grapple with questions about meaning in their lives. Members make counseling appointments to speak to leaders about their spiritual conflicts. They often experience healing in these sessions. How does this counseling differ from that of pastoral or other psychotherapies?

The *outcome* of counseling in community or in psychotherapy can be the same. Through both, conflicts can be resolved, clarity can be experienced, insight can be gained, people can be healed. However, the *relationship* between psychotherapist and client and religious leader and community member differs.

In most cases, the relationship between psychotherapists and their clients is time limited. Psychotherapists relate to clients professionally in a circumscribed manner. Their goal is to fulfill a therapeutic contract that they have made with clients who wish to make changes in areas of thinking, acting, relating, being, feeling. Religious leaders, on the other hand, have multiple roles. They have an ongoing relationship with their members. They educate, perform religious rites, and are companions on life's journey.

While some psychotherapists use brief therapy methods, for others, the project of psychotherapy takes time. It often uses special tools: the analysis of dreams, thoughts, and the relationship to the therapist; or the retraining of behavior or thinking; or "re-parenting" through a long, reparative relationship with the therapist. Many therapists help clients define their "presenting problems" and help them not only to solve them, but also to understand the reasons for which the problems were created and maintained.

Often people who come to you requesting community care do not expect *you* to find a solution to their problem. They have already decided that a solution is to be found in the religious and social service resources of your community. It sometimes takes careful listening to discern who is seeking community care and who is coming for brief counseling to solve a particular life issue.

Brief Counseling is used with those who are stuck in problems, who experience impasse in their life situation, or who wish to sort out questions around a life issue. We believe that it is appropriate that community counseling be brief, focused, and goal oriented. In chapter 6 we will demonstrate the effective use of the *Solution-Focused Therapy* method for doing brief counseling. Solution-focused therapists have discovered that although counselees come to them because of a sense of being stuck in their problems, they not only have solutions to their problems, but they have occasionally used these solutions to get "unstuck." The counselor helps clients discover what they have been doing to solve the problem — even when they were not aware of this.

We have been underscoring the use of *brief counseling* because counselors in community have only so much time to do counseling with individuals, couples, and families. Counseling that extends beyond four to six sessions would monopolize the counselor's time. Furthermore, researchers have discovered that many people go to a therapist for only one or two sessions. Many seem to sort out their problems in this brief amount of time. You can help people reach their goals faster than you might think.

"Brief counseling" refers not simply to the duration of sessions, it is also a treatment method. Although strategies of the different schools vary, most are oriented in the here and now and they help people make changes in thinking, feeling, and behavior in a focused, goal-oriented way. We recommend Howard Stone's *Brief Pastoral Counseling: Short-Term Approaches and Strategies*, which applies the methods of several schools of brief therapy to community counseling situations.

Traditional pastoral counseling methods have often been based on psychodynamic methods and theories of psychotherapy. These methods cured through the healing relationship between the counselor and counselee. Counselees "re-membered" themselves through their associations and dreams in the safety of the therapeutic relationship. Today pastoral psychotherapists often use this methodology.

But many clergy who use these techniques find themselves getting in over their heads, into the projections and transference of their counselees. Often they find themselves responding in ways that are confusing. They are caught in unexplored material from their own unconscious. The counseling becomes muddled. The counselee's goal for change is often obscured in the process.

Both psychodynamic therapy (hence, psychodynamic pastoral counseling) and brief therapy (hence brief community [pastoral] counseling) share some common ground. Both methods respect the integrity of the counselee. Both require careful listening. Both require that counselors know what to do with what they hear. But there are significant differences. The two methodologies have different relationship between past, present, and future. Psychodynamic counseling often focuses on past history to understand the counselee's problems in the present. Brief counseling focuses on the present and the future.

⚸

To distinguish a request for counseling as community care from a request for brief counseling, we will illustrate some *community care situations:*

COUNSELOR: "What brings you in?"
COUNSELEES: #1 "I need help. I'm finally going to do it. I'm going into a rehab program."
#2 "I need help. I took the test. I'm HIV positive."
#3 "I need help. Charlie and I are going to separate."

When hearing the words "I need help," many counselors in community will automatically slip into problem-solving gear. Because they cannot consider the possibility that they will not have to help *fix it,* they might not even inquire,

"What is it you need help with?" They will already be *at work getting ready to give advice.*

When hearing statements such as these, how are you to know if you are being asked to help someone discover their solution to a problem, or if you are being asked to be a bridge to community care?

In fact, you do not yet have enough information to know what is required. I have simply illustrated how difficult it is for most counselors not to respond reactively to the statement, "I need help." Many counselors grew up in families where their role was to be the caretaker or the conciliator. They have been conditioned to "fix it." In addition, clergy are *expected* to *help.* To be an effective counselor in community, you must *unlearn* your reflexive urge to be helpful. Train yourself not to say immediately, "How can I help?" Learn to wait first to discover how your counselees are helping themselves.

It takes a change in mind-set to listen for solutions—for good news. Often counselors do not expect that people will make appointments to talk about the problems that they are in the process of solving. However, community members sometimes call you to tell about their healing and to ask for prayerful support. These very people might begin with "I need help." However, it is not necessarily *your* help to which they are referring. People may call their religious counselors because they want support, not problem solving. Often they want you to be with them *in their situation*—in their living.

Listen: you will be told what is needed. Usually when people come asking to be supported in changes they are already making, they know the help they need. They may not know what *form* the support should take, but they know that they do not expect you to solve the problem they're working on. If you don't jump in to solve the problem but wait receptively, you will learn more about what the need is. Here are some examples based on the three statements listed above:

"*I need help. I'm finally going to do it. I'm going into a rehab program.*" John began his session with these words as he settled into a chair in his rector's office. His rector, Father Gregory, had known of John's struggle with drinking. He had supported him during his "off and on" attendance at Alcoholics Anonymous and had eventually referred him to a pastoral psychotherapist for counseling. He knew that in the past, John had fiercely maintained that he was a heavy drinker, not an alcoholic.

FR. GREGORY: "Wow...how did you come to that hard decision?"
JOHN: "I just couldn't pretend anymore. I was suspended from my job. Who was I kidding? I couldn't quit by myself."
FR. GREGORY: "I'm impressed with your courage and your honesty."
[Thoughtful silence between them.]
JOHN: "Yeah...well, I've come to talk...well, no really to pray... because I'm really scared that I can't make it. And I also know that

I'm leaving Nancy with a mess. I know she gets support from her friends. But I've put a strain on stuff between us."

John did not know what specific help Father Gregory could give him, but he did know that he needed the spiritual resources of his community. In this session Father Gregory found out more specifically about John's fears of "not making it." John was frightened about the physical effects of coming off alcohol. He acknowledged that going into a treatment program in a medical facility had somewhat quieted this anxiety. Father Gregory also found out more about the "mess" John was leaving with Nancy and the strain between them. Near the end of the session he made an appointment with John and Nancy together to discuss Nancy's plans for coping while John was gone. John and Father Gregory prayed together and then made a plan for John to go to the church's healing service where he would receive blessing and anointing.

In this first session, Father Gregory supported John's courage to begin treatment. He then waited and allowed time for John to state his need. Father Gregory did not get sidetracked into trying to "fix" John's relationship with Nancy or giving him a pep talk about his treatment. He listened to John's concerns and addressed *with action* John's specific request for prayer, spiritual support and a meeting with Nancy.

The form that community care takes differs in each religious tradition. In his book *African-American Pastoral Care,* Edward Wimberly gives a moving case study of the experience of a cocaine addict who used the resources of his church as he prepared to go to a rehabilitation program. Like John, the man had struggled with the denial of his addiction. A breakthrough in his healing came when he said to his pastoral psychotherapist:" You can't leave a person at a time when they are wounded the most. You can't abandon me to this problem." When Dr. Wimberly asked him to explain, he said that prayer was the only thing that could help him. He then spoke about the help his nephew, who was recovering from alcoholism, received from a small group who prayed with him. Dr. Wimberly was moved by this solution, and organized a prayer meeting with the man, his wife, the man's pastor, friends, and a goddaughter who had recovered from cocaine addiction. The meeting, which was held before the man entered treatment, was spirit-filled. The familiar ritual of the prayer meeting — prayer, words of scripture, singing, and laying on of hands — comforted, sustained, and supported both the husband and wife as they prepared for the difficult days ahead.[2]

"*I need help. I took the test. I'm HIV positive.*" After Carlos blurted out those words, Rosemarie's stomach sank but she kept quiet and waited. And then Carlos said, "And you know, the hardest thing was the years of worrying...and then, the test...and the waiting." After some silence, Rosemarie asked, "What happened in you that finally let you be tested?" Carlos was silent for a while. "Well, I knew I was at risk," he said, "and I had learned there are things to do to stay healthy for as long as possible. I guess wanting to live beat out my fear of knowing."

Carlos had come to Rosemarie because he knew that she was a social worker. As a member of the parish, she worked with people who were living with AIDS. He came to ask her help in learning to meditate because he had heard that meditating helped to strengthen the immune system as well as to give spiritual support to those with the virus. Rosemarie supported Carlos in the strength of his solution. She said, "Carlos, I'm really moved by the way you figured out that supporting your life is better than living in fear. That's wonderful."

Sometimes people who are struggling to accept a diagnosis come to you for brief counseling. Unlike Carlos, who had already dealt with inner conflict and fear by being tested, many who seek counseling are still struggling with the meaning of their serious illness. Often conflict about the illness can be resolved as they work with you in brief counseling. Sometimes, though, it is wise for you to then refer them to a therapist for support in the long process of their illness and, in some cases, death.

Many coming to you will be like Carlos. They do not see their illness as a problem to be solved, but rather a difficulty to be lived with. They will be coming for occasional support, for the comfort of your liturgical healing ministry, for referral to therapists or support groups. They might also be wanting the support and knowledge of people in your congregation who have struggled with similar life difficulties.

It is essential that you learn to listen for the complaint or situation that they are solving at the present time and then identify the *specific* help they want from you. Carlos was asking to learn to meditate. In the session, Rosemarie and Carlos prayed. She then referred him to a support group whose members prayed and meditated together. Rosemarie did not try to tell Carlos everything she knew about living with the virus nor did she invite him to tell her how he felt about the possibility of having AIDS. Facing AIDS was not the problem Carlos was solving at this time.

"I need help. Charlie and I are going to separate. "

PASTOR JOAN: "That sounds like a big decision. Tell me about it."
ADELE: "Well, you know I've been struggling...that's why you referred me to
DR. DIAZ. I guess it's more accurate to say I'm leaving Charlie."
PASTOR JOAN: "How did you make that happen?"

Adele was a very faithful member of Pastor Joan's parish. Frequently she and Pastor Joan had long discussions about scripture, particularly as it applied to Christian family life. In time, Adele was able to speak more personally. She told Pastor Joan that when her husband drank, he would "knock her around" but the next day he would be sweet and apologetic and would even pray with her for God's forgiveness and for God to help Adele be loving again. Adele believed that staying with Charlie and helping him not to drink was God's plan for her. She believed this because of the way Charlie prayed and was sweet after his episodic drinking bouts.

Adele began to doubt her belief about God's plan for her after an occasion when Charlie beat her so badly that she required medical attention. She came to Pastor Joan in great shame. She felt that somehow she had failed Charlie. However, she did not believe that a loving God would want her to be abused. At that time, Pastor Joan was concerned about Adele's safety. She and Adele began to talk about a plan for moving but Adele felt that she first wanted to sort out some conflicts. She was certain that she would feel guilty and would soon come back to Charlie. Pastor Joan had then referred her to Dr. Diaz, who specialized in crisis intervention and the treatment of people in abusive situations.

PASTOR JOAN: "How did you make that happen?"

ADELE: "Well, I guess I learned to listen to myself. Remember when I told you that I didn't think that God would make a plan for me to be abused? When I said that, I didn't really take it in. I told it to Dr. Diaz. She said, 'Wait a minute...listen to what you just said!' I let it sink in. We spent time exploring how I could care for myself, how I could value myself — at least in the ways my head knew God would want me to. Knowing that God would not want me hurt has given me the strength to leave."

PASTOR JOAN: "I think that God has placed a wise counselor inside you."

Adele was silent for awhile and then said,"You've just given me what I came for. I just needed you to hear how it happened, how I felt surprising strength and clarity."

Pastor Joan had listened until Adele told her what she needed. In the meantime, she learned what Adele was resolving and she then affirmed her solution. It is not unusual for people to come to their clergy counselors to tell them of healing that has happened in the context of psychotherapy, spiritual direction, or through their own discernment. Sometimes they come to "tell the good news," to witness to the healing, and to express gratitude for it.

At other times, people come asking for specific healing rituals — blessings, rites of reconciliation, confession and absolution. Sometimes they come knowing they need "something spiritual" and, through listening to them, you recognize that a liturgical ritual is necessary so you will use something from your tradition, or borrow from the traditions of others, or invent one in a creative moment. Traditionally, religious rituals help bring closure and binding. Today, counselors in community often participate in healing the pain of couples who have had miscarriages or who have finally accepted the diagnosis of infertility. They have been with those who are recovering from sexual, physical, and emotional abuse. They have ministered to those who separate or divorce. However, most religious communities do not have traditional rituals for these crises or transitions. Ritual would be helpful. It can be created and used in healing. We recommend Elaine Ramshaw's *Ritual and Pastoral Care* as a resource for rituals, both ancient and modern, that transcend words.

Not all requests are for help with healing and closure. You may be invited to help to *upset* a situation so that healing can begin to happen. Community members might ask you to be a part of an intervention with an alcoholic or drug addicted person. Interventions are usually planned by therapists or addiction counselors who, with family members and others, confront the addicted one as part of getting him or her into treatment.

Often you will be asked for resources to support solutions, sometimes for the names of support groups, or agencies, or you may be asked to make the referral and be actively involved in the intake process.

Community care requires follow-though. Follow-through was needed in all of the case examples I have just described. Father Gregory spent time alone with John after the healing service. In his meeting with Nancy and John, he learned that Nancy, because of her intense shyness, needed support before going to the family therapy session at the hospital. Father Gregory and Nancy met together for a session before the meeting. Rosemarie called her colleague before referring Carlos to the support group. She then met with Carlos in a follow-up session a few weeks later to support his practice of meditation and to connect him to other resources in the parish. Pastor Joan helped Adele find temporary housing and met with her for two sessions to help her plan and make her move.

Sometimes follow-through requires a simple phone call initiated by you or the counselee. At other times, the follow-through will require more telephone work for you and perhaps another session with the counselee. It is necessary to keep your focus — you are supporting a solution. Your goal is to keep to your *specific* agreement, not to become globally helpful!)

Policy for Counseling Ministry

In the not too distant past, clergy and other counselors in community did not give much thought to the legal consequences of their counseling ministries. They thought that their counseling had legal immunity because of confidential privilege. They saw it as an extension of their healing ministry, related to rites of reconciliation and forgiveness. Even clergy in faith groups that had no formal rite of confession thought of their counseling as protected because of the confidentiality of the confessional.

But times have changed. Clergy are now being sued for professional malpractice as well as for sexual misconduct and other abuse. Clergy cannot hide behind the seal of the confessional when being charged with unlawful or unethical acts. Congregations and their parent groups are learning that they are vulnerable when their clergy or other staff members are found guilty of violating trust.

Because of this vulnerability, many denominations and faith groups and their insurance carriers are beginning to set policies to protect themselves and their members from clergy malpractice. They have been particularly concerned about establishing policies for sound community/pastoral counseling because it has been established that most clergy who have been convicted of sexual misconduct had abused someone whom they had first counseled. Religious judicatories have begun to set standards for the type of counseling done by clergy and the number of sessions appropriate for them to conduct. They have policies about the counseling setting, about record keeping and fees. They also have policies on whether or not clergy may counsel nonmembers of their congregations. They have policies on requirements for supervision of the clergy counselor's work.

It is necessary for you to know what policies and standards your denomination or faith group has set and to understand the thinking behind them. The policies of many religious groups have grown out of concern for:

1. *Cost:* Religious groups have been motivated to set standards because of costly law suits; they have also been motivated by their awareness of cost to human life. Many people have been emotionally and spiritually injured by clergy counselors who practiced counseling beyond their competence and training or who abused their power in counseling relationships.

2. *Confidential privilege:* Some religious groups value the confidentiality of the confessional (priest-penitent) and want this privilege to be preserved for theological reasons. Some groups value confidentiality and expect community caregivers to maintain it, but believe that counseling in this context is also a public ministry in which the spiritual leader is also a representative of the church. It is for this reason that the Church Insurance Company requires that "where spiritual leaders provide more intensive care, ongoing supervision by a credentialed professional safeguards both parties."[3]

Other groups want counseling to be protected from litigation and therefore want their counselors to strictly abide by the rules of the confessional as they interpret them. Aaron Liberman and Michael J. Woodruff, in their book *Risk Management*, report:

> Numerous pastors and counselors want their counsel to be absolutely insulated from litigation. They conduct their pastoral counseling in highly confidential setting.To reduce the risk of later discovery or of review by third parties they take no notes. They even resist disclosure of the counselees' identity as within the scope of their confidential privilege. These counselors do well not to think of their work within a medical model. They are confessors who guard secrets appropriately and legally. Accordingly, they should stay within character, maintaining careful boundaries and making referrals to pas-

toral counselors, who integrate insights from both theological and psychological training.[4]

Religious groups have their laws (canon law), and states have their own laws about clergy confidentiality. It is important for you to know both sets, as both affect your practice. Some religious groups understand clergy confidentiality to be maintained only if the clergy counselor is speaking to a member of their congregation. These clergy counselors must refer nonmembers to other counselors. Some understand clergy privilege to be between the priest and one other person, therefore they understand couple counseling as not protected as confidential material. See W. Rankin's *Confidentiality and Clergy: Churches, Ethics and the Law* for clarification about clergy privilege. (We further this discussion in chapter 10, "Tending Yourself.")

3. *Competence:* Because of lawsuits, religious judiciaries have become increasingly aware that counselors who practice beyond their level of competence can be found guilty of malpractice. It is essential that counselors in community not hold themselves out as doing more than they are trained to do. Certified pastoral counselors function as psychotherapists and in some states are licensed as mental-health professionals. Because of the possibility of boundary violations and conflict of roles, it is not wise for certified pastoral counselors who are also religious leaders of congregations, to do long-term treatment with members. Clergy counselors are trained to use psychotherapeutic methods for doing brief counseling, but they should not refer to their work as "doing therapy" because it is misleading and increases their legal liability.

Religious groups are setting standards for the appropriate counseling practice of their clergy. For example, the Church Insurance Company, which insures the counseling work of clergy in the Protestant Episcopal Church, has made the following regulation reflecting these concerns:

> Clergy and other pastoral care providers will be required to have ongoing professional supervision or to refer the individual to professional counseling after six sessions have been held around a given life issue, and fees or donations for pastoral care will be proscribed. Anyone charging fees for counseling outside the scope of church employment must possess appropriate professional credentials and proof of separate professional liability insurance, including coverage for Sexual Misconduct, in force at all times.[5]

The Church Insurance Company recognizes that the relationships between those pastoral caregivers who practice spiritual direction and their directees are not immune to boundary violations. It is the tradition that spiritual directors seek their own spiritual direction to protect directees from their blind spots. The Church Insurance Company has given spiritual directors a more formal directive to submit to peer or supervisory review with a spiritual advisor approved by the bishop or ecclesiastical authority.[6]

❧

It is not unusual for community care and counseling to be dependent on the calling, skills and personal inclination of the religious leader.

However, religious communities that are aware of being healing networks will be interested in policies affecting their counseling ministry. Because the gifts of the entire community are utilized, their healing ministries will not simply reflect the skills of the leader. These communities will wish to be a part of decision making about utilizing their resources. They will care about the amount of time their clergy spend in counseling; whether or not trained lay people could be part of counseling teams; whether fees should be charged for counseling services; whether they should join with other congregations to sponsor a pastoral counseling agency or to create other healing resources.

Religious leaders can help their congregations set policies on community care and counseling, but they must first know where they stand on the matter. They need information about:

- How much time they can devote to brief counseling.
- How they will handle requests for counseling when they do not have time to do it.
- How the counseling done as community care differs from brief counseling.
- How the method of counseling used determines their goals and affects the number of times they meet with counselees.
- How they will carry out the guidelines set by their faith groups and how they will interpret these guidelines to their congregations. For instance, clergy whose religious groups strictly interpret confidential privilege may not be able to counsel nonmembers. Their congregations will need to be educated about this. These same congregations may then develop referral and consultation services to meet the needs of the broader community.

Clergys' answers to these questions can become factored in with the concerns of the community and be part of the mix out of which community policy is formed.

In addition to these issues, congregations need to set policies on whether fees should be paid for counseling. Some counselors feel that paying a small amount for brief counseling services helps counselees take the work more seriously. Others feel that counseling is as much a part of their ministry as preaching or administration and therefore, it is inappropriate to charge a fee. Others do not charge a fee, but have a fund to which counselees can contribute if they feel moved to do so. Sometimes the fund is used to pay for the counselor's supervision, or to help others pay for mental health treatment.

Many counselors in community who take fees for their services do not understand that in doing so they lose the absolute privilege of clergy confidentiality. Accepting money for their counseling services places clergy in the same legal position as other mental-health providers.[7]

States have rules and regulations that affect counseling done by clergy. For example, you need to know under what circumstances you must report child abuse and neglect, when you should notify parents or others when you learn of potential threats to self or others. States differ in their regulations and in their interpretation of confidential privilege. You may find yourself breaking the law because you do not know it. It is up to you to know state laws that affect your policies of counseling and referral. It is equally important to understand the law as it affects nonordained members of the community's counseling team. (We will continue to address this subject in chapter 10, "Tending Yourself.")

Most religious communities give their leaders a free hand to develop community counseling programs. While they may broadly set policy that supports ministries of counseling and care, it is up to the religious leader to carry it out. You — the leader — must develop your own policies for the conduct of your counseling practice. By developing personal policy, you do not have to do it ad hoc in the stress of the moment. Let us suggest some items to consider in advance:

- The number of hours per week you can *reasonably* spend at your work.
- The number of hours each week you can *comfortably* do brief counseling.
- The number of times you will see individuals, families, couples in a series of brief counseling sessions.
- Persons with whom you are uncomfortable doing brief counseling and will therefore refer.
- Policy for referring those who are suicidal, homicidal, seriously mentally ill, or suffering from addictions.
- Policy on reporting knowledge of child abuse and neglect and family violence.
- How much support you need in the form of supervision, peer group support, continuing education, personal therapy, spiritual direction.
- What to do when you feel "over your head" in the counseling work.

Information-Gathering Systems

Your life will be made easier if before meeting counselees you have prepared a system for gathering information, keeping records, obtaining permission for releasing information to medical sources and other professionals, making referrals and responding to emergencies and crises.

We have prepared forms that you will find in *Appendix B,* which we hope will simplify this task. They include:

- *Wholeness Network Members* card for organizing information about the members of the wholeness network of your community.
- *Care and Counseling Information Log* for you to have on hand at both your home and office to use when people call for counseling appointments. It contains space to record the counselee's personal data and the reason for calling, whether community care, brief counseling, or referral is needed, and which services will be provided. In addition, there are spaces to remind yourself to follow through with additional appointments or referrals.
- *Information for Referral Counseling Form* that we suggest you fill out to help make an effective referral. Counselees should be assured that the information gathered will be kept confidential. You will notice that we have included the questions: "Are you now working with a psychotherapist? Is medication being prescribed ? By whom?" These are personal questions that you might be reluctant to ask but which are pertinent in your assessment. Counselors in community must observe the delicate balance of respecting community members' need for privacy and their own need for information. We have included a problem check list that counselees can answer when they are asking for your help in referral.
- *Counselee Permission to Release Information* form, which counselees sign before you refer them to another for therapeutic treatment or evaluation.

Gathering information is essential to the counseling process. It is very important that you learn to listen well so that you can recall with accuracy what counselees tell you about their understanding of their problems, goals, and solutions for change. To make it easier for yourself, always take notes when speaking on the phone to those who wish to begin counseling so that you can write, in their words, what they experience their problem or difficulty to be and what they expect from you. Gathering information when you are sitting in the room with the counselee is more difficult because it is hard to make notes, maintain eye contact, and respond emotionally at the same time. However, because it is necessary for you to know exactly how the person both experiences the problem and has solutions for it, you probably need to take some notes during the session in order to record the person's own words.

We believe that it is useful to keep track of basic data through record keeping and process notes. We also believe that confidential information should be recorded in a minimal way, kept in a locked file and destroyed when it is no longer useful for counseling purposes. Basically, counseling notes are necessary *for you,* as you serve the counselee.

Since you will be seeing the counselee for only a few sessions in brief counseling, you will not have a large quantity of materials. Making notes on sessions will help you keep in mind the counselees' goals, your agreement for helping them reach their goals, and your mutual understanding of when you both will know the counseling has ended. It is your job to keep track of the process. Reviewing notes before each session will help you do this.

It is particularly important to have accurate information when you are referring a counselee to another professional. It may also be necessary to keep records of referrals for future reference. Attorney Michael Woodruff, expert on religious institutions and civil law, further illustrates the importance of keeping records when he says:

> When a counselor in community has repeated contact with a counselee, notes can document the counselee's ideational history. This may be very helpful to future treatment by another professional upon referral. It may enable the counselor to arrive at a more accurate assessment of the problem and lead to an appropriate referral. Notes can serve the counselee. Casual notes that avoid documentation of presenting symptoms and concerns, that omit a meaningful review of medical issues or problems, that do not cross-reference other treatment by physicians or take into account effects of medication, that provide no responsible axial diagnosis or identify a treatment plan/ goal, are dangerous. They may be later used as objective evidence of professional malpractice.
>
> Notes are often understood as the best objective means of assessing the quality of care, or lack of it. The failure to have notes may be tantamount to an admission of negligent practice if the prevailing practice standard is to keep notes. Counselors in community must make clear that when they keep minimal notes of personal use only, that their counseling is limited in duration, that counselees with identifiable mental health needs are referred to others as soon as practicable.[8]

Woodruff is saying that a distinction can be made between notes that are used by you for keeping track of the process, and notes that are used for records. Process notes can be thrown away after their use. Your record notes, if kept, should reflect that you are practicing within the sphere of your competence and that you have contracted to do goal-oriented work within a given time parameter and have followed through on that plan. It is particularly important that records reflect that you have referred to appropriate professionals those with "identifiable mental health needs."

Many religious counselors have not been trained in seminary to take notes or to keep records of counseling sessions. In fact, many come from traditions where counseling and the function of the confessional are somewhat merged. Counselors are apprehensive about taking notes because of fear that if the notes are seen by others, the privileged information of the confessional would be violated. Others are confused about the practice because of recent concern due to lawsuits against clergy and religious institutions. These people ask:

are we supposed to take notes of counseling sessions for legal protection, or should we not?

In their book *Risk Management,* Aaron Liberman and Michael Woodruff say that those whose religious groups uphold a strict interpretation of privileged communication because of the rite of the confessional, should not take notes. Find out what your religious body advises about keeping notes and storing records. While concern about keeping records may seem like a small matter, it can become large if under the scrutiny of litigation.

Referral Counseling

There is an art to making successful referrals. Essentially, referring involves an extension of your relationship with the person who wants a referral to another helper. Referrals "take" when counselees sense that you believe in the persons to whom you are sending them. Allowing oneself "to be referred" involves trust. If the person or agency to whom you are referring is known by your community, the trust comes more easily. If the pastoral psychotherapist to whom you are referring has preached to your congregation, or if the family therapist has led workshops, they are not strangers. If the pastoral counseling center, women and children's shelter, or community health agency has been supported by your congregation, they, too are known resources.

We are assuming that many of those in your network are not members of your congregation. Boundaries are more easily kept when you have people to whom you refer who are on your "wavelength" but who do not have to cope with the dual relationships of friendship/doctor that occur when both are members of the same religious community.

❧

We must acknowledge that the situation in which you find yourself as a referral counselor today is very unsettling. A few years ago it was easier. At that time, you probably had a consultant who was a psychiatrist trained both to talk to people about their lives and to prescribe medication. You were able to refer parishioners to him for an evaluation and then he would refer them to the appropriate professionals. This same colleague was someone you could call for supervision when you needed help with troubled parishioners. Or perhaps you did not use just one consultant because you knew the practitioners in your community. You made referrals to many types of helping professionals, including psychiatrists who evaluated and medicated.

But today your psychiatrist might be working for a health maintenance organization (HMO) and will only be able to see those who are entitled to use the services of that group. Or perhaps the person you wish to refer has health insurance that only covers a particular list of consultants — and your consultant is not on the list. Perhaps your psychiatric consultant has retired and the new psychiatrist was trained as a psychopharmacologist; she medicates but does not do "talk therapy." She is fine when you need someone to whom to send a depressed, panicky, or disoriented person, but she is not the one to supervise and consult with about your counseling.

Because of these changes, it is even more essential that you have an active healing/healers network to give you guidance. You may already be noticing a difference in your referral practice. Because primary physicians in managed health-care organizations must make referrals within their system, you may not have so many people coming to you for referral. They may come after they have seen therapists for an allotted period of time because they have found that they still need help. They may come for brief counseling. Or you may be able to refer them to pastoral psychotherapists or others who charge fees they can afford.

The present changes in health-care delivery are far-reaching. At this writing, hospitals are merging, and child-care and other social and mental health agencies are gearing up in response to managed care organizations that are either absorbing them or preparing to buy units of care from them. Health and social service agencies are being challenged to be cost effective and to deliver services efficiently. We do not yet know what health care and other social services will look like in this new corporate culture.

But faith communities will face new challenges. They may have more work to do. Because of changes in legislation, it is probable that more people will have *some* mental health care. It is also clear that in a managed health-care culture, counseling will be measured as valuable if it keeps people from using expensive emergency room service or having long hospitalizations. Medication for mental illness and brief therapy will be the treatment of choice. Most health insurance will not fund psychotherapy for personal growth, or the "soul minding" functions that have been provided in the past. It may be that faith communities will have to provide extra support for pastoral counseling centers that do this work. Faith communities may also need to do more programming for small groups, workshops, and forums that give their members a context for personal reflection and learning.

Many people will *ask* you for a referral. They come to you knowing that they need help. Some, however, may not know what type of help they need or whom to go to. For instance: A parishioner makes an appointment to speak about a daughter who is in trouble at school. The school has told her to get help for her child, but she does not have money for counseling. The mother asks you, "Where can I get help when I don't have much money?"

Sometimes people decide that they need referral in the course of their brief counseling with you. For example, a man meets his goal of getting along better with his boss. He sees, however, that he still feels blue and asks for more help.

There may be times that you will need to refer persons who could be helped by the brief counseling you do with community members. However, you might not want to do this counseling with them. It is unwise to try to counsel those with whom you have a "transference tangle" — who have placed you on a pedestal, or are in love with you, or whose transference causes them to be hostile or to be in power struggles with you. Sometimes you have difficulties with community members that originate *in you*. You should refer elsewhere those whom you do not like or to whom you are erotically attracted. Unworked through difficulties with community members often signal that you have some work to do yourself, or with your own marriage or primary relationship.

Some people need another type of treatment before they can be counseled in brief counseling. These include: those who are referred to *psychiatrists* because they need medical treatment for genetic, biological, chemical, or neurological problems; those who need *inpatient hospital* care for alcohol or drug detoxification, psychosis, or serious suicidal potential; those who are dangerous to themselves or others and for whom intervention is needed.

There will be occasions when you participate in *both/and* referral and treatment. This is also referred to as *concurrent* treatment.[9] More and more psychiatrists and other mental health workers see the advantage to working as a team. They recognize that counselors in community are essential to the team both because of their knowledge of the patient's life and circumstances and also because of their spiritual perspective. When working concurrently, you might send a community member to a psychiatrist who medicates and supervises your community member's medical treatment. That psychiatrist might, in turn, suggest that you begin brief counseling when the medication begins to be effective, and that you also provide community care and other religious community resources. You and the psychiatrist, who also continues to treat your community member, stay in touch and exchange information about the person. However, if the member needs more continuous supportive therapy, a referral should be made to a psychotherapist. You would remain on the "team" as a counselor in community.

Here are some guidelines to keep in mind when you are referring:

Plant the seed early. The possibility of referral needs to be introduced early in the consultation process, perhaps even in the initial telephone contact. It is wise to get in the habit of saying to those who call for a consultation, "I'd be happy to see you to find out what's bothering you. Then we can know what kind of help you might need and who the best helper might be."

Gather information. Usually people who come asking for a referral, or those who discover their need for it as they speak with you, will have a goal for change. They want something to be different. Seeing you to ask for a referral is part of their solution for change. They know they need help in making changes. They may not know who can help them or what form the help should take. But they come to consult with you because they know that you have resources through your network.

The *Information for Referral Counseling Form* in *Appendix B* will help you organize the data given to you. Referrals can be made more easily when you have accurate and pertinent information. In *Appendix B* you will also find the release form that must be signed by the persons being referred before you give information about them to consultants. Protect confidentiality. It is particularly useful for you to keep focused on the person's goal for change. Do not substitute your own goal for changing the person. For example: A man comes to you wanting employment counseling. You may know his situation and believe that he needs intensive psychotherapy to deal with marital problems. But you must have faith in his ability to know and follow his own path for solutions. A change in his employment may indeed be the first step he needs to take.

Find the appropriate resource. In addition to being competent and being on the same healing wavelength as your faith community, consultants have to be able to accept those whom you refer. Before making a referral you need to know whether the professional is available. You need information about the professional's fee, affiliation with an HMO or other managed care plan, and whether he or she accepts third-party payments, Medicare or Medicaid. You may also need to know about his or her license or certification for insurance purposes. When referring to other social services, health-care agencies or self-help/support groups, find out about availability, fees, and other requirements.

Matchmaking of consultants and those asking for referral can now begin. After deciding on a consultant or other resource that meets the requirements of availability and affordability, with permission you can give the consultant pertinent information from the *Information for Referral Counseling Form.* Because you are part of a network of concern, you can ask the consultant to let you know when treatment, or other service, has begun or if a plan for hospitalization or other intervention has been made.

Tell the counselee of the consultant's (or other resource's) availability and the counselee will make his or her own appointment.

Watch for opportunities to provide him, her or them with other forms of community care.

You need to know your religious body's policy on counseling those who are not members of your congregation. Some clergy are prohibited by their religious body's rules (or canon law) from counseling nonmembers because of concern for confidential privilege. If your religious body deems it inappropriate to do brief counseling with nonmembers, you will need to refer those who come to you for this service. Be straightforward about your reason. Then spend time understanding their situation so that you can make a referral to someone who will do a good evaluation and pursue an appropriate treatment plan.

Referral counseling is a ministry of holism. When you refer to those who are specialists in healing the body or the mind, you are acknowledging the mind-body-soul-team of which you are a member. Just as it is the information coded on a cell's gene that allows us to function, it is the flow of information among professionals who jointly care for individuals in community that contributes to their healing. We need to learn to speak each other's language. Many medical doctors and psychiatrists are becoming open to the language of spirituality. This is evident in the increasing number of symposia on religion, spirituality, and healing at medical, psychological, and psychiatric conferences. Counselors in community can also learn to understand the language of medical and psychiatric consultants — on behalf of those for whom they mutually care.

You should also have enough diagnostic skills to be able to recognize those persons who need medical, psychiatric, or other specialized care. However, it is beyond the scope of this book to give *all* the information you need to know about depression and other categories of emotional illness, or about human development and differential diagnostics. We will make suggestions about where you can learn more about these. Following these will not make you a psychotherapist, but they will provide you with a working knowledge of the current world of mental health.

If you have been out of seminary or graduate school for ten years or more, you should take some refresher courses in human growth and development and human sexuality. You will also benefit from refresher courses that help you understand basic concepts to use in counseling and referring those whose problems are related to alcohol, drugs, and physical and mental illness. Professional organizations for marriage and family therapists, social workers, and pastoral psychotherapists have ongoing continuing education courses to help members stay up to date. Nonmembers are often invited to attend these courses and workshops. Find out about these opportunities from your colleagues. Reading journals in the fields of pastoral and family counseling also helps you keep up with new information.

We hope that this *Check List* will be a useful tool. We pray, as do farmers and gardeners when they plant, for God to bless your work. May your soil be rich, may you be blessed with good weather, may your crop thrive.

Chapter Five
Reading and Resources

Publishing information is found in the Bibliography.

• While it is not appropriate for counselors in community to do long-term counseling with severely mentally disabled members, they do support them and their families through community care. To help you be more effective, we recommend:

Resources for a working knowledge of mental disorders.

Joseph W. Ciarocchi, *A Minister's Handbook of Mental Disorders;* Edward Bruce Bynum, *Transcending Psychoneurotic Disturbances: New Approaches in Psycho-*

spirituality and Personality Development; Wayne E. Oates, *Behind the Masks: Personality Disorders in Religious Behavior.*

Community care resources:
  Pastoral Care of the Mentally Disabled, edited by Sally Severino and Richard Liew; Paul C. Hollinger, *Pastoral Care of Severe Emotional Disorders;* Herbert Anderson, Lawrence E. Hoist, and Robert H. Sunderland, *Ministry to Outpatients:A New Challenge In Pastoral Care.* Also see Clark S. Aist's "Pastoral Care of the Mentally Ill: A Congregational Perspective," *Journal of Pastoral Care,* December 1987

Working with families of the mentally ill:
  Stewart D. Govig, *Souls Are Made of Endurance.*

• *Pathways to Understanding: Ministry and Mental Illness,* developed by Peggy Way, Joseph Barbour and Joseph Gillespie, is a training program for congregations that uses written materials and videotape to focus on the faith community and mental illness, the person and the family, community care and mental illness and community and its resources. It is available from Pathways to Promise: Interfaith Ministries and Prolonged Mental Illness, 5400 Arsenal Street, St. Louis, MO 63139-1424 Tel. (314) 644-8400 Fax (314) 644-8834.

• Resources for community care of those facing chronic or life-threatening illnesses: John T. Vanderzee, *Ministry to Persons with Chronic Illness,* and Dale G. Larson, *The Helper's Journey: Working with People Facing Grief, Loss, and Life-Threatening Illness.*
  In responding to the AIDS crisis, religious communities have been given guidance about healing ministry. Among the rich literature are: Robert J. Perelli, *Ministry to Persons with AIDS: A Family Systems Approach;* Walter J. Smith, *AIDS: Living and Dying with Hope — Issues in Pastoral Care;* Ronald Sunderland, *AIDS: A Manual for Pastoral Care;* Letty Russell, *The Church with AIDS: Renewal in the Midst of Crisis.*

• We have offered a functional recipe for referral counseling. However, the more traditional advice is that counselors should know how to assess counselee's problems and strengths and then make appropriate referrals. For an overview of this approach, we suggest Edgar Draper M.D. and Bevan Steadman, M.D.,"Assessment in Pastoral Care," and Sr. Madonna Marie Cunningham, O.S.F., "Consultation, Collaboration and Referral," in the *Clinical Handbook of Pastoral Counseling, Vol. I.* Also see William B. Oglesby, Jr., *Referral in Pastoral Counseling* and Paul W. Pruyser, *Personal Problems In Pastoral Perspective: The Minister as Diagnostician,.*

• For more resources to support your community care, we recommend: Maxine Glaz and Jeanne Stevenson Moessner, eds., *Women in Travail and Transition: A New Pastoral Care;* Valerie M. DeMarinis, *Critical Caring: A Feminist Model for Pastoral Psychology;* Margaret Ferris, *Compassioning: Basic Counseling Skills for Christian Caregivers;* Jeanne Stevenson Moessner, ed., *Through the Eyes of Women: Insights for Pastoral Care;* Christie Cozad Neuger, ed., *The Arts of Ministry: Feminist-Womanist Approaches.*

• For a basic general understanding about *mind-body-soul integration,* we recommend Ernest Rossi's essay, "From Mind to Molecule: More Than a Metaphor," in *Brief Therapy: Myths, Methods and Metaphors,* edited by Jeffrey Zeig and Stephen Gilligan, which makes the conceptual links between the new discoveries in molecular and gene biology and mind-body healing. Rossi asserts that it is the *concept of mind-body information flow* that serves as a common denominator between psyche and soma.[10] He explains mind-brain connection, brain-body connection and cell-gene connection clearly enough for lay people to understand. We also recommend Daniel Goleman's *Emotional Intelligence: Why It Can*

Matter More than I.Q. for its accessible introduction to current research on the functions of the brain and human emotion.

Change Supported by
the Solution-Focused Method

You cannot solve a problem with the same kind of thinking
that created it.

— Albert Einstein[1]

In previous chapters we have been asserting that God is in the midst of
our changing lives. God heals, we cooperate. We have been fortunate to
find a brief counseling method that reflects these principles. Insoo Kim Berg
and Steve de Shazer, founders of the Brief Family Therapy Center in Milwaukee, Wisconsin, and their colleagues have been developing a method of
working with clients that shares these assumptions. It is called the solution-
focused method.

Solution-focused therapists have observed that their clients have been experiencing change — moving toward wholeness — even before they come to their
first session. The therapists help their clients see the changes they already have
been making (of which they were unaware) and help them use their strength,
creativity, and imagination to support these changes. Solution-focused therapists have found solution *building* to be more effective than problem *solving*.
In fact, they have found that it is more useful to know what the solution
is than to understand the causes of the problem. . Most theories and methods of counseling are concerned with understanding problem formation as a
means of problem resolution. Many counselors in community skillfully use
these techniques for helping others. You may already have such a counseling method that works for you. If so, you may read about this relatively new
solution-focused method with interest and may use some of its ideas to support your work. We encourage you to take what is useful. In so doing, you
will be following this basic rule of the solution-focused method:

*"If it ain't broke, don't fix it. If it worked once, do it again. If it doesn't
work, do something different."*[2]

The solution-focused method, however, requires a change in perception.
The method itself grew out of a paradigm shift: from problem solving to
solution building.

Berg and de Shazer had first been studying problem formation theory and its application for practice from the Mental Research Institute in Palo Alto, California. (We discussed some of the Institute's basic ideas in chapter 4.) They believed that they could help people solve problems through understanding how the problems were created and maintained. At the same time, they were also open to current ideas that were postulating that change is constant and inevitable and that it comes from many sources and directions. They were beginning to observe that many clients had already started to change before coming to their first therapy session. They observed also that people were not *always* constant in their symptoms: bed wetters did not wet the bed every night; problem drinkers did not drink the same way every day; depressed people sometimes felt "lighter"; truants sometimes went to school. People experienced exceptions to their problems.

As they talked to clients about these "exceptions," they came to the realization that at those times, clients were in fact solving their problems. However, they were intrigued to observe that their clients' solutions often seemed unrelated to the problems they had come to solve!

Steve de Shazer, in *Putting Difference to Work,* uses a Japanese folk tale to illustrate the relationship of solutions to problems:

> A Japanese coastal village was once threatened by a tidal wave, but the wave was sighted in advance, far out on the horizon, by a lone farmer in the rice fields on the hillside above the village. At once he set fire to the fields, and villagers who came swarming up to save their crops were saved from the flood.[3]

Through the folk tale, de Shazer points to the farmer's problem: he wants to warn the villagers of the tidal wave but he is too far away. He cannot yell and be heard. The problem looks unsolvable. However, he has a solution. *The farmer does something different.* He sets fire to the crops on which the villagers' lives depend. They come running; their lives are saved.

Berg, de Shazer, and other solution-focused practitioners have been fascinated by the ingenious solutions people find to their problems. As in the Japanese story, they observed that for some, the original problem (difficulty) remained, but their solution took them to a new place. In the story the tidal wave came; the village was destroyed but the people were saved. In the course of their work, solution-focused practitioners became less interested in understanding problem formation because their clients' solutions often had little to do with the original problems.

Of course, people often find solutions that are not so dramatic. But *all solutions involve doing something different.* For example:

A man with deep depression sometimes takes walks and feels better. His solution: Move more. How can he do it more frequently? How else can he move?

A woman who "loses herself" in her boyfriend's problems, gets "back to herself" when she plays the piano. Her solution: get the piano tuned so she will enjoy playing more.

A man comes with his problem of heavy drinking. However, he does not drink at all the night before a morning conference with his boss. His solution: become aware of other times when not drinking the night before helps him be more effective.

Solutions begin with small steps. They are built through discovering small behaviors that make a difference to the clients' experience. As illustrated by these problems and solutions, there seems to be no clear connection between patterns around problems and solution-building activities. Solution-focused therapists have found that they can help clients *build upon* their solutions to reach deeply personal goals.

The Solution-Focused Method in Action

The staff at the Brief Family Therapy Center has found that the best way for people to understand their method is to see them at work and to participate as trainees behind the one-way mirror where they become members of the treatment team. Second best would be to view their work on video. We are left with a third — introducing you to the treatment model through the printed word where you can grasp it with your imagination. We will use highlights from a first session interview:

RABBI SILVERSTEIN: "Hello, Mark. What brings you in?"

MARK STERN: "I need help. My kid is driving me crazy! He's always in trouble and I can't get him to cut it out."

RABBI: "Sounds like a difficult situation. Is it David you're talking about?"

MARK: "Yeah... you wouldn't even recognize the kid. He looks practically punk."

RABBI: "You mean, purple hair?"

MARK: "No, not that bad. He does have an earring. The worst thing's the music. The trouble is he thinks he's a rock musician. His band is in the house all the time. And those kids are positively weird. But it's the music. It's *so* loud and I just don't get it. I never thought I'd be square, but he drives me wild."

RABBI: "Well, he does seem to be getting your attention. But what's this about trouble? Can you tell me more about it?"

Mark then told Rabbi Silverstein that for the past few months David had seemed very different. He was hanging around with a different group of kids, his grades were erratic, and he had been put on academic probation because he was getting *Ds*. He frequently missed his curfew and his room looked like a "garbage pit." Mark believed that his wife, Marcia, was "conned" by David, so he had decided to take over the discipline. However, he and David were at an impasse. The more he pushed, the more sullen David became and then Mark, in reaction, felt "crazy" — agitated, frustrated, and ineffective. He was afraid he might get out of control. They were going nowhere. And David would not even admit he had a problem.

"What are things like with you and David *when you're not stuck*?" Rabbi Silverstein's question surprised Mark because it seemed to him that he and David were "always at it." Upon reflection, Mark said,"Well, the other night we did watch the game on TV, and it was like old times." Rabbi Silverstein asked: "How did you get that to happen?" Mark replied, "Well, David was watching, and I just sat down."

Later in the session, Rabbi Silverstein asked Mark this rather strange question: "Suppose while you have been sleeping, a miracle occurred. You don't know it because you have been sleeping, but miraculously, the problems with you and David have been solved. When you wake up in the morning, *how* do you know they've been solved?"

MARK: (thoughtfully) "Well...I guess I'd go down to breakfast and see David, and he'd be wearing sort of regular clothes. And I wouldn't be irritated. He'd look good to me, and wouldn't make a crack about his get-up."

RABBI: "Umm, hm."

MARK: "And then, Marcia would be there, I'd give her a kiss and we'd talk about what was happening that day."

RABBI: "What else?"

MARK: "And then I'd go to work...and I'd concentrate better because I wouldn't be calling Marcia at work and then calling later at home to see if the school had called or if David was messing up."

RABBI: "O.K."

MARK: "In fact, I'd stay at the office and catch up with work because I wouldn't have to supervise David. Or maybe I'd get in a game of tennis."

RABBI: "And how would Marcia know a miracle had occurred?"

MARK: "Cause I'd kissed her good morning instead of growling at David."

RABBI: "And how would David know?"

MARK: "He'd be the first to know. There wouldn't be tension between us."

Rabbi Silverstein then responded: "So, you'll be less tense with David. You won't be irritated in the mornings. You'll give Marcia a good morning kiss. You won't interrupt yourself by calling home and you won't have to hurry home to supervise David. And you might even get in a game of tennis! That's how you will know a miracle has happened. What would be the *smallest* sign that a miracle has happened?"

MARK: "Well, I guess not feeling so compulsive about having to call Marcia to check on David all the time. I guess not calling so much. Yeah, then I'd know I was out of my difficulties with David when I was relaxed enough to not check on him."

What has happened so far:

- Rabbi Silverstein *listens to Mark's story* and finds that it is full of complaints about David and Marcia. He also learns that Mark is disturbed about being at an impasse in his relationship with David and is afraid of becoming out of control.
- Rabbi Silverstein develops an *empathetic rapport* with Mark.
- Through being asked about times when he was not "stuck" with David (*an exception to the problem*), Mark realizes that he was not *always* at an impasse and that David was not *always* in trouble. He gets the first glimpse of the ways he sometimes acts as his "old relaxed self." This is his first awareness that he sometimes has found solutions.
- Through the *Miracle Question*, he learns what he really wants. The "miracle" points to the results that are desired: the impasse would be over. He would be more relaxed and he could return his attention to the rest of his life: his wife, his business and his tennis. He is *out* of his problem.

Rabbi Silverstein helped Mark sharpen answers by asking, *"What will be different after the miracle?* Mark began to see that the miracle could happen "even a little bit" if he could begin to do more of the things that already helped him relax.

Mark and Rabbi Silverstein began their work together by establishing a goal.

RABBI: "Well when you first came in, you were really concerned about David — his behavior, and mainly his music. Now you'd also like to get back to your old relaxed self."
MARK: "Yeah, I think that's what I really want. Although my tension first seemed to come from my hassle with David."
RABBI: "What's the least *David* could do to help you get your relaxed self back?"

MARK: "Well, I know he's picking his grades up. I think I could let up on that and feel more relaxed."

RABBI: "What would be the hardest thing for him to do?"

MARK: "It's the music. It's too loud and I just don't get it."

RABBI: "What's the easiest thing *you* can do with David to be your relaxed self?"

MARK: "We do like to watch the game together. I'm relaxed then. It's easy to sit down and just be with him."

Rabbi Silverstein then used numbers to begin to help Mark establish goals for himself. He first used *scaling questions* to establish a "language" for them to describe Mark's progress more clearly.

RABBI: "On a scale of '0' to '10,' with '0' being where you were most stuck in the impasse and '10' being where you are relaxed and back to your own life, where would you put yourself right now?"

MARK: '4.'

RABBI: "What will be happening when it is a '5'?"

MARK: "I think I'll be getting in some tennis. I used to play twice a week. But even playing once would seem like a miracle."

Rabbi Silverstein and Mark agreed to work on finding small steps to get his "old relaxed self" back. They would begin by focusing on tennis.

RABBI: "On a scale of '0' to '10,' with '0' being when you were most stuck in your hassle with David and '10' being when you are back in your regular tennis habit, where are you now?"

MARK: "I guess '3.'"

RABBI: "What will be happening when it is a '4'?"

MARK: "I'll at least be writing 'tennis' in my calendar just to get it in my mind again."

RABBI: "What would Marcia see you and David doing if things were 10 percent higher?"

MARK: "Maybe she'd see us just talking in the den after we watch the game."

RABBI: "Before I take a break to think about what you've been telling me, is there anything else I should ask?"

MARK: (after some consideration) "No, I think you've got the picture."

RABBI: "Mark, I'm going to take a break now to think about what you've been telling me. I'll be back soon. Would you like coffee or tea in the break?"

After taking a short break to assess the session, Rabbi Silverstein gave this message, which consisted of a *compliment,* an *agreement* with Mark about his goal for change, and a *behavioral task:* "Mark, I think it's great that you came to sort this out with me today. You've been taking your parenting of David very seriously and it's obvious that you really love your son. You want to be a good parent, and that's not easy! You've realized that you've been forgetting about yourself. I agree that you don't have to wait for David to get it together before you get back to being more relaxed yourself. It's not going to be easy to get off his case and think of yourself. Between now and when we meet next, notice what is happening when things are a '5' on the miracle scale."

Rabbi Silverstein asked Mark when he'd like to come back, and Mark said, "In about ten days."

We will now look at the theory of the methodology that undergirds Rabbi Silverstein's work with Mark. We are indebted to Daniel Gallagher, a solution-focused family therapist as well as an Episcopal priest, whose description of the *Five-Step Treatment Model,* from Insoo Berg and Scott Miller's *Working with the Problem Drinker*, we are adapting for this demonstration. Dan Gallagher uses the solution-focused method in his parish counseling as well as in his work with adolescents who are problem drinkers and drug abusers, and their families. While we will be speaking of working with an individual client, the method is also effectively with families, couples, and groups.

The Five-Step Solution-Focused Treatment Model[4]

Step I: Working With the Client:
How to Form a Cooperative Working Relationship

Solution-focused therapy is more akin to coaching and conversation than to traditional psychotherapy. Through talking together, the client is helped to see what he is doing that is good for him and then he is coached by the counselor to help it continue to happen.

Many of us have noticed that in the past we have done something good for ourselves — exercised, dieted, practiced, played — but for some reason, we stopped. Solution-focused work helps people *continue* to act.

A fundamental concept in the work is *relationship:* It is the cooperative relationship *between* client and counselor, and the relationship of both the counselor and the client *to* the client's goals — both are committed to helping the client *get what he wants.*

A good working relationship, or "therapeutic alliance," is considered important in most schools of psychotherapy. This usually is understood to mean that the client cooperates with the efforts of the therapist. In psychotherapy, difficult clients often are described as those who "resist the work of therapy." Resistant clients are considered "unworkable" and they usually drop out of treatment. In the mid 1980s solution-focused therapists declared the "death of resistance." They had discovered that "resistant clients" were more likely signaling to their therapists that the types of interventions used by the therapists did not fit them. Clients did not resist therapists who understood the *type of relationship* the client had to the work and who were thus able to make appropriate and useful interventions. Solution-focused theorists then categorized these *relationships to the work* in the following ways:

Visitor-Host Relationship: Visitors are people who come to counselors with seemingly no complaints of their own. They have been sent to counseling, often involuntarily, by a parent, spouse or some authority. Someone else thinks it's a "good idea for him get help." The staff at the Brief Family Therapy Center often have referrals from courts and schools and it is not unusual for clients to come resenting the order that they go to treatment. It is also not unusual to have children sent by parents who feel the whole problem is the child's, not theirs.

Counselors in community also have counselees sent to them by others to be "fixed." Parents send teenagers for counsel; a spouse may come, not because he or she feels the need to change, but because of a sometimes implicit threat of divorce. Sometimes those "visiting" are persons whom the counselor in community may know well. The counselor can be confused by the "tentative" way a congregant relates to her at the beginning of a counseling session. The counselor is helped by knowing that the counselee may not be relating to the counselor herself, but only to the counseling *situation*. Visitors are *sent* to *counseling* — and this can even obscure their relationship to a counselor whom they know well.

It is not surprising that "visitors" resent being sent. If a counselor sees that the visitor has a problem — or *is* a problem — and tries to get the visitor to see the light, the visitor predictably will resist the suggestion. Solution-focused therapists do not try to *change* "visitors" by talking them into believing that they should "get into therapy." They work with them where they are. Therefore, with a visitor who does not see that change is necessary the first session is "pre-therapy." Solution-focused therapists use the following guidelines for the first session with "visitors:"

1. Be as nice as possible.
2. The therapist is always on the side of the person being interviewed.
3. Look for what works rather than what does not.[5]

Counselors are hospitable to "visitors." They make them feel at home and they try to see the situation from the visitor's point of view. They also give a series of compliments on the way in which the visitor is coping with a difficult session. Solution-focused therapists have noted that not infrequently visitors say, "this is the first time a professional has ever said anything nice to me."[6] *The goal of the therapist* is to create an atmosphere in which the client feels understood and senses that there might be a "fit" with an understanding counselor. At the end of the first session, "visitors" are invited to return.

Because a "fit" has developed at the first session, at a subsequent session a visiting teenager, for example, may decide that he wants help in getting his parents off his back.

Visitors can be helped to reach their goals while they remain in their visitor mode. They may not identify themselves as "being in therapy," yet they return to meet with the therapist who helps them "do what is good for them."

We can imagine that David, Mark's son, might have been a "visitor" at Rabbi Silverstein's office had his father been able to talk him into having a counseling session. Had David come, Rabbi Silverstein would have been welcoming and would have tried to see David's situation through David's eyes. David would have told him how his father had become intrusive and nagging; how his father did not appreciate how lucky he was to have new cool friends who were creative and "out there," making new music. He might have told the rabbi that his friends even had connections with clubs so that their group was going to play to audiences. David might have said that if he had any problem, it was his father, who *used to be* a supportive guy. Rabbi Silverstein might then have invited him back to see if he could help him with his problem with his father.

Complainant-Listener Relationship: Solution-focused theorists believe that therapy can begin when people come in complaining about their problems. When a complaint is made, the counselee is actively involved and there can be some expectation for change. This is true whether the problems are identified as one's own or if they are about others. The role of the counselor is to listen as the complaints are spilled out, while searching for what the client wants to be different, noticing strengths, and asking about times when the complaints are not happening.

Solution-focused therapists build a working alliance with complainants by listening to their story as they focus on the people they are complaining about. When clients see little hope for change, the therapists then use "coping questions" to help the complainant begin to talk about themselves. Most frequently, they work with data from answers to the "miracle question" to help clients focus on their solutions, as in this exchange between Mar and Rabbi Silverstein:

RABBI: "Mark, let's go back to the 'miracle day.' What else would be different with you and David?"

MARK: "Well, we'd have a real conversation at breakfast. We wouldn't just be grumbling at each other."

RABBI: "What else?"

MARK: "Well, maybe I'd ask David if he wanted to play tennis next weekend, and he'd say, 'Sounds like fun.' "

RABBI: "Umm hmm."

MARK: "And then, we might even be able to talk about the music. I'd bring it up and maybe David would even say, 'I know it bugs you, Dad.' "

At the beginning of his session with Rabbi Silverstein, Mark, like many others, believed that the solutions to his problems lay in someone else's hands. It is not unusual for someone who is in a complainant relationship with you to try to change others instead of focusing on their own lives. However, complainants do not need to changed into customers in order to discover their own solutions. The complainant relationship offers strong opportunities for solution building. The therapist cooperates with the style by asking *how the other* will see the client's situation: "What will your (son, partner, wife, etc.) notice when things are different?" and what will be different for them when the client changes: What will your (son, partner, wife, etc.) notice about you that tells him that things are different?"

Counselors cooperate with complainants by *not* expecting them to focus on their own lives. They listen to their frustrations and sympathize with the difficulties they have suffered because of troubled teenagers, or alcohol-abusing husbands, or chronically ill parents. Counselors acknowledge the sacrifices the clients have made and appreciate that their actions have been positively motivated.

People in complainant relationships with you are often surprised when their efforts are acknowledged by counselors. Often members of their families either take their involvement and worries for granted or find them annoying or intrusive. Sometimes their behavior has been negatively labeled as "enabling" or "codependent" by alcoholism counselors or other professionals. In some cases, they have been told that they are the cause of their loved one's problems.

Solution-focused therapists have found that it is easier for people who want other people to change to detach from those whom they have been trying to change when they feel understood rather than criticized. Once therapeutic relationships have been formed with counselors who are sympathetic and respectful, it is fairly easy for complainants to see that solutions are not working and that another approach is needed. At this point, they see that they can become a part of a *solution-finding* approach.

At the end of the first complainant-listener session, a great deal of information about the problem has been given. The client and the counselor may have begun to formulate goals, and some solutions are beginning to be formed. At this time some expectations for change and possible solutions are emerging, but clients do not have clarity about steps to take to make changes; and/or they believe that changes are dependent on something or someone else changing first. In couple or family counseling there are often "visitors" *and* "complainants" attending the same meeting. Sometimes in the course of the interview, a "visitor" may shift into a "complainant" relationship. It is because people frequently change in the course of a session that therapists do not make a judgment about clients' relationship to their work until therapists take their "think break."

People in a complainant relationship with you are most likely to perform *observation* tasks assigned by the therapist. ("Notice when things are different.") Visitors are not expected to perform such tasks. In couple or family counseling, the visitor may not be invited to attend the next session because it confuses or in some cases, impedes the therapy.[7] Gallagher's rule of thumb is that clients are seen separately if it is clear that they have mutually exclusive goals. However, in most instances, when family members come together, they tend to return together.

Rabbi Silverstein was confident that he could use the solution-focused method with Mark to help promote change. Mark knew that he was at an impasse with David. At the beginning of the session Mark believed that David would need to change before he could be better. It was only as the session progressed, that Mark saw that he needed to make changes in himself, as well.

Rabbi Silverstein at first saw Mark's relationship to the work as the "complainant-listener type" and he began to build therapeutic rapport with Mark by asking about his trouble with David. He listened to the ways that David got Mark's attention and sympathetically asked about how Mark had tried to change his son to make the situation better. He did not say, "Mark, I think you're contributing to the problem by being overbearing. Let's look at you." Instead, he sympathetically listened to Mark's complaints, the chief one being that he could not relax because of David's behavior. He also asked about the times when Mark and David got along better, what was different then, and how they could do those things more.

Although in this case Mark moved from first seeming to be a complainant to being a customer, it is not the goal of solution-focused counselors to change people. They can help all clients — visitors, complainants and customers — discover their own solutions and work to maintain them. The counselor's goal is not to turn a visitor into a complainant and then into a customer.

Customer-Seller Relationship: Sometimes a complainant becomes a customer when he *wants to do something* about the complaint itself and has worked with the counselor to construct "well formed goals" for treatment. At that point, the counselor becomes a "seller" of other therapeutic tasks which he is quite certain the client will do and will find useful.

Mark had come to the session aware that the more he pushed David the more sullen David became. Clearly, he already saw that doing "the same old thing" was not working. Mark wanted *to do something*. Rabbi Silverstein listened to see if Mark was willing to change *himself* or if he would continue to maintain that he could not be in a better place unless David changed first.

Rabbi Silverstein asked the "exception question:" "What are things like with you and David when you're not stuck?" Through that question Mark became aware that not only were they not always at an impasse, but in fact, *he* had created a change by sitting down with David to watch the game on TV. Rabbi Silverstein asked Mark about *other* "exceptions to stuckness" and found that both David and Mark, on occasion, had acted in the "old relaxed way." These questions about exceptions began to change Mark's perception of himself and his situation. He saw that David was not *always* in trouble nor were they *always* at an impasse.

Mark's answers to the "miracle question" informed Rabbi Silverstein that Mark could begin to think of goals for himself that did not require David to change first. In fact, in his response Mark did not dwell on David. For Mark, the miracle was that he was no longer at an impasse: he had his own life back. Instead of being preoccupied with David, he could pay attention to his business, his tennis, his wife.

Rabbi Silverstein helped him identify his goal when he asked: "What will be the *smallest sign* that a miracle has happened?" Mark had replied, "Well, I guess not feeling so compulsive about having to call Marcia to check on David all the time."

> RABBI: "When you're not calling so much, what will he be doing instead?"
> MARK: "Working, for one thing! "

Near the end of the session, Rabbi Silverstein saw that Mark was becoming a "customer" who would be able to use solution-focused interventions to help him reach his goal.

Step II: How to Begin Treatment with the End In Mind: Negotiating Well-Formed Treatment Goals

"How will I know when it's time to stop coming to talk with you?" This is a question clients sometimes *think,* but often *do not ask* their counselors. Solution-focused theorists believe that people in most therapies often do not know when they have met their goal for their therapy because the goal was not clear to begin with. Because of this, they help their clients begin therapy with an end in view: It will be time to stop when their *goal* for treatment has been met. They do not set a limit for the number of times they work with clients. However, the staff of the Brief Family Therapy Center see their clients for an average of 4.6 sessions.[8]

Because both clients and therapists must be able to determine when progress is being made and when treatment can be ended, clients' goals must be clear and well defined. The entire solution-focused interviewing process is designed to help clients and therapists work together to set and achieve the goals. Through years of refinement, solution-focused theorists have determined seven qualities of well-formed goals:

- *Salient.* The client must view the achievement of the goal as important to him or her and believe the goal to be personally beneficial. The goal must be the *client's* goal! According to Gallagher, the best goal is one that is already beginning to happen.
- *Small.* Goals should be small enough that they can be achieved. Furthermore, *small changes have a domino effect that create greater change.*
- *Concrete, Specific, Behavioral.* Vague, illusive goals such as "feel better," "be happy," "get it together," "have self-esteem" are not considered well-formed goals. Goals need to be *precise* and described in *behavioral terms,* such as: getting to work on time, enrolling in class, making five calls to temp agencies to inquire about work, etc.
- *Presence rather than the absence of something.* Goals need to be stated in proactive language about what a client *will do* rather than not do. Goals that are seen as the absence of a problem (I won't get drunk) don't contain a picture of the solution. It is easier to see when clients "get there" when they see what they *will be doing.*
- *A beginning rather than an end.* Focusing on an end point can overwhelm a client. Rather than setting a goal of "being a college graduate," the goal of beginning, "getting college catalogs," is more effective. Many clients tell therapists that they can continue "on track" after they successfully take a small next step. However, clients are not coming to therapy at the *beginning* of their journey; they are already "somewhere along the way." They often do not know that they have begun because they "do not know *what they know.*"
- *Realistic and achievable within the context of the client's life.* Often clients have failed in the past because they were trying to meet goals set for them by others. Sometimes these came from unrealistic, perfectionistic inner demands, sometimes from society ("one cannot be too rich or too thin"), sometimes from self-help books or other professionals ("I'll never eat sugar; I'll jog every day; I'll never raise my voice in anger.")
- *Perceived as involving "hard work.* "Through their negotiations, clients and counselors set goals that are not impossible to meet — just hard. Acknowledging that the behavior changes involved in meeting goals requires hard work is respectful of clients' dignity and self-esteem. Solution-focused therapists often work with people who have "failed" in other treatment settings, or who come to therapy blaming their failures on "the disease of alcoholism," or "coming from a dysfunctional family." While these explanations can salvage some self-respect, solution-focused therapists have found that perceiving *the work* of therapy as "involving hard work" promotes personal responsibility. Knowing that a goal is attainable — with hard work — also instills hope.[9]

Step III: Orienting the Client Toward Solutions: How to Interview for Change

> The primary tool of most helping professionals is the therapeutic interview. Far from being a neutral or benign process, the therapeutic interview is a powerful intervention that serves either to orient clients toward solutions or toward problems. With this in mind, the solution-focused interview is specifically designed to orient the client toward solution building by focusing on change and the client's own experiences in creating solutions.[10]

You will recognize some of these first session interviewing activities from the story of Rabbi Silverstein and Mark. We will now look at assumptions *behind* the activities. In the following section the italicized questions are adapted from Dan Gallagher's outline of the *Five-Step Treatment Model*.

1. *"What brings you here today?"* Most first sessions of solution-focused therapy begin with this simple question. Clients then tell their story while the therapist *actively* listens and acknowledges what is being said. This is done nonverbally (through nods, eye contact) and verbally (uh huh, O.K., umm). This, with lively curiosity, encourages detailed descriptions.

Because the therapist's goal is to listen for the client's solution, the therapist does not interrupt the client to ask for expansion of descriptions of the problem. Nor does the therapist encourage "problem talk" through expressions of empathy that encourage lengthy discussion of the problem. The therapist expresses curiosity about what is happening that will lead to solutions the client wants. Through *active listening* to his or her story, the therapist joins the client.

2. *"What is already changing?"* Solution-focused therapists observe that, when asked, clients have often commented that they were already beginning to feel better before their first therapy session. Because it happens so frequently, many solution-focused therapists routinely ask clients at the time they call for their first appointment to observe what is getting better between the time of the call and the first meeting. They will then ask about it at the first session. This helps construct the working relationship between client and therapist.

The request to notice change *before* coming to a session puts therapy in a context of improvement in the client's life, instead of the traditional idea that the *therapy* is the context in which the improvement occurs.[11] The "exception question" — what is it like when the problem is not there? — is another way of inquiring about "what is already changing?"

3. "Suppose a miracle happens." Once clients have a chance to tell their stories, the counselor helps them begin to identify their goals for coming for treatment. This is done through asking questions and giving them plenty of time to answer. The question most frequently asked is the "miracle question:"

> Suppose, tonight, you go to bed and fall asleep and, while you are sleeping a miracle happens. The miracle is that the problem that brought you here today is solved! But you do not know that the problem that brought you was solved, because you were asleep. When you wake up in the morning, what will be some of the first things you will notice that will tell you a miracle has happened and the problem that brought you here is solved?

This is a powerful tool because it gets to the heart of the client's hope for change. Because the change is accomplished through a "miracle," the client does not get caught up in explaining the problems, and, perhaps, his past failures, for reaching his goal. He gets in touch with his desire for change. Often people have become so caught up in trying to solve a problem that they have forgotten what they originally wanted. The "miracle question" can reawaken the memory of the wish. It also invites people to use their imagination to help identify small, concrete behaviors that a solution might create.

Dan Gallagher suggests other questions to help clients *identify* what they want to be different by being in counseling:

> Suppose that our work here together is successful. What will be different in your life that will tell you that it has been successful?

> What has to be different in your life that will tell you that coming for counseling was a good idea?

> Imagine yourself six months or so in the future, after you and I have finished working together and have achieved the goals that brought you here today. What will be different in your life six months from now that will tell you that the goal was achieved?

4. "What else will be different after the miracle?:" Gallagher reminds us that this simple question can be used many times in the interview to help clients expand and simplify their description of what they would like to be different. The more clearly they are able to picture the differences they desire, the greater chance they will have in reaching their goals and experiencing satisfaction.

Solution-focused therapists have found that asking clients to see the desired changes through the eyes of someone close helps them to focus their picture more sharply. Asking about how significant people would see these changes also reinforces commitment to change. Clients anticipate the pleasure they will feel from the compliments and good will of those significant to them. Therapists ask the questions:

> What would your (spouse, parent, employer, etc.) say that would be different after the miracle?
>
> *What else* would he (she, they, etc.) say is different?
>
> What will they be doing that tells you that things are better now?

5. *"How is the miracle already happening, even a little?"* Clients are asked about times in which they may already be experiencing success in reaching some of their goals. These instances are usually seen as "exceptions" to the problem, which the client has discounted or considered a fluke. The "exceptions" are times when the solution is already happening, even a little bit or temporarily. To elicit information about these exceptions, clients are asked:

> Tell me about the times when pieces of this miracle are happening already. What is different about these times?
>
> Tell me about the times the problem does *not* happen?
>
> Many times people notice in between the time they make the appointment for therapy and the first session that things are improving. What have you noticed about your situation?

6. *"On a scale of zero to ten...."* Through using numbers, therapists can refer to clients' problems without getting sidetracked into talk about problems themselves, thereby losing sight of clients' solutions. This communication system is also used to assess actions, to predict outcomes, and to reinforce motivation.

Near the end of the first session, clients are often asked to establish a frame of mind in which future progress may be noticed. Without asking them to expand upon a description of the problem, therapists ask that they rate where they are vis-à-vis the goal:

> On a scale of zero to ten, where zero is when the situation was at its worst and ten being the day after the miracle, how close are you to ten today?

Scaling questions are also used to help the client and therapist identify a small, realistic, achievable goal. For example, if the client responded to the first scaling question with a number three, the therapist could ask:

> On that scale then, if you are presently at a three, what will be happening when you are at four, what will you (and others) be doing?

Scaling questions are also used to assess the client's willingness *to invest effort* in achieving the goals which have been negotiated between the therapist and the client in the interview:

> On a slightly different scale, from zero to ten, where ten is that you will do almost anything to achieve these goals (or solve this problem) and zero is that you will nearly give up and sit still, where would you say you are on that scale?

7. *"What else?"* The last question that is usually asked is:

> Is there anything else that I haven't asked about that you think I should know before I take a break and think about our meeting?

While most clients answer "no," in some cases, where the session has been confusing or the client's goals have remained unclear, this simple question serves to clear up the confusion and helps clients state their goals for coming to therapy.[12]

Step IV: Solution-Focused Interventions:
How to Construct Interventions That Invite and Facilitate Change

The effect of the initial solution-focused interview is powerful because through it, clients' perceptions change. In the interview, therapists have not given advice or made pronouncements, but through active, attentive, and careful listening, have created a context in which clients feel respected and understood. In the process, a trusting alliance has been formed. While many clients come to sessions embedded in their problems, solution-focused therapists mainly ask questions but also make comments that suggest to clients that they have *already* begun to make changes. Through the therapist's different lens, clients begin to see their situations differently.

It is near the end of the session that therapists *actively make interventions* that reinforce the work of the session and lead to more change. The process of solution-focused intervention begins when therapists take a break to review the session and to decide on an appropriate intervention for the client. Before they take the "thinking break," they tell clients what they will be doing and either leave the consultation room, or ask clients to wait in the waiting area.

When solution-focused therapists take a "break," a pivotal *action* happens. Clients have been told that what they have said in the session is important enough to merit the considered thought of the therapist. And then they are left, and a space is created. This is a dramatic event! The client and the therapist each "fill" the space in ways unknown to the other.

Clients have varied reactions to the break. It is certainly an unusual occurrence for a professional to leave them to think about their situation. Some clients are curious about what the therapist is thinking, some are relieved to have the focus off them. But all clients are given space in which they, too, can reflect on the session. In this space,"the mud can settle and the water can become clear."

Many therapists who initially hear of the "break" have varied responses to "walking out" on a client session. Some feel it is impolite, or that it might be interpreted by the client as abandonment. The therapists have to work through their feelings before they are able to take the action of creating a break. However, others see it clearly as a technique that gives them space in which they can take care of themselves as well as time to reflect on the client.

The practice of taking a break began very pragmatically at the Brief Family Therapy Center when therapists stopped near the end of sessions to consult with colleagues who were watching the session behind a one-way mirror. Throughout the consultation, the therapist and colleagues reviewed the session, identified the client's solutions and designed tasks that reinforced solution building. The therapist then returned to the client with the message from the team. The "break" became an integral part of the therapeutic structure.

Today many counselors using solution-focused methods practice without the benefit of a consultation team, but they have kept the "break" in place because of its many benefits: In it they can collect themselves, review the session, assess the situation and make a plan.

Counselors in community who use solution-focused methods find themselves listening prayerfully and empathically. The method depends on counselors being able to see the *unique* solutions created by others who are *unlike* themselves. They pay careful attention to the exact words of their congregants and watch for solutions that congregants often have overlooked or considered a fluke. They delight in their congregants and in their creativity. This is the kind of vision the psalmist was describing in Psalm 1:

> *Blessed are the man and the woman*
> *who have grown beyond their greed*
>   *and who have put an end to their hatred*
>   *and no longer nourish illusions.*
> *But they delight in the way things are*
>   *and keep their hearts open, day and night.*
> *They are like trees planted near flowering rivers,*
>   *which bear fruit when they are ready.*
> *Their leaves will not fall or wither.*
>   *Everything they do will succeed.*[13]

After being centered and, as the Psalmists says, "delighting in the way things are," the counselor is then able to review his or her notes. When using the method it is important to take notes in the session so that you have the counselee's own words. (And Dan Gallagher points out that a counselee's actions are reinforced then a therapist only takes notes about strengths and solutions.) Then you can keep a clear focus on what the person wants to have happen and how this is expressed in "well formed" goals. Notes on the initial session should include:

- An understanding of the goal. You need to know what the client wants.
- Exceptions to the problem.
- The person's strengths, resources, and abilities.
- Detailed description of "day after the miracle" and times when the "miracle existed just a bit."
- Descriptions of what is happening on the scales. The actual numbers are less important, except as a momentary reference point, somewhere on the way to "better."

This information is used to create a message that is given to counselees after the break.

Compliments form the first part of the solution-focused therapist's message to *all* clients. In the interview, therapists listen carefully to discern what clients are doing that is good for them. Clients usually receive compliments with gratitude and relief, for they often have not identified the strength they have used to come to the counseling session. They are then further surprised when they discover the changes they were already making toward solving their problem before they came to the session. Compliments point out these changes and underscore them.

Therapeutic tasks are then based on the *type of relationship* clients have to the work:

Visitor-Host Intervention: Because "visitors" do not believe that they have a problem, they are not given therapeutic tasks to perform before the next session. They are given a message that compliments them specifically on something they are doing that is good for them. They are then invited to return to another session.

In their book *Working with the Problem Drinker,* Insoo Kim Berg and Scott D. Miller give an illustration of a *message* to a visitor:

> Curtis, we are very impressed that you are here today even though this is not your idea. You certainly had the option of taking the easy way out by not coming. Your willingness to put up with many demands that seem unreasonable, including being here today, shows that you are the kind of person who wants to do the right thing. It has not been easy for you to be here today; having to give up your personal time, talking about things you really don't want to talk about, having to take the bus, and so on. But we are impressed with your willingness to cooperate with us today.

I realize that you are an independent minded person who does not want to be told what to do and I agree with you that you should be left alone. But you also realize that doing what you are told will help get these people out of your life and you will be left alone sooner. Therefore, I would like to meet with you again to figure out further what will be good for you to do. So, let's meet next week at the same time.[14]

You will notice that the therapist did not make any suggestions for behavioral changes that the client would not be able to make. The positive message facilitated Curtis's cooperation and made it easier for him to return for treatment. The message did not condone his problem drinking. And it did not do what had been done by professionals in the past: reprimand, give threats or ultimatums, or remind him of past failures. Because it was new, the message given to Curtis got his attention — the first necessary step in making changes.

Complainant-Listener Intervention: By the end of the initial session, complainants through the miracle or exception questions have hopeful expectations of how their problems can change. However, they still believe that *others* must first change. These clients do not yet have hope that they can find solutions that will make changes in their *own* lives. The messages given to complainants compliment them on the concerns they have for others and on their faith in the ability of others to change. They also compliment them on something good which they are doing for themselves.

This *message* given to the wife of a problem drinker illustrates this type of intervention:

It is clear to us that you have given a lot of thought to your husband's drinking problem and noticed many things that are helpful to understand his problem. It is clear that you have tried many different things to convince your husband of the seriousness of the problem because you love him and are very concerned about the welfare of the family. It is also clear that in spite of everything you have been through, you still have hope that he may realize some day how serious the problem is.

At the same time, we are impressed that you have come to finally accept that only he can stop drinking and that he needs to learn to take the natural consequences of his drinking. We agree that this is what growing up is about. We think that your being here today is the first step toward a healthier future for both of you, and that right now is the best time to start detaching yourself from his drinking and concentrate on learning to take care of yourself. But as you know, it will not be easy.[15]

The task given to a complainant is designed to use the skills the complainant already has. She has been *observing* and *thinking* about what is wrong with her husband. The therapist asks her to continue to think and to notice exceptions in his behavior. The task assigned is this: "Therefore, we would like you to give some further *thoughts* to what else you will notice different about him that gives you hope as you continue to detach yourself."[16]

The therapist did not suggest that the client change her own behavior to help herself. The client will begin to make these changes *after* she begins to see that she need not be a victim of the behavior of others.

Solution-focused therapists help complainants become aware of their own coping skills. In subsequent sessions complainants may be given tasks to help them pay attention to their own coping activity. Eventually they may think: "If I can put out all of this creative energy and clever managing for you (my child, partner, etc.) I can do it for myself."

Customer-Seller Intervention: As with visitor and complainant interventions, customer interventions begin with *compliments — positive feedback* about what clients are doing that is good for them. The counselor agrees with clients' beliefs that it is important to *do* something to achieve the goal that brought them to counseling.

Because customers are willing to take action, they are given explicit *behavioral or action-oriented tasks*, usually with the instruction to *observe changes* that happen when tasks are completed. Although customers are not caught up in "problem talk," they sometimes need to focus their goals more clearly for change. Therapy *tasks* help them do this.

A typical task after the first session is: "Between now and the next time we meet, I would like you to observe what happens in your (pick one): family, life, marriage, relationship that you want to continue to have happen."[17] When clients return to their next session they are asked, "So, what's better? What is happening that you would like to continue to have happen?"

The *generic task* is used with those whose goals are still vague by instructing them *to notice* when they are doing more of what they want. If, for instance, the client says, "I want to have more peace of mind," the task is: "Keep track of what you are doing this week that gives you more peace of mind."[18]

Often clients have been clear about their goals and have been able to point to specific behavioral changes that occur before coming to treatment. In the course of the interview, they are helped to identify the first active, behavioral steps they should take to continue to meet one of these goals. The therapist designs tasks to reinforce and support these steps.

Insoo Berg and Scott Miller give a customer who is a problem-drinker his message, which includes *compliments, acknowledgment, and support of goals,* and *a therapeutic task:*

> I am very impressed that you have finally recognized that you have
> to stop drinking, be more responsible, and take care of your family.

It takes a great deal of maturity and strength to accept the reality that you must start taking care of your business (these are the client's terms). We agree that it will be hard work and the tough part still lies ahead, but your determination to be a better parent to your children than your father was to you is impressive. But, as you know, it will take lots of hard work and trial and error since you will be teaching yourself how to be a responsible father. The same will be true with staying sober. As a way of getting you started in the right direction toward becoming more responsible, I would like to have you continue to stay with your newly discovered healthy habits and also pay attention to what new ways you discover that increase your success.[19]

Step V: Goal Continuation:
How to Help the Client Continue Noticing Change

Solution-focused therapists expect their clients to change because they are building on changes that have already been occurring. Most clients return after their first session with positive reports. However, the challenge is to help clients *continue to act*. Clients are helped to continue through the interviewing activities of the therapist in the second and subsequent sessions.

Through the therapist's questions, clients identify and amplify positive changes. They are "trained" to notice their own behavioral changes and to recognize the differences these changes make. They are also helped to know how to think about their setbacks or difficulties. To remind therapists of their interviewing tasks, Dan Gallagher uses the solution-focused acronym, EARS,[20] which means:

Elicit: Solution-focused therapists begin each subsequent session with the open-ended question: "What's better?"

They do not ask, "Did you do your homework task?" nor do they assume that "what's better" was the result of the assignment. Therapists are genuinely curious and are open to surprise. (Later we will address how the therapist uses interviewing techniques to help clients who have had setbacks or other difficulties.)

After a client reports what is better, the therapist might ask, "What would (your son, parents, teacher, judge, spouse, etc.) say is better?

Amplify: The therapist asks for details about the changes using questions about when, who, where and how:

When did this happen? (Ask about sequences): Then what happened?
Who: Who else noticed? How did they respond? What tells you they noticed?
Where: What was going on at (a place) that helped?

How: How did you do that? How did you know that was the right thing to do? How did you think (your son, teacher, the judge, etc.) decided to do that?

Reinforce: Therapists use the interview to teach clients not only to pay attention but also to value the positive changes they are making. They teach through their own response to the client's positive changes using *nonverbal* response such as leaning forward, picking up a pen and taking notes, smiling, and *nonspecific verbal gestures* such as interrupting, asking, "Say that again!" or, "You did what?"

Solution-focused therapists have found it more effective to use indirect compliments or compliments that encourage clients to see themselves through the eyes of others. For example, instead of saying, "That's good," the therapist asks "How did you decide that was good for you?" or, "How did you know that would help?" They also ask, "What do you suppose your husband noticed when he came home last night that let him know that something was different about you?" In structuring compliments, therapists are careful to use the *same words* clients use in describing their goals.

Not all clients are comfortable with compliments. Some need to downplay them or discount their importance, saying in effect, "It's nothing much." With such clients, therapists preface their remarks with: "You may find this difficult to believe, but in my experience...I have found that it's hard for folks to stick to a plan like you are doing so faithfully, etc."

Positive changes are reinforced and internalized as clients become aware that what they are doing is good for them. They come to these realizations as they answer the question: "How did you decide that was good for you?" It is then not uncommon for them to begin to give themselves self-compliments. For example, "I decided to take myself seriously and go back to school," or "I decided to get my own energy back, so I began to jog again."

Scaling questions are also used to reinforce awareness of progress. For example, "On the scale from zero to ten, where do you think you are this week?" "What did you do to move it up a point?" "What do you want to do next week to continue to reach your goal?"

Start Again: Ask, "What else is better?"

Tasks such as the following are designed to help clients *maintain* change:

Pretend the miracle has happened. "Each night, before you go to bed, I want you to toss a coin. When it comes up heads, I want you, throughout the whole next day, to pretend the miracle has happened. When it comes up tails, do as you would usually. Observe how you feel, what you do, what your (partner, parent, etc.) notices — this coin-toss-pretending should be a secret from her (etc.). We will discuss it at the next session." When this task is used in couple or family therapy, the parents, or other family members, are instructed to try to guess which day the person is pretending is the miracle day, but they are to wait until the next session to discuss it.[21]

The Surprise Task (for couples and families), "Do at least one or two things that will surprise your parents (spouse, if doing marital therapy). Don't tell them what it is. Parents, your job is to see if you can tell what it is that she is doing. Don't compare notes; we will do that at the next session."[22]

In Appendix B we have included a *Goal Continuation Worksheet* for keeping track of the process of later sessions when the *Five Step Solution-Focused Treatment Model* is used.

Solution-focused therapists report that most clients respond to the question "What's better?" by at least saying, "It's a little bit better." Some, however, report no change and some even report setbacks.

Often a client's report that "nothing is different" indicates that she does not feel that change is happening quickly enough. It is an expression of frustration. Sometimes she is looking for *big* changes. When hearing this complaint, solution-focused therapists accept this appraisal as valid. They then review the events of the person's week to help her look for *small* exceptions to the problem. Clients are thus helped to identify how they behaved differently, even if the changes seem small to them. The changes are then positively reinforced through the EARS approach.

A report that "nothing is different" may be an indication that the therapist may have given a therapeutic task to a "complainant" whom she thought was a "customer." If she suspects this is the case, she switches to *coping* questions that help the client recognize her strengths in a difficult situation and reinforce ways in which she can begin to act on her own behalf. When clients report that "nothing is different," they can be asked, "How come last week was not worse?" If the client reports that she "barely copes" she may be asked *how* she barely copes. Or she may be asked, "How do you keep on trying?" Coping questions are used to acknowledge the client's difficult situation and to help her see that not only has she survived it, but she has not made things worse. Coping questions lead to a client's hopefulness.[23]

Solution-focused therapists have had a great deal of experience in working with problem drinkers. (We enthusiastically recommend Insoo Kim Berg and Scott Miller's *Working with the Problem Drinker* and their *The Miracle Method: A Radically New Approach to Problem Drinking.*) Through this work they have helped people move beyond setbacks. While solution-focused therapists work with all types of setbacks, we choose to give examples from *Working with Problem Drinkers*. The questions raised by therapists that are quoted below also came from this source.

The key strategy in helping people move beyond a setback is to help them remember the success they were having prior to the setback and to return to the original goal. Solution-focused therapists use questions such as these to achieve these purposes:

- "How did you manage to stop drinking when you did? How did you know enough to stop at five beers? What did you do that was different?"
- "What told you to stop when you did?"
- "What do you suppose your spouse would say you did that was different in order to stop at five drinks?"

They also believe that no one setback is the same as another and that clients can learn from setbacks to gain more sense of control and responsibility. They ask:

- "How is this setback different from the last one?"
- "What did you do differently this time (stopped drinking earlier, changed location, any sequence of events, and so on, in detail)?"
- "What have you learned about yourself from this episode? What will you do differently as a result?"

In order to be reminded to change in small steps, questions such as these are asked:

- "What do you need to do more of?"
- "How will you make sure to do that?"
- "How do you suppose that will affect your life?"

Berg and Miller have found that some problem drinkers test their confidence in their sobriety by attempting to drink again. They help these clients to continue to do what works for them by asking:

- "Could this be your unconscious way of reminding yourself that you still have a drinking problem?"
- "What other ways do you have to remind yourself that you still have a drinking problem?"
- "What do you suppose your best friend (spouse, parent, etc.) would suggest to you to remind yourself?"[24]

Sometimes, clients report new problems just as they are beginning to meet their goals. Counselors can be tempted to address the new problems and get sidetracked. The counseling would then move into an open-ended, not brief mode.

When new problems arise, solution-focused therapists acknowledge them, but point out that they can best be addressed after the gains of the present work have been solidified. In order to keep from being sidetracked clients and counselors need to keep the client's picture of the "miracle day" clearly focused and in view.

Challenges to Counselors in Community

Counselors in faith communities need to learn some brief therapy methods in order to help members deal with their life issues. Not only do some religious bodies require that clergy and lay people use brief therapy methods, but there is evidence to show that these methods can be powerfully effective.

However, many counselees find brief therapy surprising. They come to clergy and lay counselors expecting simply to find a sympathetic ear. Some hope for advice from an authority, others expect prayer. Most do not expect "therapeutic interventions" nor do they anticipate being asked to carry out behavioral tasks.

No matter which brief therapy method you choose, counselees need to be given guidelines about the process. Solution-focused therapists have found that the best way to educate clients is by doing the work, rather than explaining it beforehand. Therefore, the counseling contract is made *within* the session, itself.

By the end of the first session, counselees should know that:

- You will meet until a "well-formed" goal has been met.
- Sessions will last a stated time, from forty-five minutes to an hour.
- The goal is usually met within a few sessions. You need to remind yourself that you will not work with the counselee for more than six sessions without professional supervision.
- People are asked when they want to come back. The second session is usually scheduled within a week or ten days but subsequent sessions may be spaced further apart so that new behaviors can be practiced.

Just as counselees need to learn to be in brief counseling, many counselors in community need to learn to *use themselves differently* so they can counsel. Some counselors find it difficult to do brief counseling because of the complexity of the roles they have to play and the varied expectations of their members. Others find it challenging because of their particular leadership style.

Clients go to *secular* solution-focused therapists with the expectation that the therapy hour is for them. They expect to be helped by the expertise of the therapist and are not surprised that they are given a prescription: in this case, not to take medicine, but to *do* something. Solution-focused therapists have a clear understanding of their role: They are to find what relationship clients have to the work and then help them discover solutions they are already finding to their problems.

Counselors in community who use solution-focused methods, however, find that their role is often not so clear. Like the other solution-focused therapists, they, too, must listen for solutions. However, counselors in community also need first to listen to see if they are being asked to provide community care, or a referral. Sometimes a community member comes wanting to talk about the business of the congregation. Sometimes a congregant is dropping in to talk with his friend — who is also his pastor, or rabbi, or lay leader.

You may experience community members wanting you to perform two functions at once. For example, the president of the congregation may come in first speaking of a community problem, and then, let "slip" that he and his wife are having marital difficulties and he needs to talk. You can manage these differing expectations if you are clear about your roles and their function.

First, separate out the two roles: Are you the cleric or lay leader who "answers" to the president of the congregation? Or are you the counselor who will do a unique type of brief therapy that is goal-oriented and time-limited? You may need to explain the two tasks and the different "hats" you will wear as you do them. You will then ask which need is the most pressing because the two tasks cannot be done effectively at the same time. If the president says, "My situation at home is not good, but we've got to see where we can get money to fix the church roof," you might say, "Let's make an appointment later this week to talk about your personal situation," and then put on your "community administrator" hat.

The image of yourself as one who wears many hats is useful. When you know which hat you are wearing you can be clear about your role, what others can expect from you, and what you must expect from yourself. When putting on your "counselor using the solution-focused-method hat" you will realize what is needed to do the work effectively: you need an hour's time, the privacy of an office, and materials for taking notes. When you pay attention to these needs, you are already communicating something about the process to your community member: You take him and his situation seriously; you make adequate time for his session. And you become curious about solutions he finds to his problem.

Some counselors in community have no trouble knowing which hat they are wearing but they are hampered in using the solution-focused method either by their leadership style or by the perception that others have about their office. Counselors coming from either authoritarian or egalitarian faith communities might each have their own kinds of problems with the method.

Authoritarian: Some counselors may not themselves have authoritarian personalities, but may serve congregations that give weight to ordained clergy and whose ecclesiastical doctrine carries great authority. In these religious groups clergy are often called "Father" or other hierarchical titles and there is sometimes a belief in the congregation that Father knows best. Even when clergy in these religious groups do not experience their own authority in this way or believe that they have *the answer*, there is often an expectation that they *should* know. Members of these congregations expect to get advice from clergy. And they expect clergy to speak with authority.

The solution-focused method is challenging to those who come to it with an authoritarian mind set, for it shifts authority from the counselor and the therapy situation to the client and the client's life. The client is expected to know what is good for him and to become empowered to assume his own authority.

Often counselors who come from authoritarian traditions are relieved to learn these solution-focused methods. They have in the past been uncomfortable about being expected to give wise advice which they did not have. While it takes practice to listen attentively to counselees, these counselors learn to listen for solutions and to avoid counselees' attempts to get them to give advice that will solve the problem.

On the other hand, sometimes these counselors are more comfortable with the method than are their members, who expect the religious authority to give advice. But counselees become more comfortable as the counselor consistently and genuinely inquires about their solutions, coping abilities, and values. In some cases counselees are uncomfortable with the compliments given by the counselor because they come expecting a shaming response. Even when counselees express surprise about this unusual experience, it is important for the counselor not to get sidetracked by talking about his expectations and to continue the counseling *in order to meet the counselee's goals.*

Egalitarian: Sometimes counselors who work in congregations with a less hierarchical style also have trouble *facilitating* the method. Counselors who are members of communities and perform a counseling role, parish administrators, lay leaders, and peer counselors often have no trouble with the method itself: in fact, they like it. They do not get caught up in counselees' problems; they can identify counselees' solutions and they believe in the counselee's ability to claim her life. These counselors, however, can sometimes find it difficult to claim their own *authority as facilitator* of the solution-focused method.

Such counselors often experience a feeling of equality with those they are counseling. They *join with* the counselee in a respectful relationship. However, the role of facilitator requires them to *create an action:* by taking the "break" and by making an intervention. In this facilitation, the counselor is no longer acting in the familiar role of friend even when the counselee might be a friend.

Because empathic listening is needed to do solution-focused work, counselors must be conscious that they are *different* from the counselee. This requires a high degree of personal individuation and consciousness. It is easy for counselors who are peers or who relate collegially to sympathize — not empathize — when counseling those whom they know. Because they are sympathetically identified, they may find it more difficult to discern those unique, small solutions the counselee is already making.

The challenge for these counselors is to be prayerfully centered and aware of their separateness as they counsel those they know well. It is then that they can connect to the uniquely other.

Sometimes they must also educate their counselees who are acquaintances, friends, or colleagues that the counseling session is *for them*. Sometimes friends are uncomfortable about "taking all the time" and will try to engage the counselor in talk about the counselor's life. They may need to slide into the work through sociability. In such cases, the counselor needs to be firm about setting boundaries and clarifying expectations.

A Spiritual Tool

The solution-focused method is a tool that we can use to cultivate our own spiritual garden. It is uniquely suited to make us more discerning, hopeful and grateful.

At the heart of solution-focused work, for both the counselee and counselor, is discernment. Both are looking to see where change is already happening. In the process, both are retraining their eyes; both are being given new perception. Through this discernment process, both are becoming more open to the Presence of God.

Solution-focused work is very active. Counselees are encouraged to *do something different*. This instruction reminds us of Jesus' command to those whom he healed. They were to take an *action*: After putting mud on a blind man's eyes, Jesus told the man to "Wash it off at the pool" (John 9:6–7). In another case he first asked an invalid: "Do you want to be well?" He called upon the invalid's will and his faith. Jesus responded to the man's wish to be healed when he said, "Stand up, take your mat and walk." (John 5:6–9).

Counselees come wishing to be healed. They are supported as they learn to pay attention to the inner voice that helps them find solutions. They are helped to consider the question: "What more can you do that is good for you?" Because counselors do not have to solve their counselee's problem, the method requires them mainly to listen and inquire. This respectful, curious, and active attention can become "holy listening." The counselor might even have been "praying without ceasing." It is not unusual for the counselor to experience awe.

Counselees often leave their solution-focused sessions feeling more optimistic. They are hopeful. However, they do not experience "hope" as is often understood in our culture. The word "hope" can be used to mean "passive wishful thinking" or even "hopelessness." For example, "I can't do anything. Just hope."

The hope that these counselees feel is active. It feels similar to Emily Dickinson's understanding when she says, "Hope is the thing with feathers."[25]

Hope, like a bird, is active, in flight and expecting to be upheld by the air: held by the everlasting arms of God. It is this sense of being supported that many counselees and counselors feel when they use the solution-focused method.

Counselors who use the solution-focused method often find themselves saying "Thank you!" Both they and their counselees are grateful for the changes that are being made. Counselors are often grateful for a method that clearly allows them to know that *they are not* the healer. They are grateful for therapeutic techniques that simply and elegantly allow them to facilitate — to be a midwife — to the new life that is happening.

At the end of the session both counselor and counselee might be moved to give expression of their gratitude through prayers of thanksgiving. In some cases, counselees might offer their own prayers, or have requests for prayer which they wish you to offer. You will be led by your religious tradition to give blessing, anointing or to lift up prayers of:

> *Thanksgiving* for the solutions, change, transformation that were happening even before they were recognized.

> *Petition* for eyes to see the changes that are happening, support in the hard work of "doing something different," and trust in that support in order to feel God's everlasting arms.

Chapter Six
Reading and Resources
Publishing information is found in the Bibliography.

• For a clear overview of Solution-Focused Therapy we recommend Peter De Jong and Insoo Kim Berg, *Interviewing for Solutions;* and William Hudson O'Hanlon and Michele Weiner Davis, *In Search of Solutions: A New Direction in Psychotherapy.* We also recommend John Walter and James Peller's *Becoming Solution Focused in Brief Therapy* as a guide to help you apply the method to counseling.

• Steve de Shazer's *Words Were Originally Magic* contains transcripts of sessions illustrating the careful way solution-focused therapists listen to clients. For an understanding of the evolution of the theory, see de Shazer's *Clues: Investigating Solutions in Brief Therapy, Keys to Solution in Brief Therapy,* and *Patterns of Brief Family Therapy.*

• We recommend Howard Stone's *Brief Pastoral Counseling: Short-Term Approaches and Strategies* for its application of various brief therapy techniques to specific community counseling problems.

• Books teaching the solution-focused method to treat effectively:

> *Problem Drinking:* Insoo Kim Berg and Scott D. Miller, *Working with the Problem Drinker* and *The Miracle Method;* Insoo Kim Berg and Norman H. Reuss, *Solutions Step by Step* (with video)
> *Sexual Abuse:* Yvonne Dolan, *Resolving Sexual Abuse*

School Related Problems: Ron Kral, *Strategies That Work: Techniques for Solutions in Schools*

Child Welfare Problems: Insoo Kim Berg, *Family Based Services*

• Audio and Video Tapes demonstrating the solution-focused method can be ordered from:

Brief Family Therapy Center
P.O. Box 13736
Milwaukee, WI 53213-0736 Tel. (414) 785-9001

• Information about training in the solution-focused method can be obtained from:

The Brief Family Therapy Center (above]

Northeast Brief Therapy Training Center
Daniel Gallagher
R.R. I, Box 400 Halcyon Road
Millbrook, NY 12545 Tel. (914) 677-5954

Blanton-Peale Graduate Institute
3 West 29th Street
New York, NY 10001-4597 Tel. (212) 725-7850

～ PART III ～

Caring for and Counseling Others in All the Seasons of Life

For everything there is a season,
and a time for every matter under heaven:
a time to be born and a time to die;
a time to plant, and a time to pluck up that which is planted;
a time to kill and a time to heal;
a time to break down, and a time to build up;
a time to weep, and a time to laugh;
a time to mourn, and a time to dance;
a time to throw away stones, and a time to gather stones
      together;
a time to embrace, and a time to refrain from embracing;
a time to seek and a time to lose;
a time to keep, and a time to throw away;
a time to tear and a time to sew;
a time to keep silence and a time to speak;
a time to love and a time to hate;
a time for war and a time for peace.

                          Ecclesiastes 3:1–8

~ 7 ~

Care and Counseling
at Life's Many Beginnings

I forget and I remember
all the dim beginnings in me,
of the many lives I have had
I have had....

I begin again so often I begin again.

— Gertrude Stein[1]

Our lives are a series of entrances and exits, beginnings and endings — turning points of change. To know the importance of an entrance, you have only to watch a play: An actor makes an entrance and the whole scene changes. We do not yet know his name but his very presence makes something happen. People move, heads turn, a sentence is uttered and the action changes.

The entrances we make in life affect us, and those in the scenes with us. As happens in a play, we *need* to make entrances; to move into new places in ourselves and in the world. In addition, our entrances cause the scenarios of our families and our world to change.

The urge to make an entrance, to be *in* the action, begins in utero. It is the baby's need to move, to get going, that causes the mother's hormonal system to receive the message that starts her labor. Now in the world, curiosity and excitement propel the baby to respond, to move, to speak. Through each stage of the life cycle, the baby is drawn and propelled to make new beginnings. A child *has* to master — to ride the bike, to learn the answer, drive the car, go to school.

One cannot look at an individual baby without seeing its connection to everyone in the constantly changing "scene" around it. One must think *systemically* — seeing the baby in a family system, *that* family in the system of the community and, then, in the total system of the world.

Counselors in community help members in their life's journey when *they celebrate with them and help them prepare for and support their entrances.* Faith communities are centrally involved in "entrances." The community of faith holds and supports members as they begin and begin again on their spiritual journey of self-knowledge and self-transcendence.

Community Care and Counseling in Family Beginnings

Much of the work of counselors in community is to support members as they move into the beginning of each phase in the family life cycle. Through youth groups, family education, and community care and counseling, *adolescent* s are helped to become independent. Parents are helped to "let go" so that their children may leave home, learn skills for self-support and develop intimate relationships. Clergy are there for them when they are ready to marry. They give premarital care, perform the weddings and counsel families so that *new families* can be created. When *children* come, they are named, blessed, and covenanted. They are welcomed into the religious community and are celebrated in other rites of passage. *Parents* are supported as they nurture young children and as they both hold and let go of young people so that they may become strong enough to fly from the nest of the family. And so the cycle repeats itself.

It is useful to understand the principles of family transitions so that you can help members move through them and so that you can support and educate families who are in the midst of radical transformations, without yourself getting caught in the undertow of change.

Weddings are a time when you run the risk of getting caught in family undertow unless you know how to navigate *and* have a good map. All families are caught in ambiguity at the time of weddings. There is joy, excitement, and often the desire to put on a large affair to celebrate the new family with friends and relatives. But there is some underlying sense of loss — loss of a "child" and loss of parental roles. At the time of the wedding, often the families of the couple are strangers to one another, with different backgrounds and lifestyles. New extended families are often friendly but wary.

The young adult bride and groom have shaky feelings, too. Their newly found sense of autonomy and independence is not yet firm, particularly in the area of finance. The wedding may be costing a "small fortune" compared to what the couple is earning in their entry-level jobs. While they would like to *appear* independent, they may also wish to *remain* more dependent on their families. This inner conflict can make them testy with their parents and touchy with each other. Both the couple and their families have the developmental task of *supporting and becoming a new family*. This is hard to do when both parents and young adults are ambivalent about letting go of old roles.

If, as the counselor who is doing premarital care and/or performing the wedding, you do not understand that unsettledness is expected, you might pick up on the couple's or families' anxiety and not find ways to support the commitment of the couple. But as you support their commitment, you also help families realign themselves as both families *let go* of their children so that their children can join each other, and also so that families can *open up* to accept the new son or daughter-in-law and the enlarged, extended family.

You will get caught in undertow if you try to talk any of the cast of characters out of their feelings. By supporting the couple's commitment, you help families find some balance as they try to find a new shape.

Your understanding of second order change can help you show families what is happening to them when they experience the upset of radical change in the family. At the time of the marriage, the *entire system* changes. Children leave their families. Their separation needs to be clearly acknowledged. The parental family, in choosing to "let go," paradoxically allows the new couple to "stay connected" to them. If a family "gets its feelings hurt" by the independence of the newly coupled children, they may push them *too* far away. Families who learn how to be flexibly supportive, to have elastic boundaries, find that their children still are able to be emotionally close, but individuated.

The parental family has been radically changed. It is both smaller in number — one member has left — yet larger, for the extended family has expanded. Each member of the family has a new role and there are new rules for relating to the new couple. There is also an opportunity for the parents to rediscover each other. The boundaries of the family have been tested.

Just as children develop through stages of growth, so do families. Young people who have successfully moved through adolescence and into independent young adulthood are ready to form a new family that becomes part of the preexisting family system of two or more families.

Counselors in community are with members at life transitions. Understanding more about the family life cycle can help you be less anxious about these unsettling changes. Your knowledge can make you a more comforting companion. Family theorists provide useful maps. We have been drawing on the work of Betty Carter and Monica McGoldrick. In *Appendix C* you will find an outline of their understanding of the stages of the family life cycle.[2]

There is transformation — second order change — in each stage of the family. In each stage, there are tasks that must be accomplished before families can become emotionally accepting and move on. By understanding this process you can help those who come for community care and counseling identify where they are in the cycle and assist them on their way.

Community Care and Counseling and the Miracle of Creation

A priest or minister holds a baby and baptizes it and the child is accepted into the Community of Faith.

A child is dedicated and blessed in a Free Church service and is embraced by the community.

A circumcision is performed and a Jewish baby boy is brought into the Covenant of Abraham.

A Jewish baby girl is named and blessed in the synagogue and the family is enriched.

The religious rituals around birth and adoption are times of celebration, dedication, and thanksgiving as children enter families and their religious communities.

As a counselor in community, you are aware that these occasions of joy often have an *underside.*

You know because you have been offering community care and counsel to mothers throughout their pregnancies. You have been with families as they rearrange themselves to make room for the new baby. You know that:

Sometimes these naming services are filled with joy and thanksgiving when a baby is finally born to a couple who has had multiple miscarriages or who has had the trauma accompanying lengthy and expensive infertility treatments.

Sometimes these occasions are bittersweet when babies are blessed who have spent months in the hospital in units for premature infants, or who are still being treated for birth defects.

Sometimes babies have not been truly welcomed into families because parents are fighting or are overburdened. Sometimes a mother holds her baby alone because the father has left.

Sometimes mothers are still feeling the stress of difficult pregnancies or traumatic deliveries. Sometimes the mother is even now experiencing a serious postpartum depression.

Sometimes babies are welcomed into the community who have come into their families through long-awaited adoptions. Often these adoptions were preceded by years of heartbreak and frustration as couples tried to conceive.

The birth of a child into a family creates a *natural* crisis in life. Crisis (from the Greek, *krinein,* "to decide"), is a turning point, a time of change. It is not unusual for families to turn to counselors in community for support and wisdom when they expect a child. After the child is born, they expect to speak to clergy to plan the religious service and to receive education about the *meaning* of the ritual for their lives.

This gives you an opportunity to ask how the family is doing and to inform them that *family upset is to be expected at this time.*

The balance within marriage is upset by the arrival of the baby because of the stress of fatigue, sexual tension, financial expense, and the rearrangement of roles and chores. Underlying tensions, old hurts and arguments that the couple felt were settled often come up as well. The upset caused by the baby's arrival gives the couple *another* opportunity to work on some of the issues in their marriage and to find some deeper healing.

The entrance of a new baby into a family causes older children to have to move over to make room for a new sister or brother. After a new baby is brought home, parents often report that older children regress or act "baby-like." Before the baby was born, children often talked about looking forward to a new addition to the family. The *reality* of the baby is a different matter. In response to it, older children often become less inwardly organized. For example, the success which older children have had just weeks before — with toilet training or other marks of "being bigger" — unravel.

Families need to be told that this unsettledness is normal and that it will take more than six months before they are on an even keel again. Couples, particularly those having their first baby, are terrified when they feel their marriage is falling apart at the very time that they are bringing a new baby home. You can bring comfort to them with your knowledge about second order change by telling them that when babies enter families, the whole system changes.

Often the success couples have had in relating to their families of origin becomes strained after the baby comes. Although couples have spent months talking about possible names for the new baby, as the time draws near for naming ceremonies, tension mounts. In Jewish families children are given Hebrew names which are chosen to honor relatives who have died. Often Jewish couples have conflict as they experience pressure from their families to choose particular names. Christian families experience similar conflicts around the choice of a name.

Sometimes there are also conflicts about the amount and kind of help new mothers need from their mothers, mothers-in-law or other relatives. Mothers of new babies often experience a need to be dependent on their own mothers. They are tired. They need care themselves as well as help with the baby and other children. But they also need to be in charge. Mothers and daughters often experience tension between them at the time when they are also deeply bonded through the joy of motherhood. When a new baby is born, families have to renegotiate boundaries and rules within their own walls and with their extended families as well.

The blessing of babies connects religious communities to the cycles of nature and to the mysteries of creation. Although it is not overtly expressed, the celebration of a baby is one of the few times the Christian church acknowledges sexuality. Babies are undeniably the outcome of sexual acts. When we celebrate babies, we celebrate bodies and sensuality as well as families and commitment. The stork did not bring the baby. The baby grew out of parents' love and sexual experience — the gifts of creation. As you bless and name babies, you can give thanks for these gifts.

The Jewish tradition has been less separated from the celebration of sexuality. Unlike Christianity, which has had more puritanical and dualistic trends, Judaism has traditionally had rituals and prayers that express thanksgiving for *all* the blessings of creation. The following, a liturgy to be recited on the eve of the Sabbath by couples who are expecting a baby, is an example of such a prayer. This prayer can be adapted for Christian use as well:

> O God
> On Shabbat you surveyed your creation and found it good,
> This Shabbat we thrill at the wonder of our creation.
>
> Our love for each other
> Swept us into this most wondrous of nature's cycles;
> You created our lives;
> We joined them together under your covenant.
> Now we seek the wisdom needed to entwine yet another.
>
> We strain to imagine its reality;
> We pray for its health and perfect growth.
> Bless our family with Shabbat peace.[3]

If your religious community is ministering to the world as it is, you will be welcoming and blessing babies who will live in single parent homes. Some of these babies are in foster care or are adopted by single parents, others are born to mothers who are not married and are without partners. These mothers will parent their child alone or will be supported by their extended family.

Caring for the Modern Family in a Time of Change

Today only 50 percent of all children live in nuclear families.[4] Because the nuclear family has been the norm in the lifetime of most of us, it is easy to forget that it is a modern phenomenon. Our great-grandparents' marriages were partnerships that supported families *within extended families*. They were not self-contained units. Couples were not expected to meet all of each other's emotional, social, and friendship needs.

The nuclear family is comprised of parents and their children. It is a self contained emotional, social and economic unit. While over the years adjustments have been made in family roles, there is often a fantasy shared by nuclear families: they *should* be economically supported largely by the father whose place in the world gives the family status. Traditionally, the mother was not to earn money but was to work in the home and community. This has changed; wives work to contribute financially, although not always as much as those who have a career. Even today in the nuclear family a mother's life tends to be child- and service-centered. Children are to succeed so that their mother's work is fulfilling. The family is expected to be strong and independent enough to survive the husband's job transfers. The family, while feeling loss because of these moves, is supposed to be able to adjust, to find ways to keep in touch with extended family, and to accommodate quickly to a new community.

Post World War II suburbs, with their minimal public spaces and one-family houses, reinforced the isolation of nuclear families. While shopping malls have added to public space, they have not created communities. In suburban settings, nuclear families become private and autonomous. But it should be noted that not all nuclear families are cut off from community and extended family — some families whose ethnic culture values the extended family go to great lengths to maintain these ties.

The nuclear family has generated important social values:

- Children are valued — and are entitled to have childhoods.
- Husbands and wives have learned to be friends and partners.
- Families have learned to play together.
- Commitment to family and mutual concern uphold many families.
- Religious and other community institutions have been created and nurtured.

The nuclear family also has its downside. Fathers are often absent because they work long hours. Often they are overwhelmed by their financial and social responsibilities. Mothers may be overly involved with their children. If they have been trying "to be the perfect homemaker" as well as earn money, they are exhausted. Children feel pressure to succeed and be their parents' "meaning." They are also lonely if they have become "latchkey children." The family feels the strain of financial overextension and isolation. The arrangement of the modern nuclear family puts too much pressure on everyone.[5]

Many couples are further burdened by expectations of marriage that have been reinforced by the nuclear family ideal. People who have an idealized view of the nuclear family often believe that marriage *is supposed* to create psychological transformation because of the marriage ceremony — "the two shall become one." Their personal inadequacies will be filled through the person of their husband or wife; two half-people will become one whole. Couples then feel that it is their responsibility to supplement each other's personality and to change it. Marriages break under the weight of unrealistic expectations:

Marriage *can* be a partnership in which *each supports the other as they each become themselves.* Many divorces occur because couples had expected that, if they were to give themselves to the other, while also taking care of the other, they would *then* become their true selves. This is particularly true for women who have been trained to "give themselves away" as a part of their feminine role. While it is true that people can "find themselves while losing themselves," people must also learn to develop and be themselves. Couples become disappointed when they themselves are not fulfilled through marriage. They do not know that the *state* of marriage does not, in itself, fulfill people.

It is no wonder that couples who have brought unrealistic expectations to marriage leave it when they feel the marriage has failed them. You can help families function better by helping people change their *expectations* of marriage itself. You cannot offer a corrective to all unrealistic expectations of marriage in premarital care or a few brief counseling sessions. But through your sermons, workshops, and discussion groups, you can be speaking to unrealistic expectations in an ongoing way and can help people find corrections to *some* of the following common unrealistic expectations.

- *Expectation:* Marriage will make two people into one whole person.
  Correction: While people can grow as individuals in their marriages, they do not each become the other.
- *Expectation:* The couple should be *everything* to each other — best friend, constant companion, alter ego, lover, parent, business partner, sounding board, playmate, advocate, source of emotional support. *They should not need other people.*
  Correction: All couples perform *some* of these functions *some* of the time. It is hard to do *all* of them *all* of the time. Each member of the couple needs friends and colleagues to help meet some of these needs.
- *Expectation:* Couples should always agree; fighting is bad.
  Correction: Couples should agree at times to disagree and should learn to resolve conflicts.
- *Expectation:* The wife should be in charge of maintaining relationships with all extended family members — including the husband's parents.
  Correction: While organizing the family's social life is often a function wives perform, members of a couple also need to maintain their own relationships with their own families.
- *Expectation:* Couples should tell each other everything; wanting privacy and boundaries is wrong.
  Correction: All people have the need to nurture their own souls. This "soul work" is a private matter. People need the freedom to be private about their own inner lives which they may share with others if they choose to do so.

Community is the corrective to the isolated nuclear family. Family theorists remind us of the importance of the *natural support* of the community and of the extended family. At one time, people could expect to be in regular contact with members of their extended families. Our mobile society has changed this. However, the telephone and computer have helped many families maintain close bonds.

Religious communities offer another support for families. In them, families become nurtured by members of all generations. Children whose grandparents live far away can find adoptive "grandparents," "uncles," and "aunts." They can find their own special adult friends whom they can claim as "god parents." Older people can become close to younger people who are the age of their own children perhaps living far away. These are not "substitute" relationships. They are authentic in their own right.

The family is changing. While many in your community grew up in nuclear families and may have both nostalgia for them and conflict about them, even families who meet the description of traditional families are different. Today, in all probability, both parents work. The mother may work not only because the family needs money, but because she likes her job and finds it fulfilling. The family does not depend solely on the father's success for its identity. In all likelihood, these "traditional families" are uneasy partnerships that are making up new rules that differ from the nuclear families of the fifties.

However, many families in your community will not resemble the old nuclear family ideal. If your religious group is responding to the needs of society as it is, you will have many nontraditional families in your midst.[6]

American households are enormously varied. Some are made up of *partners,* married or unmarried, heterosexual or homosexual. Sometimes these couples have children living with them and sometimes they are guardians, not parents, of the children. The constellation of *parents* is also complex. Some families have *two parents,* who, while they are committed to each other, may or may not be married. One or both of those parents may have been previously married or widowed. Some families may have *single parents.*

Some *children* are adopted; others come through foster care. Some children are wards; some are relatives living with a family but not adopted. Some are children from previous marriages or relationships.

In *Appendix C* you will find a chart outlining the varied shape of the nontraditional family. We suggest that before proceeding, you review the different shapes of families in your community. What are their *special needs* as they make the transitions into life's entrances and exits?

The *blended family* is made up of a parent with a child or children who marries another parent with a child or children. Stepfamilies sometimes have a stepparent who has no children from a previous marriage. Many people use the terms "blended family" and "stepfamily" interchangeably.[7]

Blended families are top-heavy with adults. Children in blended families have two parents, one or two stepparents, grandparents, aunts and uncles, and various step grandparents, step aunts, and step uncles. These adults provide many role models and the new relatives are frequently nurturing resources for the children. However, these numerous relationships can also cause children to feel torn by divided loyalties and to be confused by family rules that differ in each household.

When blended families are formed, parents try to balance the excitement of their new romance and the beginnings of new marriage with the ongoing needs of parenting. While trying to live their own lives, children in blended families also have to adjust to many new beginnings — including new stepbrothers and/or sisters. Often they have to adjust to a new house and may even have to move to a new location. With all of these beginnings, there is concomitant loss.

Blended families begin again, usually in the *middle* of the family life cycle. As if they had come into the middle of a movie, parents do not have the full stories about their new stepchildren. Each parent has had a separate history with their own children and has had conflicts and painful experiences with their children's other parent, their former spouse. Blended families play "catch-up" because of the past, as they attempt to stay on track in the present.

Blended families need parents who are *strongly bonded*. However, newly remarried couples feel conflict between their desire to be together, and the demands that their children place on them. Each set of children is unusually demanding because they need to be reassured that they are still important to the parent. Counselors in community must help newly blended families by supporting the couple as they find their way into a solid relationship.

The number of *single-parent* families is increasing. The Census Bureau reported that in 1991, 24 percent of all children lived in one-parent families.[8] The 1993 census reports that among them, there is an increasingly large number of single-parent families where the mother has never married (23.7 percent).[9]

Single-parent families are often top-heavy with children and lack enough adult support. Most single mothers carry the entire load. They provide emotional support and other parenting duties while going to work to provide financial support as well. Sometimes they are supported by extended family but always "the buck stops" with them.

Although they may sometimes have a new relationship or new job, many single parents feel that they have few opportunities for truly "new beginnings." They are on an ongoing, never-ceasing treadmill, being the support for their children. There are exceptions, of course. Some communities have creative programs for single mothers that provide child care and parent education and allow mothers to finish their education and train for jobs so that a new beginning is possible.

Single parent families begin *without* the support and blessing that are given to two-parent families. Although the number of children born to single mothers is increasing, there is still stigma attached to "out of wedlock" children. Often these children are not welcomed or celebrated by religious communities through naming and baptismal rituals. This is true even though there is a growing acknowledgment of middle-class women, "media couples," and others who are not married but have children.

It is necessary to note that nontraditional families go through the same complex developmental stages as do traditional families, but with even more stress. Blended families, because of their complex structure, and single parent families, because of the extra responsibilities that are already on the parent, have extra pressures as they move through second order transformations.

Faith communities are containers for the ever-changing families in their midst. They nurture these families through their network of friendship and care and are uniquely situated to give them practical help in this time of family redefinition. Through the resources of their wholeness network, they can offer support groups and parent and family education programs. Even if your community does not do the programming itself, it can be a clearing house for information and resources.

When faith communities cooperate with each other and pool their resources, support and educational groups can be designed to meet the special needs of single parents, newly divorced, divorced, and remarried families. By being aware of the developmental issues of different forms of family configurations, religious communities can be more sensitive to their members' needs.

※

By the time a divorce has actually happened, families are usually settling into their new system. Parents live in separate households, child-care arrangements and parental visiting rights have been established, and financial arrangements have been made. By now, friends and the extended family know that the divorce has happened. But while the logistical and legal work has been finished, the emotional work of divorce may still be happening. Parents are working to overcome their hurt, anger, and guilt. Children may not have given up their dreams that their family might be reunited. The rearranged family is still mourning its loss.

However, family members might also be experiencing new growth. People often mature in the process of divorcing. Through it, they become more differentiated from their own parents. Sometimes the first marriage was made to please parents or to live out the role that was expected of them in their family of origin. To divorce, they had to "go against" a family rule. If their families are able to respect their decision to divorce and are able to view them as autonomous adults, their maturity is reinforced.

Reworking relationships with grandparents and extended family is a post-divorce task. Families learn together to make new rules so that they can comfortably give and receive support. After a divorce, mothers usually have more responsibility for parenting and are often overburdened. They need the help of concerned, extended families. They also need to be respected as independent heads of households. Often fathers who have divorced use visits with grandparents as a time when they and their children can be together. Many times these visits take place in parental homes where grandparents are used to being in charge. At these times, fathers and grandparents have to negotiate so that fathers' roles are respected. In the process of renegotiating their own parenting roles, recently divorced people often clarify their family relationships and grow in the process. . Sometimes children benefit from divorce even though they experience loss. Children are often caught in the cross fire of marital fighting. When their parents separate, they often get more attention and absorb less pain. However, in the postdivorce family they may still be feeling the tug of conflicted loyalties. Another postdivorce task is to refocus attention on the children.

While recently divorced couples may still be working it out, they often strive to continue to be connected to each other through a common concern for their children while being physically and emotionally separate from one another. Because they have separated, they are able to become individually stronger. As they continue to grow, each will become flexible enough to cooperate for the sake of the children. When parents cooperate, their children are better able to grow up and eventually leave home.

Children in divorced families need to keep contact with both birth parents. Because of the divorce, their original family has died. This does not mean that they must lose their parents as well. Often it is hard for postdivorce parents to work out visitations and living arrangements so that this can be done. Making it work is worth the effort. Custody arrangements and parenting plans usually need to be adjusted as children grow and their needs change. However, the principle still stands: Children need both parents. This view is modified when children have been abused by a parent. In this case, parental visits are often supervised by someone appointed by the courts.

In *Appendix C* we have included charts prepared by family systems therapists Betty Carter and Monica McGoldrick showing the process families go through to *restabilize after divorce*. These maps chart the way. We recommend using them with members who are going through divorce.

※

Statistically you can be certain that people in your community are preparing to remarry. And they are doing it with a great deal of hope that "this time it will work!"

Of the people who divorce, five-sixths of the men and three-quarters of the women will remarry — with the chances of remarrying being greater in the early stage of the family-life cycle. And many of the marriage services will be performed in religious communities. The Marriage Preparation Research Project found, in their study published in 1994, that clergy performed 8.6 weddings a year. Of those, 5.6 were first marriages and 2.5 were remarriages.[10]

However, a sobering statistic is that of these remarriages, the divorce rate is even higher than for first marriages. While the statistics vary according to sex and age groups, it was predicted in 1980 that, of men and women in their thirties who remarry after divorce, 61 percent of men and 54 percent of the women would again divorce.[11]

Concerned by these statistics, family therapists and theorists are asking: "What makes second marriages work?" Their studies show that *readiness* to be married *again* is a factor in successful second marriages.

Before remarrying, it is important that there be emotional divorce. New families *begin* to form *before* the wedding, when a new, committed relationship starts to form. Because emotional divorce takes time, a new relationship often begins to form before the emotional divorce is "final." A formerly married person has to recover *enough* from the trauma of the first marriage and divorce to begin to trust again. If there are children, they, too, have to deal with their fears as well as their curiosity about the *possibility* of a new stepparent. As they are recovering, they can become more open to mom or dad's new partner. Issues of trust must often be addressed in the early stages of newly committed relationships. Children need to be secure in their relationship to both their custodial and noncustodial parent to deal with their complex and ambiguous responses to the new marriage.

A period of time is needed to conceptualize and plan a new marriage and family. Everyone — parent, children, and the new spouse — will have fears about forming a new stepfamily. Family therapists Carter and McGoldrick spell out tasks that need to be accomplished as the new family forms:

- Plan for maintenance of cooperative financial and coparental relationships with ex-spouses.
- Plan to help children deal with fears, loyalty conflict, and membership in two systems.
- Realignment of relationships with extended family to include new spouse and children.
- Plan maintenance of connections for children with extended family of ex-spouse.[12]

If couples who are remarrying have had education about family reformation, they are more prepared for transition into blended family life.[13]

Through support groups, forums and workshops, your community can share information with postdivorce parents that can help them better understand their experience as their family *restabilizes*. Working through the developmental tasks of postdivorce will ready them for a remarriage if they choose to make it. Workshops and other educational venues for couples who are *preparing to remarry* can help them think about questions whose answers have bearing on the new family that is beginning to form:

- What were the issues in the first marriage that led to divorce? How have they since been worked on?

- Has there been an *emotional* divorce created through the first marriage being mourned, and anger and hurt addressed? Does the divorced person feel that he or she has *recovered* his or her self?
- If there are children: To what degree has parental cooperation been achieved in the parenting plan? How have the children responded to the divorce? To what degree has their loss been dealt with?
- What is the couple's view of the previous divorce(s). What is their view of this remarriage?
- What is their relationship to their families of origin at this time?
- What values and beliefs do the new couple share?
- What is their relationship to your religious community? Do they benefit from its support and nurture?
- What strengths do they recognize in the new family configuration?

It is essential that before remarrying, parents have time for their families to restabilize. Carter and McGoldrick have charted the *developmental tasks of the postdivorce family,* which we have included in *Appendix C.* We have also included Carter and McGoldrick's outline of the *formation of the remarried family,* which we suggest you use as an educational tool with those preparing to remarry. These materials come from their book, *The Changing Family Life Cycle* in which they discuss women, ethnicity, and traditional and nontraditional families in depth.

Premarital Care

Counselors in community are at the center of families in the ambivalent process of transition. This transition takes time. The shock waves of change begin at least six months before the wedding and can last for well beyond another six months after the marriage takes place. Through premarital care, clergy play an important role in helping couples create new families in this unsettled time.

A recent study of the Marriage Preparation Research Project showed that nearly 100 percent of the Protestant ministers surveyed did premarital counseling. Of those, 94 percent personally felt that such counseling should be required of *all* couples before marriage. The same study showed that approximately 50 percent of the clergy had received no formal training to do this counseling. Of those who had been trained, 39 percent had had a course in premarital counseling, while the rest had had one unit in a course on pastoral counseling. Clergy know that the premarital care or counseling they do will, in all probability, be the only *formal* marriage preparation the couple has. Many clergy experience stress when doing premarital counseling. *They believe in its importance, but they are not trained to do it.*[14]

Perhaps you feel pressure to help facilitate and enrich the couple's relationship and to assess the couple's readiness for marriage. Underlying these goals is your awareness of the present high divorce rate. Maybe you feel personally responsible to do counseling in such a way that couples will not later divorce.

Certainly, clergy have an opportunity *to do something* with couples prior to marriage. Most couples expect that they will meet with their minister, priest, or rabbi before their wedding. They are receptive to the meetings. But what is it reasonable for you to expect to do in that time? It certainly is not reasonable for you to believe that you are personally responsible to keep couples from divorcing because of your premarital *cram course.*

One of the most significant benefits of premarital care is that it connects the couple to you and to the resources of your community. In chapter 2, we said that communities are places where people can communicate to others who they are. Their differences can be celebrated and conflict is possible. In them, people are learning to love themselves so that they can love and accept others. These are the characteristics that help *families* work, as well. If your community provides ongoing support and education in skills that facilitate community, and if those who marry can be included in the community, you will not have to be cramming information into a few premarital sessions. This means that in premarital care you do not have to attempt to teach all communication skills or techniques for fighting fairly: An impossibility. You will be giving a wedding gift to couples if you relieve them of impossible expectations about marriage and invite them to be supported by the community.

Solution-focused thinking is important to use when doing premarital care, for it reasons that premarital *counseling* is a misnomer. To many people, counseling implies the need to solve problems. Most people who are getting married do not believe that they have problems with their relationship or with their plan to marry. If they do have doubts, they are usually trying hard to deny them. They believe that in their decision to marry, they have found a solution to prior problems. It is best to think of the work you do with couples prior to marriage as community care in which you use solution-focused thinking. Your chief function is to support their resolve to be committed to each other.

In the course of premarital work, you have an opportunity to teach the couple some of the basics of family dynamics. This education will help them understand that much of the conflict that couples have after they are married is caused not so much by their problems with each other, but by the ways in which they are still tied into their families of origin. They are tied to their families because someone else in their family needs to change. It takes more than one family member to tie a knot. You can teach them the following:

- All people repeat roles they learned in their families. And when they understand these roles, they can choose to change.
- All families go though changes after children marry. Some families try to hold on to adult children too tightly; others react by pushing them too far away.

- All families have myths about marriage that get played out through the generations. By learning of these myths and expectations they can identify them and, as they begin to play them out, choose to change "the script."
- When they make a *major* move, such as choosing to marry, they will rock the boat of their extended family. If they can remain firm in their commitment to each other and begin to establish their own rules and boundaries, they can help their families change: Their families will then have a new, strong family unit to which to respond. *They can expect that their movement will cause someone else in the family to react.*

A good way to find out about family patterns is through encouraging the couple to tell each other detailed family stories about parents' and grandparents' courtship and marriages. Even when the "facts" are not available, family myths are. Myths live on through the generations and shape families. In telling these stories they will discover assumptions that their families have made about marriage and family life. As they begin to be conscious of the assumptions that their families believe are normative, they can begin to see what some of their own expectations are. Usually, couples do not experience what their differing expectations are until they have their first marital fights. You can predict that these fights will happen and suggest that when they do, they look to see if they can find the underlying assumptions that are in conflict.

To be able to tell each other family stories, couples will need to go back to their families to find information and to "get their stories straight." Often it is through asking about details that family secrets are revealed. For example, when asking, "Grandma where were you married? What was your wedding like?" it may be revealed that Grandma and Grandpa were not married in church. That information might elicit another question that reveals *the secret:* They *couldn't* be married in church; Grandpa had been married before.

Until people begin to inquire about their family history there is often a "conspiracy of silence" around family secrets. No one had ever directly asked Grandma about her wedding before. The family had been "trained" not to ask. However, when a family secret is told, the air is often cleared. Things make sense! Grandpa and Grandma had been married for over fifty years. Throughout their lives, their children and children's children had felt that Grandmother's relatives looked down on them with disapproval. Grandpa and Grandma's family members never could figure out why they felt stigmatized. Now they know. Grandma's family did not feel that she was *really* married. Grandma's revelation allowed her own family to have compassion for her. It also allowed the family to celebrate its legitimacy.

※

You undoubtedly have a format that you use in premarital work with couples. The Marriage Preparation Research Project found that, in their counseling, clergy incorporated the roles of: facilitating (encouraging couple discussion), enriching (relationship enhancement). moral teaching (sacred nature of marriage), evangelism (enrichment of personal faith), screening (assess preparedness for marriage), rehearsal (preparation for the ceremony), resource identification (to identify clergy and others).[15]

We invite you to incorporate storytelling and to adapt solution-focused methods into the work you already do. This work helps support the commitment that the couple has to each other and to "plant seeds" that will help them to appreciate their differences and to know the importance of learning to resolve conflict. We are suggesting a four session course in which you:

- Support the commitment of the couple through using the solution-focused "first session task."
- Help the couple identify their families' myths about marriage, and help them understand whether their family deals with transitions through overinvolvement (fusion), or underinvolvement (cutoffs).
- Appreciate each other's differences and give permission for conflict and its resolution.

Session One

PASTOR MCDONALD: "So, how'd you make this match happen?"
MAX GANIN: "Well, it wasn't easy!"

With this kind of opening question, Max is invited by his pastor to tell his story of the courtship. Tricia enjoys the story of Max's "triumph" of romantic pursuit.

PASTOR: "Tricia, Max takes credit for this triumph, but what were *you* really doing to make this happen?"

The pastor's question gives Tricia an opportunity to tell her version of the courtship story and to be able to claim her *active choice* of Max. The pastor uses these questions to learn about the couple's courtship and the wedding that they are anticipating.

He then asks the solution-focused question: "What *difference* has it made for you to be together?" This elicits answers that illuminate both the solution as well as problems that are being resolved or reworked by the approaching marriage. The commitment to marry produces second order change. Life is clearly demarcated as "before I met you" and "after I met you." The individual's "system" changes in the process of falling in love and then committing to marry. Couples who decide to marry work through and rearrange personal issues in order to say "yes." The issues that are "rearranged" usually reappear and are reworked in the marriage itself. For example, in response to the question, "What difference has it made for you to be together?:"

> TRICIA COLLINS: "I never thought I would trust men again after my first husband ... and then I met Max."

Tricia had a very difficult first marriage. She identifies lack of trust as being the problem she hopes to solve through this marriage.

> PASTOR: "Tell me more about how Max has helped you learn to trust men again. "

While the potential for a future problem has been identified, Pastor McDonald focuses on the *strengths* that Tricia has found in Max and the happiness she has found in being able to trust again. Through the question, Pastor McDonald is also able to find out something about Tricia's first marriage and to see whether or not she is emotionally separated from it. Some people can be *divorced, but not separated.*

> PASTOR: "Max, what difference has it made for you to be together?"
>
> MAX: "Until Tricia, I never thought I'd want to have kids. I just couldn't imagine feeling consistent about anyone. Before, I was always on the move. When I'm with her, I only want to be *with her.* "
>
> PASTOR: "What is it that she does to let you feel so satisfied ... to be able to stay?"

Max has identified a problem concerning constancy. Pastor McDonald does not ask about Max's need to be "always on the move." Instead, his questions help Max identify *what Tricia did* to help him feel comfortable and also show *how Max responded* to her. He then gives them this assignment:

> PASTOR: "Between now and our next appointment, identify some more good things in your relationship which you wish to continue to have happen. Don't tell each other what they are. We'll talk about them together."

Session Two

> PASTOR: "So, what are some of the good things in your relationship that you want to keep happening?"
>
> TRICIA: "Well, it may seem like a small thing, but when Max says he'll call, he calls."
>
> PASTOR: "Max, does it surprise you that Tricia feels that's important?"

MAX: "I hadn't particularly noticed I did that. After what she said about trust last week, I can see why it matters. You know, I like to call. She doesn't make me feel I have to. And when I do, I know she's glad to hear from me."

PASTOR: "Max, what would you like to keep happening?"

MAX: "I like knowing that Tricia cares."

Pastor McDonald uses their discussion to introduce some family dynamics principles.

PASTOR: "How have your families been helping to make good things happen for you?"

TRICIA: "My Mom likes Max and that's a help."

MAX: "My parents can't believe I'm settling down. In some ways, they want to help too much."

Pastor McDonald wants to know how both Tricia and Max's families are doing in this life cycle transition. He will use family histories to see how their families have helped them prepare to create a new family. For Tricia and Max to smoothly move into this next phase of life, they need to be financially and emotionally independent of their families. At the same time, their families need to be supportive yet able to let go. Pastor McDonald is also interested in knowing how their families are adjusting to the approaching wedding. He knows that Tricia has already tried to form a partnership that ended in divorce. He wonders what was going on with Tricia's family at the time of her first marriage.

PASTOR: "Your marriage will be affected by how your families react to it. And you know, your parents' marriage was affected by your grandparents. Let's take a look at your family stories. First, let's see where you fit into your families. Max, let's start with you."

Pastor McDonald takes out two large sheets of paper to make a diagram of Max and Tricia's family trees, as a way of charting their family histories. He uses the insights of family theorist Murray Bowen, who noticed that *families repeat themselves*. By looking at a family over at least three generations, Bowen was able to see how families transmit patterns of behavior, problems, myths, and rules through the generations.

Pastor McDonald is using family histories to see how Max's and Tricia's families have been encouraged and supported through the generations. First, he needs to organize data to outline the basic "shapes" of their families. At the next meeting he will help them put family stories into the outlines.

Pastor McDonald asks questions to obtain basic family information:

1. Names and dates (birth and death) of: grandparents and their siblings; parents and their siblings and Max and Tricia's siblings (arranged from oldest to youngest) and other persons living in their families.
2. Where family members are living now.
3. Dates of divorces, separations, remarriages, liaisons of all family members.
4. Ages when family members married or left home.
5. Family members who never married but stayed with parents; members who "disappeared" or were "cut off."

Both Max and Tricia are unsure about many of the dates they need and they also lack information about certain relatives. They make notes of what they need to learn to fill in missing pieces. Pastor McDonald encourages them to ask their parents stories of their own courtship and marriage and to find out their grandparents' response to it. He encourages them to find out about their grandparents' marriages as well. He reminds them that if they cannot find "facts," stories will do as well.

Session Three

PASTOR: "Well, what did you learn about your families?"

MAX: "It was fascinating! I learned why Mom has been behaving so inconsistently about our wedding. She's been enthusiastic, almost pushy. But she's also been angry."

TRICIA: "I learned that Mom and Gram had been having a fight at the time of my marriage to Johnny, which I had been totally unaware of. It explains a lot of things."

PASTOR: "Let's fill in the missing pieces in the family diagram and then we'll add these stories to it."

Max's Family Stories:

PASTOR: "Max, tell us more about what you learned that has helped make sense of your mother's attitude about your wedding."

MAX: "I had no idea that Mom thought she was going to lose me to Tricia's family. She believed I'd be like Dad. I found this out when I asked her about Grandpa Robinson's reaction to her marriage. She said, 'He thought he was getting his son back.' This confused me because I'd never heard that Mom had had a brother."

While Max knew that his Grandfather Robinson was close to Max's father, Charles, he had never known that his grandfather felt that Charles was a replacement for a son who had died when three years old. The name of the son was never uttered by his grandfather or by anyone else in the family because their grief was "unspeakable." Not mentioning the little boy's death was an unwritten family rule. When Max's father (Charles Ganin) married Janet Robinson, Mr. Robinson felt that a hole created by his son's death had been filled. Max had often heard his Grandfather Robinson say, "Ganin men make great sons-in-law!" — but he always felt that Grandfather Robinson was really calling his father "son."

Max also knew that his Grandfather William Ganin had been *his* father-in-law's favorite. Max remembered Grandfather Ganin for his charm and slight Irish accent. His grandfather had come from Ireland when he was a young man. Intent on becoming an American, William Ganin cut himself off from his Irish Roman Catholic past when he married a young Protestant woman, Alice Brewster. Max's Great-Grandfather Brewster admired William and eventually took him into his business as a partner. Max's father, Charles, thought of himself as a member of the Brewster family.

Max's mother had been unaware that she thought Max would join Tricia's family until Max had asked her, "Do you think I'm going to be like Dad and Grandfather Ganin?" She said, "I guess so. You've always pushed me away."

MAX: "She's right about that. I've pushed because she's always wanted to do everything for me. I said, 'Yeah. I've wanted some space from you. But that doesn't mean I want to be cut off from the family!'"

PASTOR: "If zero stands for your family being unsupportive of your marriage to Tricia by either holding on too tightly or pushing you away and cutting you off, and ten stands for your family's support and acceptance, where would you put them right now?"

MAX: "If you had asked me that three weeks ago, I might have said a three. Dad is pleased for me, although he lets Mom run family things. He just lets himself fit in. Mom confuses me. Sometimes she acts like the 'mother of the bride.' It's like she is trying to pull Tricia into our big family. At other times, she's distant. Now I know where she is coming from. I guess, after our talk this weekend, I'd say seven."

PASTOR: "What would need to happen to make it an eight?"

MAX: "I'm not sure. Things are changing in our family anyway. My great aunt who lived with us is in a nursing home. My parents have never traveled, and now they're planning a trip to Europe for their thirty-fifth anniversary. My Dad wants to go to Ireland. And Mom's excited about going with him. Mom doesn't seem to be thinking so much about me. That's a help already."

PASTOR: "It looks like your family is shifting. That realignment might make a difference. It seems good that your parents are planning that special trip. Perhaps your mother might get a break from being a professional family caretaker. If she decides she doesn't need to take care of you, maybe you won't have to stay so far away. And then she won't try to pull you in so tightly."

Tricia's Family Stories:

> PASTOR: "Tricia, you will see the world differently than Max because of your family experience. What came up for you through talking with your mother and grandmother?"
>
> TRICIA: "I remembered how I used to love to look at my parents' wedding pictures. I used to dream of being a beautiful bride like my mother. I'd get my mother to tell me stories about the wedding. I'd always thought I'd have a wedding just like theirs. I can't believe how awful my wedding to Johnny was. We were going to elope, then mother found out. She said that even though she thought our marriage was a bad idea, we should at least have something with the family. We were all miserable."

Tricia grew up in a traditional nuclear family with romantic ideas about weddings. As a child, she assumed that she, too, would grow to lead a "perfect" suburban family life. When she was fourteen her perfect world began to fall apart. The fall that her sister went to college, her father, Roger, was diagnosed with bone cancer. By the time she was sixteen, her father had died.

Prior to her father's death, Tricia's family had been self-contained. She had relatives in a neighboring state and she went to grandparents on holidays, but her family had few close friends. Because they did not have a community to rely on, her father's illness placed a great strain on her mother, Mary. Because Tricia and her mother cared for Roger, they were even more closely bonded. Eventually, the strain became too great for Mary. Uncharacteristically, she asked for help from the hospital social service department, and they referred her to a cancer-care support group. To her amazement, Mary was able to reach out to strangers. The group became a support community for her. They were with her in her grief when Roger died. Because of her experience in the group, Mary began to change.

> TRICIA: "By the time I left for college, I felt like my world was falling apart. I was leaving home, but home was also leaving me. My sister, Karen, announced her engagement. Mom had to sell the house because Dad's illness ate into our savings. She went to work. Her personality also changed. She sort of opened up. I really felt hurt when she stopped relying so much on me and began to make friends in the cancer group. And then she got involved with Ed. I felt completely betrayed when they decided to marry."
>
> PASTOR: "Did your grandmother support their marriage?"
>
> TRICIA: "At the time I thought she did. Everyone in our family's so polite. When I was getting these family stories, I found out that she and Mother were having a terrible time with each other. My grandfather had died a few years before and Gram had assumed that she would

live with Mother like my great-grandmother had lived with her. She was mad that Mother wasn't living by the rules."

PASTOR: "What rules?"

TRICIA: "The family rules that say you don't depend on those outside the family and that you keep your business to yourself. Gram felt it was Ed who influenced Mother to break the rules. Mother had met Ed on some Cancer Care committees. He's much more open and emotional than my dad was. He says what he thinks. I think he'd changed through his experiences around his wife's death. Gram wasn't totally wrong. He really supported Mother and helped her stand up to Gram. *Now* Gram says it's the best thing that could have happened. Gram still lives independently in an apartment complex sponsored by her church."

PASTOR: "How did your wedding to Johnny fit into all this?"

TRICIA: "I was so hurt and angry when Mother and Ed decided to get married. I said, 'To hell with them!' I'd been going out with Johnny who was rowdy and immature. His folks liked me and thought I was a good influence on him. Johnny and I were both at the same place. We didn't really know how to grow up. We just sort of play-acted together. Although I never would have admitted it, I wanted to feel close to Johnny the way I felt close to Mother after Dad died. I think when I decided to marry him I just wanted a family. Mother tried to talk me out of it. But basically I was mad at her. If it hadn't been for Gram, I might still be in the marriage. Johnny started messing round right away. I knew it was a disaster. But I was trained to not be a quitter. It was Gram who told me that I didn't have to put up with his nonsense." PASTOR: "Did your family respect your decision to divorce Johnny?"

TRICIA: "Yes. But I went back to the old family rule — with a vengeance! I decided to be *totally* self-reliant. I went to law school and then got a job in the firm where I met Max.

I'm just coming back to a more middle position. Max has helped me trust again.

I think I was afraid of being as dependent as I was on Mother after Dad died. I sort of lost myself then."

PASTOR: "If zero stands for your family's being unhappy with your marriage, and ten for your family supporting your commitment to Max, what number would they be at now?"

TRICIA: "I'd say nine. My family's excited. Its like I'm getting married for the first time. When I married Johnny, everything was so chaotic. Everybody is in pretty good shape now. Even Mother and Gram are in a good place. I feel like now they can concentrate on me. It feels good."

PASTOR: "What would it take to bring it to ten?"

TRICIA: "I said nine because I don't know how my Dad's family feels about me and Max. We didn't see much of them after Mother married Ed."

PASTOR: "Well, Tricia and Max, your families are both showing a healthy degree of unsettledness. I've got to congratulate you for picking a good time for your wedding. Your families both seem in good places. Your parents are involved with each other. That's terrific. Tricia, your family seems to have settled down some. You certainly were overloaded at the time you married Johnny. Although it wasn't the way you planned it, you did seem to grow up through your experience with him.(To Max) "Max, I think some excellent changes are going on in your family. It's really helpful that your mother is getting her dream trip. Make sure to send them some champagne for the trip! It's their wedding present to you. If they go on a second honeymoon, you'll get yours. I'm glad you see that you don't have to leave your family to get some space for yourself. (To both Tricia and Max) I'm going to give you an assignment. Pay attention to ways that you are different from each other. What are the differences you value about the other? Don't discuss them with each other. We'll talk about them together next week."

What Pastor McDonald Has Learned and Taught So Far:
You will notice that Pastor McDonald spoke little. The power in the session came from the *telling* — not from an interpretation — of the stories. Couples learn through telling their stories, that they come to marriage with different customs, rules, and expectations that affect their perception. The awareness of their different family experiences becomes a *background* that they will be able to move into the *foreground* when they begin to have marital arguments. They will be able to say, "Just because you did that in your family...." Through being able to describe differences, they can begin to resolve them.

You will notice that Pastor McDonald's questions elicited information about the support that Max and Tricia's parents received from *their* parents and the support that Max and Tricia were receiving from their parents *now*. The ways this support was given revealed *family style*. Max's family was an *"including family"* that took members in. It was hard for Max's mother to accept that Max and Tricia were doing the wedding "their way" rather than in her family's elaborate style. Max's family was working to respect the new family. Before Tricia's father's death, her family had been small and insular. After Tricia's mother's marriage to Ed it became a *blended family* that was trying to find a new family style. Tricia's family was supporting her marriage to Max by being more embracing and celebratory than they had been when she married Johnny.

Pastor McDonald said, almost in passing, "You come from families with very different styles that operated by very different rules." He did not go into these differences. He was planting a seed of awareness.

He also noted the *family patterns* that were evident through the generations. The cutoff that began with Max's Great-Grandfather Ganin had been repeated in the next generation. It was not a surprise that Max's mother sensed that it could happen again. Her need to hold on protectively to Max was driving him away and could have led to a repeat of the pattern. Pastor McDonald also noted the ways in which *unfinished business with the previous generation* played itself out in their families. Mary's secret fight with her own mother was about the roles mothers and daughters had played in her family for generations. Daughters were not to "put themselves first." They might seem emotionally distant from their mothers, but they were to care for them in their old age. In Max's family, the unhealed grief about his mother's brother directly affected him. His father was a "replacement" for this dead uncle and he was treated by his mother as if he, too, were vulnerable.

Through asking Max and Tricia to find out about how their families had dealt with the new beginnings of families, Pastor McDonald helped them talk together about family expectations and patterns. In this process, Max and Tricia were able to see how their families were making corrections and adjustments to their own histories. Because Tricia's grandmother was able to accept her daughter's right to "put herself first," Gram had adjusted and now enjoyed living more independently. Tricia was able to be married without having to worry about taking care of her own mother. Max's mother might begin to see that she did not have to worry about her son because he no longer had to be a "stand-in" for her dead brother. Max's father might begin to feel less obligated to make his wife's family feel "whole."

Session Four

PASTOR: "What differences do you like about each other?"

TRICIA: "I love the way Max is easy with people. He fits into every group. I feel more at ease when I'm with him."

MAX: "And I love the way Tricia's calm and has things under control. She just assumes I've got it together, too. She doesn't nag me. I never feel guilty around her. We were just saying, though, that it's not our differences we think about. We're amazed to have found each other because we have so much in common."

TRICIA: "Yes, after our meeting with you last week we started talking about how different our families really are. Of course, we'd already run into this when we started planning the wedding. But most of the time, we get out of family stickiness by doing what we like to do."

PASTOR: "Sounds like you are already discovering that you have solutions to problems with family differences. What was your solution? "

Pastor McDonald used solution-focused questions such as, "What happened?" "What did you do next?" "How did you get that to happen?" to help them see the facility they already had in solving problems. In an offhand way he said, "If you can find solutions to problems with your families, you're going to be able to solve fights with each other."

Max and Tricia were quite comfortable appreciating and talking about their perception of each other's differences. They were also interested in talking about the ways they had found to navigate between their families' styles as they planned the wedding.

Not all couples are comfortable in talking about their differences. When asked Pastor McDonald's question "What differences do you like about each other?" some might reply, "We're really very much alike," or "We can almost read each other's minds," or "We never fight." When couples respond in this manner, it is important not to try to "enlighten" them. You might respond, "Well, when you do find that you differ, you need to know that that is all right, too. Now, tell me more about the things you have in common."

Partners who are not able to acknowledge and appreciate each other's differences are usually in the stage of their relationship in which bonds need to be reinforced. When falling in love, couples are bonded through sensing how much they have in common, how "at home" they feel with each other, and how close they are together.

Some couples are more threatened than others by awareness of their differences. If you have discovered in previous sessions that parents are unsupportive of the couple, you may find the couple is particularly interested in speaking of their commonality rather than their differences. As they feel your support, they may be able at least to *hear* the suggestion that it is important to know and accept each other's differences. You will have planted a seed that can sprout after the wedding service is over and they feel more differentiated as a newly married couple.

People who have grown up in *enmeshed families* often are uncomfortable talking about differences. In their families, they are expected to be like each other. Often people from enmeshed families are attracted to others who *seem* very different from themselves. They may have chosen someone from a different religious, social, or ethnic background. These folks might be uncomfortable talking about the less obvious ways in which they are different from each other.

People who are marrying are in the process of differentiating from their families. As they become comfortable with the boundaries of their new family, they will begin to experience their own uniqueness in a fresh way. *Newly married people experience transformation* that comes through feeling their spouse's love and experiencing separation from their family of origin. Premarital care lays a groundwork for couples when it suggests that marriage brings surprises. Marriage produces second order change that includes change in the individual partners themselves.

The traditional understanding of "the two shall become one" is helpful when it supports and recognizes the new family unit. Religion's blessing of the new family protects it from those in their families of origin who may still be trying to pull their "children" back to themselves. However, it is important when doing premarital work that you let couples know that marriage will not make them "one person." In fact, often the opposite occurs. When people marry they often feel more separate, more uniquely themselves. When this happens, they sometimes worry that something is wrong — perhaps they've fallen out of love, because they do not feel "fused."

It is for this reason that following an exploration of the ways Max and Tricia had found to differ from their families, Pastor McDonald discussed with them the part of the marriage service that speaks about "the two shall become one." He told them that in his wedding homily he would encourage them "to agree to differ and resolve to love." In his homily he also would speak about creating a home that, because of their deep respect for each other, would be safe. In their home they, and their children, would be free from violence and physical, emotional, and sexual abuse. He was interested to know what they made of those ideas.

Some clergy use the Myers Briggs Personality Inventory,[16] which assesses personality styles, or other tests that describe different thinking styles, as ways of helping couples understand and appreciate their unique characteristics. Through their use, couples can identify their thinking styles so that they can say: "I'm not wrong. I'm just different."

Premarital care supports the couple's commitment and plants seeds. Because your work reinforces separation from families and also gives permission for couples to differ, couples will feel comfortable returning for coaching *if* they need it when these events occur. Because you have invited them to partake in the riches of your religious community, you are also letting them know that there are resources when the inevitable growing pains in marriage occur.

Pastor McDonald often predicts that conflict will occur and asks couples to watch for it. When couples see it happening they will say, "Well, Pastor McDonald was right. He also said we had pretty good techniques for working things out. Look how we dealt with our folks."

Sometimes in the course of premarital care, couples discover that they have problems that they wish to talk to you about, and they wish to make an appointment for *brief counseling*. Usually this occurs when you have not pointed out problems to them. They might say, "We know you'd like us to ask our families about their marriages, but we are really having a problem with them that we need to discuss with you." You might then reply, "This changes our agenda a bit. We have been doing marriage preparation, which is not really counseling. Tell me what you are trying to solve, and then we'll see what to do next."

Caring for and Celebrating the Lives of Single Adults

How are the lives of the *single adults* in your religious community celebrated? How are the beginnings and endings in their lives marked?

Families have public rituals that are "outward and visible signs" of the inner changes in the lives of both individuals and in the family itself. Religious communities are principally organized around families and couples. There is often a lack of awareness of the ways in which communities offend their single members by assumptions that exclude single people or that ignore their special needs.

Your community has many single adults. Some have never been married and are single by choice. Others are single again after being divorced or widowed. Although "single" status is defined as "not married," some single people are in fact partnered or coupled. Some live together, others although not living together are emotionally and physically intimate and committed to each other. Some would marry, but cannot, often for financial reasons. (A growing number of older people, who do not remarry because they would lose pensions or other retirement income, fit this category.) Other singles do not have a "significant other," but they do have a loving network of friends. Some live with their own parents, often caring for them.

Although single adults live in various situations, they share a commonality: they must cope and find their way in a married world. While single people experience somewhat less stigma than many did in earlier times, they still live with society's expectation that they will "grow up, be married, and have a home and children." In addition, they have learned that "love and marriage go together." And in most religious communities, they have been taught that "sex and marriage go together."

Single people who have *never* been married usually feel the burden of these assumptions most intensely. Parents and friends worry about them and pressure them to marry. Parents and other family members treat them as if they were not quite grown up. Parents want grandchildren and women feel the pressure of these expectations as well as the ticking of their biological clock. Men are expected to have children who carry on the family name and tradition.

Single people pick up their families' anxieties about the necessity for marriage. Some families are highly anxious; because of cultural expectations, some are shamed if they have an unmarried daughter, others want to have grandchildren, particularly if in other generations children have been lost in a holocaust or in war. Other families are less anxious: they value independence and achievement and expect their children to be successful in work before being married. Single people from those families feel they "have more time."

Not only family, but society as well, adds to the pressure. Women are taken less seriously at work and are paid less than men, because they are viewed as temporary — they'll be leaving soon to marry. Men do not feel pressure from work to be married until midlife when being married is considered an asset to career advancement as well as a signal to employers that they are stable and responsible. While there is variation of this pressure in different cultures and ethnic groups in America, marriage is the norm.

Some single people, frantic to marry, do so unwisely, to get out from under the pressure. Others internalize the pressure and feel that something is wrong with them; they compare their lives with those of married people and experience themselves as being on hold, waiting for *real life* to happen. Often those who join the ranks of singlehood *after divorce* again experience those same inadequacies. They had known the "higher status of marriage." Although they are happy to be out of a bad situation, they feel marginalized when they are single again. In our society *being* married counts!

In their thirties, many single people find it necessary to consult with psychotherapists because of their sense of failure for not marrying. Because of their increased experience, therapists — particularly family therapists — are acknowledging that in some ways, both therapists and psychological theory have themselves contributed to the problem. Like society, many therapists have presumed marriage to be normative for themselves and clients and have considered "not to be married" a problem. Some therapists have looked for "what was wrong" with unmarried clients and often described their problems as: "has problems with intimacy," or "avoids commitment," or "is passive or dependent or avoidant." Other therapists have acknowledged that although some people do not marry because of their own personality problems or because they are stuck in unfinished business with their families of origin, others do not marry for different complex cultural, economic, demographic, and personal reasons. While for others, not marrying is a matter of preference.

As a corrective, some family therapists have begun to study the "never married state," to find its strengths and to help their unmarried clients live their lives more fully in the present, rather than "waiting until I get married." Family therapists Natalie Schwartzberg, Kathy Berliner, and Demaris Jacob through their Clinical Project of Singlehood have researched and charted the stages and the emotional processes of the single adult life cycle. Their findings are useful not only for understanding the experiences of those who have never married, but also are invaluable in helping those who reenter single life deal with its challenges. We have included their map of *Stages of the Single Adult Life Cycle* in *Appendix C.*[17]

Many families, and singles themselves, have equated "being married" with "being grown up." Because singles are not married, neither they nor their families truly grant them adult status. Usually, young people are not conscious of their own interpretation of what it has meant for them to think, "When I grow up, I'll get married and have a home and kids." Often, only in his or her early thirties, an unmarried person might finally say, "It's time to get a grown-up bed, I'm sick of my college futon but I guess I'll wait," or another might say, "I'd like some nice china, but I'd feel silly buying it unless I was getting married." For them, "being grown up and having a home" does not seem possible unless they are married.

Not feeling entitled to "grown-up things" affects the lifestyle and well-being of singles. Some feel that to furnish a home by themselves is an admission that they are never going to marry. However, a benchmark for singles comes when they are able to give themselves a pleasant home without first being married.

Families, too, often treat singles as "children" who must be worried about. Yet, paradoxically, they also expect singles (more than the married siblings who have their own families to care for) to be more available to meet emotional and familial needs of others. But, single adults have the same "emotional job" their married siblings have: they need to find ways to be close to their families of origin while also having their own independent lives. Because families do not automatically grant their single children adult status, single people have to claim it for themselves. They have to find ways to signal their adulthood to their parents, siblings, and other relatives. In some cases, this might mean assuming responsibility for tasks that their parents have been doing for them — managing money, making appointments, filling out tax and other forms, dealing with relatives, etc. For others, it might mean inviting family to come to them, rather than their going to relatives houses for meals and celebrations. It is often a sign of growth when singles invite their families for dinner or a party or a family trip.

Often those who again enter the single state after a divorce or the death of a partner find that they have to reestablish their adult status with their families because families often try to pull them back into old roles. This also is true for singles who are parents themselves. Being married had given them license and permission to be more independent from their family of origin; this independence now needs to be reestablished.

Single adults need to separate their equation of love with marriage to know that they can be loved without having to be married. Love takes many forms. For some it will come through intimate friendships that might include sex. For others it will be a close, emotional but not physically intimate friendship. Others will find love in friendship and extended family. By changing the belief "I can only be loved if I'm married," singles can open themselves up to being nurtured and treasured.

Friendship is the most important and valued resource for singles. Because of cultural expectations, women learn early to value relationships. They usually have developed skill in communicating their feelings and needs to their friends. Single women tend to have the support of rich friendship networks. Men, on the other hand, are trained to expect women to manage their friendships and their social lives. These social and emotional needs also are often met by the women men date, and a vacuum is created when they break up. Men are often lonely in single life. The most challenging task for single men is to learn to make friendships that are emotionally nurturing and in which they feel safe enough to be self-revelatory. Men need to learn communication and relationship skills to have a satisfying single life. Homosexual men, on the other hand, usually have more developed friendship skills.[18]

The task for single women is to learn to take care of themselves practically and financially. Often, women have been taught that holdover belief of the nuclear family: "When you get married your husband will take care of you." Single women need to learn to be bold — to take themselves seriously, to make money, and to plan for the future. Because they have not had many role models, they need to find mentors to coach them.

Both single men and single women have to face the disappointment and anger that their dreams of being taken care of have not come true. It is not unusual for single men and women to say to their counselors, "I'm so tired of always having to take care of myself!" Women are tired of having to assume practical responsibilities; men are tired of managing their own emotional lives and their interactions with family. However, as both men and women become skilled in these tasks, their lives can become richer in the present; they are also learning what many of their married peers must later learn.

The forties are pivotal years for singles. For men, it is a time when many will marry. A U.S. Census Report cites that in 1993, 40 percent of men at age forty are yet to marry. Of these only 6 percent will be unmarried in the next decade.[19] Many of these men will marry women younger than they, not the single women who are in their age bracket. Many single women who are not married at forty will begin to accept the possibility that they might not marry and will begin to integrate a self-image of being a single person who can have a satisfying life, rather than a single-person-waiting-to-be-married. As part of the process of self-acceptance, many of these women will mourn the dream that did not come true. They will also assess their present life and claim its positive value. This is what Schwartzberg et al. call "defining one's authentic life."[20]

While many singles at midlife mourn the probability that they will not marry, others are even more sad not to have had their own children. As single women hear the ticking of their biological clocks, many consider having children as single parents. Some choose this option.[21] Other single women are adopting or caring for foster children. For many women, being single has not meant a deprivation of motherhood.

Research is showing that single women fare very well. In fact, they are physically and emotionally healthier than their married counterparts.[22] Never-married women also have a head start on the married women who will be joining them when they become fifty. At age fifty, 51 percent of all women are single. Women entering single status later than fifty must learn the skills of independence, self-confidence, and fulfillment that never-married singles have been practicing for years. At fifty, many never-married singles are enjoying financial stability and freedom. They are having a good time.[23]

Single men, both those who have never married and those who become single through divorce or death of a spouse, do not fare as well as single women. During the period after fifty when 51 percent of all women are single, 81 percent of the men are still married. At age seventy -five, 67 percent of all men are still living with their spouses (while only 23 percent of women over age seventy-five are living with theirs.)[24] Older divorced or widowed men have often not developed the emotional and social skills that would enrich their lives: tending to emotions and relationships was their wives' work. Because so much of men's self-esteem and meaning comes from their work, men who lose their wives and their work in the same period are often devastated. This is reflected by the poor emotional and physical health and the high suicide rate of white men over seventy — three times more than white women or black men or women. The white, over-seventy men who commit suicide are the highest of any group in the family life cycle.[25]

※

Single adults are drawn to faith communities: communities meet their needs for affiliation, friendship, and service.[26] Many singles who have never had children fulfill their need to nurture when they teach children or lead youth groups. Through this involvement, they contribute to the lives of the next generation. Singles play significant leadership and service roles in faith communities; Undoubtedly, you have single members in your wholeness network or lay ministry team. Singles make a difference to communities — and communities make a difference to singles when singles are fully acknowledged and appreciated by them.

Authentic communities already know much of the data about singles that we have just reported because in them, singles have been able to talk about themselves and to tell of the pressures and struggles they confront. Hopefully, the singles in your community are developing their authentic selves in your midst. Perhaps your community has groups and educational opportunities for singles that address their particular concerns. And undoubtedly, singles have come to you and other counselors in community to find ways to affirm their lives and to make plans for enriching them as well as to mourn the loss of their dreams of marriage and/or children.

Singles need their communities' blessings of their blossoming and thriving lives. Through the often painful process of becoming responsible for themselves, many singles have developed their talents and skills, have nurtured friendships and have become spiritually mindful. Sometimes this growth began as compensation for the marriages that were not made or the babies who were not born. But gradually, these singles claimed their lives and their rights to have them. Sometimes, however, their families, and others, have given them messages that say: "You should feel guilty for spending money and attention on yourselves, when we're having to give ourselves to our children," or "You should be paying attention to us, your poor parents." Earlier in life, many singles felt devalued because they had no husband or wife. Now they are devalued or shamed because they have their freedom and greater opportunities to nourish and develop themselves further.

Because there are few traditional communal rituals that recognize and celebrate singles, communities need to watch for opportunities to create them; observing important milestones can be one way. Communities can affirm singles by celebrating their professional accomplishments, by honoring their community service and significant anniversaries. Some communities show interest in singles' travels or other explorations or learn from their deep spirituality or other knowledge.

An area where communities often do less well is in helping single members deal with their conflict about having sexual experience. Most religious groups teach that sex should be reserved for marriage; some teach that sex is primarily a gift to be used to create children; some that while it is preferable to have sex in marriage, it is permissible to have sex in a committed relationship. While the teachings on sex differ, most religious groups do not help their members resolve inner conflicts between the pull of emotional and physical needs, and of conscience and religious instruction; the pull of life experience (some have never had a committed relationship, some have had satisfying sexual experiences, some are recently divorced or widowed) and the pull of personal relationships. Nor do communities address their single members' anxieties about wanting sexual experience in this time of AIDS.

The dis-ease about sex is not simply going to go away in religious communities. This dis-ease will be felt even more strongly by the increasing number of singles in religious communities. (It is estimated that 67 percent of those married after 1990 will divorce. While many will remarry, they will spend some time as single adults.)[27] Many who are conflicted about their sexual activity or who feel guilt or shame develop emotional and physical problems. Some, because of these conflicts, leave their religious community. Others project their guilt about their sexual activities on to others. Using the psychological defense mechanism of displacement, they deny their own guilt about their sexual activity and project blame onto others whom they consider "deviant" — prostitutes or homosexuals.

Communities that have the capacity to ask hard questions without giving easy answers and that have techniques for resolving conflicts, will be helpful to singles — and *all* their members — as they address sexual experience. In such communities, singles will feel compassion and understanding as they forge their lives in a married world.

Community Care at Midlife's Reawakening

We know from those who have studied adult development that all adults experience the transition of beginnings and endings in their *inner experience of individuation.* A significant aspect of becoming an adult is that of knowing oneself — and this is a spiritual journey.

The adult midlife crisis occurs when people realize that they have become lost in the life of their work and families. Robert Kegan, in *The Evolving Self,* speaks of this as becoming *embedded* in the very place that one had once yearned to be but now no longer gives a sense of life. When adults feel lost in their lives, depression and mourning set in. They yearn for themselves. Daniel Levinson, in *The Seasons of a Man's Life,* speaks of this as trying to reconnect to a lost dream. Most young people in their twenties are connected to dreams for themselves that they use to begin their adult lives. These dreams are often romantic and unrealistic, but they contain enough reality that young people find direction for themselves. In midlife, adults "wake up" and wonder what happened to their dreams. Levinson says that at this point adults have an opportunity to transform the lost dream into a *vision.*

All adults in your community need support in midlife as they begin the spiritual task of taking stock and finding their lost dreams — which can be transformed into visions. This is an inner journey of meaning making. It can be a time of rebirth. Adults need a space, a place, and companions to whom they can tell their stories and with whom they can express doubts, confusion, disappointment — and dreams.

Adults need to know that this personal second order change is natural. *It is inevitable and unsettling.* At midlife every aspect of life is reevaluated. It can be a time of job change and divorce. Adults who are supported through this transitional time can be helped to see that this at its core is an inner process. In some cases, the radical moves of divorce and relocation are appropriate — when they are part of the vision. At other times, they are an "acting out" of inner movement that is not sufficiently understood.

It is essential when giving care and counseling with those in midlife that you do not automatically see these changes as problems. The midlife transition is a process. The upset, of course, can cause some problems. Religious communities need ongoing groups where people can be supported as they explore and define their visions. They need study groups and retreats. Solution-focused brief counseling will sometimes be appropriate for resolving some of the problems that this transition creates. You must be careful, however, not to *create problems* by absorbing the anxiety of the unsettledness or by understanding the transition in a *concrete* way. Those who are coming loose from an experience of being embedded in the life of work or family may speak as if they wish to leave their job or family. If you listen closely, you will hear that *they want to find themselves again.*

All adults in religious communities need an opportunity to affirm the new beginnings they are making in midlife and to be comforted as they mourn the dreams for themselves that did not come true.

Community Care for Older Adults: Beginning Again

> *I am growing older knowing*
> *That my disappearing youth*
> *Hides itself in my uncertain wisdom*
> *Growing younger all the time.*[28]
> — Nancy Woods

We have been considering the many ways that religious communities care for their members in all the seasons of life. The ages of late summer and early fall have lengthened in our time. Middle age lasts longer and extends with more vitality into old age. Old age is another time of beginning. In old age we become wise. Old people experience freedom as they "get it together." In old age the self becomes integrated.

Many older Americans, the fastest growing segment of our population, live in relative financial security and with adequate medical care because of social security and retirement insurance benefits, savings, privately or publicly subsidized housing, and Medicare or Medicaid. Because of their growing numbers they have political power and advocacy through such groups as the American Association of Retired People. Many mature adults are careful with their money, but they live comfortably. And they have time for themselves.

While numerous women in their fifties and sixties still find themselves "in the middle," caring for their own elderly parents while also being helpful to their children and grandchildren, many mature adults are finding that they have time to "have another life." Some are still working at the second career jobs they began after taking early retirement. Others are retired and are creatively engaged in volunteer work, hobbies, and personal interests, traveling, sports, and other physical activities. Yet others are involved in the leadership or maintenance of civic and religious institutions or good works. And some are finally having a chance to devote themselves to their "real" personal work that had to be set aside while they earned a living. In retirement they seem to come alive.

Some, however, find it difficult to use this time to "ripen" into maturity because they are living out a self-fulfilling prophecy about being old by a certain age. Our society has suffered from ageism in which older people have been marginalized or devalued. Unlike cultures that value sages — the wise grandmothers or wise old men — our society has taught us that those who no longer earn money or are physically incapable of conceiving children are "over the hill."

In our complex society there are exceptions to this devaluing attitude. Native Americans learn from their elders. In the African-American church, women leaders known as church mothers are held in high regard. Asians, our newest wave of immigrants, bring with them the long tradition of honoring their elders. But because of devaluing attitudes, many of us have internalized a form of "age-phobia." As awareness of "age-phobia" is raised to conscious-ness, older people can fight against the biases they have against themselves and look upon this time with more appreciation. Current research on the bi-ology of aging and the studies of gerontologists provide information that can counter some of the stigma and myths about older Americans.

Many of the bleak stereotypes about older people are not true. Most old people in America do not live shut away in nursing homes nor have they lost their minds to Alzheimer's disease. Only 5 percent of people over sixty-five are residents of nursing homes and less than 10 percent will ever be. Only 5 percent of those over sixty-five suffer from Alzheimer's disease today.[29]

Instead of a predetermined decline of intelligence in old age, there is now evidence to show that there can be intellectual *growth* if people have en-vironmental stimulation. Betty Friedan, in her enormously useful book *The Fountain of Age,* refers to the work of Paul Baltes and his colleagues at the Max Planck Institute of Neurological Research who say that while there is a decline in the maximum use of the basic mechanisms of intelligence after seventy-five, most people have "great reserve capacity and potential for new learning and growth."[30] These findings are compatible with the work of George Vaillant, whose longitudinal study of men and women show that the ego's adaptive skills mature with age. People can become wiser.[31]

Stereotypes about aging are dangerous, particularly to old people them-selves. Old people who have internalized the biases of ageism *expect* them-selves to be declining. Their attitudes cause them to have chronic mild depression. They do not question their symptoms of depression; these seem natural. Indeed, feeling "helpless, hopeless, worthless" is an appropriate re-sponse to their belief that they are destined to lose their individual potency and become useless to society. They become what they fear.

Religious communities are perfectly placed to help older people dispel myths about aging. People sixty-five years and older make up from 20 percent to 40 percent of religious communities. This is in contrast to the 12.1 percent of old people in our general population. David Moberg, a social gerontolo-gist, estimates that one half of religious community care involves ministering to this older population.[32]

Many religious communities are already providing excellent support and care to their older members. These communities provide occasion for lively in-tellectual and social stimulation. Old people participate actively, not passively. They are affirmed.

Through listening to the stories of older people, religious leaders discover ways in which the community can be helpful. Older people have a multiplicity of needs. For some, it is for more home visitation; for others transportation to meetings; for yet others, assistance with the paperwork of insurance and other forms or for family counseling with themselves and their adult children to help them make a variety of decisions. Some need help in adjusting to wid-owhood, others need support as they live with their bodies' deterioration or with chronic illness. When using solution-focused thinking in care and counseling, religious leaders encourage congregants to state their needs and goals and to identify their own solutions.

As communities become intentional in their ministry, they often find that they need to become aware of the social policies affecting older people. They may need to lend support to programs that fund housing, nursing homes, hospitals, and other social services. Sometimes they need to be advocates for older people at city council meetings or community planning boards when decisions are being made affecting the quality of seniors' lives.

Perhaps the faith community's most unique role is to help mature people do the *soul work* of aging. Erik Erikson, who devoted his life to studying the human life cycle, contributed greatly to our understanding of the life tasks of mature adults. He taught that the central task in *mid-adulthood* is to become *generative,* to contribute to following generations by leaving a legacy of care. For some, this is done through the care and nurture they have given to family or other treasured people; for others, it is their contribution to religious or social causes and groups. For yet others, it is the mentoring they have given to students, or their artistic, scientific, or scholarly contributions.

Those in mid-adulthood are actively involved in making their mark both through generative activity and their own acknowledgment of it. When adults are successfully generative, they have learned to care. Those who fail to do so become stagnant. They are rejecting of others and their thinking becomes authoritarian. Those who learn to care, enter old age with strength.

Erik Erikson believed that the developmental task of *older adults* is to *become integrated* — and *wise*. Those who are unable to do this come to the end of their lives feeling despair. They treat others with disdain and use dogmatic thinking to find assurance for living.[33]

Old age is a time of meaning making. Many philosophers, religious leaders, and thinkers have made their weightiest contributions at the end of their lives as they have reviewed, synthesized, and integrated a lifetime of experience and reflection. Research on the brain has shown that the intelligence factor called "crystallized intelligence," the ability to make judgments on the basis of accumulated information, range of world knowledge and fluency and richness of communication — actually *increases* into the ninth decade of life.[34] This is the intelligence factor necessary for gathering wisdom. Erikson believed that it is the life task of all people to become wise, to make meaning of our own life experience. Remembering is necessary for meaning making.

In his brilliant lecture "Making Sense of Soul and Sabbath: Brain Processes and the Making of Meaning" given at the National Institutes of Health, pastoral psychotherapist and theologian James Ashbrook understood this kind of remembering to be *"soul work."*[35] He believes that the capacity for soul work is built into the very cells of our bodies and is at the heart of being human. He quotes neurosurgeon and brain researcher Richard Bergland who believes that *every* cell of the body "contains the well-chiseled molecules that give life to the soul and guidance to the mind."[36]

Dr. Herbert Benson, Harvard University cardiologist, who for thirty years has researched the relationship of faith to well-being, has also concluded that we are "hardwired for God." He argues that humans have a genetic blueprint that has made belief in an Infinite Absolute part of their nature. He says:

> By the process of natural selection, mutating genes deemed faith important enough to the survival of our forefathers and mothers that we were endowed with the same tendencies. Ironically then, it can be argued that evolution favors religion, causing our brains to generate the impulses we need to carry on — faith, hope, and love becoming part of the neuromatrix with which we approach living.[37]

The hunger for knowing our soul — remembering who we are — was planted into the being of everyone at Creation. In chapter 4 we referred to Dr. James Ashbrook's work that asserts that the soul expresses meaning and that the making of meaning depends on a working memory. This memory helps us gather our past events — the history of our unique self — so that we can make purposeful meaning of it. The soul, says Dr. Ashbrook, "constitutes that which each of us can call our own, that which distinguishes us from everything else in creation."[38]

From this earlier reading, you will recall Dr. Ashbrook's assertion that we do the soul work of reflection, synthesis, and experiencing because of the biorhythm of brain-mind. We have built into our bodies the cycle of work, rest, reorganization, creation. He sees that the biorhythm of the brain-mind reflects the gift of Sabbath: Sabbath has been built into the biochemistry of our bodies. Sabbath was given by God who worked, created, and rested because God looked upon creation and found it good. God has built that cycle into our bodies so that we might become intentional about doing the work of soul: We remember our experience, find God's presence in it, become aware of God's creation and sense its goodness — and learn to rest.

Faith communities need to help all their members learn to do "Sabbathing" — to rest and to reflect on God's presence and goodness. Many older people who have been workaholics, a condition fueled by the American work ethic and their own anxiety, must be taught to keep Sabbath. At the time of retirement they do not know how to rest and to reflect. For some, particularly men, retirement causes such stress that they soon become ill and in some cases, die. They experience time without work as a terrifying void. For them, learning to rest, to reflect on their lives and to find God's presence in it could make the difference between life and death. When religious communities help their members become intentional about soul work, they teach them how to become wise and to be ready for the dying process, where letting go and "resting in the Lord" leads to transformation.

We have been considering the relative comfort of many of our older Americans. Unfortunately, there are also many old people who live on the edge of poverty and even more who are poverty stricken. Most of these impoverished ones are women. The highest proportion of the elderly are women. Women have had a lifetime of earning less than men, therefore their savings and benefits for old age are less, too.[39] Many of the comfortable older people we described earlier were couples. After widowhood, many women's financial status changes dramatically. By the time women are sixty-five years old or older, 15 percent of all white women, 50 percent of all black women and 25 percent of all Hispanic women live *below* the poverty line.[40] The financial plight and lack of security of older women needs to be understood in the context of women's lifelong vulnerability to poverty. We recommend Pamela D. Couture's *Blessed Are the Poor?: Women's Poverty, Family Policy and Practical Theology* for its careful social analysis, theological reflection, and advocacy for shared, responsible action.

In spite of being worn down by the effects of poverty, many economically marginalized older people live highly generative lives — often nurturing their children, grandchildren, and great-grandchildren with wisdom and compassion. They often do deep soul work. Unfortunately, many do not get enough Sabbath rest. They work hard in some way or another until they die.

✂

Be a Gardener. Community care and counseling at life's beginnings draw us back to our metaphor. Counselors in community assist God's children as they grow in the natural cycle of life. A gardener must observe Nature to find how plants grow and develop. The counselor, too, must learn how God's children grow to become themselves — to thrive, blossom, die, and be transformed. This knowledge helps the counselor know how to *support the natural process* in our many beginnings. Counselors in community do not make these new beginnings — birth, maturation, independence, falling in love, new families, vision quests, meaning making — happen. Like the gardener, they are present at these times of beginnings and are *in awe.*

Chapter Seven
Reading and Resources
Publishing information is found in the Bibliography.

• The *insights of family theory and therapy* have contributed to community caregivers effectiveness. David C. Olsen's *Integrative Family Therapy* explains basic family therapy concepts and J. C. Wynn's *Family Therapy in Pastoral Ministry* shows how family theory can be applied by community caregivers. While Laurel Arthur Burton's *Religion and the Family: When God Helps* is addressed to family therapists, her understanding of how faith and spirituality can be a resource for healing family problems is useful to community caregivers. Herbert Anderson's spiritual insights and theoretical knowledge makes his *The Family in Pastoral Care* extremely valuable to caregivers.

In *Transforming the Inner and Outer Family: Humanistic and Spiritual Approaches to Mind-Body Systems Therapy,* Sheldon Z. Kramer uses meditation as well as holistic and family systems approaches to heal people's "internalized families" as well as their present family relationships.

• Deborah Anne Luepnitz reminds us that we must examine the underlying concepts of the theories and therapeutic techniques used in healing. See *The Family Interpreted: Psychoanalysis, Feminism, and Family Therapy* for her thoughtful *feminist critique* of the problem solving and systems theories that are used in this text.

• Robert C. Fuller's *Religion and the Life Cycle* is organized around Erik Erikson's developmental tasks and augments the family systems material that has been presented in this chapter. Margaret L. Hammer's *Giving Birth: Reclaiming Biblical Metaphor for Pastoral Practice* extends the "beginnings" metaphor that has been used. We also recommend Herbert Anderson and Susan B. S. Johnson, *Regarding Children: A New Respect for Childhood and Families.*

• Both the need for new coparenting roles and the reality of single-parent families have underscored the *need to support and nurture fathers* in their changing role and also to help families raise sons who will be effective fathers. See *Men's Changing Roles in the Family.* edited by Robert A. Lewis and Marvin B. Sussman; Ann F. Caron, *Strong Mothers, Strong Sons: Raising the Next Generation of Men;* and Frank Pittman, *Man Enough: Fathers and Sons In Search for Masculinity.* James B. Nelson, *The Intimate Connection: Male Sexuality, Masculine Spirituality* contributes to an understanding of this crisis.

• The *family is in transition* because of its new forms and demands. See Bonnie J. Miller-McLemore, "Women Who Work and Love: Caught between Cultures," in Maxine Glaz and Jeanne Stevenson Moessner, eds., *Women in Travail and Transition.* We recommend Betty Carter and Monica McGoldrick's *The Changing Family Life Cycle* for its overview. Also see Barbara H. Settles, Daniel E. Hanks, and Marvin Sussman, eds., *Families on the Move: Immigration, Migration and Mobility,* and Jeanne Stevenson Moessner, ed., *The Handbook of Womencare — Through the Eyes of Women: Insights for Pastoral Care.*

To understand the variety of *new family forms* more thoroughly, see: Patricia Kelley, *Developing Healthy Stepfamilies;* C. Margaret Hall, *New Families: Reviving and Creating Meaningful Bonds;* Shirley M. H. Hanson et al., eds., *Single Parent Families: Diversity, Myths and Realities;* and Teresa D. Marciano and Marvin B. Sussman, eds., *Wider Families: New Traditional Family Forms.*

• Many religious communities are becoming sensitive to the particular needs of their *gay* and *lesbian* members. For their depth of understanding we recommend Joretta L. Marshall's "Pastoral Theology and Lesbian/Gay/Bisexual Experiences," in *Journal of Pastoral Theology,* Summer 1994, and her *Counseling Lesbian Partners.* For spiritual resources see: Chris Glazer, *Coming out to God: Prayers for Lesbians and Gay Men, Their Families and Their Friends;* John J. McNeill, *Freedom Glorious Freedom;* Craig O'Neill and Kathleen Ritter, *Coming Out Within: Stages of Spiritual Awakening for Lesbians and Gay Men;* Eittredge Cherry and Zalmon Sherwood, eds., *Equal Rites: Lesbian and Gay Worship, Ceremonies and Celebrations;* and Larry Graham, *Discovering Images of God: Narratives of Care Among Lesbians and Gays.*

• Resources for ministering to *singles:* Kay Collier-Slone, *Singles in the Church: New Ways to Minister with 52% of God's People;* John R. Langraf, *Creative Singlehood and Pastoral Care,* and Natalie Schwartbert, Kathy Berliner, Demaris Jacob, *Singles in a Married World: A Life Cycle Framework for Working with the Unmarried Adult.*

• For *premarital care and marital counseling* see Michael E. Cavanagh, *Before the Wedding: Look Before You Leap;* and Charles L. Rassieur, *Pastor, Our Marriage Is In Trouble: A Guide to Short-Term Counseling.*

• Among the resources for *marriage enrichment* are: Herbert Anderson and R. Cotton Fite, *Becoming Married,* which develops the importance of autonomy and community in marriage. Herbert Anderson, David Hogue, Marie McCarthy, *Promising Again* focuses on the importance of renewing marital vows periodically in the face of significant changes. Jeanette C. Lauer and Robert C. Lauer, *Til Death Do Us Part: How Couples Stay Together* uses research of over 100 couples who have built a fulfilling marriage. Also see Pepper Schwartz's *Peer Marriage: How Love between Equals Really Works.*

How to Have a Happy Marriage is a practical six-week program for marriage enrichment developed by David and Vera Mace.

• Resources for ministering to *adults in midlife:* Mark C. Tennant and Philip Pogson, *Learning and Change in Adult Years: A Developmental Perspective;* Elizabeth Liebert, SNJM, *Changing Life Patterns: Adult Development in Spiritual Direction;* and Harold G. Koenig, M.D., *Aging and God: Spiritual Pathways to Mental Health in Midlife and Later Years.*

• Resource for ministering to *adults in later life:* Zalman Schachter-*Shalomi and Ronald S. Miller, *From Age-ing to Sage-ing: A Profound New Vision of Growing Older;* James J. Seeber, ed., *Spiritual Maturity in Later Years;* Thomas B. Robb, *Growing Up: Pastoral Nurture for the Later Years;* William M. Clements, ed., *Ministry with the Aging;* James N. Lapsley, *Renewal in Late Life through Pastoral Counseling;* and Margaret Fowler and Priscilla McCutcheon, eds., *Songs of Experience: An Anthology of Literature on Growing Old.*

Care and Counseling
at Life's Many Endings

O Earthmother from whom we grow;
  sandy gravel into whom our roots branch wood
    and sap deep down,
  bless us in our night-sleep, in our death and decay.

Bless us, dark earth as we give back
  that which we have received
  as we make a forest of blessing a ridge of blessing
  for the future to grow upon.

Chinook Psalter[1]

Those who live close to the earth have always known the cycle of beginnings and endings. They have observed that all return to the earth to enrich it so that new life may grow. "The grass withers, the flower fades" and are then plowed under the ground in autumn for new life in the spring. The psalmist proclaims that while grass and flowers wither and fade,' " The steadfast love of the Lord is from everlasting to everlasting." (Psalm 103:17)

And so it is with the human life cycle. We are drawn into new beginnings that must have endings if we are to move on to another place. Endings are exciting, for change is happening, but they are also times of loss. Our loss causes yearning for another time — when we were totally dependent, resting in our mothers; when the world was new; when we were innocent and playful children; when we were discovering our sexuality and that of others; when work was new and interesting; when we were consumed with new babies and the joys and confusion of parenthood; when our bodies were stronger and more agile; when our memories were clearer and more accurate.

When we remember those times that have ended, we remember the selves we were then. We would like to go back — sometimes to do it differently; sometimes to savor it. The admixture of excitement and loss, dependency and independency, is experienced at every ending and beginning in the life cycle. Children experience it as toddlers and again as first graders; when they enter college or whenever there is leave-taking from the family. They again experience excitement and loss when they form an intimate partnership and create a family. They experience it as they become embedded in work and family and then again, when they emerge from that embeddedness — trying to find and be themselves in a more singular way. And, near the end of life, they experience curiosity, wonder, and loss as they anticipate death.

The ambiguous nature of beginnings is true of endings as well. When you understand the ambiguous response people have toward all change, you can help them be more self-accepting and less frightened. Often people believe that they are *supposed* to feel a certain way — joyful at beginnings; sad at endings. They are confused when they feel sadness at the time of their wedding or relief as well as sadness at a funeral. They fear that something is wrong with them when they experience what is really an understandable mixture of emotions.

People often do not know when some endings occur. They look back and only then realize an ending has happened. It is after someone is in a new job that he or she will look back and say," I really 'left' my old position four months before I left to come here. I see now that when we finished that big project, I was no longer engaged in the work." We, as counselors, also have experienced this confusion in marriage counseling when we worked with a husband and wife who both seemed engaged in the counseling but the counseling did not help. We only learned later that one or the other had not known that they had emotionally left the marriage even as we were trying to help them *be* married. The husband or wife discovered after being with a new partner that they had "left" their former marriage much earlier.

At yet other times, endings are painfully obvious and the loss is immediately experienced. This is particularly true when one has lost a loved partner through sudden death, or a corporation moves and one must relocate or lose one's job, or one has a catastrophic illness.

Endings and the beginnings that accompany them *offer second chances for the uncompleted endings of a former time.* No one ever completes all of the work of each stage of life. No child is totally ready for first grade; no one has matured enough to be completely ready to leave home; no one has resolved all issues with parents before they marry or form other committed relationships. Most people may not be completely grown-up, but they are grown up *enough* to marry. No one has worked out all of their problems before a second marriage. No one has finished all of their parenting job or their personal issues with their children before the children leave home. All people have left unfinished business behind, which they absorb as they go on to the next stage.

In our discussion of the formation of new families we described how young children become more babyish when a new child comes into a family. At this time children experience an *ending* to their established place in the family. Regression is their second chance — when their parents understand it as such — to complete some unfinished business. Older children need additional attention and a chance to be dependent, as well as to be rewarded for being "bigger." When their regressive needs are patiently met they will not have to live their future lives being *overly* independent, not expecting nurture. Nor will they be overly needy and dependent, trying ineffectually to get in adulthood what in childhood they missed. Parents who help their children take care of the "unfinished business" of infancy will allow it not to have to be addressed — at least not so powerfully — in another stage of life.

Because you understand the principle of "second (and third — and more) chance" you can educate and support people who are at the points of endings or beginnings to take advantage of those occasions to grow. It may be in a home visit that you learn the young parents are frightened as they bring a new baby home. Parenting seems overwhelming. They may laughingly say, "We have this baby, but the hospital did not give us the instruction book." In addition, they are letting you know of their wish that someone was taking care of them. When you label their somewhat embarrassed desire to be "cared for" as "unfinished business," which eventually must be attended to, although it may need to be put on hold for a few weeks, young parents do not feel so out of control.

Young parents will be particularly comforted if they have already heard you speak about "unfinished business" in sermons or in some other community-care context. Marriage brings an ending of young people's need to be fiercely independent, to stand apart from parents. With this ending comes another chance for a new dependency. Young couples particularly need understanding about a "second chance" if they are not to be frightened by the natural regression that occurs when people marry. Because marriage is a second chance to meet old needs, new couples are often confused when they find themselves acting "young" and wanting a partner to supply needs for parenting that they had forgotten they had. If couples do not know that it is common, they may not only feel strange but frightened and alienated. When couples understand that they are not really asking their partner *to be a parent*, but rather to help them get something that they did not get earlier, they can relax.

You have many opportunities to offer community care and counseling to those who experience life's many endings. Because you understand the complexity of life transitions, you can help your members move through these transitions with insight that will also help them to receive the grace of the "second chance."

Not all endings are an outgrowth of the *family* life cycle. Some occur dramatically and traumatically in the *human* life cycle when bodies age or are ill; some occur when relationships are ruptured, when couples separate and families experience divorce, or when friendship fades. Some are caused when jobs are lost or people retire. Some are the result of changes in communities. Some are caused through death. All endings are occasions for your care and counseling.

Loss When Marriage and Friendships End

"Pastor, is there such a thing as a funeral for a marriage? Maybe if there were, I could accept my divorce better. I feel as if someone had died. If there were a service, I could invite my friends and let everyone I care about *know at once.* I hate the messy way I tell people about it. I try to put a civilized spin on it, but I'm still so angry. I feel so betrayed. I also feel stupid. I should have known he'd leave. But he always said he wouldn't leave like his father did."

Religious communities have an uneasy truce with the concept of divorce. While Jewish, Roman Catholic, and Orthodox Christian groups have had methods whereby members could have approved ecclesiastical divorces or annulments, all religious groups have considered marriage sacred and have expected members who marry to be committed for life. Some groups will still not marry those who have divorced without religious sanction.

Now with one half of the new marriages performed ending in divorce, clergy are having more and more experience with counseling and then offering support when couples divorce. Often, prior to the divorce, clergy have done brief counseling, and then made referrals to marriage counselors as the marriage strained and then broke. Sometimes one of the partners leaves the religious congregation at the time of the divorce. At other times, both members and their children remain in the religious community, which then has to deal with the reality of the family's brokenness.

While we have not heard of public funerals for marriages, some form of healing liturgy for broken relationships would be helpful to those suffering from divorce. Some couples arrive at divorce reluctantly, after deciding that their differences are unreconcilable. In these instances, both partners may have spent years trying to change each other — and themselves — to fit an idea of marriage. They married an idea, not each other. Often, through psychotherapy or other processes of self-reflection, they have given up their idealized version of marriage and have found some peace. Such couples would welcome a liturgy where they could ask each other's forgiveness, experience God's forgiveness, and release each other from their vows with respect and care. Such a service would be painful as well as freeing. Because such healing liturgies do not typically exist, you might feel called upon to create them.

Many divorces end with more acrimony than the one we have just described. While the marriage itself has been painful, the respective lawyers may have "upped the ante" for the sake of larger divorce settlements. Often child-custody battles have also been fought in the process. People who end a marriage amidst this contentiousness often need to be healed from the process of divorce itself. They are full of rage, pain, and humiliation.

Because in our time 50 percent of marriages end in divorce and 61 percent of remarriages end in divorce,[2] it is necessary for counselors in community to have a way of conceptualizing this phenomena. Family theorists see it as an interruption or dislocation of the traditional family cycle. Even when families divorce, life has to go on — preschoolers begin kindergarten; children become teenagers. But the family is in disequilibrium; when parents' relationships change, all the emotional relationships in the family change. If emotional issues are not resolved, all family members will be hindered. Often remarriages fail because the emotional work of the first marriage was not finished.

Family theorists Betty Carter and Monica McGoldrick believe that those who succeed in the emotional work of divorce are able to retrieve themselves from the marriage. They say, "Each partner must retrieve the hopes, dreams, plans, and expectations that were invested in the spouse in this marriage. This requires mourning what is lost and dealing with hurt, anger, blame, guilt, shame, and loss in oneself, in the spouse, in the children, and in the extended family."[3] Families after divorce need to restabilize. When counselors in community understand the developmental sequence that restabilization requires, they can be helpful to families. Carter and McGoldrick have charted *dislocations that divorce causes in the family life cycle*. We include it in *Appendix C* for your use.

Counselors in community are often baffled about how to give community care to those injured in the divorce process. Sometimes those hurt will come to religious counselors for counseling or referral. Many times they are too embarrassed and have a difficult time even coming to religious services. It is often through home visits that clergy and lay counselors will be able to speak with them about their pain. Community caregivers are also often troubled by their knowledge of the continued toxic effect of the divorce on the children and in those visits sometimes are able to speak plainly to the parent about their concern.

Counselors in community sometimes have difficulty dealing with anger — either their own or that of other people. After a divorce, people are often angry or depressed. It is preferable, in most instances, that one be angry rather than be depressed. Depression is sometimes anger turned against the self. Sometimes, in counseling recently divorced people, counselors in community try to get them to drop their anger saying, "It does you no good." Usually this advice is *unhelpful*.

The person seeking counseling following divorce is usually a woman. Women tend to remain in religious communities as heads of households following divorce. Women are often deserted by their husbands before divorce and they have very good reasons for being angry. Expression of this anger is often helpful. If women are helped to become assertive and to express their feelings, it gives them energy that they need to carry on.

In doing community care with recently separated or divorced angry women, it is important that counselors carefully listen to the reasons for their anger. In all probability, they were not able to be heard and understood by the people who left them. Underneath the anger is the pain caused by abandonment. And, with that pain, is shame. It is humiliating to be left. Even if one has initiated the separation and divorce, there is often unresolved anger to be experienced and faced. It is only after some of the anger and pain are unloaded in the presence of a counselor who listens with concern and respect that the member can move on.

The recently divorced woman often takes the blame and feels the stigma for the fractured family. In addition to living with the humiliation, she is also the one who must now care for the children and possibly support them financially. While this is almost always the case with lower income women, middle income women, too, *functionally* bear most of the burden for child care after divorce.[4]

Faith communities need to discover how to be of practical help to families who live with loss caused by divorce and then who must adapt as single-parent families. Communities, through self-examination, can begin asking: "How can we provide an arena where women can express the anger they feel by being left, without adding to their humiliation?" "What practical help do single parents need and can we provide some of it?" "How can we help fathers to be able *not* to leave?" "Have these fathers had their own absent fathers?" "Do these fathers have a fatherly self identity with skills to be a husband and father?" "Can our community be a place where parenting skills can be learned?"

After asking and seeking answers to these questions, faith communities can respond to the needs of divorced people and single-parent families by opening or referring to day-care centers or programs for continued education and job training for single mothers; having classes, forums, workshops on issues facing single parent families; sponsoring support or social groups for single parents; having workshops for religious education teachers and youth leaders on the special needs of children and adolescents who grow up in single-parent families.

Faith communities who are listening to the needs of families after divorce may find that counseling individuals is not enough. Many families suffer not because the single parent is not managing responsibly, but because she needs more money if her former husband is not paying child support or better health insurance policies because her part-time job does not provide benefits or more adequate after school care. To help parents meet these needs, religious communities need to support public policies on behalf of children and families.[5]

Marital separation and divorce are *public* — your community knows when members suffer loss because of them. But other members in religious communities may, at the same time, be suffering more *privately* over the loss of a personal relationship or family connection. Counselors in community need to be sensitive to those who mourn these more private losses so that care can be extended. Sometimes you learn of these losses when a member comes for community care or brief counseling. At other times, you will learn about them through the grapevine.

Private loss is lonely and hard to bear. However, when religious communities are open, members can reach out to each other and share their pain. It is through prayer that care can be extended to those suffering loss without revealing identities. Communal prayers can be offered for the healing of hearts that are broken through ruptured relationships. Those with private pain often respond to such prayer, and come out of "hiding."

Loss: When Work Is Ended
— Voluntarily or Involuntarily

Freud believed that to be able to love and work, and we would add, play, was what healthy adulthood was about. Many in American society would declare, "And the greatest of these is work."

Undeniably, work is a significant experience in our lives, an *anchor* to which our self-esteem, identity, friendships, and sense of purpose is tied. While people need to work to make money to live, many believe work is more than their means of survival. It is a way they express themselves. It is the way they "spend" their lives.

In our society there has been a difference between "men's work" and "women's work." "Work," as the term is usually used, means "working for money." Because the work of a homemaker is hard — but unpaid — many women feel that their work does not count. Men's work has more status, power, higher pay, and bigger benefits, than even the comparable work done by women. Usually women's "money" work tends to be in service industries or support services. While "officially" women have less status, functionally they often "hold the business together." It's not uncommon to hear, "She's just the secretary, but she knows more about what's going on than the Dean," or, "The nurses here know more than the doctors" (although one can no longer assume that those doctors are men). While women chafe because of the inequality of their income and benefits in the workplace, they often enjoy the knowledge of their competency and the importance of their role. They also value the friendships they have made at work.

Workers — both men and women — whether they are in white or blue collars, whether they do domestic, service or factory work, find meaning and satisfaction in the jobs they do. People count on work. When their jobs end they are often destabilized. They feel lost.

Counselors in community have long been aware of the stress people experience when they retire or lose their jobs. It is not uncommon that they become depressed or physically ill in the year following this change. Often, even those who have adequate retirement income and have been planning for retirement find this adjustment difficult. It is not uncommon for retirees to change too many of their "anchors" at once. A stress overload occurs when work ends through retirement. With it there is a change of status, daily routine, work friendships, and the personal validation that came through the job. For most, there is the adjustment to having less money, but more time. Some move out of a house and into an apartment. Others move to another part of the country. Friendships, church or synagogue affiliation, family ties become disrupted in this move. And stress is placed on the marriage: Partners must rely on each other to meet most of their needs until they make new friends in their new location.

Counselors should be able to help members become knowledgeable about the stressful nature of retirement so that they can plan to avoid as much stress overload as possible. It is also helpful to inform people that *it takes time to adjust to major life moves.* Often people believe that, because they have settled into a new apartment in six months, they have adjusted to this major life move. But they have merely coped with the move, they have not integrated and assimilated its effect. It usually takes three years to synthesize the information about internal changes; This includes *all* the major changes of life — work, relocation, divorce, death of a loved one. There is a neurological basis for this. It takes time for our brains to reorganize, assimilate, and consolidate memories of the past "worker self" so that a new identity of the "now retired from work self" can begin to be formed.[6] When one stops working, either voluntarily or involuntarily, self-identity is changed. This is what Gertrude Stein meant when she said, "I forget and I remember all the dim beginnings in me; of the many lives I have had."[7]

In addition, many people in our society experience loss not from the absence of work, but from the ways in which work itself is changing. Americans make fewer things, and industries that service and support the financial, information, media, and computer sectors are growing. Many who work in these service industries have a different relationship to work itself. For example, entering data into computers requires little use of one's self; one does not see an end product. While factory work on an assembly line was thought to turn people into machines, workers at least had the satisfaction of knowing that they were helping to create a car. While some people who work in the world of computer technology find that job satisfaction comes almost completely from the salary, others are intellectually challenged and are learning to think in new ways.

The work location also is beginning to change. Many people no longer work in offices; they work at home using personal computers that tie them into central offices or databases. More and more workers are self employed, selling their services to clients on a project basis. These workers spend more time on the telephone, often working with cellular phones, even as they drive. The social interaction and friendships that developed in the workplace are now missing.

While there may be less unemployment than a decade ago, more people are working at part-time jobs. Many in the so called "Generation X," those graduating from college in the late eighties and nineties, have found it difficult to get "real" full-time jobs that include health insurance and other benefits.

If college-educated young people are having difficulty crafting work identities, impoverished young people are in an even more difficult position. Many poorer high school graduates face a future in which they may never make more than minimum wage, which guarantees that they will never adequately support a family. The plight of high school dropouts is even more grim. Education and skills divide those in the workforce. This division is seen when one compares the wages and benefits of college and high school graduates: In 1992, male college graduates earned 83 percent more than men with high school diplomas. In 1993, employer-sponsored health coverage was available for 76 percent of college graduates, 60 percent of high school graduates, and 36 percent of high school dropouts.[8]

Often the loss that people feel about the unreliability of the place and nature of work is not articulated but it contributes to attitudes of cynicism and feelings of depression. Some come for community care or counseling because they are experiencing anxiety about work. As companies and corporations merge or downsize, those who are not laid off work harder and longer. They are more exhausted and anxious. Others are discouraged by the changes in the system and seek early retirement, for which they are emotionally unprepared. Others are laid off or are expected to find some other niche within their company. For many, the emotional security they felt because of their work has been replaced by apprehension. Their company or corporation is no longer the "family" that they can depend upon to take care of them during their working lives or provide security for retirement. Many middle-class workers are anxious; they hold jobs but are uneasy about their job standing and fearful about their children's future.

Faith communities are finding a ministry in supporting their members in this changing work environment: In one congregation, business executives meet at their church with those who have lost jobs to help them write their résumés. Other congregations have formed support groups for those who are unemployed and who need counseling and retraining. Some have periodic lunch meetings for those who are socially isolated because they work at home as independent contractors.

Religious communities that proactively address issues of work in discussion groups, workshops and sermons create an atmosphere in which members do not have to bear their anxieties alone.

For many, changes in the shape, place, and constancy of work has offered them an opportunity to grow spiritually. They have time to reflect on who they really are. The Protestant work ethic, which became America's standard, not only placed an emphasis on the value of work and thrift, but also implied that the more successful one was as a worker, the more one was blessed by God. Many who lose their jobs feel that not only have they failed themselves and their families, but they have lost favor with God.[9] Until they lost their jobs, many did not know that they had internalized the belief that God loves only those who are successful workers. This belief contradicts the Judeo-Christian message that God loves us for who we are, God's children, not what we do. When those who have lost their jobs are ministered to through community care and counseling, they have the opportunity to discover they are accepted.

The loss of a worker's identity is a kind of death. When people are retired, laid off, fired, or given an enforced early retirement they go through the same stages that Elisabeth Kübler-Ross describes as the process of death and dying — *denial, anger, bargaining, depression and acceptance.*[10] Those suffering the loss of work identity need help in moving through *all the steps* of this process. They need to know that the healing will take time.

In the meantime, many must move on and find work that tides them over. In some cases they can find work that is even more satisfying if they identify *what* about their previous job they miss most. Do they miss the work itself? Or having a place where they belonged? Do they miss the validation that was given them by others or by their success? As they discover what their loss is about, they may find other ways to meet these needs. For many, the time after job loss can be one of self-exploration and meaning making. Those going through this journey need the support and love of their religious community.

Loss When the Holding Environment of Community Changes

Most people take their neighborhood or community for granted although it is the supportive environment that is a holding container for their lives. For most, it is their own home and their own family that is their main focus — until there is change.

Forty years ago when a young family would build a house in a new suburb they expected it to be pristine and "modern" forever. That suburb, once the home of young families, now is filled with older people. The houses have increased in value; middle-class young families cannot afford them. The older people resent paying school tax. The churches and synagogues, which once had large religious education plants, now have unused space. The community now needs services for the elderly. Nursing homes are needed, not nursery schools.

Communities change. Main Streets become deserted because business is now being done at shopping malls. Middle-class neighborhoods deteriorate. Working-class neighborhoods are gentrified. Although their parents' houses have increased in value, adult children cannot afford to buy a house in the old neighborhood. Orchards are uprooted so that housing developments can be built. City apartments are demolished so that office towers can be constructed. Only buildings that have the protection of "historic preservation" remain the same. After a neighborhood has been transformed, its inhabitants often ask: "How did this happen?" "What happened to our church, our synagogue, our community association?"

Counselors in community can help their members by reminding them about change: everything changes. Changes in a community need to be seen in a larger context; these changes reflect the flux of the economy, population shifts, and cultural metamorphoses. When these changes come, the religious communities change also. Old families move away; new ones come. Some come from different traditions within the same denomination. Southern Baptists move to the North; Korean Presbyterians move to Brooklyn. The prominent families of the synagogue move to Florida. People come with new needs and expectations, and many congregations find it hard to adapt. They hold on more tightly to old traditions. They are anxious about the unknown shape their community is forming.

Communities that are knowledgeable about change are not as shocked by it. They have been helped to find ways of adapting to it and welcoming it. They can discover that change can be revitalizing. Inner-city churches that were closing have been invigorated by Asian immigrants. Suburbs that had been geared to young families can find new ministries as they respond to the needs of the older people who live there.

Those who lead congregations in transition need to pay attention to the mixture of anger, loss, relief, and celebration that are part of the community's response. When congregations are growing because new people are moving in, a congregation may be happy but it is also mourning members who have left. Clergy need to help members acknowledge both feelings. Communities, like individuals, experience mourning. However, this mourning does not indicate that a community is not open to change: communal mourning is a necessary part of change itself.

Change in community self-identity takes time. Just as with individuals, communities have memory — corporate memory. It takes time for the community to assimilate and synthesize the self it was — when the strong, patriarchal minister was there; when it had a large youth program; when it was predominantly white, not Hispanic; when it was small and struggling — so that the old identity is consolidated and can make way for realistic awareness about the way the congregation is now.

People want their religious communities to be unchanging and stable, to be a given. But life does not work that way. Communities that acknowledge change, and struggle with it, can be places of living education for their members. It is when institutions deny their flexible boundaries that they become ossified. Rigid institutions, like rigid people, easily break.

Communities try to understand the complexities of change in light of their religious tradition. These raise ethical and theological questions for congregations as they look at the changes in the traditional family, in the attitudes of their young people about religion, in the demographics and economic base of their community, and in medical treatments that prolong life.

Living religion has always been in dialogue with life's changing ways — to make sense of it, to find God's purpose in it, and to minister in the midst of it. Often it is your religious community, itself, that needs your ministry of care as it lives with change.

> *God of change and glory,*
> *God of time and space,*
> *When we fear the future,*
> *Give to us your grace.*
> *In the midst of changing ways,*
> *Give to us still the grace to praise.*
> — Al Carmines[11]

Community Care at Life's Endings: Facing Our Fears

Communities — religious and secular — expect clergy and other counselors in community to be experts on life's final endings: death and the rituals around dying. Clergy, in fact, manage matters around death: wakes and viewings, eulogies and rituals, care for the mourners. But often clergy and other counselors in community share our culture's aversion to the process of dying. They, too, are afraid of death. In trying not to think about death, they become preoccupied by obsessive concerns about health and dread aging. They value youth because they fear death.

Counselors in community, like other Americans, are not prepared for dying because they are protected from witnessing it. Fifty years ago most people died at home. Today 80 percent of Americans die in hospitals.[12] Because death has become "unspeakable" they also lack information about the dying process. Recently more information has become available to the general reader. For example, Dr. Sherwin Nuland, in his book *How We Die*, removes the medical mystique as he explains the actual processes of dying of cancer, heart disease, and other illnesses to make them more understandable and to help his readers be less afraid. Marilyn Webb's splendid book *The Good Death: The New American Search to Reshape the End of Life* thoroughly examines end of life issues and our growing openness to prepared dying.

Our fears have caused us to bracket consideration of death. Although religious Americans may have theological understandings that give them hope, many still share our society's fear of the dying process. Many American religious communities are not aware that they wish to deny death because the *theme* of death is central to their religious practice. After all, many of the primary events in Jewish life are the High Holy Days of repentance, renewal, and remembrance of those who have died. In Christian practice, Jesus' death and resurrection and the hope Christian believers have in eternal life are at the heart of their religious experience. Because of their faith, they believe that after death they will be with God in Heaven. Nevertheless, they are afraid of the act of dying.

Many religious people compartmentalize their understanding of death. They believe the *physical experience of dying* belongs more to a category labeled "hospitals and mortuaries." They put *being dead* into a "spiritual" compartment and focus on eternal life.

Often counselors in community truly do not know what to say when ministering to dying people. They are busy pushing away their own fear of dying. Because of their fears, sometimes they do not acknowledge that the dying person *is* dying. Instead they will ask the person about the results of the latest test that has been performed to prolong life. Sometimes they collude with medical specialists who try to prolong life through technical means. When both their doctors and their minister or rabbi have invested in the cure, it is difficult for the patient — who often knows instinctively that he is dying — to speak about his experience. Therefore, he is alone.

As you help your community be a place where fear of dying can be examined, you can ask yourself if you, too, become frightened when you look at your aging face in the mirror. Are you forced to push these fears aside as you try to perform your tasks of community care? Perhaps because of your faith you do not fear death. But perhaps you too are afraid of the *dying process*. You may already be conscious of these fears and are facing them. However, some of your fears of dying may be hidden. Uncovering them can bring relief.

You might ask yourself, as you do a self-inventory: "Have I had actual experiences with dying people that frightened me? Do my fears come from what I've seen on TV? Am I afraid of dying because I fear pain or don't want to give up control? Have I seen too many people linger on life-support systems? Do I feel guilty because of unfinished business with people who have died? Am I afraid I will die alone? Do I feel helpless when ministering to dying people because of the unknown?" As you address these questions you may feel the need for support and counsel from trusted friends, professional peers, or other counselors. You may also need more information about the dying process from courses, reading, and the supervision of your ministry.

When you have faced your fears you can, *together with your community*, grapple with questions asked of you in the course of community care such as: "I'm getting old and I hate it. How can I have faith?" "Why has God let my child have cancer?" "What is my suffering good for?" "Who's going to tell my husband that they can do no more?" "I've been advised to have a radical mastectomy. I don't know how to think about it. Can you help me?"

Communities that struggle with these questions *together* are integrating their physical experience with their religious experience. *Fears are lessened as they are talked about.* Not only can you address the subject through preaching and prayer, but there can be workshops, support groups, and classes to address the complexities of this concern in such topics as:

"Our bodies are changing: issues for women around menopause."

"What happens to our bodies when we age?"

"What spiritual practices prepare us for death?"

"How can we truly live till we die, even when we are sick or old?"

"What needs to be considered when planning for health-care proxies or living wills?"

"When we think of dying, what has scared us the most?"

"How can I love my body when it hurts me?"

People who suffer from fear of death are often unconnected to their bodies. Even those who *seem* connected because they are preoccupied with not aging, or who compulsively exercise, or who are worried about their health, are usually attached to *an idea about how their body should be.* To help decrease their fear of dying, they need to be helped to be comfortable and accepting of their body — *as it is.* As they experience body-spirit connection, they can become more accepting of their bodies and their bodies' limitations. This acceptance will help them not to expect modern medicine to perform an impossible miracle, the elimination of death.

Those who are less frightened about death will be able to experience the *awareness of their bodies' limitations as a gift.* When in midlife their bodies catch their attention through the beginnings of arthritis, or high blood pressure, or eye strain, they can receive these symptoms as messages from the body that say: "Don't take me for granted. Appreciate and care for me. I've been good to you." When this message is received, they can listen to their bodies to find what is needed. Is it more attention? More rest? Less food? More movement? It is easier to learn to respect and care for one's body when one is not afraid. Then it is also possible to experience the joy and pleasure of being alive.

Community Care for the Sick and the Terminally Ill

Although being expert about the body has not been religion's job description, being compassionate and caring for the sick has been a major concern of religious groups. Jewish children learn from their families the importance of performing *mitzvahs,* active compassion for those in need. This religious belief has shaped the vocation of many doctors and scientists. Christian children have learned from their families stories of Jesus' care for the sick and the outcast. Because of this core belief, religious institutions have founded and supported hospitals, medical research centers, nursing homes, hospices, and other institutions that care for the body as well as the soul. Today, religious professionals are pretty much the only ones who continue to make house calls on the sick and infirm.

While it is the clergy's role to visit those who are in hospitals, nursing homes, hospices, or at home, lay members of religious communities often share in this ministry. Some communities have programs where members, in addition to visiting the sick, drive those who are ill to doctors' appointments or wait with them while they have chemotherapy or other procedures. Other congregations make and bring meals to those who are elderly or sick. Some sponsor day programs for the elderly. In addition to caring for individuals, some communities have groups supporting those who are ill. We will describe such a program sponsored by a local congregation:

In the early 1980s, a small congregation, largely composed of young adults and small families, felt as if hit by a plague. In a six-month period, five young women — mainstays of the community — were diagnosed with breast cancer. The women, their families, and the religious community were totally unprepared; most had only been in a hospital to have tonsils removed or babies delivered. They did not know how to *think* about cancer. They could not even ask questions about their condition that would give them the information they needed to make decisions about proposed surgery and treatment. As one after another were diagnosed, the congregation went into denial. No one wanted to believe it was happening. However, soon the congregation awakened.

In the next two years, because of community involvement, the women, their families and the congregation had a crash course in the etiology of cancer and its treatment. The women learned to talk to doctors without being intimidated. They learned how to be patients; their families learned how to maximize their care in the hospital. They and the congregation learned about ways to support health through diet and nutrition, visualization and relaxation techniques, and meditation. All learned about the possibilities for alternative treatments. Some families worked with a family therapist to resolve issues and tensions so that healing could be enhanced. The community listened to the women as they struggled to make meaning of their cancers. The women asked questions: "I've been healthy; I've lived reasonably. Why has this happened?" "Is it my fault?" "What's going to happen to my children?" "The treatment doesn't seem to be working." "Do I have the right to say 'no' to more treatment?"

The community had healing services. They also had parties where those who were ill were celebrated. At these parties friends shared loving memories with them — the kinds of things usually reserved for eulogies at memorial services.

Within three years, all five of the women had died. The community continued to gather together. They learned about mourning and about being healed from grief. In gratitude, the family of one of the young women established a memorial fund for the congregation to use to share what it had learned about caring for those with cancer. This money was used to staff a weekly support group.

The congregation wished to continue this as a ministry for their local community because they felt that they had been given a gift. They had learned that *to be healed* did not necessarily mean being *cured* of cancer. Although their members had died, they had each become more *whole*. Through their experience, the congregation had learned how to be with and care for those with cancer. They had knowledge to share. Because of their friendships with hospice nurses and doctors, they already had a referral network. They let these professionals know that they were forming a new group and invited them to send people to it.

This support group was led by an oncology nurse who had become aware of the congregation through the loving concern they had shown to her patient, their member. She had begun to attend their religious services and was delighted when the board asked her to lead the support group. She was assisted by members of the congregation, who by now had become knowledgeable about cancer care and could share their knowledge as well as prepare nutritious lunches. Members also taught relaxation and visualization techniques and led in meditation and prayer.

In these weekly meetings, group members talked about their fears and other concerns and felt group support. They were able to ask the leader questions about cancer and its treatment and were able to get coaching — both from the nurse and each other — about coping with the side effects of treatment. They learned about ways to be healthy even with cancer. They learned about the special stress caused by cancer and its treatment and the beneficial role of diet and supplements. They learned visualization techniques to support healing.

Two group members went into remission but stayed in the group to support others. Several members died. The group had helped them prepare for dying as they listened to their concerns and supported them in prayer and meditation. Even though they had cancer themselves, several members visited them in the hospital and comforted them by being a quiet, loving presence.

The cancer support group is a small community within the community of the congregation. The original leader has taken a break, but other members are there to step in. While there has been no complete "cure" for cancer, the group has found that there is a "cure" for the isolation — and sometimes, stigma — which accompanies cancer. That cure comes through the loving support of knowledgeable friends.

Helping People Die: A Time of Loss and Transformation

> *Today is a very good day to die.*
> *Every living thing is in harmony with me.*
> *Every voice sings a chorus within me.*
> *All beauty has come to rest in my eyes.*
> *All bad thoughts have departed from me.*
> *Today is a very good day to die.*
> *My land is peaceful around me.*
> *My fields have been turned for the last time.*

My house is filled with laughter.
My children have come home.
Yes, today is a very good day to die.
                              — Nancy Woods[13]

Until recently in our culture, the job of helping people die has fallen through the cracks. The role of doctors and medical scientists has been to keep people alive. Doctors have not been expected to be experts on preparing their patients for death. Clergy, on the other had, have tended to focus on preparing their members for the afterlife. Or to help them plan their funerals or memorial services, and to comfort their survivors in mourning. Usually, clergy and other counselors in community do not help people know what to expect of the dying process — or to prepare for death.

Today this is changing. Because of the Hospice movement and the response to the AIDS epidemic, counselors in community are learning with others to help people prepare to die. Like Marie in the following case study, they are discovering that people often know when their death is approaching and will let others know about their needs.

Learning to Translate Nearing Death Awareness

ELIZABETH: "I need you to come now. It's time. No one believes me!"
MARIE: "I'll change my appointments and be on a plane in the morning."

Marie remembered their conversation three years earlier. They were sitting in a coffee shop. Elizabeth had just come from the oncologist. Her tests for breast cancer were positive. Elizabeth said, "I'm going to beat this. Lots of people do. But, just in case, will you be there for me if I don't?" Marie recalled that she said, "Of course," but at the time, neither of them felt it would be necessary to keep the promise. Now the call had come.

When Marie arrived at the hospital after her transcontinental flight, she wondered if she had misunderstood Elizabeth's veiled message. Elizabeth looked sick, but she was full of strong will and purpose. She was talking about the new medical protocol that her doctors were trying. She was concerned about grading papers so that her students' midterm grades could be completed. Her husband was speaking about a drug that they had ordered from France. Her daughter was excited about being invited to a dance. Marie thought: "Maybe I got it wrong. Maybe she's not dying."

Arrangements were made for Marie to spend the night on a cot in Elizabeth's hospital room. About ten o'clock Elizabeth seemed to change. She began vomiting violently and had diarrhea. She was weak and she seemed to be "slipping." Marie was scared; never before had she cared for someone who was *really* sick. Elizabeth's nurses assured Marie that these upsets were a reaction to treatment, and with Compazine, Elizabeth would get a good night's sleep.

About midnight, Elizabeth dozed off. But soon she woke with a start, called Marie and then seemed to slip into what Marie thought was a trance. Marie took her hand and sat on the edge of the bed. Elizabeth's eyes seemed far away as she looked at Marie. Her usually remarkable, lucid thinking seemed strange. She seemed desperate to convey a message that had something to do with friendship. She was speaking complete sentences, but Marie did not catch their meaning. Marie, who had had years of psychotherapy in which she had worked with her own dreams, suddenly realized that Elizabeth's talk was symbolic. She was speaking in the language of dreams. Marie began to listen to her friend with a "dreamer's mind."

Elizabeth said something about "going on a long bus ride to see Daddy." Marie remembered that when Elizabeth's child, Ann, was small she and the child had great adventures as they went to see Elizabeth's late father. Marie asked, "Is Ann with you?" Elizabeth rather impatiently shook her head, "No!"

Marie had been holding Elizabeth's right hand. Suddenly, Elizabeth gave Marie her left hand as well and indicated for her to pull. Marie pulled hard and, with that, Elizabeth came out of her trancelike state. Elizabeth then said, "Don't be afraid. I was in a very restful place, like where I go in self-hypnosis or meditation, only much, much deeper."

Elizabeth seemed to come out of the experience refreshed and reorganized. Even though it was the middle of the night, she said: "Call my sister Jeannie. We have some family business to take care of. Ask her to call my brothers. I need them all to come." Elizabeth needed to talk to them about their mother's death. She was the youngest and her mother had died in childbirth. She felt that they had protected her and had never told her the whole story behind it. The sense of "not knowing" had bothered her all her life.

She also had the energy to talk about her husband's denial of how close she was to death. She told Marie that they had not talked together about their daughter's future. She needed to grieve with him over what she would be missing: her daughter's graduation from high school and college and her life as an adult women. She needed to grieve and then talk with him about his plans for Ann.

After this remarkable night, Marie was in the hospital corridor going for coffee when she met Elizabeth's oncologist. "What's going on?" she asked him. "I think Elizabeth is dying, but no one around her acts like she is!" To her amazement, the brusque doctor turned his head away as his eyes filled with tears. He mumbled, "I'm so angry. She's the most remarkable patient I've ever had. I just wanted to save her. I guess I need to give her husband the real prognosis."

Soon, Elizabeth was sent home with hospice care. In the three weeks before she died she was able to meet with her brothers and sisters, be open with her husband about her grief, speak with her husband and her daughter about her love for them, and even get her tutor assistant to grade her students' papers.

Her husband related Elizabeth's death to Marie: "As she was dying, she said to me: 'I have to get off the bus now. Is it all right?' I said, 'Yes, Betta. It's all right.' She closed her eyes and died."

Elizabeth was communicating to her friend out of what hospice nurses Maggie Callahan and Patricia Kelley refer to as *"nearing death awareness."*[14] They describe how dying people are able to communicate through symbolic language, dreams, and body language to those who are close to them that they are nearing death. In that communication they become aware of what they need to do before they can die peacefully and they are able to let their friends and family know what they are experiencing so that their loved ones can be comforted as they let them go.

Hospice workers, who act as midwives in the dying process, hospital chaplains, and those who work in AIDS ministry have been acquiring empirical knowledge about the dying process. As they share this information with those who are dying, their families and others who minister to the terminally ill, the terror about dying — caused by ignorance and lack of experience with those who are dying — is being quieted.

Because they have been with hundreds of dying people, these workers gain experience out of which they can answer a person with a terminal illness who asks: "I'm not afraid of death because of my faith, but I'm afraid of dying. What is it like? Will there be pain? Will I know when it's coming? How do I prepare?"

A hospice nurse who is asked the question, "Will I be in pain as I die?" can honestly answer, "No. You will be given medication for pain. I have been with many people when they die. They have died comfortably." It is necessary to note the context out of which the nurses speak. For the most part, those whom hospice nurses care for die at home where they are with family and friends who love them. The nurses and family have worked to minimize pain and maximize the comfort of the dying one. The nurses have also helped families understand the dying process so that they can be with the person as a "nonanxious presence." Most people however, die in hospitals, often alone, although hospitals, too, do their best to make people comfortable in their dying.

Whether they are dying in the hospital or hospice, people who are mentally alert have nearing death awareness out of which they communicate. When they are understood, they are able to prepare for their dying and their loved ones are helped to let them go.

Although nearing death awareness is related to "near death experience," it is not the same. Near death experience happens *suddenly* when one is drowning, has a heart attack, or is in a fatal accident. Reports of near death experience come from those who have been clinically dead (without heartbeat, breathing, blood pressure, or other signs of life.) After being resuscitated, they speak of experiences that are remarkably consistent, even when those report-ing them come from a variety of cultures. They report being "jerked back" from having seen their lives flashing before them; they report a place of in-describable beauty, a place of radiant light; they describe hearing beautiful music, seeing someone they love who has already died and who has come to meet them, and being in a place of deep peace, free from pain. Near death experiences are explored in Kenneth Ring's *Heading toward Omega*.

Nearing death awareness is more gradual. People who are dying slowly are in a process in which they often seem to be moving back and forth between the life of this world and that of the next. They can usually talk while they are in the midst of it, although they may not seem to be talking to you. Some-times they appear to be staring with a glassy-eyed look; sometimes they are distracted or look secretive. In other cases, they may be pointing to, or reach-ing for something or someone unseen. Sometimes they are waving. Sometimes they are picking at the covers or trying to get out of bed. At other times they will be agitated or distressed when they are unable to make the caretaking person comprehend their message.[15]

It is at the point in the process that Kübler-Ross calls *acceptance* that near-ing death awareness usually occurs. Elizabeth, when she called her friend Marie, had entered the place of acceptance: she knew intuitively that she was near death. During the previous years, she had vigorously fought her disease. She lived the experiences that Kübler-Ross describes — denial, anger, bargain-ing, and depression. Because she was an intellectual and social activist she did not spend much time bargaining with God. She fought and read and acted. She ate brown rice, she meditated, visualized, and studied the literature. And she was angry. By the time she called Marie, she had moved into another place; she was accepting that death was near, but she needed help to let go.

Elizabeth had always been a gifted communicator so she used her gifts to die well. She instinctively knew enough to call a friend who would understand her messages. She and Marie had collaborated on writing and other creative projects over the years; they understood each other's deepest meaning. Intu-itively, Elizabeth knew that Marie would not discount her symbolic messages as "ramblings," or "confusion," or "hallucinations." Unfortunately, the mes-sages of dying people are often dismissed by medical professionals or family as being a byproduct of illness or a reaction to medication. Marie did not know about the phenomenon of nearing death awareness, so she was unaware that many people when communicating out of this state speak of getting ready for or going on a journey. She simply knew that Elizabeth was telling her some-thing important as she talked in a rambling, symbolic way about going on a bus ride. After Marie asked Elizabeth if her daughter, Ann, was with her, and Elizabeth shook her head, "No," Marie understood that Elizabeth was telling her that she was on a journey, alone, to see her father, who was dead.

People in nearing death awareness often communicate their experience of "getting ready to leave" to those to whom they are close. Often they will ask about maps, or they will speak of needing to pack a suitcase. They will speak of train or plane schedules. They are communicating that they are getting ready to leave. Some will let friends know where they are going — like Elizabeth told of her journey to be with her father. Others seem to be seeing and speaking to someone who is there in another place waiting for them. They are not alone.[16]

Nearing death awareness helps people know what they need to do to be able to die peacefully.[17] Elizabeth also told Marie that she had asked Marie to pull her back from death because she was not ready to go. She had business to finish with her brothers and sister, her husband and her daughter before she could die peacefully. Elizabeth's husband told Marie about the peaceful look on Elizabeth's face as she died. While they were at the hospital together, Marie had told him about "the bus ride." They both believed that Elizabeth got off the bus and found her father waiting for her.

Hospice nurses, chaplains, and AIDS ministers have learned to communicate to people as they are dying about the experience of dying itself. By learning to recognize when people are experiencing nearing death awareness you can learn to decode their symbolic messages so that you may *be with them* as they let you know about their dying experience. Often counselors in community are chosen by dying people as the ones to whom to give messages. They will let you know what they need in order to die peacefully. Often people feel held back from dying because of concerns about those whom they are leaving behind or about other unfinished business. If you can understand their message you may be able to communicate the dying person's concern to the wife or husband. Sometimes, when the wife learns of her husband's reluctance to leave her, she can reassuringly convey a message such as: "I'm going to be all right. I have a plan to visit our son. I'm glad we moved out of the big house. I'll be fine in the apartment. You can let go now." Often, this provides an opening for the couple to speak together about the husband's fears and concerns. Sometimes you will learn that the person is waiting to die until a reconciliation is made or a loved one can come to the bedside. When you make this discovery, you can let family know.

When the dying find that their messages are received, they are relieved to know that even as they are dying, they are aware of their deepest needs and can ask to have them met so that they may die in peace.

> Jesus said: "Ask, and it will be given you; search, and you will find; knock, and the door will be opened for you. For everyone who asks receives, and everyone who searches finds, and for everyone who knocks, the door will be opened." Matthew 7:7–8

When those who are dying know that they have been heard, they are more able to face death with openness and trust.

Many cultures have practices that help people prepare for dying throughout their lifetimes. Traditionally, Native Americans of the Plains prepared for death by developing the death chant. In the adolescent rite of passage, young people would go out into the wilderness for a time of prayer and fasting and would then look for *their own* healing — or death — chant. The chant could be given to them by the Great Spirit or it could come from a grandfather or a dream. It was received at a time of deep centering. The chant was used *continuously throughout their lives* to keep their hearts open and their minds clear any time they were in danger or in need of healing. Its continuous use created an inner path, a way to healing and clarity. At death, one could trust "the way" to the Great Spirit as the chant was sung or heard by the dying one.[18]

Counselors in community are sometimes asked, "What will it be like when I'm dying? Is there something I should do?" How you will answer that question depends on your religious tradition. Some traditions have prayers for those to pray if they are still conscious at the moment of death; others have instructions, such as "let go; trust in the Lord; speak Jesus' name." Others instruct dying people to say the Rosary or recite the Jesus Prayer. Some traditions use candles and incense at the time of death to convey spiritual meaning. Native Americans are given crystals in which a person can see all the colors of the rainbow on which to meditate so that their souls may move into rainbow light.[19] Others are given religious icons to gaze upon in their dying.

Whatever your tradition, it is essential for you to help your community find spiritual practice that members learn to use in life to prepare for death, to help them not to be afraid, to know perfect love that casts out fear (I John 4:18).

Because the moment of death is often kept out of the family's sight in medical facilities, people are often not even aware that they do not know what to do with dying people. They need information.

Most people die in hospitals or nursing facilities where many die in their sleep or under heavy sedation. Often family and friends are kept from the person in his or her dying — sometimes because he is on machines in intensive care units, sometimes because a last, intense procedure is being used to revive him, or sometimes because hospital staff does not want to deal with the confusion of a grieving family. In such instances, a doctor or nurse may come out into a waiting area and say abruptly to a worried family, "I'm sorry, your father is gone."

There are times when family should be able to be with those who are awake and aware in the moments before they die. When dying, people need to be in the presence of those who love them. However, without the help of a chaplain or loving nurse, some family members may sometimes be frightened in this situation and could become hysterical and intrusive. They would not be able to provide the calm serenity their dying loved one needs.

To prepare your community, you may need to turn to other traditions — or to memories of your own — to know what was done when dying took place at home, usually with clergy present. Older Irish Catholics will remember that their grandmothers had a special place for candles and holy oil for anointing so that when the priest came when one was dying, all was prepared for last rites. They were not anxious about dealing with the body; everyone knew how to do a "laying out." Jewish families knew that a group of women who were specially trained would come to help with the ritual washing and preparing of the body. Every Jew knew the funeral customs — the burial, in a simple wooden coffin, would happen within twenty-four hours; they knew where to find the boxes for sitting shivah. There were always candles in the house. Everyone knew the prayers. And Protestants knew that the community would bring food and comfort to the house after the service and burial. The minister was with them, saying prayers, reading Scripture and knowing what to do.

When someone dies in the hospital, it is much less real. After death, the family is usually allowed briefly to see their loved one, who is now referred to as "the body." The family is left to wander, shocked and aimless, in the halls. Some need to make phone calls. Where do they go next? The ground has fallen out from under them.

Clergy, community caregivers, and hospital chaplains can make a difference. With the intervention of hospital chaplains, families are often allowed to be with their loved ones as they are dying. Now, not only chaplains, but members of community care teams can be there to show families what to do. Because members of congregations are being trained to know how to give comfort to dying people and their families, as more people are dying at home with hospice care, clergy and lay people can be with the family. As in this example:

Sheila, a member of her congregation's ministry team, was with the family and John, who was taking his last breaths. She said: "Let's gather around the bed now, and hold hands and just be together." To his wife, she said, "Hold his hand; you can speak, he still hears you."

As he is dying, she prays:

> Into your hands, O merciful Savior, we commend your servant, John. Acknowledge, we humbly beseech you, a sheep of your own fold, a lamb of your own flock, a sinner of your own redeeming. Receive him into the arms of your mercy, into the blessed rest of everlasting peace, and into the glorious company of the saints in light. Amen.
> *Book of Common Prayer*[20]

They are silent together as John's breath slips away. After more silence, she prays for the family. She then holds and comforts each member as they sob and hold each other. Their grieving is unrestrained; she has been real with them.

With the trend toward hospice care and the shorter hospital stays mandated by health insurance, more and more people will again be dying at home.

Religious communities have an opportunity to teach their members to die in serenity supported by their faith and rich religious traditions.

Facing death is liberating and life affirming. Many people dream — and daydream — about their funerals. They create scenarios about what is said about them in eulogies or who at the wake seems most upset about their death. These daydreams are important because they reveal the dreamer's goals and values. If, in the dream, a man's child is talking about his "wonderful father," the dreamer, when waking, will recognize that he will have to tend to his relationship with his son so that those words can actually be said at his funeral.

Spiritual gifts often come out of another's pain and suffering. So it is with our present understanding of dying and mourning. Much of the present attention to dying and the literature about it comes from the testimonies of those dying from diseases that they could not fight because of their impaired immune systems, and from the testimonies of those who have worked with them.

In this country, the human immune virus (HIV) first spread among homosexual men, in contrast to the rest of the world where heterosexual women first contracted the disease. When these men became ill many — who were well educated, articulate, and proactive — formed organizations to care for those who were ill and actively fight AIDS. They also raised the public's consciousness about death. Until the time of AIDS, Americans did not see death being center stage in movies, TV shows, or Broadway plays. Now dying is talked about.

In response to the epidemic, many religious communities have supported organizations that provide housing and care for those who have the virus or who, because of it, are sick with opportunistic diseases. Others have themselves provided support groups for those with HIV or AIDS. While these groups provide ministry to those with the infection, often it has been the religious community itself that benefits most because of the gifts of spiritual wisdom that those in the groups give them. The following tells the story of one such support group.

※

In responding to a new member's question, "What's this group like?" Bill replied: "It's like a life raft in the middle of a lake. It's always here when you need to swim onto it to rest or be supported."

The group was started by an urban church that, in the late 1980s, had developed a deep concern about the AIDS epidemic. Some of its members had the virus; others were professionals in AIDS work, and many of the members had already lost friends and colleagues to illnesses related to AIDS. In trying to decide what to do, the congregation developed a task force that, among other issues, considered the spiritual needs of persons with HIV and AIDS. Out of this concern, an AIDS support group was formed.

The group was open to anyone with a concern for AIDS. Over a six-year period, the group met weekly and was made up of people with HIV or AIDS, their friends, partners, and parents. It was also open to professionals who worked with those with AIDS, chaplains, a psychiatrist and nurse, AIDS educators, pastoral psychotherapists. It also had volunteer AIDS "buddies," mourning friends who had died and those who volunteered their time to care for children with AIDS and who were there to mourn babies — who felt like their own — who had died. The group was held together by an awareness that their spirits were aching. The AIDS crisis demanded a spiritual response.

The meetings began with individuals sharing "where they were at the moment" — what they needed, what their concerns were for others, what they wanted from the group that night. After the members had connected to each other, they practiced spiritual meditation growing out of Quaker practice. Before moving into centering silence, members named those they wished to "hold in the light,"; they were then led in a body relaxation and breathing exercise that helped their bodies relax and their minds clear. There then were brief readings that could be used to meditate on as the group moved into a half hour of silence. Out of that silence members then shared the "messages" that had come to them — some in images, some in thoughts. The group closed with all present holding hands in silent prayer and then giving each other the kiss of peace.

When the participants developed their format for meeting, they had no idea that they were being given a gift that would help members in their dying. This practice is just what is needed to prepare for death: relaxing, centering, letting go; being one with one's breath; feeling the love and support of friends and family; becoming comfortable with silence; listening to one's deepest longings, and believing that needs will be met. When members became too ill to come to group, the group went to them in the hospital or at home. By the time they were bedridden, members with AIDS had meditated with others in hospital rooms and now the group was coming to them. Group members were often with them at their deaths, holding them in the light and breathing with them until the last.

In the silence, members were given wisdom about living with AIDS. Because people do not die of AIDS, but become ill of a disease they cannot fight, many of the group's members lived with AIDS for a number of years. In an early meeting of the group, they had received the message from Scripture: "Choose life so you may live." The group continued to struggle with what it meant for them to "choose life." Some felt it was to learn to live with positive, not negative, energy. This meant that they must become forgiving and live with compassion. They must learn to forgive those who hated them. Those with the AIDS virus have been scorned; they have been treated as modern lepers; they have been stigmatized. Yet group members knew that they were to "pray for those who persecute you." Members struggled with how to do this.

It finally became apparent to them that the best way to prepare for their deaths was to live their lives to the fullest in the present. This meant helping each other live with the virus or the complications of AIDS. They became knowledgeable medical experts, sharing information about the disease, its treatment and side effects. They helped each other learn about nutrition. They gave massages. They assisted in wading through the red tape of medical forms and welfare systems. And they did this with humor and style.

Birthdays were celebrated; at death, people's lives were celebrated. At the next meeting following a member's death, the group invited friends and family to come to the meeting. By this time, the group knew many of them because they had met at the hospital or cared together for their member at home. These special meetings were times of celebration and deep grieving, when memories were shared out of profound silence.

The group borrowed Eastern Orthodox liturgy using an ancient prayer that ends, "May his memory last forever." Holding the memory of members "In the light" became an essential part of the group's practice. Often, as members were approaching death, they would become aware of the presence of members who had gone on before them. And often the room was filled with "a cloud of witnesses" who seemed to be giving comfort and guidance.

The group had many experiences of listening to messages of nearing death awareness. In some instances, members knew "it is time to go home," to return to their family. One returned to his family in Puerto Rico and another to his family in the South; both were accompanied by their partners, also group members. They died soon after they returned to their families. Their lives were celebrated by the group when their partners returned. Other members knew what they needed before they died. One asked the group to pray for "buoyancy." He died peacefully the next day. Another knew that he should move from his walk-up apartment. Before his last illness, his friends moved him into a new first-floor apartment where he could be cared for easily.

Many of the members had to learn to receive care. They were independent, strong willed, resourceful people. Some had been professional caretakers of others. Often, even in their illness, they were worried about failing to take care of others. One of the lessons they had to learn was to release some control and let themselves be loved and taken care of. A message that was often received in the silence was: "Let go. Learn to be loved."

By the time the sick members of the AIDS group faced death themselves, they had come to their own understanding of what it was "to die well." One, on his deathbed said, "Dying is such a big responsibility." In his dying, he was concerned about how his family was coping; he was also wanting to die with honesty and integrity. Some members died with full consciousness and clarity. One died before he had truly accepted that he was at the "dying stage"; he did not have the chance to say "good-bye." Another died with group members around him, although he had been in a coma for over a month. One member died reconciled with his family around him. Another died more pained by his family's desertion of him than he was by death itself.

After so many group members had died, many in mourning suffered survivors' guilt. For them, "seek life so you may live" was hard, for it seemed like betrayal. They, like their friends who died, were in the prime of life. Their many losses made them seem older. They prayed for courage to live with vigor and to be able to love again.

Faith communities that have groups supporting those who are dying know that those who are faithful companions until death must be very committed. Some members have the energy to keep many dying people company. However, sometimes companions cannot walk all the way on the journey because they must pay attention to themselves. They know they are burning out.

It is necessary that caregivers be encouraged to take care of themselves — to rest, take some time off, eat well, and think of themselves. Family therapists know that it is essential when helping someone recover from a serious illness that the caretaker be attended to. Sick people get better when all the attention is not on them. People who are dying do so with more ease when they do not have to worry excessively about their partners and friends whom they are leaving behind. Those who take the long walk toward death with their friends need to learn when to "take a break," to become refreshed. Those who are dying find a guilty, worn-out companion to be a pain in the neck.

Being with friends who are dying stirs up feelings, many of which are negative. Sometimes the dying person seems demanding, impossible to please. Sometimes caretakers are angry and feel abandoned, even before death has taken their friend. Sometimes the caretaker feels taken for granted. Sometimes, when being with those who are having nearing death experience, caretakers feel frustrated because they are uncertain that they understand the message. It is important that caretakers not push away these unpleasant feelings. Sometimes it is not possible to deal with them directly with one's dying friend. However, it is helpful to acknowledge these responses and when possible, to be alone to experience them: to be in a room and experience the anger in one's body — to stay with it, breathe into it, and watch the anger change into another emotion. Often the anger becomes pain, but the pain is curative and will lead eventually to peace.

Those in the AIDS group just described were able to walk on the long journey toward death with their friends because they had had time in group to be quiet and to experience their own feelings. They could feel and discharge emotions and not let them build up. Any support group that cares for those who are dying needs to have some method by which people can acknowledge, express and accept the negative feelings that come up in the course of "faithful companioning."

By practicing regularly to rest, letting go and relaxing into openness; listening into silence to hear God's message; trusting that when one asks, one receives; being with one's own breathing and becoming aware of the breath of others: letting go of control and accepting love — one is living life in the present and also preparing for death.

> *Empty your mind of all thoughts.*
> *Let your heart be at peace.*
> *Watch the turmoil of beginnings,*
> *But contemplate their return.*
>
> *Each separate being in the universe*
> *Returns to the common source.*
> *Returning to the source is serenity.*
>
> *If you don't realize the source,*
> *you stumble in confusion and sorrow.*
> *When you realize where you come from,*
> *you naturally become tolerant,*
> *disinterested, amused,*
> *kindhearted as a grandmother,*
> *dignified as a king.*
> *Immersed in the wonder of the Tao (Way)*
> *you can deal with whatever life brings you,*
> *and when death comes, you are ready.*

—Tao Te Ching 16[21]

Blessed Are They Who Can Mourn: They Shall Be Comforted

Mourning is the process that all who experience loss must go through to be able to begin again.

The infant feels anxious when she discovers that she is separate from her mother — but she is comforted as she "takes her mother in with her eyes." Her comforting mother becomes internalized. The toddler who ventures off from her mother carries her favorite teddy bear so that she will not feel "lost." When she goes to nursery school the teddy bear goes with her, while her mother cries in the corridor because she is losing her "baby."

How do we bear a lifetime of losses — losses that are necessary for our new beginnings? We are more able to bear grief if we have "taken in" comfort — our comforting mothers and their stand-ins, the transitional objects of teddy bear and other nurturing presences. God in us was first known by us in our mother's arms. Our image of God as comforter reflects these internalized experiences.

Many, however, bear their losses without enough internalized comforting presences. Some mothers were not able to be emotionally holding. Therefore, their babies were unable to become attached to them. Some children were physically and emotionally abused and therefore did not have a safe inner space to return to for comfort. Some children have lost a parent by death or have known the loss of a secure family because of divorce and feel a sense of emptiness inside. Yet, even those who are not sturdy grow up and, amazingly, keep beginning again.

What is the process by which grief is lived through? How do abused children move into life without losing hope? How do widows who were married for forty years reorganize their inner experience to become independent, to think of themselves as "I," not "we"? Where does this courage come from? The human spirit is fortified by Grace.

Counselors in community ask themselves these questions as they seek to give words of comfort to people who mourn the multiple losses of life. When one grieves one is mourning for one's self, the self that was connected to and was a part of that which was lost. All grief work is about the "reworking of the self" because of loss.

Many pastoral theologians and researchers conclude that successful grief work is about reintegration and redefinition of both the individual mourner's self and the family as well. Wayne Oates writes about mourning leading to "the acceptance of loss and the affirmation of life itself."[22] D. K. Switzer sees loss activating the reexperiencing of early losses and "the loss of the other is experienced as the loss of one's own self." Therefore, it is the self that needs repair.[23] Kenneth Mitchell and Herbert Anderson say, "Loss of any kind requires reaffirmation of the self."[24] They also say "All change involves loss, and where there is loss, there is grief. If a family is able to grieve, it is more able to adapt to change."[25]

It helps us to know that it takes time for the brain to synthesize and assimilate images of the "old self," the person one was when the loved one was alive or "before the children left," or "when I still had my old job." Mourning cannot be rushed; it takes its own time. Counselors in community must convey this information to those who are grieving and then reinforce it.

Because the reintegration of the mourner's self is done through memory, counselors can encourage those who are mourning to reminisce about the person who died and about their life together. It is most helpful when the whole family does this together, so that the family memory can be reknit. The person who died must be seen for the real person he was, warts and all, before the family can put him in another place and then experience the gap his leaving created. Encouraging families to make scrapbooks or family picture albums gives them a chance to remember. Looking at old home movies or video tapes revives old memories. Giving away clothes and possessions with thought and care, rather than "getting them out of here," is also a way of keeping memory alive and honoring relationships. Being together on the deceased's birthday and on other important anniversaries also keeps memories alive. Counselors in community can help the process by keeping track of the deceased's birthday and date of death to send notes of remembrance to the family on those days. In the first year following a death, the family task is to remember, not to forget. Remembering helps the brain synthesize past events. This frees those who are mourning to live in the present.

Some mourners resist the pain of remembering, particularly early in the process. They find it easier to have a fixed picture, sometimes romanticized and idealized or even vilified, of the person they lost. Early in the mourning process people are in shock and often are numb or depersonalized, feeling separated from themselves. Remembering can warm the soul and cause numbness to thaw; it is a psychic microwave. With this thawing necessary feelings, good and bad, are allowed to be felt.

It is helpful for community caregivers to make frequent home visits to those who are in the early stage of mourning to support them as they courageously remember and then deal with a mixture of feelings — grief, anger, guilt, love — that are felt as the early numbing thaws. As mourners accept conflictual feelings and thoughts, they can sort them out. Mourning is a process of letting go. Conflict needs to be named, sorted, resolved before one can let it go. Letting go usually requires forgiving — forgiving one's self and forgiving the one who left. Mourning is a spiritual activity.

People in the first year of mourning feel disoriented and disorganized; they often say, "I just can't get anything done." They are unaware that they *are* working — as they sort out memories, identify and resolve conflicts, try to know the "real person" they are grieving so that they can allow him truly to go. Counselors in community can be reassuring to those who feel discouraged for not "snapping out of it." Counselors and caregivers can point out that they are being *inwardly* active.

In the highly instructive practices of mourning in the Jewish tradition, there is predictable movement and understanding. The dead are buried within the first twenty-four hours. The reality of a loved one's death is faced immediately. After the burial and for the next seven days, the family sits together — to bear the shock, to allow the heart to break, to remember together. The religious community cares for the family, bringing in food, saying prayers, and being with them in the presence of the candle that is lit in memory of the loved one's soul.

For the next thirty days, the mourners do the work they have to do, but they are still tender with themselves. They do not go out to entertainments. They allow space for their pain to surface, for memories to come up, for the reality of the loss to sink in. It takes at least a year for inner reorganizing to be accomplished after such grief. It is not until a year after the death, when the family again gathers to dedicate the deceased's tombstone, that those in mourning are encouraged to *fully* move out of mourning and to embrace life. Jewish mourning practices are all about helping those who grieve to be able to live. Even the kaddish, the prayer said throughout the year in memory of the dead, praises God for life.[26]

The timing of these practices is right. This is the amount of time it takes for mourners to disconnect from preoccupation about their dead loved one and to become engaged and hopeful about their own lives. Much can be learned from these traditional practices.

Grieving is not a disease to be cured; one does not "get over" a loved one's death like "getting over" the flu. Even when grief is worked through, it later resurfaces. A father may feel deep pain at a daughter's wedding because his wife, her mother, is not there. A certain food, or special place, can cause her memory, and grief that seemed healed, to emerge suddenly. Even when a widow or widower is happily remarried, pain of another's death can be unexpectedly felt. Community caregivers can let mourners know that this is predictable. It is not a betrayal of a new relationship, but rather an indication that one's past lives in one.

The death of another, even when it is expected, is experienced with a certain degree of disbelief. However, grief is greatly affected by the quality of the experience with the deceased while he was dying. When family members and friends are able to be with one who knows and accepts that he is dying and is able to say "good-bye," they are not left with such a sense of regret and incompletion, feelings that often torment those in grief. When family members are aware of their loved one's wishes because they have understood the messages that come out of his nearing death awareness, there is less unfinished business to be grieved over later.

When a death is expected, often families are able to speak with their dying loved one about her wishes for her funeral service — music, Scripture, prayers. These conversations can be extremely painful because the approaching death becomes very real, but they also can be times of comfort. The person who is dying is able to talk about her faith and about her sources of comfort. And the family can be both sad and moved by the sense of completion she is experiencing. Emotions that are experienced before a loved one's death lighten the load of grief.

There are a number of variables that affect the grieving process and its outcome. Individuals and families *can* experience life and renewal when a loved one dies. On the other hand, grief denied can lead to depression, family fragmentation, and even suicide.

The shock that comes when a family learns of sudden death or when they are not allowed to be with a loved one in the hospital as he is dying is compounded by not knowing what to do next. When families do not know about the dying one's preference for where he wishes the funeral service to be or whether he wishes to be buried or cremated and whom he wishes to officiate at the service, they find making these arrangements even more painful.

Family therapist Rabbi Edwin Friedman speaks of death and funerals as "rites of passage" that allow families to regroup themselves and to heal. This rite of passage is a chance for families to learn to communicate more clearly and for individuals in the family to become more self-differentiated.[27] Families need to begin to make these changes *before* their family member dies. Families that pay attention to the messages of nearing death awareness are given time to begin to change. Often it is a *family* matter that a person wants resolved before death. The dying one might ask to speak to his brother, from whom he has been distant. Or he may need to speak of a worry about a child.

When family members, including extended family, communicate with each other before a member dies, the shape of the family already begins to change. It is necessary for each member to deal directly with the person who is dying rather than have the communications delivered by someone else. *Each* family member needs to say good-bye and to affirm his relationship with the person who is dying. Making these contacts before a person dies reconnects the family and starts building support for those who will soon be in mourning.

Mourning is not done in a vacuum. When families are functioning well, they come together to support each other as the family rearranges itself. This is a time when family roles can change as well. A member who has been the family "worrier" can resign from her job. A member who has been too distant can come closer and assume some responsibilities. Secrets that have been kept, such as a nephew's "secret marriage," can be revealed. And family anxieties can be lessened. Friedman observes that in the year after a death there are often significant changes in a family — marriages occur, children are born, and individuals make significant moves in their lives.[28]

Of course, the way families deal with a loved one's death can also cause the family to be less healthy. Families do not provide a healing function when the cause of a member's death is withheld, or not all members are notified about the death, or secrets are alluded to but not revealed, or people are criticized for showing too much grief — or not enough.

Counselors in community who understand how families work can help them become stronger when death reorganizes them. When planning the funeral, clergy can find out who *all* the family members are, even those not present. In this way, the cleric can learn if the family has members who are cutoff and can inquire about them. When preparing the eulogy, it is useful to have the *entire* family together — spouse, brothers, sisters, children, parents, sons and daughters-in-law, grandchildren, grandparents, "adopted" family members — *everyone,* so that each person can say something that can be woven into the eulogy. The family, in hearing everyone, can experience itself as a whole entity. While the family may not be fully experiencing the gap — after all, the dead one is very present in memory — they will soon have to reorganize without him. This is easier when there has been shared memory.

The experience of grief is greatly affected by the nature of the illness, the cause of death and the stress that these have already placed on the family.

Sudden death gives the family no warning and the family reacts with shock. Whether the death happens before birth — stillbirths, miscarriages, and abortions — or whether it is caused by suicide or homicide, sudden illness or accident, the family has had no time to say good-bye or to resolve relationship issues. The intensity of the grief reaction to these deaths is greater than with more prolonged or "natural" deaths.[29] Often, because of the nature of some deaths, speaking of them becomes taboo. Families begin to have many difficulties that are caused by the stress of secrecy although family members do not consciously relate their problems to the death.

The age of the person who dies is another variable in the grief response. The death of a child profoundly affects the parents' relationship. Researchers have found that when children die in hospitals, their parents undergo such stress that following the child's death, 70 percent to 90 percent of them separate or divorce.[30] The statistics are not so staggering in the cases of children who die at home with home care. Family therapists have found that the impact of a child's death is particularly great in families where the child is unduly attached to the parents' sense of well-being or sense of self.

Terminal illness and then loss through death of a parent has lasting impact on a young family. It has been shown that in the first year of a spouse's death, the remaining parent is vulnerable to suicide or serious illness. This is particularly true for men. The effect of parental death is very much tied to the family life cycle: the death of a mother or father when children are small has a different effect than when children are adolescent. No matter when in the cycle it happens, however, a death that occurs when the parent is in the prime of life leaves a gap that can never be filled. It causes profound disruption and continued stress. It is difficult for grief work to be completed. The remaining parent has to work twice as hard to fulfill financial, domestic, and emotional responsibilities, and children often suppress their grief to make it easier on their parent, particularly if the parent is trying to hold back his or her grief, to get on with it. They need help.

Counselors in community can play a valuable role in supporting families that lose a parent or a child. Because you have in all probability been with families as they tended for those who were terminally ill, have been with them at the time of death, and have conducted the funerals, memorial services, and burials, you are trusted and you can lend support as families regroup. It is important that you immerse yourself in the literature of dying and mourning so that your interventions can be the most helpful. But you cannot do it alone.

Community Care for Those Who Are Bereaved

Providing community care for the bereaved is the work of the *entire* religious community. It is too big a job for clergy to do alone. It is labor intensive. Mourners need regular home visits and other support to move through grief work. Some will need brief counseling or referral to a psychotherapist or a specialist who can medicate for depression. Families that have lost a parent will need practical help and support as they find ways to adjust to their one-parent situation. Often elderly couples who together have been able to manage independently, become destabilized with the death of the spouse. After this death, the widow or widower will need help in managing daily tasks, such as remembering to take medications. Sometimes, friends from church or synagogue step in to help the widow or widower establish systems for managing or for moving into a supportive housing situation.

To care adequately for those in your community who are mourning, you need to engage your entire *wholeness network*. In addition to trained laypeople who do home visitation, perhaps you will need psychiatrists who can evaluate mourners for depression. You will need the resources of a social worker who can help destabilized families reorganize and elderly widows or widowers make plans for supportive housing or other care. You will need to be able to refer to grief groups that offer both support and socialization.

The year following a loved one's death is a dangerous time. Sometimes it is difficult for those who have close contact with mourners to know whether the sadness and pain they express is normal grief reaction or if the person is clinically depressed and needs psychiatric attention. Often callers from religious communities are privy to the mourner's true emotional state. When laycallers visit they are often told "how I really feel." These callers are placed in a position of enormous responsibility. They need to know how to judge whether the mourner is appropriately sad or in need of professional help. Then they need to know to whom to go with their observations so that appropriate interventions are made.

Many religious communities train laypeople to do grief work, helping them become empathic listeners, understand the process of mourning, assist those who are stuck in the grief process, and recognize danger signals for depression. Sources for appropriate training materials are listed at the end of this chapter.

※

People in mourning often become frightened by the depth of their grief. They worry that they are suffering serious depression. You can help them by educating them about the normal course of mourning. People are reassured when they learn that early stages of mourning resemble clinical depression. But the acute symptoms pass with time.

The emotional state that we commonly call "depression" is complex. Sometimes the term is applied to people who seem to have depressed personalities, sometimes it is used to describe a depression that has come on quickly and seems to tackle the person to the ground. At other times, depression describes a part of a mood cycle that may include bouts of mania. The American Psychiatric Association has named, defined, and systematized these disorders and described them in the *Diagnostic and Statistical Manual of Mental Disor-*

ders, IV. We will use their distinctions to help us understand the relationship of the "normal grief" of bereavement to a "major depressive episode."

Grieving comes on quickly following a loved one's death. The mourner displays symptoms that are similar to those of major depressive disorders. Those suffering grief need to be told that their response is normal and appropriate to their loss. When ministering those in grief you might at times suggest that they consult their doctors for medication for sleep or appetite. However, you need to tell them that medication will not take their sadness away. Their loss needs to be felt.

It is normal in the first few weeks after the shock of a loved one's death for mourners to be distraught and profoundly sad. They will say, "I'm so depressed. I have no appetite. I have difficulty sleeping (or I sleep too much)." Some will be anxious and agitated. Others will think pessimistic or even suicidal thoughts: "I can't face life without him," "It should have been me; I just want to die."

Many mourners will display the signs of depression: they experience themselves as *helpless, hopeless*, and *worthless*. They will have disturbances of appetite, sleep, concentration, energy. They will cry easily or they will be blocked from feeling. All of these are also symptoms of major depressive episodes.

Those who experience "normal mourning" will, with time, find their intense grief lifting. Although they will feel sad and will continue to do grief work, they will have returned to themselves. C. Parkes, a researcher who has studied bereavement, has found that, in the first stage of grief, which he calls "numbness and denial," the mourner feels numb and is in shock. These experiences last from five to seven days. The second stage, which he calls "yearning," lasts for several weeks. The mourner experiences intense longings for the deceased, is preoccupied with thoughts and has occasional visions. Often, there are feelings of self-reproach and suicidal thoughts. The third stage, "disorganization and despair," lasts for about a year. During this time, the intensity of the yearning and other feelings gradually diminish and there are various degrees of apathy and aimlessness. In the last stage, "reorganization," the bereaved person begins to see a hopeful future without the deceased.[31]

Those who are mourning naturally will move in and out of grief. They may remember a funny experience with their loved one that makes them laugh. They may forget their sadness for a moment as they become distracted by the antics of a grandson. And then they move back into a memory that causes pain.

At the beginning of the process of mourning, people have a distorted sense of time, which soon becomes corrected. They speak of their loved one in the present, not the past tense. Time seems to move more slowly or more quickly than clock time. There is confusion about the sequence of time.[32] In both major depressive episodes and grief reactions, there is a *distortion* of time:

the past seems more real than the present. The hopelessness of depression is related to the sufferer's inability to project through imagination into the future. As natural mourning progresses, the past becomes the past; the dead are buried and good-byes are said.

People mourn at their own pace and they use their own coping styles. Counselors and caregivers who are involved in the community care of those in bereavement need to respect the individual's process and not give a message that implies that the mourner is "not doing grieving correctly." Mourning takes time.

But time does not heal everyone. There are some mourners who, after learning of a loved one's *sudden* death, seem to remain in a state of shock. They continue for months to experience the death as unreal, and they feel themselves to be "unreal" as well. There are some who do not move in and out of sadness, but are *stuck* in depression. Often those who are stuck in some part of the mourning process, who do not seem to be moving toward a reorganized sense of themselves, have had a history of anxiety, panic attacks, or depression. Sometimes the present situation has reactivated a loss from the past. These mourners need special help.

Because of breakthroughs in psychopharmacology and research in the neurochemistry of mood, there are new medications that are helpful to those who are reacting to grief in acute ways. These medications do not take the grief away. Rather, they allow people to regain a neurochemical balance. Mourners may then remember the past so that they can redefine themselves and live in the present.

Cultures differ in the length of time that feels "normal" for acute grief reaction. A rule of thumb, however, is, if after *two months* you observe that the mourner still has any or some of the following you may consider that *an evaluation by a professional is appropriate:*[33]

1. *acutely* sad and depressed and has *lost* his/her capacity for happiness,
2. "slowed down," functioning poorly in daily tasks,
3. obsessed not only with thoughts about the deceased or her relationship to him, *but with other thoughts* as well,
4. *continuously* self-reproachful, even when he knows rationally that he is not at fault, guilt-ridden or feeling worthless,
5. believes that she or he would be better off dead,
6. having psychotic symptoms — hallucinations, delusions — that *do not* include the deceased.[34]

What may have begun as an appropriate response to loss may have moved into a major depressive episode. Also, if after two months a mourner is still feeling "numb" with "not me" feelings or still not able to believe his loved one is dead, or still experiencing anxiety or panic, he or she should be referred for consultation.

Before you make a suggestion that a referral is in order, it would be help-ful if you could gently ask questions that would give you more information. You will begin to get a history of the mourner's past emotional upsets. People who are depression prone have usually had bouts of depression throughout their lives. Sometimes these have been accompanied by obsessive thoughts or compulsive activity, and anxiety. It is helpful to know if one who seems stuck in grief was depressed *before* his or her loved one's death.

It is sometimes hard to judge how a mourner who often seems to be slightly depressed, is progressing with mourning. Such people *may have an untreated dysthymic disorder in addition to suffering from grief.* Dysthemic disorder is the diagnosis of those who have had a depressed mood *for two years,* most of the day, more days than not. In addition, those with this condition have at least two of the following: poor appetite, or overeating, insomnia, or hypersomnia, low energy or fatigue, low self-esteem, poor concentration, or difficulty making decisions.[35]

Not everyone whom you observe as having a severe grief reaction would describe themselves as having a history of depression. Some might say that they are shy and "overly sensitive" to slights or rejection. Often in marriage, those sensitive to rejection have been protected by the closeness of their mari-tal relationship. When their spouse dies they experience the death as rejection and they are thrown into deep depression; This condition is called "rejec-tion sensitivity." Others, who have not shown previous signs of depression, might be sensitive to stress. The stress overload of caring for someone who dies after a long illness can cause the stress sensitive person to destabilize and to become seriously depressed.[36] Others who suffer depression may feel guilty about unresolved issues with the person who died; their depression is related to internal conflict.

As you are sorting out for yourself whether your community member is suffering from "normal grief" or depression, you need to get a picture of his or her past experience. You can begin by asking her to "name" her emotional state: "When you are feeling this way, what do you call it?" She may say "ter-rible," "depressed," or "desperate." Then using her word for her condition, you can ask: "Have you felt _____ before? What was going on? What other deaths have you suffered and did you feel _____ then? How far back can you remember feeling _____? Did anyone else in your family feel _____? If you felt _____ before, what did you do to feel better? Have you ever had professional help for this problem? Did it help?"

Solution-focused questions are also useful: "Is there an exception to the _____ (feeling) ? How do you make that happen?" The miracle question: "If there was a miracle in the night and these depressed feelings disappeared, how would you know? What would you be doing?"

These questions will give you information you can use to paint a picture of your community member's situation. You will know if she is worried about herself. The solution-focused questions will let you know if, even in imagination, she can think of what "feeling better" would look like. An inability to answer the "miracle question" can sometimes be the sign of depression.

In the discussion on making referrals (chapter 5), I described community care and counseling sessions in which members were already in your office and had moved to the place in which *they were asking* for help. In ministering to those in mourning, it is highly likely that you have gone to your member's home and it is *you* who is reaching out to her with the suggestion that she seek professional help. How do we square this with the maxim, "Don't try to change people" ? Your situation is compounded by an additional problem; when people are severely depressed they cannot think clearly. Often a symptom of depression is passivity, and the inability to take initiative on one's own behalf. Depressed people often hold on to an idea that they are helpless and everything is hopeless, that nothing will make a difference. If the mourner was also the caregiver in her spouse's long terminal illness, she may also be fed up with doctors. However, your intervention in these cases is not "to change" but to refer for emergency triage.

In spite of difficulties, you have a responsibility to make a helpful intervention in the life of one who is in danger. Untreated depression can be fatal. Thankfully, because of medication and the skills of sensitive psychotherapists, many people no longer have to suffer the debilitating pain of depression.

Your questions can also help a mourner remember what he or she has experienced in this condition before and how in the past he or she has changed. The following questions invite these memories to surface.

CALLER: "Have you ever had professional help before?"
MEMBER: "Yes, I did see a doctor before. He gave me medicine, but I didn't like the side effects."
CALLER: "Did you keep using it anyway?
MEMBER: "Well... yes."
CALLER: "Did it make a difference?"
MEMBER: "Yes it did...I eventually felt better...maybe it helped...I don't know."
CALLER: "It might make a big difference. Why don't you give your doctor a call?"

❧

CALLER: "So, if while you were sleeping a miracle happened and this terrible heavy feeling was made to go away, how would you know it?"
MEMBER: "I would know something had happened if I didn't dread getting up in the morning. And I wouldn't be exhausted. You know I just can't sleep anymore. I guess a real miracle would be if I felt like having breakfast."

CALLER: "Well, if you could get up in the morning and not be tired and then felt like breakfast, would that make a big difference for you?"

MEMBER: "Oh, yes. I might have more energy and be less blue. I haven't felt that way since before John died. I guess I just can't expect to feel that good again."

CALLER: "But you think it would make a difference if you could sleep and felt like eating."

MEMBER: "That sounds like a simple thing. But for me, that's hard. Do you think I could ask my doctor for something?"

CALLER: "I'm sure your doctor could give you some help."

There will be other times when the mourner's depression is so intense that he does not remember ever feeling better. In this situation, it is as if his depression has taken over and is doing the talking. It is imperative in this case not to try to cheer up the mourner or talk him out of his sadness. You might ask him if, on a scale of one to ten — one being the worst he has ever felt in his life and ten being the time when he didn't have this feeling — where he would place himself now. This question could cause him at least to imagine a time when he felt better and would give you an indication of his evaluation of his situation. You could ask him what would make him feel one half a point worse or one half a point better.

You might say: "I know that medication has made some people feel better. Although it might not make you feel better, it might be worth a try. But even medication would not make you feel immediately better." In speaking this way, the mourner might know that you are taking his situation seriously, you clearly know he feels terrible. But you are also giving him a ray of hope and inviting him to pick up on your suggestion.

It is important when calling on those who are depressed that you *join* them, that you let them know of your empathy. It is empathy, not sympathy, they need. Sympathy says: "I'm so identified with you that I feel the way you do." Depressed people need to know that you know what they are experiencing, but they also need you to be separate so they can lean on you, or so you can throw out a lifeline.

Sometimes people who are deeply depressed or anxious will say, "I don't think there's anything that could help me but if you do, I guess I could give it a try." You can join them by saying: "Well, maybe it won't do much, but I think it's better to try than not to try. Why don't we call my colleague, Dr. Williams, and see if he could see you. I have a lot of respect for him."

Your genuine concern and the authority of your religious calling can help people make a leap of faith out of their despair and into a helping situation. There may be times that you will need to explain to a member that you understand his resistance to medication, that you can appreciate his not wanting to take pills. However, it is your opinion that, until his thinking is clearer, you do not believe he is able to make reasonable decisions for himself. You would suggest that he be evaluated for antidepression medication. After taking pills for a few weeks, he could see how he was thinking. If his thinking was clearer he could make a reasonable decision about continuing the medication.

※

And of course, the religious resources of prayer and Scripture are essential for you to use, as well. Reading the laments of David from the Psalms is a helpful way of joining those who are depressed. The Psalms are full of testimonies of others who have been in the pit, have felt alone and deserted and yet they have cried out to God.

Counselors in community must respect their members' right to mourn in their own way. They also know not to give unwelcome presents of well meaning advice. But they can give their *presence* to those who are mourning. Praying for them, listening to them, walking along beside them on the journey, laying on healing hands and anointing oils, using the rites and rituals of religious tradition, and affirming faith in God's love and salvation are also medications counselors in community can give to heal the brokenhearted. So many endings. So many losses. How do people find the courage to begin again?

> *Within the circles of our lives*
> *we dance the circles of the years,*
> *the circles of the seasons*
> *within the circles of the years,*
> *the cycles of the moon*
> *within the circles of the seasons,*
> *the circles of our reasons*
> *within the cycles of the moon.*
>
> *Again, again we come and go,*
> *changed, changing. Hands*
> *join, unjoin in love and fear,*
> *grief and joy. The circles turn,*
> *each giving into each, into all.*
> *Only music keeps us here,*
>
> *each by all the others held.*
> *In the hold of hands and eyes*
> *we turn in pairs, that joining*
> *joining each to all again.*
>
> *And then we turn aside, alone,*
> *out of the sunlight gone*
>
> *into the darker circles of return.*[37]

— Wendell Berry

Chapter Eight
Reading and Resources
Publishing information is found in the Bibliography.

• This chapter has examined the many losses that are experienced in the course of life. See Herbert Anderson and Kenneth Mitchell's *Leaving Home* for additional information about *supporting young adults and their families in this life transition.*

• For more information about *changes in the workplace* see *Cross-Cultural Perspectives on Families, Work, and Change,* edited by Katja Boh, Giovanni Sgritta, and Marvin B. Sussman. Roy Lewis's chapter, "Pastoral Care to the Unemployed," in the *Clinical Handbook of Pastoral Counseling, Vol. 2,* describes one of the possible pastoral responses to these changes.

• We again direct you to Betty Carter and Monica McGoldrick's *The Changing Family Life Cycle* for an overview of the *marital separation and divorce* process. For additional information on the ways that gender and culture affect divorce see: Sandra S. Volgy, ed., *Women and Divorce/Men and Divorce: Gender Differences in Separation, Divorce, and Remarriage;* and Craig A. Everett, ed., *Minority and Ethnic Issues in the Divorce Process.*

Among the books that you can use to support divorcing families are: Constance Ahrons, *The Good Divorce: Keeping Your Family Together When Your Marriage Comes Apart* and Judith S. Wallerstein and Joan Berlin Kelly, *Surviving the Breakup: How Children and Parents Cope with Divorce.*

Tim Emerick-Cayton's *Divorcing with Dignity: Mediation, the Sensible Alternative* gives information about the skills of divorce mediators. Divorce mediators can be valuable members of your Wholeness Network. For a *caring response to divorce* see: Randall Nichols' *Ending Marriage, Keeping Faith.*

• There is an extensive body of literature on dying, death, and bereavement that you can use to support your ministry. See this book's bibliography as well as *Death and Dying: A Bibliographical Survey,* complied by Samuel Southard.

Marilyn Webb's *The Good Death: The New American Search to Reshape the End of Life* is an excellent companion to this book.

For family systems and cross-cultural resources see: Froma Walsh and Monica McGoldrick, eds., *Living Beyond Loss: Death in the Family;* and Donald P. Irish, *Ethnic Variations in Dying, Death and Grief: Diversity in Universality.*

We strongly recommend Maggie Callahan and Patricia Kelley, *Final Gifts: Understanding the Special Awareness, Needs, and Communications of the Dying* and Stephen Levine, *Who Dies? An Investigation of Conscious Living and Conscious Dying.* Kenneth Mitchell and Herbert Anderson, *All Our Losses, All Our Griefs* is another valuable resource. Among others are: John Cobb, *Matters of Life and Death* and Ernest Morgan, *Dealing Creatively with Death: A Manual of Death Education and Simple Burial.*

• Mourning can be a time of spiritual awakening. This is explored in Martha Robbins' *Midlife Women and the Death of Mother: A Study of Psychohistorical and Spiritual Transformation.*

• Ten-session course to train lay volunteers for grief ministry: Donna Reilly and Jo Ann Sturzi, *Grief Ministry: Helping Others Mourn with Facilitator's Guide;* Resource

Publications, Inc., 160 E. Virginia Street, Suite 290, San Jose, CA 95112-5854 Tel. (408) 286-8505.

• Nonprofit publisher and supplier of grief-support literature: The Centering Corporation, 1531 N. Saddle Creek Road, Omaha, NE 68104-5064 Tel. (402) 553-1200.

• Information about hospice programs: National Hospice Organization, 1910 North Moore Street, Suite 901, Arlington, VA, 22209 Tel. (703) 243-5900.

• *Resources on depression:* Because women are more prone to depression than men, it is essential that caregivers understand the complexity of this phenomenon. Christie Cozad Neuger in "Women's Depression: Lives at Risk," in *Women in Travail and Transition*, edited by Maxine Glaz and Jeanne Stevenson Moessner, clearly shows how women's depression is rooted in cultural sexism and that the anger underlying depression is fueled by their experience of oppression. Low self-esteem, which is at the heart of women's depression, can only be changed through corrective action in which women learn to "undo" their adaptation to sexist roles that they have internalized.

Although women are much more frequently diagnosed for major depression, a study reported in the *Journal of the American Medical Association*, July 1996, showed that the numbers were about the same for men diagnosed for bipolar disorder, often called manic-depression. Men tend not to speak to others of their depression, to mask it through self-medication or to act it out through anger.

Useful resources for working with depressed men are: psychotherapist Terrance Real's *I Don't Want to Talk About it: Overcoming the Secret Legacy of Male Depression* and *Darkness Visible*, Pulitzer Prize-winning author William Styron's personal memoir of his own depression.

In his book *A Mood Apart: Depression, Mania, and Other Afflictions of the Self*, Peter C. Whybrow clearly distinguishes between grief and depression. Depression also has a neuro-chemical component. Peter Kramer in *Listening to Prozac* explains its chemical complexity to the nontechnical reader.

Hopelessness is one of the properties of depression. Although Andrew Lester and Donald Capps' s treatment of hope is far-reaching, their books are useful resources to those giving care to depressed people. See: Andrew Lester, *Hope in Pastoral Care and Counseling;* and Donald Capps, *Agents of Hope: A Pastoral Psychology.* For intervention in depression see *Dealing with Depression: Five Pastoral Interventions*, edited by Richard Dayringer.

• *Resources for families coping with loved one's depression* are offered through calling the *"Connexions"* program. The program includes free brochures on depression — "Coping," "Talking," and "Family" — and a telephone program that offers model conversations with a depressed love one. Toll-free number (888) 222-1213.

~ 9 ~

Care and Counseling
in Life's Daily Round

Just to be is a blessing.
Just to live is holy.

— Rabbi Abraham Heschel[1]

The Parable of the Annoying Pebble

Father Lawrence of the Monks of New Skete, Cambridge, New York, once preached a profoundly simple sermon about his annoying experience of walking on a country road and having a small stone enter his open-toed sandal. He first felt the pebble, but pretended it was not there. He kept on walking. Finally he began to wiggle his toes and then he tried to arrange his foot around the stone. And he kept on walking. In exasperation, he decided not to think about it. But then, *all* he could do was think about it and feel discomfort. Finally he stooped down, took off his sandal, and shook out the pebble. As he stood up and looked around he realized that he had walked a quarter of a mile on a lovely road but had not seen a thing. He had been preoccupied with the rock.

He told this story to invite the congregation to become aware of the "pebbles" that most people try to ignore, that keep them from taking pleasure in the daily walk of life. He believed that if "pebbles" could be acknowledged and their effect experienced, people would remove them. They could then look about and take in the beauty around them.

Counselors in community invite members to identify their "pebbles," experience their effect, remove them, and then look around and see God's world. Some people have been so preoccupied with the rock in their shoe that they have forgotten where they were going. They need help to reorient themselves. Through community care and counseling, people are helped to move from experiencing life only as a problem and can become free to feel their own liveliness and be aware of life as a blessing.

In this chapter we will be discussing some of the ordinary "pebbles" that counselors help their community members identify and "remove," such as the response to stress, the effects of addiction, and the pain of abuse. It may seem strange to apply the metaphor of "pebble" to conditions as serious and all-encompassing as these. Unlike stones that irritate feet, these conditions are usually not experienced as being small nor outside the self. Often people lose their sense of self or become numbed by the pain. Sometimes the "pebbles" become embedded; at other times people become identified with the "pebbles" themselves. However, through graceful interventions even burdensome "pebbles" can be removed and selves recovered.

First let us discuss intervention in acute crises. Such crises feel more like boulders that often unexpectedly hit people on the head. But they are also part of life's daily round.

Intervention in Acute Crises

You regularly provide community care and brief counseling to those who come to you in crises. These crises arise at points of change when decisions must be made. They cause upsets that allow unfinished business from the past to emerge. They provide another chance for growth and integration. "Normal" crises upset the stability of one's life and family but they can also be experienced as being "in the order of life."

There are other kinds of crises that cause panic and disorder; these are *life-threatening*. Some come from out of the blue, like car accidents or death from sudden illness. Others, like suicide, happen suddenly, but usually there has been the antecedent of depression that no one believed would really lead to suicide. Other crises may seem sudden and unexpected *to you* because the systemic problems out of which they arose had been kept secret.

Because of the secrecy, you learn, only after the call about his tragic car accident, the extent to which a member of your youth group has been abusing alcohol. You learn about family incest after an elementary school principal calls to tell you that a child in your church school is receiving emergency care because her father — also a church member — has been sexually abusing her. You learn that a member has been living with an abusive husband after you are called to a hospital emergency room where she is in serious condition from having been battered.

Acute-crisis counseling differs from brief counseling. You step in to intervene in an acute crisis. Your goal is to help your community member find a solution for *managing* the crisis by first doing "counseling triage." Your first priority is to help "stop the bleeding."

Often these urgent calls are unsettling even when you are prepared with telephone numbers of resources to be used in emergencies.Your anxiety can be reduced when you can give those who call *step by step procedures* that they can follow.

Because the resources and the most effective way to use them vary in each community, we cannot give a standard set of instructions. We will remind you of those categories of emergency that you need to know how to handle:

Pleas for help from *suicidal persons:* When someone lets you know he is thinking about or planning suicide, the danger is real and you can do something about it. If you think there is immediate danger, the suicidal person should not be left alone and medical help should be called immediately. If a person telephoning you is alone, give him the number for a suicide hotline and tell him to call it while you call the appropriate emergency number. Before you hang up, ask him to make an agreement with you not to hurt himself. A promise to you will reinforce the impulse that allowed him to reach out for help. See the checklist for dealing with suicidal people in Liberman and Woodruff's *Risk Management.* Your community mental-health association also can provide resources for suicide prevention and intervention.

In all probability, you have already had experience in ministering to someone who eventually committed suicide and to families and friends of that person. Suicide is the eighth-ranking cause of death in the United States, the second leading cause of death for those between the ages of fifteen and twenty-four, and the thirteenth for those over sixty five. More people die from suicide in this country than from homicide. Researchers have found that between 65 percent and 80 percent of those who commit or attempt suicide have tried to communicate their intentions to someone, although these communications were often not received.[2] *Appendix D* includes material on the signs of suicide and what can be done to help. We encourage you to make this available to your congregation.

Family violence, rape, child abuse, elder abuse: In preparation for such emergencies, become acquainted with the police department or sheriff's office and family violence unit. Also become aware of the resources of the local child protective services and the children's services in the Department of Welfare and have their phone numbers and names of contact persons available. You also need to know how to help battered women and their children find *immediate* emergency housing and counseling services. Know how child abuse is defined and what your state law requires you to report.

Crises arising from *alcohol or other chemical substance abuse.* Often it is when people "bottom out" or their families "have had it" that those suffering from chemical dependencies are ready for treatment. In many cases you will need to know how people can be admitted for medical treatment *immediately,* and how to refer to treatment agencies and counselors and Twelve Step groups.

Survival emergencies — loss of housing, need for emergency food:. Often religious communities have a social service function. You should have a procedure and people for responding to these *emergency* requests. Know the civic, governmental, and private agencies that are available.

Illnesses — cancer, AIDS, serious mental Illness, etc.: These seriously disrupt families. Sometimes you will be called in the midst of a health crisis for pastoral functions or to help people find solutions for the myriad problems that arise as they are treated for and live with serious illness. You must have resources available.

Legal problems or need for legal protection: "Pastor, I'm at the police station. I've got a problem." You need to know procedures to help members find legal counsel and also to find the legal means to protect themselves and their children when they are threatened with family violence or other forms of abuse.

Members of your community's wholeness network committee can lend their expertise in helping you set up step-by-step procedures. With these procedures established and telephone numbers at your finger tips, you are prepared to do acute crisis counseling.

Many times you are called upon not to do problem solving personally but to give information so that someone else can take immediate action to carry out their solution, as in this example. A parishioner's sister called: "I'm Willie Mae James's sister. She's here in terrible shape. Jack's beat her. Do you know how to get her into a safe house — you know, a women's shelter? I'm scared, too."

Mrs. James's pastor, Dolores Hinton, was asked for *specific* information. However, she was able to *volunteer* more of her expertise to the crisis. She knew that in addition to a safe place to stay, Mrs. James might need medical attention. She needed care for her children. She also needed protection from her husband. Pastor Hinton suggested to Mrs. James's sister that calling the police's family violence unit would be the quickest way to get help for these multiple needs. While she gave the phone number for the women's shelter, she also gave information *which the caller did not even know to ask for.* Often people don't know how to think in an emergency — they need your help.

Crisis intervention counselors have developed methods of organizing the *data* of the crisis. A method frequently used is the The "ABC Process of Crisis Management."[3] This is similar to solution-focused therapy: The counselor helps organize the crisis through the questions she asks. *She does not take over and solve the problem herself.*

ABC Process of Crisis Management

A: *Achieve Contact*

Often you learn of the emergency through a telephone call. In most cases you are talking to someone you know, but in some cases a stranger may be calling you on another's behalf. Before getting details about the problem, make certain you know to whom you are talking and about *whom* they are calling. If you are speaking to the person in crisis either on the phone or in person make contact before jumping in to problem-solve. Usually contact will be made quickly because you will be using the goodwill of an established relationship. Often the person is in a state of distress and will need you to help her settle down through helping her focus on breathing, giving her a glass of water, or handing her a tissue, thereby giving "permission" to cry — before she can begin coherently to speak of the problem.

B: *Boil Down the Problem*

Ask the person to briefly describe what has just happened. If the person is in shock, this may be difficult because she may already be distancing herself from the trauma. However, encourage her to tell you what has happened as if it just happened. Ask what is the most pressing problem *now*.

Use the *exception question:* "If it were not (for the stated problem), would you feel better right now?" "Have you confronted a similar problem before? How did you handle it? What worked?" Review what you heard as the primary problem. Check to see if you have it right.

C: *Cope with the Problem*

Help the person in crisis find her solution to the problem:

1. What does she want to happen?
2. What is her *most* important need, the bottom line?
3. What does she feel to be the best solution?
4. What is she willing to do to meet her needs?
5. Help her formulate a plan of action based on her use of available resources, current activities, and time.
6. Arrange a follow-up appointment, or make a referral, or take an action.

The next morning, when Willie Mae James came to see her pastor, Dolores Hinton used the "ABC Process of Crisis Management" to help her continue to manage her crisis.

A: Pastor Hinton had already begun to make contact with Mrs. James through her phone conversation with her sister the night before. When she entered the office, Pastor Hinton took her hand and Mrs. James began to sob and say, "I was so scared."

B: Pastor Hinton helped Mrs. James describe what had happened the night before, how she got to her sister's apartment, what happened when the officers from the family violence unit arrived and what her experience had been at the shelter. Mrs. James found that her most urgent problem at the moment was, "Should I press charges against my husband?"

C: Pastor Hinton helped Mrs. James *listen to herself* as she said that for her, the "bottom line" had to be her safety and the safety of her children. After sorting out her options, she knew that a restraining order was necessary and that the counselors at the women's shelter could help her obtain one.

She still needed to talk with Pastor Hinton of her concern about being a good Christian wife and her fear that getting protection for herself meant splitting up the family. Pastor Hinton was able to reassure her by saying that she felt God would want Willie Mae and her children to be safe. Then she prayed with Mrs. James:

> O Loving God, You care for all your children. We ask for a special blessing on Willie Mae, the children and Jack. You know how hard it's been for them. You know about the pain. Now we ask that they may know the light of your love and that each in the family can begin to be healed.

You often do more than help people problem-solve at the time of their acute crisis. An acute crisis affects entire family systems, which need the attention and care of your religious community.

When Willie Mae James and her children found safety in a woman's shelter her whole world changed. Her husband had made all-important family decisions and controlled the money. After she left him, she needed to learn to make decisions for herself and her children and to take charge of her life. She needed her religious community to support her. And her husband needed attention as well.

Congregations move in quickly to support their members who are in acute crisis. But after the beginning phase has been managed, they think the work is done. In fact, the family's healing is just beginning and they need their community's support for the long haul. Congregations can be educated about the ways they can support families in recovery. Resource materials are listed at the end of this chapter.

The acute crises of others can draw you into a new and deeper ministry. For example, it was through being a companion to a family that was having to flee from an abusive father that Pastor Hinton's congregation learned that their community's resources for victims of family violence were sorely underfunded and overburdened. Pastor Hinton became challenged to be an *advocate for change.* This awareness caused her congregation to become involved in supporting public policy. Some in her congregation volunteered to do child care in the women's shelter; other families took in children for temporary placement while their mothers got reestablished.

It is your comforting presence and the presence of others in your congregation that is needed at the time of acute crisis. Often these crises have caused those suffering them to feel shame. Because of their past experiences, many expect religious communities to shun them or to stigmatize them when what they need is to be loved. A family needs special support if it has

- suffered a member's suicide,
- had a parent enter a chemical dependency rehabilitation program,
- had a parent removed from the home because of abusive behavior,
- experienced any other crisis that some in the congregation might deem unacceptable, such as a member's having AIDS or having broken the law.

A family in acute crisis finally has the chance to change because the upset opens up new possibilities and allows old roles to be revised. Most congregations do not draw special attention to families who might feel stigmatized. However, the word about them and the congregation's treatment of them gets out. When your community is loving, accepting, and helpful to individuals or families in acute crisis, other families learn of it. These families, with their own painful secrets, will know that your congregation is a true community in which they might some day reveal themselves.

Now we will move on to consider in more detail several of the problems of daily life — "pebbles in their sandals" — which your members come to you to help them remove.

Response to Stress

By understanding how stress works, you will have a foundation for helping those who come with problems of depression, anxiety, and other stress disorders, and alcohol and drug addictions. These problems all have stress in common.

BOB SCHMIDT: "Pastor, I'm all stressed out. I don't know if I can take it any more."

PASTOR VAN NESS: "Tell me how you've been handling it."

BOB SCHMIDT: "Well, I've been doing my best to try to relax. I know that's what you're supposed to do. I guess I'd better tell you. I know I've been drinking too much. It used to help."

Counselors in community are frequently asked for help from "stressed-out" members. Sometimes the request is to help them with the symptoms caused by adaptation to stress: agitation, anxiety, irritability, emotional tension, insomnia, physical exhaustion, confusion, impulsive or compulsive behavior. Sometimes people come to tell you of fears about their health because they have physical symptoms: sweating, diarrhea, indigestion, queasiness in the stomach, vomiting, migraine headaches, premenstrual tension, pain in the neck or lower back that they may or may not know are stress-related.[4] Frequently, people have already consulted their doctors about these symptoms — but their problems persist. These physical symptoms are signals that there is trouble brewing.

At other times, members will be coming for help with their *solution* to stress. *This solution has now become a problem.* Many times people begin to use alcohol, drugs, or addictive behaviors to self-medicate their stress.

Dr. Hans Selye, a Canadian medical researcher, introduced the concept of "stress" in the late 1950s through his study of the "fight-flight" response. This response is activated by the complex hormonal (endocrine) system of the body that sends messages to the brain (through the autonomic nervous system) when people are in danger. The neural impulses from the brain send messages back to the hormonal system and more stress hormones are released, among them adrenaline and cortisol. They charge up the body with energy needed for fleeing from danger, or for aggression for fighting.

Dr. Selye had become aware that some people reacted with the fight or flight response to situations that were actually not a matter of life or death. For example, he noticed that a person could be as upset over misplacing car keys *as if* he were being chased by a tiger. Another person was anxiously upset when he had won a prize and was asked to give a speech in response. Dr. Selye's research showed that *stressors* could be positive as well as negative; positive stressors are called "eustress," negative stressors, "distress." *Stress* is one's response to stressors.

While people could have any number of responses to stress, Dr. Selye's work showed that most people responded with anxiety, and then a cycle began. Anxiety causes additional stress. In a dangerous situation the hormonal and brain system goes to work and the energy that takes over is useful and appropriate. However, when one's body sends a message of danger even when one's existence is not threatened, the body produces *more* stress hormones to respond to *that* stress. The body then becomes dangerously overloaded with toxic chemicals that damage various organs and their tissues.

In the past thirty years, an enormous amount of research has been done on the nature of stress and its effect on the body. The evidence is clear that stress has a part in causing the physical illnesses of peptic ulcers, ulcerative colitis, heart disease, strokes, arthritis, high blood pressure, and a variety of headaches.[5] Studies of the neurochemical response to stress shed some light on *why* a person who has lost his car keys responds as if a tiger were chasing him. People who have experienced early loss, other childhood traumas, or trauma later in life are vulnerable to emotions triggered by loss, rejection, and other stress. These emotions themselves cause stress. Because sensitized people easily experience stress, their hormonal system is frequently disrupted and supplies the body with excess stress hormones. Stress begets stress.

There is now research that shows how stress also creates readiness for depression because of its effect on the neurochemical system. Through research that looks at depression from many angles — studies of nerve cells, the glandular system, psychopharmacology, longitudinal studies of depressed people — there is evidence that stress changes the "hard wiring" of the anatomy of the brain. This, in turn, affects the way DNA and RNA produce chemically complex substances that encode trauma and create a chemical hypervigilance to potential trauma.[6]

Through studies of epilepsy, it was discovered that trauma is translated into *anatomical* changes in the brain that come before the illness starts. It is being hypothesized that depression is caused in much the same way. Children experience severe stress if they have suffered trauma caused by loss, particularly loss of their mother, sexual and physical abuse, or neglect. In response, stress hormones are released that affect the anatomy of the children's brains. Little children are in fact in life and death situations at the time of this trauma, and are helpless to do anything about it. In these situations the stress systems of their bodies are in high gear and appropriately send out massive amounts of hormones. These hormones affect the cells of the brain in such a way that the *trauma is encoded in the cells of their bodies*. The trauma is not just stored in memory to be cognitively retrieved later. The bodies of traumatized children "remember" and become sensitive to potential trauma. This causes their bodies frequently to be in a state where stress hormones are activated.

It is hypothesized that as their life goes on even a slight amount of stress can get a stress reaction going in a person who has been traumatized in childhood. Often children with a history of early trauma and neglect appear to be shy and sensitive and they are not obviously depressed. They become depressed later in life.

This theory is being tested through a longitudinal National Mental Health study of young women who were sexually abused as children. Already, this research shows that these young women have, compared with a normal population, a much higher level of the stress hormone, cortisol. A disruption of the stress hormone system correlates with high levels of depression. This depression generally comes some years after the abuse.[7]

Adults, also, can have traumas that create a predisposition to depression. Psychosocial stressors such as pain, isolation, confinement, and lack of control can also lead to structural changes in the brain. These changes can bring on depression later in life. Sometimes adults who have suffered trauma in adulthood appear, at the beginning, to cope without depression. However, they may eventually experience "late onset" depression. This is frequently seen in older men who as war veterans experienced severe trauma. In their later years they have nightmares, insomnia, and depression.[8]

Depression seems to be a *progressive* illness. Because it is related to the neurochemical system of the body that, like all parts of the body, wears with age, people become increasingly vulnerable to depression with age. When depression has a late onset, its effects are more severe and suicide is more possible.

Not only can stress produce depression, it can also create shock. In our discussion of mourning, we described people who go into shock when they learn of a loved one's violent or sudden death and who are then unable to mourn. Some of those to whom you minister may experience this response, which is called an *acute stress disorder.*

Acute stress disorders last for a minimum of two days, and a maximum of four weeks, and occur within four weeks of the traumatic event. *The Diagnostic and Statistical Manual of Mental Disorders IV* gives this diagnosis to a person who has witnessed, experienced, or been confronted with an event that involved *actual or threatened death or serious injury,* or *a threat to the physical integrity of self or others.* The person's response was fear, helplessness or horror. Either while experiencing the event or following it, the person develops at least three of the following dissociative symptoms:

- a subjective sense of numbing, detachment, or absence of emotional responsiveness.
- a reduction in awareness of surroundings.
- feelings of unreality (derealization).
- being detached from oneself (depersonalization).
- inability to recall an important aspect of the trauma (dissociative amnesia).

The person has anxiety symptoms, has difficulty functioning at work and relating socially. Even though there is an attempt to avoid stimuli that cause the person to recollect the trauma, the trauma is often reexperienced.[9]

Counselors in community recognize this disorder not only in those who have been shocked by the sudden death of a loved one, but also in those who have been sexually or physically abused, or who have witnessed violent acts. Because domestic violence is so common, counselors need to be aware of members who may be suffering acute stress disorder.

Sometimes people come for counseling because they have remembered a trauma that occurred years earlier, or because they are having acute stress reactions but do not know why. Often they are experiencing a *posttraumatic stress disorder.* They have had experiences that would cause an acute stress disorder, but their symptoms are delayed for at least six months — and sometimes years — after the traumatic event.[10] Even when a reaction to trauma has been greatly delayed, many experience the trauma with intensity, as if it just happened.

People suffering this disorder cope by trying to avoid stimuli associated with the trauma. For example, a woman who has been raped might feel aversion to sexual activity. Later, the trauma is *reexperienced* through intrusive recollections of the event. Distressing dreams in which the event is replayed, often in symbolic coding, and body memories are also means of remembering. Sometimes posttraumatic stress disorders develop after the traumatized person is in a place where she feels safe to reexperience the trauma.

New medications are being developed for treating depression and stress disorders that can interrupt the pattern of "stress begetting stress." Through your referrals to knowledgeable consultants who can evaluate and medicate, you can help those who suffer from the trauma.

We need to be reminded that not only negative events but also positive ones, can be stressful. Dr. Selye's findings stimulated research in the field of social science as well as the physical sciences. Researchers Thomas Holmes and R. H. Rahe compiled a "Social Readjustment Rating Scale" (1967) and through this instrument discovered that some events that would presumably be positive were experienced as more stressful than some with negative connotations. A major change either way in one's financial state — "being a lot worse or a lot better off" — was experienced as equally stressful.[11] In our discussion of life's beginnings and endings, we have already become aware of the stress that is caused by *change* in the family life cycle.

This information can be useful in counseling those who come for help who are experiencing stress even though they are having success at work or are happy in a new relationship. Often their stress is compounded by confusion; they had expected to be happy and full of well-being. When they learn that stress is predictable, their anxiety is relieved.

With *distress* being implicated as the cause of many physical and emotional illnesses, it is not surprising that the 1970s and 1980s were times when theoreticians in the physical and social sciences seriously worked to find interventions to ameliorate the effects of stress. As psychopharmacologists prescribed medications for those most severely affected by stress, it became obvious that other therapeutic measures were also needed to mitigate stress. In response, at least three categories of interventions were developed:

Cognitive-Behavioral Therapy Interventions

Because stress is an inappropriate fight-flight response to a stressor, cognitive and behavioral psychologists reasoned that people could *learn* more adaptive ways to respond to stress. In our discussion of the physiology of stress, we saw how hormones themselves become the teacher telling a child, through a surge of adrenaline and other hormones, "something dangerous is happening, prepare for trouble." The child repeatedly feels the signal of danger but does not know what to do. The child *learns to be helpless.*

Both cognitive and behavioral therapists have been concerned about rectifying the experience of "learned helplessness" that they believe is a major component of depression. Cognitive therapists believe that through changing thoughts about, and perceptions of a stressor, people would change their behavior, and their emotions would become correspondingly appropriate. For example, someone who becomes upset about misplacing car keys would be taught to say: "Hey, a tiger is not chasing me. Slow down, breathe and think." Cognitive theory posits that realistic thoughts will help a person change behavior. This will create a change in helpless feelings; anxiety will be diminished.

Cognitive therapists also work with belief systems. A woman coming to a cognitive therapist to overcome phobia when riding in an elevator will be taught to listen to her "self-talk" when she is in the elevator. She will then observe herself saying: "I hate this. It's too small. It's like a coffin. I bet there isn't enough air in here. I'll probably get stuck. I've got to get out." She and her therapist will examine this inner-talk for irrational content and find its underlying belief system. Sometimes visualization techniques are used to help her practice new behaviors in her imagination. Through this she will learn to pay attention to her new way of speaking to herself. She will then monitor her inner talk as she rides in elevators.

Behavioral therapists believe that after one learns appropriate behavior for a stressful situation, thinking and feelings will change. Many behavioral therapists use desensitization techniques based on the theory that people can learn if they are *first in a relaxed state* and if the feared *task can be broken down* into small parts. A person who has a fear of riding in elevators learns to break the task into small steps, and then think about those steps without anxiety. She begins with the easiest part: imagining herself entering the building, moving toward the elevator, standing in front of the elevator, until she can imagine doing the hardest part: seeing herself *riding* in the elevator. Step by step, with the support of the therapist, she eventually rides the elevator. Behaviorists believe that as one performs the feared task, beliefs and feeling about the task will change with time and experience.

Behavioral and cognitive therapies help people change through the use of systematic, graduated exercises that take time and commitment. Neither system offers a fast cure, but both have proved to be effective in helping people deal with stress, phobias and other anxiety symptoms.

Stressor Management

Unlike the interventions of cognitive and behavior therapies that affect people's *response* to stress, another type of intervention was created to change *stressors* themselves. In the 1980s, managers in business became concerned that the workplace was a stressful environment. Consultants developed methods to analyze work procedures, decision making, empowerment systems, and the work environment to identify stressors and then to try to modify them. Consultants involved both workers and management in making changes.

Business and industry have developed stress management courses that use some techniques of cognitive and behavioral therapies to help employees change attitudes such as: "I can't do anything about the stress in my life." "Stress is the curse of modern man." Such courses are designed to help those whose beliefs are based on learned helplessness discover their values and goals, to set priorities and to take charge of their own lives. A popular book like Stephen R. Covey's *Seven Habits of Highly Effective People* is an example of such a stress management tool.

Methods for Activating the Body's "Health System"

While many were focusing on understanding and mitigating stress, others were investigating the systems in the body that activate and support the body's health. Many researchers were interested in discovering how the body could find better *balance,* particularly in light of its excess stress. They reasoned that the natural resources for health must be reinforced.

Just as the body has a hormonal system for *activating* the fight or flight system, it also has a hormonal system for helping it *relax and restore* its equilibrium. This homeostatic mechanism is mediated by the parasympathetic branch of the autonomic nervous system and is under the control of the hypothalamus. Among its functions are to reduce muscular tension, metabolism, and oxygen consumption, slow the heart rate, lower blood pressure, dilate the peripheral vasculature that causes skin temperature to be warmer, and increase alpha brain-wave activity.[12]

Those in some cultures have known for centuries the calming and relaxing benefits of the practice of yoga, meditation, and Tai Chi. In 1975, Dr. Herbert Benson's book, *The Relaxation Response* caught the American public's attention with his message that relaxing has curative value and that this could be scientifically supported. Benson, a Harvard University professor and cardiologist, had clinical evidence that showed that relaxation lowered stress. This, in turn, had a beneficial effect on heart patients. His book and the proliferation of behavioral and cognitive therapy that used relaxation techniques for visualization, popularized a variety of relaxation methods. Dr. Benson's new book, *Timeless Healing: The Power of Biology and Belief,* further illustrates the importance of relaxation to well-being and health.

Progressive relaxation, yoga, Tai Chi, meditation, hypnosis, and self-hypnosis, mantras and other autogenic techniques have all been used effectively to help people relax. Some people employ biofeedback, which uses machines that monitor and measure the degree of relaxation, to verify and reinforce the relaxation process. More recently the study of *"wellness"* has biochemists, biologists and neurologists researching the neurochemical systems that support health. Nutritionists, physiologists who study the role of exercise and health, physical therapists, as well as those who investigate "alternative medical paths," hard scientists, and "new age" practitioners all contribute their findings and experience to this new field of endeavor.

Community Care and Counseling:
Providing Graceful Interventions

Religious communities have always treated stress, even before the word was coined. The interventions used by religious communities are similar to the modern interventions for stress that have recently been developed. Religious practices create thoughts and attitudes that help modify "learned helplessness," affect stressful situations, and activate the "health system" of the body. We will be using examples from Christianity, but there are parallels in Jewish tradition.

Jesus frequently tried to help people *change their attitudes about worry and anxiety.* Some people in his day, like those in ours, believed that worrying does some good. They were like today's people who say to their children, "When you were late last night, I was so worried about you," or "I'm exhausted from worry." These people convey a message: "When I'm worrying, I'm really *working* on your behalf." They believe that worrying will really affect the outcome of a child's behavior. They confuse worry with care.

Jesus taught that worry does not accomplish anything: "Therefore I tell you, do not worry about your life, what you will eat, or about your body, what you will wear. For life is more than food, and the body more than clothing. Consider the ravens: they neither sow nor reap, they have neither storehouse nor barn, and yet God feeds them. Of how much more value are you than the birds! And *can any of you by worrying add a single hour to your span of life?*" (Luke 12:22–25) (Italics mine.)

Modern scientists have identified the trauma of *loss* as being a central factor in the creation of the stress syndrome that then fuels worry and anxiety. Jesus understood this. He helped cure people of their anxiety by helping them become *attached* to a loving God — a God who pays attention to the small details of our lives: "Are not five sparrows sold for two pennies? Yet not one of them is forgotten in God's sight. But even the hairs of your head are counted. Do not be afraid; you are of more value than many sparrows" (Luke 12:6–7).

At the end of Jesus' life, he also addressed *abandonment anxiety* when he said: "If you love me, you will keep my commandments. And I will ask the Father, and he will give you another Advocate, to be with you forever. This is the Spirit of Truth, whom the world cannot receive, because it neither sees him nor knows him. You know him, because he abides with you and he will be in you. I will not leave you orphaned; I am coming to you" (John 14:15–18).

Many of Jesus' teachings helped people live in the present: "I have come that you might live life in its fullness." His teachings changed behavior through affecting his followers' sense of helplessness, which underlies the avoidance of living. Jesus knew that anxiety prevented living life abundantly. Modern religious communities need this message, and if they become intentional in giving it, their members can experience a change in attitude and behavior that will affect their stressful lives.

Members of your community also need information about the many ways their bodies' own "health system" can be supported. By teaching them about "sabbathing" — that cycle of work, rest, reorganization, and creation that has been built into our very bodies — you can help them experience renewal and balance.[13] To "keep the Sabbath" means to observe the *rhythm* that all yearn for — withdrawal for refreshment and return to activity. Abraham Heschel calls this a "sanctuary in time" in which people are released from the tyranny of work production. He says it is a time of soul work when people become open to the *Sabbath keeping them* in a place of inner serenity where they sense the timelessness of the eternal.[14]

Because, in fact, our minds, bodies and souls are unified, spiritual food nourishes our bodies and minds. There is a growing body of research that is finding scientific verification of this holism. Some of this research is cited in Dr. Benson's *Timeless Healing*. Dr. Larry Dossey also explores this theme in *Prayer Is Good Medicine*.

※

Many people attempt to self-medicate to soothe their feelings of anxiety, anger, and depression, which are related to stress. They use food, alcohol, prescription, and illicit drugs and other substances as "medication." Often this solution creates other problems, which in turn adds to stress.

Young people begin to self-medicate early in life. While drug use among young people is tapering off, the trend toward alcohol consumption is increasing at even younger ages. Daniel Goleman, in his book *Emotional Intelligence*, reports a survey that found half of college men and 40 percent of college women had two binge-drinking episodes a month. Of these college drinkers 11 percent called themselves "heavy drinkers" (Goleman suggests substituting the word, "alcoholic"). He reports another survey that found that 35 percent of college women drink to get drunk.[15]

The alcohol consumption of young people creates other problems. Alcohol related deaths are the leading cause of death among young people between fifteen and twenty-four.[16] On college campuses there is a correlation between heavy drinking and rape. In 90 percent of the rapes reported, the assailant or victim or both had been drinking.[17] Let us now return to the pastor whose parishioner's "pebble in his sandal" was stress.

BOB SCHMIDT: "Pastor, I'm all stressed out. I don't know if I can take it any more."

PASTOR VAN NESS: "Tell me how you've been handling it."

BOB: "Well, I've been doing my best to try to relax. I know that's what you're supposed to do. I guess I'd better tell you. I know I've been drinking too much. It used to help."

PASTOR: "Can you tell me a little more about being 'all stressed out'?"

BOB: "Yeah...I guess it began when the company moved down South and just left a small office up here."

PASTOR: "Umm hmm."

BOB: "I really didn't want to move because it's our son's last year in high school. I guess this is part of the stress, too. We're waiting to see where he's been accepted and we still haven't figured out all the finances."

PASTOR: "Yeah, it's a tense time."

BOB: "But a tough part is the work itself. The competition for staying was pretty great. I got to stay, but they've really piled on work. None of us on the staff can complain much because we want to make it look like we have it under control. None of us want to move. I guess that's why I'm drinking more. I go with the guys after work just to let down."

Pastor Van Ness asked Bob the "miracle question." In response, Bob described a morning in which he started the day rested and without a hangover. He and his wife were on good terms, and he was able to talk with his son about his son's anxieties about college admission without being defensive. His "miracle day" was hopeful.

PASTOR: "Is there a time when the miracle day is happening, just a bit?"

BOB: "Well, I'm only hung over when I've had too much the night before. Yeah, most nights I don't drink too much."

PASTOR: "What's happening then?"

Pastor Van Ness used solution-focused methods to help Bob identify and reinforce the solutions he already was using to deal with the heavy stress in his life. Bob was worried about his drinking; his own father had had a drinking problem. However, his solution of self-medicating, while *becoming* a problem, had not eclipsed the stress problem. It had not become the more obvious problem of addiction.

Pastor Van Ness did not try to solve Bob's concerns about drinking. Rather, he listened to the things Bob was already doing to make things better. In response to his question, "What's happening when it's different, when you're not drinking?" Bob had said: "You know, I thought I was drinking every night. But I guess I don't. I still play handball once a week at the 'Y.' On those nights I just come home and have dinner. And when we're with friends, I might have a glass of wine, but I don't feel I have to have more. At the end of the day, I feel I need a drink. It's the feeling of *needing* to drink that's bothering me." Through using the solution-focused interviewing techniques, Pastor Van Ness helped Bob continue to do those things that he was already doing when he was not drinking.

Insoo Berg and Scott Miller's *Working with the Problem Drinker* can help enhance your brief counseling skills for working with those who have been using drinking and other types of self-medication to ease the pain of stress. Some in your congregation will also be coming to you for referral to another professional. Often those who have been self-medicating are addicted to more than one self-medication, often alcohol and prescription drugs. And usually, they also have untreated depression or other stress-related illness. They need your ministry of referral counseling.

Community, itself, can soothe stress. In prayer and meditation, those undergoing stress can "Let go and let God." They can be upheld by God's everlasting arms. The religious message of faith in God inspires worshipers and gives them the hope to go on. Communities in which people feel safe are places where members can share their personal concerns, be supported, and get practical help.

❧

We have been looking at the remarkable way our bodies are designed to protect us from the stress of life. When we are experiencing threat or danger, our neurochemical systems pour out adrenaline, cortisol, and other hormones to rev us for flight or fight. They also secrete neurochemicals to calm us and make us responsive to pleasure. Not only our brains, but our entire personality systems have evolved so that we might not only survive, but thrive. Psychodynamic therapists call this self-protective system the *ego and its defenses*. These defenses help us resolve conflicts and minimize stress as we move through life.

Dr. George Vaillant, Harvard psychiatrist and researcher, has studied how adults thrive in the midst of the conflicts of their lives. We will be using some of his findings to understand how human conflicts are formed and how people then resolve them. Vaillant calls the points of conflict "lodestars." He describes how a sailor finds a star (lodestar) upon which he fixes his gaze as he navigates his boat. As he concentrates on the star he feels pulled by it. When one is in conflict, one is aware of more than one lodestar and feels conflicting pulls that compete for attention. The lodestars that pull are:

conscience — cultural taboos and imperatives, superego;
people — whom we cannot live with or without;
reality — facets of our external environment that sometimes change faster than we can adapt;
desire — passion, emotion, affect, instinct, id, drive.[18]

Sitting in the midst of these pulls — in the boat — is the self, and its organizing ego. It is the self's job to sail the boat through these competing tides. Because the self cannot carry out the demands and requests of all of the "stars" at once, it has to ignore some as it sets priorities. It is protected or defended against these pulls by ego defenses. These defenses *deny, distort, and repress* the competing pulls of inner and outer reality so that the sailor is able to make the necessary decisions about direction in order to sail on. Some sailors have more effective defenses than others.

No doubt when people have come to talk to you about unresolved conflicts, they have described themselves as pulled in all directions or being tied in knots. Their bodies are in conflict. Conflicts are not simply problems to be solved, they are conditions affecting the entire self.

Conflicts affect people's bodies in similar ways, although they seem to come from different sources. Some people will speak of an inner conflict that involves their conscience or their emotions. Sometimes the conflict is with a person or a group, or they are in conflict with an introjected person who lives inside them — their mother or father whose voice they have internalized. Sometimes the conflict is between an inner desire and the constraints of what is possible in the external life situation. Even though these conflicts seem to arise from different sources, all conflicts involve tension among one's inner feelings and drives, one's conscience, one's relationships (including those that are internalized) and one's external reality.

Most of the time, people's inner navigation equipment works well enough so that the process of inner negotiation is unnoticed by them — it is unconscious. Even when people come for brief therapy, they soon discover that they have had solutions to conflicts or problems of which they were unaware. While the cause of our conflicts remains constant — we are navigating among pulls of conscience, relationships with people (including those we have internalized), desire and reality — our solutions are influenced by the maturity of our navigation equipment. This equipment — our ego defenses — becomes more efficient as we grow. A simple understanding of the categories of ego defenses is helpful in understanding stress and conflict:[19]

Psychotic defenses are similar to those of infants who must cope with overwhelming emotions and physical sensations. A psychotic person who is overwhelmed with the terror of dementia, hallucinations, etc., does not experience his inner conflicts, but projects them onto the world through a system of dissociation, denial, and delusion.

Those with *immature defenses* do not resolve inner conflicts either. They manage their conflicts through being *dissociated* from them or *acting them out* or being *passive-aggressive* or *projecting* their conflicts onto others to make it "their fault." They also remove themselves from their conflicts through *fantasy* or *somatizing* them in their bodies.

Neurotic (good enough) defenses are used to control one's own thinking and feeling rather than controlling others. This is done through *intellectualization, repression* of one's conflictual thoughts, reversing one's thinking about a conflictual situation (*reaction formation*), or through transferring one's wishes, feelings or conflicts onto another object (*displacement*).

Mature defenses allow people to care for themselves as well as to take others into account and care for them. This is done through *altruism*. When one is being altruistic, feelings are sometimes claimed indirectly through *sublimination* or postponed through *suppression*. Those with these defenses are able to plan for future anxiety-filled events through *anticipation* and they are able to lighten situations through the use of *humor*.

Stress and Sexual Conflict

JEANNE: "Reverend, I've got to talk with you. I don't know what to do about my daughter. You know, Leah. She's pregnant."

Jeanne's minister, Pastor Washington, was not surprised to get her call. He had just finished a counseling session with Leah who was resolving her conflict about an unplanned pregnancy. Even though it was painful, Leah had decided to have the baby, but then to place it for adoption. Pastor Washington knew that Leah's mother was less upset by the fact that she was pregnant than by the way she was resolving her conflict.

When Pastor Washington spoke to Jeanne, she exclaimed in anger, "In our family, we don't give our babies away!" She had assumed that Leah and the baby would live with her, just as she and Leah had lived with her mother.

Jeanne had a conflict that she consciously thought was between herself and her daughter. The pastor, who knew her family, was aware that it was more far-ranging. Leah's pregnancy was a repeat in a family cycle. Jeanne had given birth to Leah when she was still in high school. Leah had been her "little doll" — the special person she could love and who would love her back. Although being a single parent had been difficult, she now missed her baby. Leah had acted out her mother's wish to have another baby in the house.

However, in her counseling session with Pastor Washington, Leah had realized that her mother was in the process of breaking the family pattern in which children were the main resource for meeting emotional needs. Jeanne had had several promotions at work and was now being trained in a highly technical job. Jeanne's work was gratifying. Leah herself was on a college track. Neither she nor her mother was prepared to give a new baby what it would need. And a baby was not what either she or Jeanne needed to give them self-affirmation and assurance of worth.

Often counselees come to counselors in community with issues that *seem* to be about sex but that reflect other concerns. Leah's pastor could have understood her predicament to be about the "sin of having sex outside of marriage." He could have shamed her and added guilt to her already burdened soul. Instead, he saw her pregnancy as a reflection of a family pattern that would not be effectively broken through moral teaching ("It is wrong to have sex before marriage") or sex education ("Why weren't you using birth control?"). Pastor Washington knew that Leah and Jeanne needed to be seen in family therapy to continue to work on changing their family pattern. Leah would need support for the painful separation she would feel at the time of the adoption. Jeanne would need support and validation as she found ways other than being a grandmother to be loved. Jeanne would also need help in letting Leah become independent so that she could leave home without being cut off.

And so it is with other conflicts that seem to be about sex. People come to their counselors and talk about having affairs. As the sessions progress, they discover that while they were distracted by the sexual nature of affairs, they were really avoiding facing the conflicts in their unhappy marriages. Sometimes affairs are an indication of sexual addictions that are more about obsessive compulsive behavior than they are about sexual pleasure. When the sexual activity is part of marital rape or incest, the real issue is power abuse. Those who come to see you to resolve sexual conflicts will be navigating among conflicting pulls. They will use their ego to help them manage and adapt:

Conscience: Your community's moral teachings on sexuality will play a significant part in informing conscience. Your members will also bring with them experiences in which they were shamed because of their bodies or made to feel guilty because of sexual curiosity. The conscience of one who has been loved and accepted in early childhood will differ from that of one who has been treated harshly and whose conscience (superego) is punitive and inflexible. In the conscience reside beliefs about sex being good or bad, permissible or not permissible. Cultural attitudes and mores about sex also become factored in.

People: Some who come to resolve sexual conflicts may need to address inner voices of introjected authority figures whose attitudes are influencing their present sexual experience. Others may be consciously unaware of people who sexually abused them. However, they have taken in these experiences and have introjected the presence of those who now cause them to be panicky about sex. Others might be experiencing personal conflicts with their sexual partner. For some the conflict is around the emotional intimacy of sex; for others, it might be around having difficulty sexually pleasing or being pleased.

Reality: The person coming to resolve sexual conflicts will factor in his or her age, health, relationship status, availability of sexual partner, in addition to all the other external realities affecting one and one's sexual situation.

Desire: Sexual conflicts are fueled by the power of sexual drive and passion, sexual orientation, ability to experience delight, as well as other emotions that become stirred up in a sexually arousing situation. Inhibitions against the expression of sexuality also provoke countering emotions and anxiety.

You can help those who come to you sort out these strands and see where their conflict lies. The ease with which they can resolve their conflict will depend on the maturity of their ego defenses. Those with immature ego defenses may be somewhat disconnected from their bodies or have defenses that do not allow them to acknowledge fully and give pleasure to their sexual partner. Those with mature defenses will be more able to enjoy sex and to give pleasure in a relationship that is based on mutuality and consent. They will be able to intertwine love and sex.

Even though you will not be able to help all those who come to you with sexual conflicts to resolve them in brief counseling, you can help them label their conflicts, and in many cases, refer them for additional help. Some people will also have sexual dysfunctions (inability to experience sexual pleasure or to have orgasms; premature ejaculation; tightening of the vagina) that can be overcome through sex therapy. Others have difficulties communicating their sexual needs. They and their partners may be helped through relationship counseling.

Others whose pleasure is inhibited because of a harsh conscience might be most appropriately helped by you to become more accepting of their sexual selves. Often people whose sexual function is impaired by a punitive conscience have internalized a fearful God. They also may not understand your religion's more positive understanding of the gifts of sexuality. Often your acceptance of them and your ability to provide an educational corrective will help them to be more appreciative of their physical selves. Through your counsel, they may be able to be healed and to say: "God is good. Sex is good."

It might be useful for you to reflect on your counseling experience to see how frequently counselees bring sexual issues or concerns for consideration. If they are rarely mentioned in sessions, perhaps even though you are open to talking about them, members of your community may not be expecting you to be. Some in your congregation may feel conflicted about talking about sex with a religious counselor. They do not expect that you will be able to help them sort out their conflicts because:

- They expect that you will tell them what they *should* do. Their conflicts lie in what they *do*.
- They expect that you will use fear to try to make them become sexually acceptable.
- They are leery of the helpfulness of religious teachings on sexuality because of the widely publicized clergy sexual misconduct and sexual acting out and abuse in some religious communities.
- They expect negative thinking about sexuality that will not help them find a way to cope with today's sexual climate.

Your community members will know more realistically what to expect from your counsel if they hear you preach about the gift of sexuality and its role in life. If your community has workshops and forums that address the complexities of sexuality, these will also have an opportunity to serve a corrective function.

Members of religious communities need more than "thou shalt not's," reinforced by fear, to help them make appropriate moral decisions about the place of sexuality in their lives. Parents also need help in guiding their children in a time when, on TV, and in the cinema, images of sexuality are violent and depersonalizing. Children and adolescents need to learn that sex can be experienced in loving relationship in which there is mutual consent and mutual pleasure. To offer this positive corrective, the blessings of sex must be talked about in community.

Effects of Addiction

When your community care and brief counseling are in response to addiction, you are dealing with people who abuse or are dependent on alcohol, drugs, or other chemical substances. Often you help them receive treatment or find their way to Twelve Step groups. You also help them and their families deal with the *effect* their drinking or drugging has upon their lives. Couples come for counsel about marital problems that are related to addiction. Drinking is often a part of the picture in family violence and child abuse. Families come for help to stop colluding with their substance-abusing member so that healing can happen.

It is important that you understand the *illnesses* of chemical abuse and dependency, which can be treated. However, addiction is a condition that is more comprehensive than the illness itself: it also is a *syndrome* that affects the person's mind and spirit, thoughts and actions, and is supported by an entire family system. Following are some medical descriptions:

Dependency is at the heart of addiction. It is in part a physiological response. The body *needs* the chemicals of the substance to feel pleasure and to avoid the state of withdrawal. To obtain the needed chemical, the person then *depends* on a system of obsessive thinking and compulsive behavior. Addiction is driven by the need for *more* of the substance to get the desired high. Obsessive thoughts ("When can I have it?" "Where can I get it?") and compulsive actions compel an addict to fulfill the need.[20]

Addiction is a form of *chronic* adaptation to the body's *reward system.* Dr. Steven Hyman, Director of the Mind, Brain, Behavior Initiative at Harvard University, says that in alcohol addiction the brain's reward circuitry is bombarded by the chemical, ethanol. This bombardment causes molecular changes in the brain that in turn responds to alcohol. The brain "learns" that *more* alcohol feels good. Once this occurs, the alcoholic becomes dependent on the message of reward to feel good; however, more and more alcohol is needed to produce the effect. The brain demands it. Dr. Hyman notes that there are individual genetic, developmental, and environmental factors that determine who will get addicted to alcohol and how soon, although we are still learning about these. More research is required to learn *who* could become an alcoholic.[21] Studies show that children of alcoholics are at risk, but not all members of alcoholic families become alcoholic. And some alcoholics come from families where no one drank.

Recent studies are showing that it is the affect of the addictive substance on the brain circuitry itself that causes the craving. Anyone using substances such as amphetamines, heroin, alcohol, or nicotine can become addicted. With the advent of sophisticated research equipment such as PET scans (positron emission tomography), scientists have been able to do fine-grained studies of brain cells, capturing images of the brains of addicts as they crave addictive substances. They have discovered that all addictive substances activate a single circuit for pleasure — the neurotransmitter dopamine. The neurons in the circuitry for pleasure become damaged when addictive substances repeatedly flood the brain's circuitry damaging the neurons. This damage causes the brain to become starved for dopamine. The starvation in turn triggers a craving for the addictive substances that will once again activate the pleasure circuitry. Although the brains of addicts change because of the assault to the dopamine receptor, they can become almost normal after a year without the addictive substance.[22]

To define our terms, *alcoholism* is a progressive, potentially fatal, but treatable chronic *disease*. It is complex, involving genetic, psychosocial and environmental factors. It is supported by social context. It is an illness that affects the total person and his or her social and familial relationships.

Those who *abuse* alcohol are debilitated by it in their daily lives. Their work and home life suffer. They are physically endangered by it and they endanger others, for instance, by driving while drunk. They are prone to legal difficulties — for drunk driving, fighting, family violence. They are *compelled* to drink even when they know that their drinking causes problems. They are out of control.

Alcoholism progresses from abuse to the state of physiological *alcohol dependence*. In this state a person needs to drink more and more to get the desired "high" and to avoid alcohol withdrawal. Alcohol withdrawal occurs twelve hours or so after drinking decreases. With it, come symptoms of sweating, tremors, agitation, anxiety, nausea, etc. Those who depend on alcohol use it compulsively and think about it obsessively. Their thinking becomes distorted and they use the defense of denial.[23]

The forms alcoholism takes differ. Some alcoholics are binge drinkers who abstain from drinking between episodes. Others may not drink to intoxication, but may drink steadily and maintain a high amount of alcohol in their system. Yet other alcoholics are steady drinkers who also periodically go on binges.

Many alcoholics and drug addicts trace the beginnings of their addiction to experimentation in their early years. Most kids experiment with alcohol as teenagers, yet they do not become alcoholics. Why do some? In his book *Emotional Intelligence,* Daniel Goleman cites statistics from the Institute of Drug and Alcohol Abuse showing that 90 percent of all high school students experiment with alcohol while only 14 percent will become addicted. Of the millions of Americans who have tried cocaine, only 5 percent become addicted.[24] Why are some susceptible to addiction and others not?

While researchers continue to answer the question, "who becomes addicted?" it is becoming clear that people are biologically predisposed to alcoholism and that the causes are brain-based. Some biological markers are being identified in those who are drawn to alcohol to calm anxiety. The marker *GABA,* a neurotransmitter that regulates anxiety, has been found to be too low in those who use alcohol to soothe their nerves. Goleman reports a study of sons of alcoholic fathers who had low levels of GABA and were highly anxious. Their GABA levels rose and they became less anxious when they drank.[25] Those with this neurotransmitter deficiency *crave calm.*

Another route to alcoholism is taken by those who have a deficiency of the neurotransmitters serotonin and MAO, which soothe agitation. People who have a high level of agitation, impulsivity, and boredom often self-medicate with alcohol and other drugs to quiet their agitated emotions. Others use alcohol and drugs to medicate depression and chronic anger. Both depression and chronic anger are supported by irregularities in one's neurochemical systems.[26]

One's socioeconomic situation also plays its part. People living in high-crime neighborhoods, where drugs and alcohol are readily available, have easy access to them if they have money or the job of selling them. The stress of poverty and the boredom of unemployment create emotions in many that they ease by taking drugs and alcohol.

Dr. Paul McHugh, psychiatrist-in-chief at Johns Hopkins and director of the Blades Alcohol Research Center there, ties alcoholism to stress — which differs at different stages of life. He observes that younger alcoholics are reacting to the stresses of an active life. However, many people do not become alcoholics until they pass middle age. Dr. McHugh observes that older people begin to drink when the stresses of work and family life have lessened and when the structure of work is no longer present. Retirement creates a new stress.[27] Those who begin drinking heavily during or after middle age are called reactors. They are responding to difficult life changes, loneliness, bereavement, or depression. Late onset-reactors are often responsive to treatment. However the clues to their alcohol problem might be hard to detect because the changed structure of their daily life makes it harder to monitor their drinking behavior.

Researchers at Yale University and the University of Connecticut have found that there are two distinct types of alcoholics. Those who begin drinking heavily later in life are called Type A. They have fewer early risk factors, less severe dependence on alcohol and milder physical, psychological, and social consequences from drinking. Type A alcoholics respond better to residential treatment and suffer fewer relapses than Type B alcoholics, who begin drinking at a young age. Type B's have more childhood risk factors and more severe dependence on alcohol and they suffer more physical, psychological and social consequences from their drinking. They consume more alcohol than Type A alcoholics and are often dually addicted to tranquilizers and illicit drugs. Type B alcoholics return to heavy drinking sooner following treatment, and drink more upon relapsing, than type A alcoholics.[28]

Understanding the typology of alcoholics can be helpful to you as you help your congregation address the problem of self-medication of stress. The Yale University and University of Connecticut researchers have documented what we have observed about young people and heavy drinking; the consequences can be devastating and long-term. Religious communities need to proactively educate their young people and their larger social communities about alcoholism. This must be done in such a way that it does not create another problem: nagging kids not to drink does not work. However education and intervention are not enough if *the stress* that young people are facing is not also addressed and they are not helped to *learn skills to cope with it.* This is equally true of older people.

Addiction, as a concept, has recently expanded to include not only substance abuse, but also those who use work, food, sex, gambling, etc., to get a psychological "high." These addictions use the same obsessive, compulsive behaviors to satisfy their need. Not all of them produce the same types of toxic poisoning nor do they cause the same physical illnesses. However, all addictions produce a seductive relief of tension, as hormones are released producing feelings that people want to feel again. Those who get "hooked" on compulsive sex or work become *dependent on the good feelings* that are released by the brain's neurochemical reward system. While the addictions of sex, work, and gambling may not be chemically toxic, they are pernicious. They can wreak havoc in personal and family life.

All addictions follow the same cycle. It begins with a belief system that says: "When I drink (have sex, take drugs, etc.) I feel better," "I'm more attractive," "I'm more worthwhile," "I'm not empty." This is followed by obsessive thoughts focusing on when and how to get the next drink or other "fix" and compulsive actions to obtain it. For a period in the cycle, the drinking, etc., produces good feeling, a period of "high." Because of the effects of chemical dependency, it takes more and more alcohol to feel high or to avoid the experience of withdrawal. Following the good feelings comes intoxication. In this state, there is uncontrolled behavior, and sometimes blackouts. When the person is more sober, he experiences embarrassment, shame, guilt, and these lower self-esteem. To reinforce the self, the cycle begins again. The addictive system is a conditionally reinforced habit.

To function in this system, the addict must be able to deny the consequences of the habit. This results in impaired thinking. A person who is addicted to sexual activity might tell himself: "I can slip into this strip joint.

No one from the office will see me." He tells himself he is safe even when it is likely that he might be observed by colleagues. As a result of denial, impaired thinking, and compulsive activity, the sex addict's life can become unmanageable. However, in spite of the disarray, the behavior must go on.

Drinking is a way of medicating a psychological or spiritual pain. However, drinking causes *physiological* dependence on a substance that poisons the body and causes damage to the brain. People drink, etc., to "cure" the effects of stress. They are supported in these addictive patterns by their families and friendship groups.

Families support those who drink to avoid separation and loss and in turn to avoid distress. They have the *need* to stay together. People need relationships that are constant, even if the constancy is stressful. Those who study alcoholic families have shown how each member colludes with the addicted person not to change so as to keep equilibrium. Even when family members try to stop the addicted person from drinking, there are other forces that keep the behavior going. They use methods to change him or her that rarely work and that reinforce the very behavior they are trying to change.

When the addicted person is the father, the mother is often described as being a codependent, "addicted" to the good feelings she has when she feels needed by the addicted person. Although she may be angry and hurt about his drinking or other dependent behavior, she eventually forgives him and continues to take care of him. She *needs* to be needed. These roles are often reversed when the wife is the addicted person. Everyone in the family has a role to play to keep the equilibrium and *to keep the addicted person in the family.* A family organized around a member's addiction becomes very closed, both because of the need to keep the problem secret and because they must use their time and energy to keep the family system going. This system makes it difficult for the family to reach out for help.

A driving force behind addiction is the need of the addicted person to feel calm, to quiet distress, and to feel alive. However, the "medication" produces just the opposite effect — chaos. Children of alcoholics or other addicts speak of the *excitement* in their families. Addicted people are unpredictable and the family's response contributes to the high drama. Families of addicts are usually chaotic and unstable and the children become adjusted to excitement and chaos. When they are in calm environments, they feel as if something is wrong.

To stop the addictive cycle, the person must stop drinking, taking drugs, working compulsively. To help addicts and their families "take the pebble from their shoes," counselors in community need to know which methods work and how to make referrals.

Sometimes those with chemical dependencies need to have medical treatment for withdrawal from chemical substances and for other cures. They also need treatment for depression and other stress-related illnesses that they have been trying to self-medicate. Most then need support of their abstinence from

Twelve Step groups or other support groups. Some are helped by individual or family psychotherapy. Their families also have to learn new behavior or they will pull recovering addicts back into old familiar ways. Use your community's wholeness network to find addiction counselors, Twelve Step groups, pastoral psychotherapists, and medical consultants to whom you can refer, and with whom you can consult.

As addicts recover, they need support in living life fully. Brief therapy is often useful for helping them discover the solutions they have been using to solve their problems and support their strength. Counselors in community can use solution-focused methods to help reinforce these positive changes.

Because chemical addiction is a relapsing and progressive disease, stopping drinking once is never enough. The recovering alcoholic or drug addict has to stop over and over every day. However, if one *only* focuses on *not drinking,* one can ironically become preoccupied with "not drinking" and this can become another pebble in the shoe.

The absence of drinking does not in itself guarantee that one will have a fulfilling life. This is also true about stress. Taking away stressors is not, in itself, enough. Something needs *to be added to prevent a void.* Remember again, Jesus' teaching about casting out demons. He said that unless *good spirits* were invited to *fill the house* that the evil spirits had left, many, many more evil spirits would return.

The "house" — the life — of recovering addicts and their families needs to be filled with inner calm, a sense of being alive, knowledge about how to live life, and connection to loving relationships.

The founders of Alcoholics Anonymous knew this to be true. The work of Twelve Step programs helps people learn how to live. The program helps recovering addicts face themselves and acknowledge the effect of the addiction on themselves and on those close to them. Then they are helped to take responsibility for repairing injuries to old relationships and for renewing their relationship to God — their Higher Power. The program helps recovering addicts connect to a *new reward system.* Life, itself, becomes rewarding as they help others in order to help themselves. Although their brain circuitry has been altered through addiction, their spiritual circuitry has been rewired.

Pain of Abuse

Counselors in community are often responding to those who have been or are now being abused, but they do not know it. Abuse has not been presented as the problem. The member comes for help with problems that are the result of abuse.

Many families, even religious ones, are violent. In fact, some people who abuse support their actions by religious belief. Many who come to their religious counselors for help are victims of violence although they may not describe themselves that way. No faith community is without a story, often undisclosed, of the pain of abuse.

Counselors in community need to be well prepared to assess and minister to the pain of abused people. Because the entire issue of abuse is so painful, many religious communities deny its existence altogether. In this respect, the community's reaction is itself an *acute distress reaction.* When confronted with abuse, the community responds with fear, helplessness, and horror. It becomes numb and detached from the issue. Abuse becomes unreal and may even be forgotten. Perhaps this has been your personal reaction as well.

Before finding ways to heal your community's acute distress reaction to abuse and minister to those suffering its effects, you may need to become more comfortable when thinking about abuse. Pay attention to your anxiety level. If you feel symptoms of anxiety, stop, breathe, and use relaxation techniques or meditation to become centered again. Coming into contact with abuse *is* stressful. Minister to yourself when you deal with it.

There is an extensive bibliography of material on the phenomenon of abuse, the role of religion, and processes for healing. See Reading and Resources at the end of the chapter, and the bibliography. By becoming familiar with this material, you can help overcome your own perfectly understandable feelings of helplessness. Also take advantage of experiential workshops and groups on abuse sponsored by community organizations or your religious body. Pastoral studies programs, seminaries, and local colleges also offer courses.

In addition to being fortified by better knowledge of the subject, it is necessary that you examine your own preconceptions and biases about abuse. Do you feel personally conflicted about it? How has theology informed your ideas about abuse? What has been your personal experience with it? If you remember abuse, have you been in a process of healing? You may not remember being abused but, as you read about abuse, you might recognize in yourself some of the symptoms of those who have been abused. If the readings stir up severe discomfort, you might wish to speak to a therapist. You may be on the brink of a possibility for rich healing.

I have found among the seminary students I have taught a high incidence of childhood physical, emotional, and sexual abuse. My students, who were in the process of healing, were drawn to ministry as "wounded healers." In many instances, belief in a loving God was the lifeline they grasped as children in the terror of their abuse. Others were in seminary to find or come to terms with the God whom they felt had let them down in the nightmare of their childhood. Many in ministry are grown-up abused children. Caregivers whose wounds have been healed can use their experience in the community care and counseling of those who come to them with the pain of abuse. However, those who are still in denial of their own abuse are often unable to hear or believe those who come for counsel and referral.

When a person who has been abused tells her counselor about her child-hood experience and is believed by one who does not condemn her or trivialize her experience, her healing can continue. It has already begun — that is why she came to you.

Some who come to you will need to speak to you about the pain of abuse in the past and its continued effect on their lives in the present. Others will come for help because they are living in the midst of family violence *now*. To minister effectively to them you need a frame of reference in which to think about family violence; and information, resources and skill to deal with child abuse, battering and sexual abuse.

Child Maltreatment: Neglect and Abuse

Many families are not safe places for children. Through surveying child protective service agencies, the National Committee to Prevent Child Abuse found that in 1995 at least 1,215 children died as a result of abuse and neglect. This number of fatalities is low. Many more cases of death were reported and were being reviewed at the time of the study. New York alone had 43 cases pending. As consistent with data from other years, the vast majority who died from maltreatment were very young; 45 percent were less than one year old and 85 percent were under the age of five.

The number of children who are maltreated is alarmingly high. In 1995 nearly one million children were confirmed as victims of maltreatment and became new cases accepted on to child welfare caseloads. Over 3.1 million children were reported as victims of child abuse and neglect. Overall, the total number of reports of abuse has increased 49 percent since 1986.[29]

The National Committee to Prevent Child Abuse Study also documents the *problems* of families that were reported for child maltreatment. Substance abuse was named as the top problem (81 percent). Poverty and economic stress were second cited (49 percent). Among the problems accompanying poverty are poor housing and limited community resources. Lack of specific parenting skills due to mental health problems, poor understanding of a child's normal developmental path, or young maternal age were also reported by 43 percent of the respondents. A significant percentage of adult clients struggle with domestic violence and often presented their own history of battering.[30]

While the cyclical phenomenon of family violence is complex and has no single cause, the *neglect of children* is often at its core. It is easy to see how substance abusers — by far the largest percentage of abusing parents — could neglect their children. It is also easy to see how the problems of poverty can contribute to parental stress.

However, neglected children can be found in all classes of families. Some have nannies, others baby-sitters. Some are latchkey children whose baby-sitter is television. Some are in day-care centers. Others are with their mothers at home, although their mothers do not pay attention to them. Neglected children are not attached to their parents. Parents who have mental illnesses, who have a poor understanding of child development, who are children themselves, or who were neglected or maltreated in childhood often do not know how to connect to their own children.

When we think of neglected children, we often visualize them as hungry, unkempt, sick, battered. Such physical neglect is tragic, and it often results in a child's death. However, the emotional neglect of children is often not so easily detected, but its effect is extremely serious. When mothers and then other caretakers do not connect to children, the injurious effect is far-reaching. It shapes the child's experience of himself in the world and it creates an inner condition that allows the child to adapt to a life of abuse, and later, perhaps to the abuse of others.

Children become attached to their parents in infancy, first to their mothers, and then to other loving family members. Some mothers, because of their own experience, do not form a bond with their babies. When their babies are born they feel emptiness or indifference. When they try to care for them they feel inadequate. Some begin to believe that their babies are rejecting them. Although they may try to be "motherly," even their babies, who recruit them with engaging smiles, fail to help the mothers attach to them. Babies and mothers who connect spend hours memorizing each other as they gaze into each other's eyes while the babies are nursing. As this happens, the "mother-baby" experiences wholeness. When this does not happen at this early time of life, the baby already begins to experience an incompleteness that leads to an inner self-fragmentation. A baby who has known "mother-baby-wholeness" eventually experiences a "good-baby-self" and knows that the mother is another, separate "whole-good-person."

Children who have not bonded with their mothers begin to experience the nonconnectedness as "there's something wrong with me." For them, their mother's neglect becomes their fault. Because children need their mothers, they cannot bear to perceive them as "bad mommy." Rather than blame their mothers for something being wrong, they internalize a sense of "bad me." Children who have not known sufficient attachment and nurture grow up feeling empty. They also have an *illusion* of being loved because they have created the loving mother themselves by calling themselves "bad" and their mother "good."

There lives an internalized cast of characters in neglected children: "bad me," "neglected-unseen me," "good mother," "unseeing mother." These children grow up feeling empty and split. Mothers who do not attach to their children do not really see them, so they do not take care of their children's physical selves. In turn, their children do not learn to take pleasure in their own bodies, to care for them and to learn to soothe themselves. Even if these children have good clothes, they are anxious and do not develop self-confidence.

Many neglected children do not come to the attention of child welfare authorities because their families "have it together" enough to see that they get to school. In fact, many come from families that care a great deal about "what the neighbors think." Parents who emotionally neglect their children can at the same time be overly involved with their social and academic performance. They see themselves in their children. The children are treated as their extensions and are expected to do their families credit. Nonetheless, the children grow up getting into abusive relationships themselves because of the neglect they have internalized.

Parents who neglect their children because of lack of attachment often physically and emotionally abuse them as well. Sometimes a parent has unconsciously identified a child as being like herself — the part of herself she does not like — and she strikes out against it. Parents who are not emotionally attached to their children can hit them without feeling remorse; they are already objects. They can also freeze them out and cut them off. Violence can be cold as well as hot.

Children are born with the capacity for empathy — the ability to know how another feels. Studies of developmental psychologists and physiologists show that in infancy a child will become upset when he hears another infant cry. This response is a precursor of empathy. Even toddlers, who have begun to distinguish their own feelings from the feelings of others, will respond in a variety of ways to comfort another child who is distressed.[31] Neurologists who study the biological basis of empathy are learning that the capacity for empathy is built into our very brains.

However, studies show that children who have experienced repeated beatings do not respond empathically. In one study of toddlers in a day-care center for children from high-stressed, impoverished homes, half of the children were physically abused, the others, not. The abused children had already lost their bent toward empathy. Unlike the unabused children, who comforted other children when they were distressed, the abused children reacted to these distressed children with fear, anger, and sometimes violence. They were mimicking the way they were treated by their parents who hit them when they cried to "make them stop" or who hit them again to "give them something to cry for."

The behavior of the abused children was caused by more than simply mimicking the behavior of their parents. The trauma of their abuse had affected the shape of their brain leaving a lasting imprint on the amygdala — the emotional brain. The amygdala is the site of the brain that stores emotional memory. It is also the site that alerts the neurochemical system of life-threatening emergencies. The distress of their classmates triggered memories of the abused toddlers' own trauma of abuse. Flooded by emotion, they then responded with the flight or fight response. They did not "see" their distressed classmates. They could not respond empathically.[32]

A parent's nonattachment and neglect is certainly not the only cause of child abuse. Poverty, and its many accompanying problems, also contribute. Parents are often abusive when they are drinking or abusing drugs. They "lose it" when they are "stressed-out," fatigued, irrational. They displace onto children anger that is rooted in their own helplessness and frustration. For the children of your congregation to be treated tenderly, you must help parents acknowledge their own anger and learn to love all of the parts of their fragmented selves.

Some in religious communities come from authoritarian families where harsh discipline was a duty growing out of belief that to "spare the rod is to spoil the child." Alice Miller, in her book *For Your Own Good,* helps us understand the cruelty of this approach that reinforces belief in the God of fear. Religious communities can help parents learn better ways to discipline children and to resolve family fights. In fact, of all social institutions, they can be the most effective family educator. People come to church and synagogue to learn to love.

Family violence is occurring somewhere in your faith community. Through sermons and prayers, the community can lift up their concerns. Because you know the congregation, you might also know families that are at risk because of the abuse the parents experienced in childhood. These families need special attention.

For child abuse to stop, families need to be supported through many forms of education. This includes workshops and parent groups where they gain mutual support and learn parenting skills and techniques for dealing with anger. Just as children can learn to be more "academically" intelligent, they can also learn to become more emotionally intelligent. Empathy can be learned. The heart can learn to think. Daniel Goleman in *Emotional Intelligence* describes emotional learning proposals for schools. As a leader in your community, you can be an advocate for this important addition to your schools' curricula. These programs can also be adapted for religious school curricula. (See Reading and Resources.) Psychotherapy for children and adults can also be an occasion for emotional learning.

Battering: The Cycle of Domestic Violence

Domestic violence is usually undetected by outsiders until its victims are treated medically or unless they reach out in fear and desperation. This violence is maintained by complex human relationships, held together through power imbalance, and protected by secrecy. Even when the secret is revealed, the pattern of the violence is difficult to interrupt.

Perhaps you have had a counseling session when a wife found the courage to claim that she was being abused. She then backed down as her husband pointed to her defects or behaviors that "made him" respond to her in anger. Her husband sounded as if *he were the victim* of her stupidity or insensitivity. You might have been confused when the wife did not challenge his explanation. And maybe you did not know the extent to which she was frightened of the consequences. Perhaps you were further confused because you knew her husband's socially acceptable behavior and thought he was a nice guy. Because the wife "took back" her complaint, you missed her plea to protect her from danger.

Women are by far more at risk for domestic assault and homicide than men. Attacks by husbands on wives result in more injuries requiring medical treatment than rapes, muggings, and automobile accidents combined. Twenty percent of all emergency-room visits are the result of battering; one third of all women homicide victims are killed by their husbands.[33] Women caught in the cycle of domestic violence are assaulted repeatedly. In one study, it was found that 32 percent of those assaulted at least once by a domestic partner in the previous six months were victimized again in the next six months.[34]

Even when wives leave their husbands the violence is not over. A number of studies conclude that women are at the most risk of violence *after* they separate or divorce.[35] One out of every three or four wives is living in danger of assault or death.[36] Partnership violence is not mostly a low-income or minority issue, it occurs in all sectors of society and with all racial, economic, and religious groups.[37] More low-income battered women seek assistance from public agencies and are therefore counted in official statistics than are middle or upper-class women, who have private resources for treatment and protection.

Although there has been publicity about husband abuse, the 1990 Bureau of Justice statistics report that men are victims in only about one in ten misdemeanor spouse assaults.[38] However men, too, are battered by women. Sometimes this battering is physical, but often it is emotional and verbal and is not statistically recorded. Sometimes these men are afraid to defend themselves because they know they are stronger and if they seriously hurt the women, they will be viewed as aggressors, not self-defendants.

How are we to explain the secrecy that shrouds these alarming facts? Secrecy is an aspect of the phenomenon of family violence itself. Domestic violence occurs in the private space of the family. The dependent relationships of the family are not easily broken; they are held together by loyalty and economic dependency. In a violent family, the bonds are also forged by fear. Although the cycle of domestic violence has eruptions of violence, it is rooted in *psychological abuse;* the wife is controlled in much the same way that prisoners of war are psychologically tortured. Abusive husbands verbally batter their wives through diatribes or persistent derogatory and demeaning comments until wives are too weary to fight back. Women who are being abused by their husbands do not talk about it.

Battering is the result of power imbalance and it occurs in both heterosexual and homosexual relationships. It is rooted in a need for power and control and is a violent obsessive compulsive disorder. Battering is supported by sexism and corporate memory of times when women were the property of men and children were possessed as objects. Some batterers use religious teaching to rationalize their violence. When men and women are battered in gay and lesbian relationships it is often caused in part by internalized homophobia and sexism.

Like the cycle of addiction, with its reward of pleasure as well as its pain and shame, family violence has a pattern that keeps it going. At its heart is denial and the dissociation common to acute stress disorders. The batterer will deny, justify, minimize, or blame the victim of his actions. Often the batterer had been an unseen, neglected child. Although he does so unconsciously, he uses macho strength to force his partner, whom he perceives as his "unseeing mother," to love him. When his partner disappoints him, he is enraged because he feels (as he did with his mother) that he gives much and gets nothing. He then strikes out.

Sometimes, when battering, the person seems in "another world" and "out of his head." Perhaps at these times he is reliving earlier violence he has witnessed or experienced. Research shows that children who witness or experience violence are at seven hundred times greater risk of becoming a batterer or being battered in their own marital relationships.[39] Violence is passed down to the next generation in families.

The person being battered also copes with it through denial. She, too, is living out her neglected childhood experience. She has grown up feeling unworthy of love and believes that she has to earn love. She believes that her partner would love her if she only tried hard enough. However, as with her mother, she tries to please but she can never do things right enough. She is tied to her partner by her sense of failure and her emotional, financial, and social dependency.

The cycle of violence is held together by the lack of power that the wife and children experience. A wife in an abusive system is extraordinarily attuned to her husband's moods: he becomes more tense and she becomes more cautious. The children pick this up and they, too, walk on eggshells. It is in this tense, stress-filled atmosphere that eventually the husband strikes out violently, and then the air is cleared for a time.

But the cycle is also sustained by the pleasure that the wife feels in the "honeymoon period," when after the violence the husband is penitent and sweet. In some cases although they are not having a "honeymoon period," tension has lifted. Because the wife often has loving as well as frightened feelings toward her husband, the period of "making up" keeps her hoping that perhaps things between them will not get so bad again. But the pattern repeats. The cycle of abuse is a dance in which the batterer leads but his partner follows, trying to appease or accommodate his demands.[40]

The batterer will tend to have the following characteristics:

- *Unrealistic expectations:* He expects his partner to meet all his needs.

- *Isolating:* The batterer will try to cut his wife off from all her resources of friends and family.
- *Blames others for his problems.* He tells his wife that it is her fault for almost anything that goes wrong.
- *Blames others for his feelings:* "You're hurting me by not doing what I want you to do."
- *Hypersensitivity:* The abuser is easily insulted. He says he is "hurt" when he is really mad. He takes the slightest setbacks as personal attacks.
- *Cruelty to animals or children.*
- *"Playful" use of force in sex.* He might like to the throw the woman down and hold her during sex or may want her to play out his sexual fantasies in which she is helpless.
- *Verbal abuse:* He says cruel things that are meant to be hurtful, degrade her, run down her accomplishments, and tells her that she is stupid and unable to function without him. This behavior may involve waking her up to verbally abuse her and not letting her sleep.
- *Rigid sex roles:* The abuser expects a woman to serve him, stay home, and obey him. She should perform menial tasks. He sees "his woman" as inferior and stupid and believes that she cannot be a whole person without him.
- *Threats of violence:* Breaking or striking objects and using physical force during an argument occur as tensions mount, leading to an outbreak of battering and other abuse.[41]

It is not uncommon for wives of battering men to describe their husbands as "Dr. Jekyll and Mr. Hyde." These men show to the world the self they showed to their wives before marriage: kind, generous, and very loving. Occasionally the wife might have had a glimpse of bad temper, unfounded jealously, intrusive behavior, or unreasonable expectations. Frequently a wife's relationship with a battering husband began with quick involvement. He came on like a whirlwind and pressured her for commitment.

At the beginning of a relationship, women are flattered by the very characteristics that are signs of the battering personality. In courtship, the potential batterer is extraordinarily attentive and says that his jealousy is a sign of love. After marriage, this jealousy has nothing to do with love, it is a sign of possessiveness and lack of trust. In courtship he is controlling, but says he is only concerned about her safety. In time he may not let her make personal decisions about her clothing or her use of time. He controls the money and may even make her ask permission to leave the house.

Because many counselors are incredulous that a woman would stay in a life-threatening situation, they have identified the woman, not the man, as needing treatment. They have diagnosed the woman as a masochist who unconsciously takes pleasure in being hurt or as one who seeks punishment because of self-loathing. Researchers have found that this simple profile of the battered woman is inaccurate. (See Reading and Resources at the end of the chapter.)

Women of various personality types are attracted to the "Dr. Jekyll-positive personality" of the battering male. "Dr. Jekyll" is sometimes an athlete, a rock star, a professor, a minister. His need to control is misperceived as strength. His pursuit of her is perceived as strong attraction and love. It is only later that she learns that it masked his possessiveness and fear of abandonment.

The battered wives' reasons for staying in the relationship are equally complex. Some include:

- Commitment to their marriage vows and concerns for keeping the family together for the sake of the children. Those who married the most dangerous batterers did not know that they might risk "till death."
- Debilitation created by the conditioning of psychological battering. With it, comes loss of initiative, self-esteem, and belief in their own right to freedom. They have become psychologically, socially, and financially dependent on their husbands. Many do not even know how much money their husbands make, even when they sign joint tax returns.
- Learned helplessness. Their husbands' controlling behaviors have created a climate in which they learn that they are unable to make changes. They have become depressed and, in some cases, hopeless. Some have already learned to be helpless in childhood.
- Isolation. Because their husbands often insist that they cut off their relationships with family and friends, they have a narrow view of possibilities for resources and networking. They also do not have positive feedback or experiences of being seen and known by others.
- Realistic appraisal of their danger. The statistics showing that wives are in greatest danger of violence when they separate from their husbands prove that women who stay in their marriages because of fear may be being realistic.

Those battered wives who are vulnerable because of early neglect and parental nonattachment are also held by the recreation of their familial relationships. They are in a relationship where again they experience *an illusion of love*. They often try hard, as they did with their own mothers, to create a family life filled with love. They supply the warmth, but they give their husbands the credit. This is often done even as their husbands complain that they do not give them what they need. They then try harder. Sometimes, after a fight, their husbands seem warm. Sometimes they even cry because of the wives' pain. The wives mistake the husbands' tears as remorse. In fact, a husband who is cut off from his own feelings, senses *his* dissociated pain in his wife's tears. He is not feeling love for her. Again, she is experiencing an illusion. Women who have internalized an "unseen self" return to battering husbands because they believe that it is their fault; they have not loved enough.

While battering is often accompanied by alcoholism, it is *not caused* by it. Many batterers do not drink. Some batterers use getting drunk as an excuse to beat their wives. Strangely enough, it is sometimes drinking that leads a batterer to treatment for both addictions. Sometimes wives of alcoholic batterers who would be afraid to speak of the abuse itself, are empowered to go to Al-Anon or other Twelve Step groups where the teachings of the program and the fellowship help them become more self-protective.

Families caught in the cycle of violence need treatment. Because of the complexity and the length of time it takes for a family to change, working alone with battered families is inappropriate. You need to be part of a team that cares for the family. In most cases, the husband and wife must separate while the husband is treated by a therapist who has specialized in working with battering husbands. The wife and children will also need treatment.

The religious community has an important role to play in the family's healing. In addition to interventions that you may need to make by reporting the physical abuse of the children, you may also be the one to refer the wife and children to a shelter or other social and treatment services. Wives will then need support as they learn again to become self-confident and in charge of themselves. Those who have a history of early neglect will need special attention and opportunities to be deeply "seen" and appreciated. The spiritual resources of your community are invaluable to them.[42]

Sexual Abuse of Children and Adults

The sexual abuse of children and adults is often unreported; sometimes knowledge of it is repressed. However, researchers have provided these modest estimates:

- One in three girls and one in six boys are sexually abused by their eighteenth birthday.[43]
- In 1995, over 109,230 children were reported as being sexually abused.[44]
- One woman in four has been raped and there is a correlation between rape and earlier sexual abuse. In Diana Russell's study of women who had been incestuously abused in childhood, two-thirds were subsequently raped.[45]

Children are sometimes abused by strangers, but not with the frequency commonly assumed. Researchers from the National Opinion Research Center of the University of Chicago, in their in-depth survey of sexual practices in America, found that only 4 percent of the men and 7 percent of the women who had been sexually abused as children were abused by strangers.[46] Children are molested by members of their family, family friends, or their caretakers, those whom they trust or who have authority over them. It happens in a familial relationship. They cannot run to safety because they are home already.

Where child sexual abuse is detected and reported early, children can be treated and their suffering relieved. However, as with battering, sexual abuse of children is a family affair. It is protected by secrecy and silence. In most cases one parent, most often the father, stepfather, or mother's boy friend, performs the sexual assault, with the mother in collusion through "not knowing." Often the mother's "not knowing" is related to the dissociation of her own past sexual abuse. However, mothers also actively sexually abuse their children. So do women who are child-care workers. Boys are abused as well as girls.

Most sexual abuse is correctly called incest. While some states' courts define incest as only occurring between blood relatives, the rest include in the legal definition other familial relationships as well. Stepfathers or stepmothers, mother or father's live-in partner and other members of extended families commit incest if they sexually abuse a child in the family.[47] Children experience emotional incest when child-care workers (parental substitutes) or when teachers or religious leaders (those in authority) sexually abuse them. Incest and child abuse by others is an adult disorder. Sexual abuse is never the fault of children.

Why do adults sexually abuse their children? Many theories have been posited and are being tested empirically. One of the most comprehensive studies on father-daughter incest has been conducted by David Finkelhor and Linda Meyer Williams, sociologists at the Family Research Laboratory of the University of New Hampshire. They found clearly varied patterns of abuse related to the type of abuser. They categorized the fathers as: sexually preoccupied, regressed in adolescence, self-gratifying, emotionally dependent, or retaliating angrily against the child's mother or another woman. (See Notes for a fuller description of these categories.)[48]

Finkelhor and Williams have reviewed recent studies on the characteristics of incestuous fathers and have concluded that while these point to a wide range of problems in family background and psychological makeup, the following are particularly notable:

1. incestuous fathers are consistently reported to have difficulties in empathy, nurturance and caretaking;
2. social isolation and lack of social skills are also widespread,
3. histories of being sexually abused themselves are given only by a fifth of offenders, fewer than the popular stereotype suggested,
4. a history of physical child abuse is more common than sexual abuse, and other maltreatment, particularly rejection by fathers, is quite common,
5. a certain proportion of incestuous fathers, estimated to be between a fifth and a third, show signs of general sexual arousal to children, while a more widespread response is a pattern of low sexual arousal to, or even disgust with, normal adult sexual partners,

6. studies have failed to find that incestuous abusers are identified with traditional masculine sex roles but rather, they seem more likely to have weak masculine identification.[49]

The extent and frequency of women who sexually abuse children in their care is now beginning to be explored. Psychologist Ruth Matthews studied adult women and adolescent girls who were sex offenders and found that they could be grouped in the four categories of: teacher-lover; experimenter-exploiter; predisposed, and male-coerced.[50]

Researchers believe that sibling incest is even more common than parent-child incest. There are problems with numbers and definitions of coerced and consensual sexual activity with children. Some researchers say that an age gap of five years implies coercion. Others factor in the children's size, power in the family, and intellectual giftedness as they define sexual coercion (See Vernon R. Wiehe's *Sibling Abuse: Hidden Physical, Emotional, and Sexual Trauma*). Because of the complexity of incest, abusers are hard to treat. The recidivism of those who abuse children is very high. However, when the family system of the incested family is treated, the chances of breaking the cycle are better.[51]

Counselors in community have an opportunity to be helpful to incest perpetrators during the sensitive time when they are first confronted by their abuse. In a study conducted by Parents United (a group that treats incest abusers and their families) of responses of clergy, perpetrators said they were most helped by their religious leader who said:

- "Get help and get it now!" They were most helped by practical suggestions of whom to see, where to go, and how to pay for treatment.
- "Turn yourself in." Many religious leaders encouraged the perpetrators to self-report, leave home, and get help for the rest of the family. They felt helped by the advice: "Call the social service department and tell them you need help."
- "Change your ways, pray for forgiveness, and look to the Lord." The perpetrators felt relieved by the reassurance of some form of spiritual recovery, particularly when the advice also emphasized change and treatment.
- "I'll be there with you." This response was the most helpful. Offenders felt supported when clergy offered not only to pray for them, but to accompany them to the authorities or to court.[52]

Hope for breaking the cycle of child abuse is increasing because society is learning that adults who were abused as children *can* eventually be healed, even when they remember their abuse later in life. We have seen how those in acute stress situations can block out, dissociate, from their painful experience. They "leave their bodies," "play possum," "go somewhere else." This dissociation can lead to the forgetting found in posttraumatic stress disorders.

Recently there has been debate about the validity of the "repressed memory syndrome." Some clinicians and accused parents have felt that many women recovering memories of childhood sexual abuse have in fact been victims of psychotherapists who "planted" false memories by suggestion. Because there is the possibility of influencing suggestible people, many psychotherapists have become extremely cautious about jumping to a quick diagnosis of traumatic stress disorder as originating in childhood sexual abuse.

It is possible to diagnose an adult incorrectly as having symptoms caused by childhood sexual abuse. However, for many, this diagnosis is appropriate. We know that many adults bear the wounds of childhood sexual abuse. And certainly, the more than a million children whose abuse has been substantiated in the past few years are wounded. Will those children forget the abuse? If they remember it later, will they be believed if they tell their experience?

There is evidence that people who have been abused in childhood *can* forget the abuse. Researchers at the Family Research Laboratory of the University of New Hampshire studied 129 women who had been taken to hospital emergency rooms as children where their sexual abuse was documented. The researchers found that 38 percent of the women had forgotten the documented abuse and some of the eighty who remembered it said that there had been times when they forgot it.[53]

We also know that early traumatic experience can eventually be remembered by those who find a safe place. Religious congregations are often such safe places. You may be surprised when a member of your congregation reports that in the midst of a worship service she remembered an early abuse. There might have been no overt invitation to healing. However, because she was experiencing the love of God and the support of the community, the memories came — unbidden.

You may have such members who come to you to talk about childhood sexual abuse that they are now remembering or that they feel strong enough to deal with. Believing those who tell you about their experience is the gift you have to give. Some who were sexually abused in childhood told an adult then, but were not believed. Some were afraid to tell their parent because they did not expect to be believed or thought they would be blamed. Not being believed, but being blamed instead, adds another layer to the abuse. The abuse confuses and frightens them and leaves them feeling conflicted and filled with self-disgust. When they tell another person and are not believed, not only do they feel betrayed again, but their own sense of reality becomes confused. Later, they ask themselves: "Did it happen? Did I make it up?"

❧

Because healing from abuse takes time, it is inappropriate for you to do long-term counseling with those who come to you to speak about it. It is important that you use your skills in referral counseling to find appropriate therapeutic helpers. However, it is essential that you listen, be a companion, and stand by those who are healing. In your listening and believing, you offer a corrective to the original betrayal. You can also comfort them as they experience pain and mourn the childhood that was violated.

Researchers of the impact of childhood sexual abuse have found that, in adulthood, many of those who suffered this abuse had the following difficulties: depression, self-destruction, anxiety, feelings of isolation and stigma, sexual dysfunction, failure to trust, substance abuse, poor self-esteem, and a tendency toward revictimization.[54]

It is not unusual for a grown-up child of sexual abuse to come to you for help with one or several of the problems listed above. As you listen, you may recognize that a cluster of these difficulties might point to an underlying history of childhood sexual abuse. As you continue listening, keep the possibility in mind, but do not boldly check out your hypothesis by asking: "Were you sexually abused as a child?" Even if you make the connection, keep your speculation to yourself. A person who is not ready to remember might feel blamed or shamed if you ask directly about abuse. However, you can ask open-ended questions that invite the person to speak about childhood trauma if he is ready.

For example: a woman comes to talk to you about her unhappy marriage and the guilt she feels because she gets panicky as she and her husband begin to make love. This causes her to feel depressed and anxious. You might hypothesize to yourself that she has had some sexually abusive experience in her background. She has *several* of the components of this pattern. To check your hypothesis, you can begin to inquire about *how far back she can remember* being anxious about sexual experience. This question invites her to speak about the past. If she is ready, she might tell you about some early abuse. If this happens, you can then respectfully listen to her story without doing so in a voyeuristic or judgmental manner.

If your questions do not elicit information that confirms your hypothesis, do not continue to probe. Instead, pay attention to the problem that is presented to you. Proceed to assess the problem and to decide whether to do community care, brief counseling, or referral counseling.

For many who have been sexually abused in childhood, *healing comes first — and then, remembering.* In the previous example, the woman may first need to get into a healing, supportive, therapeutic relationship in which she experiences trust before she can begin to understand the roots of her panic about lovemaking. After she has been in a therapeutic process in which she feels secure and supported, she may then recover the memory of her abuse. This memory will help her make sense of the aversion she feels when having intercourse. You and your religious community can continue to provide community care as she does the painful but curative work of recovery.

We have been using examples of women who have been sexually abused in childhood. While more girls than boys are sexually abused, boys are sexually abused, also. They, too, need to heal. The bibliography includes books written by both men and women about recovery from childhood abuse. We recommend that you read them for a deeper understanding of both the damage done by childhood sexual abuse and the journey of recovery.

%

Women continue to experience sexual abuse in adulthood. In the extensive study conducted by the National Opinion Research Center, 22 percent of all women interviewed said that they had been forced by a man to do something sexual. Again, the abuse by strangers was negligible — 4 percent by strangers and 19 percent by acquaintances. The rest was by someone whom the respondent was in love with (46 percent), spouse (9 percent) or by someone the respondent knew well (22 percent).[55] Only 1.3 percent of the men in this study were found to be forced to do something sexual by women.[56]

Other studies show rape (marital and other) to be even more extensive. Diana Russell, in her classic study, found that one in four women are raped and, of those incestuously abused in childhood, two-thirds were subsequently raped. It is hard to know the full extent of sexual abuse suffered by women. Because it occurs in the intimacy of family or love affairs, it is rarely reported unless it is accompanied by battering severe enough for the woman to go to an emergency room. Women who are raped by strangers usually go through a long period of being afraid, particularly of their physical safety. Women who are raped by their husbands are often more traumatized by a violation of trust. Husbands who force their wives to have sex or who force them to participate in acting out their particular hurtful sexual fantasies often rationalize that their wives are only carrying out their marital duties. However marital rape is not about loving sex; it is an abuse of power and control.[57]

Date rape is also a common occurrence. Because young women are becoming more aware that they do not have to be victims, date rape is more readily reported to college authorities and statistics of its occurrence are beginning to be counted.

Marital, date, and other rape are violent power abuses supported by sexist beliefs. Their effects are severely damaging. In the large study conducted by the University of Chicago's Research Center, it was noted that of the women who were sexually abused only 31 percent were not part of religious communities. Of the rest, 21 percent were mainline Protestants, 25 percent were conservative Christians (that is, evangelical, fundamentalist, and some others) and 17 percent were Roman Catholics. Studies of battered women also show a similarly high percentage of women from religious backgrounds.[58] These statistics refute the stereotype that only "bad women" who "ask for it" are raped. Good women are raped and it is not their fault.

When you are called to assist someone who has been raped you are asked to respond to an acute crisis and you need to be prepared to use the ABC intervention method:

A When a woman has been raped, she has lost control of her body and her life. If she is calling you soon after the rape she may be sobbing out of control or she may be speaking in a flat calm voice. Rape creates post-traumatic shock. In making contact with her, know that she is "not being herself."

B Find out where she is in the rape process — has it just happened? First make certain that she is in a safe place and then give her information she needs as she gets her thoughts together. She should be told to preserve the evidence.

C As she copes with the problem she needs: someone to go with her to the hospital for medical attention and to collect the evidence; telephone number of the rape crisis center; encouragement to report the rape to the police. She will also require psychological counseling and legal assistance.[59]

Because she is in a state of shock, she will need someone with her. When a community's wholeness network is in place, you will be ready to respond quickly to the initial stage of this crisis. Follow-up community care is necessary for the victim, and also for her friends and family. They, too, will be experiencing the vicarious traumatization of the violence of rape. For more guidance, see S. Amelia Stinson-Wesley's excellent chapter, "Daughters of Tamar: Pastoral Care for Survivors of Rape" in *Through the Eyes of Women*, edited by Jeanne Stevenson Moessner.

Religious communities are sometimes the last to know about the physical, emotional, and sexual violence in their midst because their members expect judgment, not help. However, when you speak directly about family violence from the pulpit and in educational settings, you will have an opportunity to intervene not only with the victims of violence, but with those who repeat their own abuse in the violation of others. Some may come to you and other counselors in community for help. Your understanding that abusers have often been abused does not mean that you believe that they are excused from responsibility. However, understanding makes you more compassionate.

Finding the Ways of Peace

Religious communities are in need of soul-searching: Why is it that so many of those in religious groups that preach love are violent to each other? Do these members, in fact, worship a God of fear? Religious groups must attend to *radically changing* the violence in their midst. Counselors in community can help members address the ways in which violence and hatred in the culture support the violence in families.

Peace is not created through the denial of anger and pain, it comes when pain and destruction are fully experienced, when people have enough. Fighting stops; peace comes through forgiveness. Religious communities can become leaven in the loaf, a light in the darkness. Communities that intentionally support healing through accepting people as they are and then experiencing together the accepting love of God can become peaceful places.

Counselors in community have gifts to bring to their members. Their religious tradition teaches about God's forgiveness; their counseling training helps them to help others stop fighting, resolve conflicts, and learn to forgive. However, many counselors need additional training to do this. As clergy, you need skills to help congregations resolve conflict, build consensus, and use the diverse gifts of your members. As counselors, you need special knowledge, practice, and supervision to help people resolve inner and interpersonal conflict. As religious leaders, you need to know how to show your members the path to forgiveness. Happily, you can continue to learn to do this through utilizing educational opportunities.

When fighting ceases, peace is possible — if forgiveness is experienced. You have undoubtedly counseled those who have broken the bonds of family violence but are not at peace. Sometimes the victim is still blaming herself for having been in the situation; sometimes she is waiting for her husband to be healed enough to see what he has done so that he can ask for forgiveness. Then she can respond; then she can drop her burden. If she is ready, she can then forgive.

Often those who abuse others erroneously believe that they know how to ask for forgiveness. In the "honeymoon period" when the abuser is sweet and says, "I'm sorry," he or she is sorry about the broken connection, not the hurt that was inflicted. Because abusers deny their ability to hurt another, they do not experience themselves. They do not truly perceive the ones they hurt. Asking forgiveness requires more than saying, "I'm sorry," and then being in the position to "do it again."

Before those who hurt others are able to ask for forgiveness, they must be able to see the other and truly comprehend the ways in which they inflicted the pain. It is through this acknowledgment that the hard knot of pain in the other can melt. Being acknowledged allows one to forgive.

But what is one to do if the one who has injured has not grown in awareness and therefore, is not able to ask for forgiveness? If the abuser is still in denial? If the one who caused the hurt is dead? If the abused is being blamed for bringing her troubles on herself? Forgiving is a response to the question, "Will you forgive me?" Often, people blame themselves for being unforgiving, even when they have not been asked to forgive.

Those who have been injured and have not been given the opportunity to forgive are often left with this problem: they are affected by the hurt and feel shame. They feel unloving toward their offender and feel guilt. They believe that they must stop being "sensitive" or "grudge-bearing" and forget it. But suppressing awareness does not work. They need to be helped to live with the hard knot of unacknowledged hurt until it can be melted in another way: Through healing religious practices, they can be helped to become restored without denying their experience even when the offender has not been able to change.

Jesus on the cross did not forgive those who were killing him. They did not ask him to. Jesus asked God to forgive them "because they do not know what they are doing." Christians and Jews struggle to comprehend and rely on their forgiving God, even in the midst of persecution. Jews ask where God was in the midst of the Holocaust. Christian blacks called to God in the midst of their enslavement. Those marginalized by social discrimination, poverty, and the stigma of disease call on God, not only for God's presence and support, but to help them carry the burden of their response to their persecutors.

Religious groups differ in their theological understanding of suffering and ways to live out the requirement to "forgive your enemies; pray for those who persecute you." They also have various liturgical gifts and practices for healing and restitution. But both Christians and Jews know that peacemaking begins with a change of heart—which is made through God's grace:

> Seek the Lord while the Lord may be found,
> Call upon God while God is near;
> Let the wicked forsake their way,
>   and the unrighteous their thoughts;
> Let them return to the Lord, that
>   the Lord may have mercy on them,
>   and to our God, for God will abundantly pardon.
> For my thoughts are not your thoughts,
>   nor are your ways, my ways, says the Lord.
> For as the heavens are higher than the earth,
>   so are my ways higher than your ways
>   and my thoughts than your thoughts.

Adapted from Isaiah 55:6–9

Sometimes those abused in childhood do not consciously know that they have experienced injury that has become unforgivable. They know that something is wrong within them but they believe that what is wrong *is* them — they are "the bad seed." Because they do not remember that they suffered injury to their innocence, that their trust was violated, they believe that not being whole is their own fault and they are unforgivable. Before some of your members can know peace, they may first need to discover that others, not themselves, are in need of forgiveness. And they will need God to help them bear the burden of that knowledge.

We all need help both to learn to ask others for forgiveness and also to become softened so that we can forgive others. It is sometimes small slights that, when held onto, become heavy burdens. The human condition requires that all people learn to see others with new eyes and to think thoughts with a clarity that comes through God's grace before relationships are made right.

Right relationships, a new heart, melted pain, eyes that see, transformation. God gives these gifts. God has also given us communities where through our relationships with each other we can be healed, loved, and supported. In our communities, we can become brave enough to ask for forgiveness. And we can be given grace to forgive. The kiss of peace can become both a sign and a reality.

Just to be is a blessing.
Just to live is holy.

Chapter Nine
Reading and Resources
Publishing information is found in the Bibliography.

• For additional readings on *ministering to people in crisis,* see Howard Clinebell's chapter, "Crisis Care and Counseling," in *Basic Types of Pastoral Care and Counseling.* Also see David Switzer, *Pastoral Care Emergencies* and Wayne Leaver, *Clergy and Victims of Violent Crimes: Preparing for Crisis Counseling.*

Classic counseling tools are found in: Charles Gerkin, *Crisis Experiences in Modern Life;* Eugene Kennedy, *Crisis Counseling, A Guide for Non-Professional Counselors;* and Howard Stone, *Crisis Counseling: An Introduction to the Theory and Practice of Crisis Counseling.*

• To enrich your *understanding of stress and its effect,* see Hans Selye, *The Stress of Life;* James J. Gill, S.J., M.D., "Anxiety and Stress," in the *Clinical Handbook of Pastoral Counseling, Vol. 1,* edited by Robert Wicks et al.; Peter Kramer, *Listening to Prozac;* and Richard Parson, *Adolescents in Turmoil, Parents under Stress.* For more understanding of Posttraumatic Stress Disorder see Judith Herman, M.D., *Trauma and Recovery;* N. Duncan Sinclair, *Horrific Traumata: A Pastoral Response to the Posttraumatic Stress Disorder;* and David Foy, Kent D. Drescher, Allan G. Fitz and Kevin R. Kennedy's chapter, "Posttraumatic Stress Disorder," in the *Clinical Handbook of Pastoral Counseling, Vol. 2,* edited by Robert Wicks et al.

Thomas E. Rodgerson's *Spirituality, Stress, and You* is an excellent book to use with congregations to help them understand and manage stress by using spiritual resources.

• In the Bibliography you will find an extensive list of books on the *etiology of addiction, its treatment and pastoral resources.* Excellent resources for information on addictions and codependence are Barbara Yoder's *The Recovery Resource Book* and Stephen Apthorp's *Alcohol and Substance Abuse — A Clergy Handbook.* For articles giving an overview of addiction see: Jo Ann Krestoan and Claudia Bebko, "Alcohol Problems and the Family Life Cycle," in Carter and McGoldrick's *The Changing Family Life Cycle;* James E. Royce, S.J., "Alcohol and Other Drug Dependencies," *Clinical Handbook of Pastoral Counseling,*

Vol. 1, edited by Robert Wicks et al.; and Howard Clinebell's article, "Alcohol Abuse, Addiction and Therapy," in the Dictionary of Pastoral Care and Counseling, edited by Rodney Hunter.

Resources for ministering to alcoholics: Gerald May's Addiction and Grace is grounded in spirituality and has an excellent chapter on the neurological nature of addiction. Also see John E. Keller, Ministering to Alcoholics; Paul D. Lininger's "Pastoral Counseling and Psychoactive Substance Abuse Disorders," in Clinical Handbook of Pastoral Counseling, Vol. 2, edited by Robert Wicks et al.

Sources for information and literature on addiction:

National Clearinghouse for Alcohol and Drug Abuse Information, P.O. Box 2345, Rockville, MD 20847-2345 Tel. (468) 2600, (800) 729-6686.
Alcoholics Anonymous, World Service Office, Inc. Box 459 Grand Central Station, New York, NY 10163 Tel. (212) 870-3400.
Narcotics Anonymous World Services Office, Inc., 19737 Nordhofs Place, Chatsworth, CA 91311 Tel. (818) 700-0700. Fax: (818) 773-9999.

• We recommend Sexual Assault and Abuse: A Handbook for Clergy and Religious Professionals, edited by Mary D. Pellauer, Barbara Chester, and Jane Boyajian; and Abuse and Religion: When Praying Isn't Enough, edited by Anne Horton and Judith A. Williamson, for their understanding of the etiology and issues of sexual abuse and their suggestions for the religious community's response. Additional resources: Suzanne Sgroi, ed., Handbook of Clinical Intervention in Child Sexual Abuse; David Finkelhor, ed., A Source Book on Child Sexual Abuse; and W. L. Marshall, D. R. Laws, and H. E. Barbaree, Handbook of Sexual Assault: I Issues, Theories and Treatment.

Ave Clark, O.P.'s Lights in the Darkness: For Survivors and Healers of Sexual Abuse, offers rich spiritual resources both for survivors and for counselors ministering to them as well as a helpful bibliography and list of resources.

For other theological responses to sexual abuse, see Marie Fortune, Sexual Violence: The Unmentionable Sin: An Ethical and Pastoral Perspective; James Poling, The Abuse of Power: A Theological Problem; Carolyn Holderread Heggen, Sexual Abuse in Christian Homes and Churches; and Nancy Ramsey's chapter, "Sexual Abuse and Shame: The Travail of Recovery," in Women in Travail and Transition, edited by Maxine Glaz and Jeanne Stevenson Moessner; Pamela Cooper-White, The Cry of Tamar, and Joanne Stevenson Moessner, ed., Handbook of Womancare: Through the Eyes of Women.

For legal information see Mary Winters' Laws against Sexual and Domestic Violence.

• For broad overviews of family violence in American families see: Mary Koss et al., eds., No Safe Haven: Male Violence against Women at Home, at Work and in the Community; Leonard D. Eron et al., Reason to Hope: A Psychosocial Perspective on Violence and Youth; Carol J. Adams, Woman-Battering; David Levinson, Family Violence in Cross-Cultural Perspective; Albert J. Reiss and Jeffrey Roth, Understanding and Preventing Violence; and David Finkelhor, Stopping Family Violence.

For a theological response to family violence see: Jo Ann M. Garma's chapter, "The Cry of Anguish: The Battered Woman," in Women in Travail and Transition, edited by Maxine Glaz and Jeanne Stevenson Moessner; James Leehan, Pastoral Care for Survivors of Family Abuse; Andrew Lester, Pastoral Care with Children in Crisis; Melissa Miller, Family Violence: The Compassionate Church Response; Marie Fortune, Violence in the Family: A Workshop Curriculum for Clergy and Other Helpers; J. M. K. Busseret,* Battered Women: From a Theology of Suffering to an Ethic of Empowerment; and Joanne Carlson Brown and Carole R. Bohm, eds., Christianity, Patriarchy, and Abuse: A Feminist Critique. You will find additional resources in the Bibliography.

Forgiveness and healing is thoughtfully explored by John Patton in *Is Human Forgiveness Possible? A Pastoral Care Perspective* as well as by Beverly Flanigan in *Forgiving the Unforgivable: Overcoming the Bitter Legacy of Intimate Wounds.* Also see Marie Fortune's excellent chapter, "Forgiveness: The Last Step" in *Abuse and Religion: When Praying Isn't Enough,* edited by Anne L. Horton and Judith A. Williamson.

• Training for prevention of family violence:

Working Together to Prevent Sexual and Domestic Violence, Center for the Prevention of Sexual and Domestic Violence, 1914 N. 34th, Suite 105, Seattle, WA 98103-9058 Tel. (206) 634-1903 Fax (206) 634-0115. Marie Fortune, executive director.

Quaker Materials: Stephane Judson, ed., *Manual on Nonviolence and Children,* and Kathy Bickmore, *Alternatives to Violence: A Manual for Teaching Peacemaking to Youth and Adults,* Friends General Conference (publications catalog), 1216 Arch Street 2B, Philadelphia, PA 19107 Tel. (215) 561-1700.

• For information and published materials:

National Council on Child Abuse and Family Violence, 1155 Connecticut Avenue, NW, Suite 400, Washington, DC 20036 Tel. (202) 429-6695 and (800) 222-2000. (Provides counseling referrals.)

Incest Resources Inc., 46 Pleasant Street, Cambridge, MA 02139 Requests no phone calls. (Provides educational materials for incest survivors.)

National Clearinghouse on Child Abuse and Neglect, P.O. Box 1182, Washington, DC 20013 Tel. (703) 385-7565. (Provides referrals, information, and publications on all aspects of child abuse and neglect.)

National Committee to Prevent Child Abuse, 332 South Michigan Avenue, Suite 1600, Chicago, IL 60604-4357 Tel. (312) 663-3520. (Holds conferences and training programs on child abuse and neglect.)

Giaretto Institute, 232 E. Gish Road, First Floor. San Jose, CA 95112 Tel. (408) 453-7616. (Provides education about family sexual abuse to clergy as well as instruction materials for the intervention and treatment of child sexual abuse.)

National Coalition against Sexual Assault, 912 North Second Street, Harrisburg, PA 17102-3119 Tel. (717) 232-7560.

National Coalition against Domestic Violence, P.O. Box 18749, Denver, CO 80218-00749 Tel. (303) 839-1852.

Internet Resources:
Sexual Assault Information Page: http://www.es.utk.edu/bartley/saInfoPage.html. (Contains complete set of web links.)
Internet Resources: http://www.feminist.org/other/dv/dvinter.html. (Lists sites related to domestic violence.)

• Resources for programs for emotional learning (cited in Daniel Goleman's *Emotional Intelligence: Why It Can Matter More Than Your I.Q.*)

1. W. T. Grant Consortium on the School-Based Promotion of Social Competence, "Drug and Alcohol Prevention Curricula," in J. David Hawkins et al., *Communities That Care* (San Francisco: Jossey-Bass, 1992).
2. Karen Stone and Harold Q. Dillehunt, *Self Science: The Subject Is Me,* Santa Monica: Goodyear Publishing Co., 1978.
3. The Collaborative for the Advancement of Social and Emotional Learning (CASEL), Yale Child Study Center, P.O. Box 207900, 230 South Frontage Road, New Haven, CT 06520-7900.

4. Resolving Conflict Creatively Program: National Center, 127 E. 22nd Street, New York, NY 10010 Tel. (212) 387-0225. (An initiative of Educators for Social Responsibility.)

❧ PART IV ❧

Our Changing Ways

Grandfather,
Look at our brokenness.

We know that in all creation
Only the human family
Has strayed from the Sacred Way.

We know that we are the ones
Who are divided
And we are the ones
Who must come back together
To walk the Sacred Way.

Grandfather,
Sacred One,
Teach us love, compassion, and honor
That we may heal the earth
And heal each other.

Ojibway Prayer[60]

~ 10 ~

Tending Yourself

> They heard the sound of the Lord God walking in the garden
> at the time of the evening breeze, and the man and his wife hid
> themselves from the presence of the Lord God among the trees
> of the garden. But the Lord God called to the man, and said to
> him, "Where are you?" Genesis 3:8–9

God called Adam and Eve, the first gardeners, out of hiding, asking, "Where
are you?" and established a living relationship with men and women.

"Where are you?" God asks counselors in community. It is easy for counselors to become lost in the lives of others and not fully become themselves —
to be out of relationship with God.

In the Genesis story Adam and Eve were in hiding. "In hiding" was not
so much a place, it was their *condition* of shame and guilt. Today, God helps
counselors in community become conscious of their condition. And their need
to be found.

In the course of reading this book you may have found yourself identifying with the conditions of those who were affected by stress or who had
unresolved conflicts. Counselors in community are affected by the human
condition. Sometimes they become lost in it.

Maybe you are unaware of your personal condition because you have become absorbed in the lives of others. Perhaps this absorption feels natural. In
fact, if because in childhood you were the caretaker or rescuer, you may experience your identification with the lives of others *to be* your condition. You
may be disconnected from yourself but not know it.

Ministry and other helping professions are dangerous for those who are
disconnected from themselves. If your body, mind, and soul are disconnected,
you cannot receive messages from yourself about your condition. You will
not know if you are starving spiritually. Because you must continually preach,
pray, counsel, and be a spiritual resource for your community, you need to be
continuously nurtured spiritually. Many clergy and other counselors in community feel guilty about spending time in the week being unavailable to others
when they are being available to themselves and to God. They do not feel they
can "take time" to pray, meditate, study, and just be. They also are reluctant
to go on retreats, find a spiritual counselor, take study leaves or replenish

themselves through relationships, listen to music, be in nature, paint or draw or do whatever they need for nurture. Because they do not believe they have *the right* to be filled, they go on empty.

Counselors in community who believe they do not have the right to have their own needs met often come from families where they were rewarded for meeting the needs of others. They were special because they gave, not received. However, this sense of being special made them feel *entitled* to position and status. But position and status do not feed the soul. Children who are taught to give themselves unremittingly away are strangely proud, yet self-denying. Often they have a hidden hope that comes from childhood: "If I take care of others, maybe they will *finally* take care of me." And they wait, hoping this will happen. If this resembles your childhood story, you may recognize that it is hard for you to ask for what *you* need. You *hope* that the boards and committees of your congregation will see what you need and, in appreciation, offer it to you.

Religious institutions do take care of their clergy: they usually provide housing and other benefits. However, clergy must negotiate with their congregations for the specifics of scheduling, time off, funding for study leaves, and time for renewal. Those clergy who are waiting to be appreciated because they have given themselves away are passive and sometimes passive aggressive. When their community does not "read" their needs, they may not speak up for themselves. They become resentful. They remain disconnected.

While ordained clergy are particularly vulnerable to burnout due to the reinforcement they get when "giving themselves away," all counselors in community need to be aware of the necessity of being connected to themselves as they care for others. Most lay counselors in community have full-time professional responsibilities and they volunteer their time as counselors and caregivers in their religious communities. Although the life of their community feeds and sustains them, they nevertheless must pay attention to the balance in their lives and to set aside time for Sabbathing.

The problems of burnout and sexual acting out are rooted in disconnection from one's self and one's situation.

Held in the Light: Not Burning Out

Burnout is not uncommon to helping professionals. It is also experienced by overly involved community members and other activists who habitually give themselves away to others. Often those who are burned out keep on going even when they no longer find their work meaningful. They go through the motions, but underneath they are cynical and disaffected. In other instances, those who are burned out have turned their despair into illness. They develop stress-related illnesses or try to medicate burnout pain with alcohol. Others collapse in exhaustion. Burnout is spiritual malaise. It is also a stress disorder.

Doing "more of the same" creates burnout. Those who burn out often have an insatiable internal system that requires them to give to others in order to fill an inner void. At the beginning of their calling, the void seems to be filled by the community's appreciation of their outreach and caregiving. But eventually, they feel empty again and so they try harder to give to others, repeating what has not worked, leaving them exhausted.

Some counselors in community burn out quickly. Others grind on year after year. Although they appear to be like the Rock of Gibraltar, they finally crumble. Burnout is a form of unrecognized self abuse. Caregivers who in childhood were abused or were conditioned to be "automatic givers" will not consciously compute the stress they are under; their neurochemical systems will pour out the needed adrenalin and other hormones until the system collapses. As with other types of abuse, the abuser is in denial.

Burnout is related to "acting out." Counselors who are in the process of burning out are acting out their past. Sometimes they are acting out beatings that they disguise as a form of self-neglect; sometimes they are acting out childhood experiences of not being seen, by not seeing themselves. Counselors whose parents did not appreciate them for being themselves, experienced "soul abuse." Their acting out is a form of dissociation. When dissociating, they do not feel in conflict about their self-inflicted pain. In fact, they believe that their work is "doing it to them" and they are helpless to change their ways.

All clergy and lay ministers are vulnerable to burnout because of the work they do. It is not correlated only to early abuse or narcissistic parenting.

Burnout can also be understood as a reaction to stress, a form of vicarious traumatization. Because of your exposure, you may develop the vicarious traumatization of an acute stress disorder. Counselors in community bear witness to pain and violence as you give care and counsel. You are on the scene in an emergency room, being with a member who is dying from a fatal accident. You listen with your feelings and imagination as you counsel one who is remembering abuse. You are in the room with a couple who are cruelly attacking each other with words. You have "witnessed, experienced, or been confronted with an event that involved actual or threatened death or serious injury or a threat to the physical integrity of self or others." (This is a description of some of the antecedents to an acute stress disorder.)[1]

Counselors in community also experience *the stress of the workplace.* Faith communities and their situations are changing. In some cases the stressors are positive — the church is growing or a collegial ministry team is being formed. Sometimes the community is in distress, fighting for its survival. As a leader of a faith community, you absorb stress that is related to change.

Women clergy and women counselors are even more at risk for burnout because of the stress of the sexual harassment that they may endure in their ministry.

Preventing, or recovering from, burnout requires more than adding exercise to one's weekly schedule or developing a hobby. For many counselors it will require second order change. They will need to let themselves be found — by sitting still.

When you feel burned out and lost, take the advice parents give small children before entering a large department store: "If you get lost from me, just stand still. Don't go anywhere. I will come to find you." Most adults forget this advice. When they feel lost from themselves, they get panicky. They go off in all directions trying to find themselves.

In the Genesis story, God came looking for Adam and Eve. Because they heard God calling, they could answer. God's question, "Where are you?" allowed them to respond and to be found. Adam and Eve were not running. Although they were hiding, they were standing still. In the midst of your ministry, you must first stand still. To be still. To listen. To let God find you. When you are found, you can begin the process of self-discovery.

The next step is to let another be your companion in your process of self-discovery. Find a wise psychotherapist and/or a spiritual director, or group of colleagues. You will learn what you need. If you have been raised in a narcissistic family — one in which your mother and/or father expected you to be an extension of them or to live out their dream — you may find yourself doing the same, expecting your children to be an extension of you. You may be living out your dreams through your children. The process of knowing and being yourself takes time. In the meantime, you may begin to get clues about yourself as you discover the quality of your investment in your children. Through observation, you may learn that you would like to play tennis or sing or act or sharpen your intellectual tools because that is what you are pushing your children to do. You may also discover that you have been neglecting your own children and have been perpetuating the cycle of "not-seeing."

Burnout occurs when you try to live out another's dream. Healing happens as you discover your own dreams, as you revise them, and as you live them out. There are systems that you, as clergy, lay ministers, and counselors in community, can put in place for support, protection and nurture:

- Find resources for spiritual nurture. Feed your soul.
- Decide on a reasonable number of hours to work each week and stick to your decision.
- Find other eyes to observe you and your work. You might be a self-abuser in denial. Meet regularly with a community personnel committee (pastor-parish committee); encourage the community to pay for supervision of your counseling work by a pastoral psychotherapist or other supervisor; join a clergy and/or professional support group.
- Shift your focus from your work to your home and personal life. If you have been overworking, your family and close friends are probably mad at you or have distanced from you, causing you to feel lonely.

Schedule time for family and time alone with your spouse or partner or closest friends. Join a clergy or lay-couple support group. Play with your children.

- Find a balance of work, play, rest, relationship in your *daily* life. Let the Sabbath keep you. Remember the image of the gymnast on the balance beam — be in motion; often slight changes are all that are needed.
- Follow an interest, an avocation, that *gives* to you.
- Become connected to your own body. Learn to care for it and find pleasure in it.
- Ask yourself the "miracle question": "If a miracle occurred in the night and restored me from burnout, when I wake up, how will I know this has happened? How will my spouse (or other close person) know?"

The properties of community prevent burnout. In community, you can be yourself and let others know who you are; resolve conflicts; accept diversity and tolerate ambiguity; learn to accept and love yourself so that you can love others.

People become friends in community. Counselors in community need friendship. It feeds their souls.

It is the *lonely* counselor in community who burns out or acts out. There is a parallel between dysfunctional clergy and counselors in community, and fathers and mothers in dysfunctional nuclear families. Male dysfunctional clerics and laycounselors are like isolated and lonely fathers, who overwork, often as "lone rangers," assuming unrealistic responsibility for the community's life that "takes up their time." Women clergy and laycounselors can *lose themselves* in their work, as do overworked dysfunctional mothers. They, like the men, may simultaneously be living dysfunctionally in their nuclear family roles at home. They are personally unfulfilled.

The corrections for the expectations of husbands and wives (given in chapter 7), apply to clergy and lay people who "give themselves away" in ministry. Those men and women who become "married" to their work, perhaps without knowing it, expect their religious communities to meet their needs for friendship, social life, status, financial security, meaning. These expectations are usually not voiced. In fact, clergy are more focused on what they believe their communities expect of them. They are often unaware of resentment when their unreasonable needs are not met. Clergy who act out sexually often rationalize that they *deserve* to do this because they are not appreciated.

Community is God's gift to the family — in all its forms. The emerging "community of peers" is a gift to religious professionals who increasingly have opportunity for collegial relationships. Team ministries of clergy or clergy and lay people, are increasing. Female and male clergy and lay leaders serve together on task forces, boards, and committees.

As more women are graduating from seminary and are serving religious communities and assuming positions of leadership and power, the ministerial profession is becoming more gender balanced. Women are bringing to ministry their experience and "ways of knowing" that value relationships, mutuality, and decision making through consensus. Clergymen are learning to listen to women without feeling threatened. Women are learning to trust that their male colleagues will not disregard or bully them.

And in many cases, professional collegial communities are being formed. In community, men are learning how to be emotionally intimate. Women are learning to claim their strength. Male and female clergy and layministers are making efforts to talk to and understand each other. Diversity is being acknowledged. As the community deepens and trust grows, so does the potential for conflict. Ministry peer groups can become places where differences can be acknowledged and conflicts resolved.

You need a community in which you can be and become yourself. Most people belong to more than one community. In addition to the community of clergy or other professional colleagues, you most likely have a community of family and friends. Perhaps you also find community with those with whom you share committed action in a cause for social justice or an interest in art, music, sports. Here you may be "just one of the group."

But how do you relate to your religious community if you are in charge? As your congregation is becoming open to grace, which creates community, you are living in the midst of resources for healing. But can you completely be yourself? On the one hand, your community is a potential resource for your own liveliness; on the other hand, you may feel conflict about how to fulfill the *role* of religious leader and still be open to it.

Those who are members of various communities where they can be themselves are often less conflicted about their role in their religious community. If they have a satisfying intimate relationship and friends who are not members of their congregation, they can more easily be themselves in their clergy role. They do not have to fend off others in reaction to their own neediness or become inappropriately attached. They can be comfortable. They can learn to be ministered to by those whom they serve if they have learned to receive.

※

Single counselors in community, especially, need to pay attention to themselves so that burnout can be prevented. Married clergy and other counselors have spouses to run interference for them and to protect them from overly intrusive community members. While the roles of clergy spouses are changing, married counselors in community still have buffers that single counselors do not have.

Often religious communities expect single clergy and other single counselors to be "married to their ministry" and to be on call at all times. This is particularly true for celibate clergy and consecrated members of religious orders. These expectations are similar to those of families that do not recognize the adult status of their unmarried children. Even when a single clergyman is called "Father" and treated with respect, his unmarried status still leaves him vulnerable to familial pressures — the church family acts like "family." Single counselors in community need to assert their personal independence and to set sensible limits to *unreasonable* demands on their time and attention, in much the same way they have already done with their families of origin.

Single counselors are, on the other hand, often more vulnerable to being given "unasked for presents." They need to be able to find gracious ways to say, "Thanks, but no thanks." It is not unusual for members of communities to try to "take care" or their single clergy, staff members, and other counselors by making them food, "mothering" them, inviting them to family and other celebrations, or trying to "fix them up" — sometimes with themselves! Sometimes their care feels nurturing, at other times it is annoying. And it often raises questions about boundary keeping. Counselors in community are particularly vulnerable to "being taken care of" when they are on the verge of burnout. Sometimes their growing dependency on their caretakers adds to their problems. While it is imperative that all helping professionals find ways to be nurtured, it is particularly important for singles to learn to be good to themselves and to operate from a position of *enlightened self-interest*.

The research on single adults cited in chapter 7 indicated that single women at age fifty fare better emotionally, psychologically, and physically than single men and their married women counterparts. These statistics, one assumes, hold true for single counselors in community. Single women counselors in community are probably thriving, very much because of their skills in forming deeply satisfying friendships that are emotionally nurturing and in which they can be self-revelatory.

Even though the training of male counselors in community has taught them communication and relationship skills and although many have had some psychotherapy, men are challenged to learn to be friends in a *deeper way*. Many single male counselors have friends with whom they *do* active, socializing things — golf, travel, go to dinner, etc. However, they also need friends with whom they can *be* themselves. Men need to learn to be emotionally close in their friendships, with both men and women. Women are socialized to do this; men need coaching. Sometimes men can get this coaching in marriage or other intense relationships. However, finding ways to learn to be close and self-revelatory is essential for single men in ministry — for their well being.

Bearing Our Burdens Lightly

"Come all of you who are tired and who carry heavy loads. Learn from me. Take my yoke — it is easy and my burden is light." Jesus' words reach the hearts of caregivers who are weighted down with the needs of their communities, the demands of their roles, and their own inner pulls.

How do we learn to bear our burdens lightly? People of faith would say: through grace, and through becoming grown-up: "When I was a child, I spoke like a child, I thought like a child, I reasoned like a child; when I became an adult, I put an end to childish ways. For now we see in a mirror, dimly, but then we will see face to face. Now I know in part; then I will know fully, even as I have been fully known. And now faith, hope, and love abide, these three; and the greatest of these is love." (I Corinthians 13:11–13.) As we mature as caregivers we become more able to respond to life with a sense of humor and the ability to anticipate — to think ahead.

Laughter is a gift of the spirit. It helps us keep perspective and it lightens our load. As we grow up, our humor changes. We move from laughing at people to laughing with them. Laughter helps us with hard times. Paul Goodman, social scientist and man of letters said, "Jewish jokes are humorous anecdotes based on absolute despair."[2]

Professional caregivers can lighten their hearts by learning to think about their professional roles and ethical responsibilities in an active — rather than reactive — way. Many clergy and other helping professionals have been required to attend training sessions to consider professional ethical issues when crises arise because colleagues have violated others and their faith group has been sued for malpractice or misconduct. Often it is difficult to think in such a session because of the fear and anxiety the subject engenders. Instead, you react. When you find ways to lower your anxiety level, you can begin to think and actively seek educational opportunities for learning about pastoral ethics and professional identity development. Such courses might not have been taught when you were in seminary or graduate school.

Through anticipation, you can *think ahead* and make a reasoned personal policy about intimate involvement with community members and about other professional and pastoral practice issues.

Researchers have found that many clergy use their *feelings* to know right from wrong. They do not have the support of cognitive ethical understanding when making decisions about their intimate behavior with community members. In their study, Karen Lebacqz and Ronald Barton found that clergy first rely on a subjective sense of appropriateness when making decisions about setting sexual limits. Those clergy who are able to set appropriate sexual limits have *internal* signals that warn them to be careful because they are feeling sexual desire that would be inappropriate to act upon. Some have signals that help them anticipate trouble or let them know that something is wrong (e.g., physical arousal, inordinate sexual fantasy, using a publicity test — "what would others think?").[3]

It is dangerous to have a sexual limit setting policy based *only* on a subjective sense of morality. Sexual feelings often overpower the "should" of the superego. Decision making needs to be based on thought as well as feelings. Counselors in community need information to help them say "yes" to their *professional* selves.

Karen Lebacqz and Ronald Barton have provided three basic guidelines that can help you reinforce your subjective signals for setting sexual limits.

We recommend their book, *Sex in the Parish,* for its thoughtful discussion on making ethical decisions. They believe that all sexual conduct should be informed by these guidelines: sexual contact that is morally acceptable must be loving and based on mutuality and valid consent; those having sex together must be legally competent, and sex should not be forced.[4]

In discussing their guideline, *"mutuality and valid consent,"* Lebacqz and Barton introduce a consideration of the *power* the clergy person has in relationship to congregants. This requires them to ask: Is it possible for a sexual relationship between a cleric and a congregant or a counselor and a counselee to be based on mutual consent, or does the power inequity between the two invalidate the relationship?

They remind clergy of their position of power in the congregation. Even ministers of churches that emphasize the doctrine of priesthood of all believers have a "priestly" function in their community because they give God's blessing. They also do counseling. This power differential, Lebacqz and Barton believe, causes a church member and her clergyman to stand on unequal ground. They say "mutuality is missing in the pastor-parishioner relationship. The pastor has power, and the parishioner is vulnerable. The very freedom of access to parishioners' lives means that pastors are dealing with people who are often extremely vulnerable. The core of professional ethics lies in the recognition of this power imbalance between the pastor and parishioner. It is this that makes sexual contact problematic."[5]

In some instances, Lebacqz and Barton believe that a clergy person and congregant would have equal power so that they can mutually make "valid consent" (especially if the clergyperson has not been her counselor). In most cases they think it is impossible for clergy and congregants to consent validly on a sexual relationship because the community member does not know that in doing so she risks losing her "priestly relationship." In some instances it also repeats earlier familial sexual abuse.[6] Professor Donald Capps develops the consideration of the clergyperson's *paradoxical power* in relationship to counselees and illustrates Lebacqz and Barton's position.

Paradoxical power is illustrated in the relationship of a clergy counselor who becomes sexually involved with a community member and who is also unfulfilled in his own marriage. He is needy and feels unappreciated. When his counselee tells him of her loneliness and unhappiness, he replies *sympathetically,* "I know exactly how you feel." He then tells her the details of his situation. The counselor *joins* the counselee emotionally. The counselee might feel upset that the focus has shifted off her, but she also feels honored to have him confide in her. She is moved by his "sensitivity and openness."

When counselors begin to share their own feelings of pain and need with women counselees, they find it easy to move from emotional intimacy to sexual involvement. Men are culturally conditioned to express their feelings genitally. For most men, emotional intimacy merges into genital intimacy.[7]

Inappropriate counseling technique and personal vulnerability work together to blur such a counselor's professional boundaries.

The counselor loses sight of the counselee's vulnerability, which he knows in detail due to the counseling he has done with her. Because of the power of the sexual attraction and because she has helped him feel more sexually potent and attractive, his perception has changed; it appears to him that she has power. To keep a sense of his role, however, he focuses on her weakness and encourages her dependence. He might rationalize and tell her that "through our love you are being healed and this is how you can know God's love." To meet his needs, he fools himself and gives her false hope. For a time she feels special.

Professor Donald Capps points out that ministers who become sexually involved with their parishioners often *consciously* believe that they are helping them by sharing in their pain *as an equal*. They believe that the authority that clergy are given stands in the way of *being with* those in their religious community. They try to lessen the power differential that exists between clergy and congregants. In our last example, it appeared that the clergyman who disclosed his personal vulnerability was not "placing himself on a pedestal." In sharing his woundedness, it *appeared* that he was trying to reduce the power of the clergy-congregant hierarchy. This is what Capps calls "the paradox of pastoral power."[8]

The clergyman in our example used the seduction of his neediness to become close to his counselee. He appeared to be putting aside his professional role to relate as an equal. However, by "stepping down" and sharing personal confidences, he increased his power over her. As they became intimate, she became increasingly dependent and his power over her increased.

A red flag must be raised when a counselor extensively self-discloses in a counseling session. Researchers studying clergy sexual misconduct have found that it is excessive self-disclosure, not excessive touch, which is the most common precursor to a sexual boundary violation.[9]

The concept of pastoral power is currently being debated, particularly by feminist and womanist theologians. Although there is consensus among them that professional religious leaders should not sexually and emotionally exploit and abuse community members, they hold various understandings of the nature of pastoral power and the means of abuse. Some (Carter Hayward and Beverly Wildung Harrison) think that others (Marie Fortune and Peter Rutter) understand clergy's power in a way that reinforces the concept of patriarchal hierarchy (power over) and underestimates the power of mutuality and friendship (power with). Carter Hayward believes that abuse can occur when friendship and closeness are *withheld* by religious professionals (particularly in the counseling relationship) as well as when inappropriate sexual behavior is acted out. Marie Fortune, on the other hand, believes that it is dangerous to lose sight of the necessity for religious professionals to withhold intimate contact for the sake of the other.

This debate is clearly articulated in *Boundary Wars: Intimacy and Distance In Healing Relationships* edited by Katherine Hancock Ragsdale. Counselors in community will be interested in its consideration of the powerful relationships between community members as well as the power differential between religious professionals and laity. In her chapter, "Walking the Bounds: Historical and Theological Reflections on Ministry, Intimacy, and Power" Fredrica Harris Thompsett reflects on these matters from her perspective as an Anglican laywoman.

✂

The concept of professional boundaries grew from the work of psychotherapists as they developed strategies to work with transference and other projections placed on them by clients and as they sought to maintain an objective stance to support their own empathy. This working style, grounded in ethical concern, is highly boundaried: dual relationships are avoided. Ideally, therapists and clients do not develop social friendships or business relationships. These boundaries are reinforced by adherence to a professional code of ethics. (The American Association of Pastoral Counselors Ethics Code found in the Notes demonstrates an attention to boundaries.)[10]

Life in religious communities does not lend itself to minding uncomplicated, clear boundaries. We have already discussed the complexity of these relationships in community. Clergy and laity have both professional and nonprofessional relationships; lay people — not just clergy — experience and cooperate with God's healing power. It is because of these complex experiences that religious professionals are helped by the consideration other health professionals give to the concept of boundaries.

Boundaries are overstepped and members harmed when religious professionals use their office for their own gain. When a clergyman ingratiates himself with elderly parishioners in order to be remembered in their wills, he is violating a professional boundary. Boundaries are also violated when confidentiality is broken or when services are provided beyond a clergyperson's expertise. Crossing these can cause serious harm.

Marie Fortune, in her pioneering study of sexually abusive clergy, underscored the importance of understanding and living within clear professional boundaries. As she classified types of sexual abusers, she described the *wanderer* who was unable to maintain boundaries. He is conflicted and anxious, does not take care of himself and uses touch as a means of control and interaction. He "falls" into a relationship with someone who is also emotionally vulnerable but who holds him in high regard. He takes the risk of becoming emotionally or sexually involved with a community member.[11]

The desire to prevent "wanderers" (and others who sexually abuse congregants) that has caused religious judicatories and their malpractice insurance carriers to create policies to reinforce boundaries. Because of these policies clergy counselors are instructed to avoid touch, to seek supervision of their counseling, and to observe other protective measures.

While the definition of professional roles — including limiting boundaries — has contributed to clarity in pastoral practice, definitions of boundaries, like those of power, are being debated. Those engaged in the debate are united in their support of policies that protect members from sexual exploitation and the debaters are in solidarity in their identification with and their care for victims. Because of the wholeness in their community, feminist and womanist thinkers can disagree with each other about the role of distance in healing. When querying the relationship of distance to healing they ask: Is distance necessary? Does it impede (or is it necessary) for making connections, being nurtured and giving mutual support? How is appropriate distance determined? About the role of touch they ask: Should touch be avoided as a preventative measure? Where is the place for healing touch? Does the prohibition of touch contribute to fragmented experience ? Again, we recommend the lively conversations in *Boundary Wars* that explore these topics.

We believe that *respect* be used as a measuring stick to set boundaries. Intimacy grounded in respect is safe. The root of "respect" is *respecere*, to look. To respect others means to see them, to be in relationship, to have a connection with, to regard. It is the distance of respect we see in African-American churches when members are referred to by honorific titles: "Brother," "Sister," "Deacon.". These members are respected — looked up to — not because they have power over, but because they are known and recognized as "being somebody."

Respecting the boundaries of others means to see them truly, not as an extension of yourself, but as to know *who* they are. Your relationship to them and the connection you make depends on knowing yourself well enough to decide how close you wish to get as well as perceiving their signals inviting you to know and come toward them. *Relationships are made when the boundaries of selves are respected.*

It is necessary for all caregivers in community — lay and ordained — to understand the concept of the boundaries of the self that are experienced and maintained when people see and respect themselves and each other. Though acknowledging each others' boundaries, we can determine and signal to each other how much closeness and distance we wish to keep. It is through observing boundaries — our own and others' — that we can refrain from offering or accepting unasked-for presents. And it is through observing boundaries that we create a comfortable context for care.

Looking at the Shadow

Lurking behind our consideration of learning to live with lighter burdens has been the ominous reference to those clergy colleagues, and lay people as well, who abuse power; who sexually, emotionally, and spiritually exploit others.

This awareness may have caused you to be concerned not only about potential victims of abuse, but about yourself. You might wonder, "Am I at risk? Under what condition could I exploit someone?" According to one study the risk is high. Almost one in four religious leaders have been inappropriately sexual with a community member.

The Lebacqz and Barton study on which their book, *Sex in the Parish,* is based found that 10 percent of the clergymen in their in depth survey had had intercourse with women in their congregation. In a study conducted by *Christianity Today,* 23 percent of those surveyed said that they had engaged in sexual behavior with a parishioner that they felt was inappropriate — 12 percent sexual intercourse and 18 percent passionate kissing, fondling, mutual masturbation. Of these, only 4 percent said they were found out.[12]

As we look at the phenomenon of clergy sexual abuse we ask about the characteristics of abusers. We have already referred to Marie Fortune's description of the "wanderer." Another description has been drawn by an insurance carrier of the American Association of Pastoral Counselors who researched information about members disciplined for sexual misconduct. They were described as older, esteemed (Fellows or Diplomates) who *overworked* and were not involved in peer or other professional activities. They were undersupervised and were not in personal therapy. They were isolated and believed themselves to be special; they felt that the rules of the ethics code did not apply to them.[13]

Psychologist Gary Schoener, director of the Walk-In Counseling Center, which has seen over 3,000 cases of sexual abuse, notes the wide variety of abusers. Some are psychotics. Others have severe character and personality disorders. Marie Fortune describes these as "predators:" sociopaths who are often charming, charismatic and are also controlling, coercive, predatory, and sometimes violent.[14] Some are sex addicts. Others are pedophiles who victimize children exclusively. Some who sexually exploit may be chronically neurotic and isolated, or naive, or situational offenders. However, in their consultations Schoener and his colleagues see offenders from a variety of situations. We have included his descriptions in the Notes.[15]

While cause and personality type vary, many who sexually exploit others share a common characteristic: they are not conscious; they are not aware. The abuser does not see his victim or himself. Many abusers were not seen by their own caregivers. Many sexual abusers resist treatment. Schoener and his colleagues have found that some violators can be rehabilitated — particularly if they are caught in their first offense, if there has been only one victim, if they express true remorse and concern for the victim, and if they are confused about why the abuse happened and are motivated to get help to discover why. Sexual offenders require the help of especially knowledgeable professionals.

Protecting yourself from becoming an abuser is a spiritual task requiring discernment. Even when we are born again, we must grow in grace. We search our souls as we ask: Do I see myself? Do I let others see me? Do I really see and know others?

Ministry is a profession that is attractive to many who were not truly seen by their parents. Their childhood experience is repeated as they stand in the pulpit, the center of attention, focusing on their community, caring for it, while not being responded to *personally*. Liturgy and preaching, for many, reinforce their lifelong experience of not feeling seen. Just as physical and sexual abuse are passed down from generation to generation, so is narcissism — that condition of being center stage, while not being known, first by parents and then by oneself. Narcissistic people are manipulatively self involved. They "arrange" for others to give them what they want because they cannot directly claim their own dream or admit to their needs. They see others as an extension of themselves who will carry our their desires. They repeat what was done to them: they do not see others as they *are*.

Often charismatic religious leaders, who appear charmingly interested in others, feel inwardly empty and unseen. They project a warmth that they hope to receive, but that they often cannot take in, because they did not have an early experience of "mother-baby-wholeness." To feel warm, they need constant reflection and validation. Through their charisma, they draw warmth toward themselves.

It is not unusual for members of congregations to fall in love with such clergy. However, the minister or rabbi honestly does not mean to be sexually seductive even when he is intimately attentive. He does not want a real relationship. He wants the warm response of intimate attention, although he may be uncomfortable with real intimacy. Women who fall in love with him suffer confusion, rejection, and humiliation. If they were to confront him or to tell him of their love, his reaction might range from apology ("I'm sorry. I had no idea"), innocence ("I never meant to imply") or annoyance covered by politeness ("I don't know where you got the idea. After all, I'm your pastor").

The "unseen-unseeing self" cleric or lay leader *does not experience his effect on others*. Although he does not know it, he is emotionally abusing those whom he unconsciously leads on. Often he engages a woman in intense, intimate conversation. He looks at her deeply, *as if* he truly sees her. He does not see her; he is looking at her *as he wishes to be seen*. The "unseen-unseeing self" cleric is also adept at manipulating committees of the community to meet his agenda. He creates a sense of openness that encourages members to engage in discussion and participation. However, he "manages" members to reach decisions he favors but often does not publicly state. He often is unaware of the degree to which he manipulates. He is doing to his community what his mother or father did to him. He repeats the abuse of not seeing others as they are. He uses them as an extension of himself.

"Unseen-unseeing self" clergy often have *ideas about* community but have a hard time with it. They did not grow up in a family in which they could be themselves, celebrate diversity, resolve conflict, or know self-acceptance. Because of this, they often do not know how to lead a true community.

In midcareer, many "unseen-unseeing self" religious leaders experience crises. *They sense themselves,* sometimes for the first time. The pain of not being known breaks into their awareness. Some respond to this pain by having an affair in which they hope to be known. Others respond by burning out or by using some type of self-medication. Change has begun. Because of the pain, they know they exist. They are now ready for psychological and spiritual counseling in which they can become seen and known.

Women, clergy and counselors, can also have "unseen-unseeing selves." They, too, can be unknowingly emotionally abusive. They cannot see others as they truly are and they treat them as extensions of themselves. They, too, use their ministry to fill an inner void. Their psychological dynamics are similar to those of the men whom we have just described.

And other religious leaders can be emotionally abusive in ways that are blatantly controlling and authoritarian. The clergyman is "king." His emotional control is similar to that of battering husbands who create dependency and deny self-agency. (David Koresh, leader of the Branch Davidian compound, was an extreme example.) Most emotional abuse by religious leaders is more subtle and confusing. Sometimes the emotionally abusing leader is a moving preacher or moral leader who champions causes of justice and righteousness. Members of his community are confused by behavior that is also seductive and manipulative. They are confused by one who speaks to them warmly and intensely, but who in the next moment disregards them, leaving them to feel unknown. They feel used.

Even when abuse has been subtle, it is still accomplished through the misuse of power: power that has been invested in clergy through the religious office or in a counselor or teacher through religious tradition and professional authority. Sometimes the power is used in mildly abusive ways when leaders demand time, attention, and service. When doing this, these leaders do not respect members' autonomy, their needs or their ideas. When leaders demand blind obedience, the abuse is overt. They expect members to give up personal freedom and critical thought.

Sometimes the abuse comes by the leader's interpretation of religious teachings and rules. Then the teachings are used to reinforce uncritical allegiance to the leader. Sometimes the leader uses the power of his office or his interpretation of teachings to persuade people to stay in situations that are not good for them, that are physically dangerous or spiritually or emotionally abusive. This is often done through interpretation of scripture such as, "turn the other cheek" or "wives submit to your husbands." The leader is abusing power over others to fulfill hidden personal needs.

A religious leader who uses a community member to meet his needs is hurtful. Those leaders who are not connected to themselves but who relate to others *as if* they care are wounding. Emotional abuse, particularly when it is subtle, is disrespectful.

As a religious leader you are blessed with community — the community you serve and various others that nurture you. Marie Fortune believes that you are helped to think of your religious group as community, rather than family, because the concept is protective, even though many religious groups use the paradigm of the family to describe their life together. (Through the use of this model religious communities have inspired their members to build relationships of love and support. In our transient culture, the "religious community as family" has become the spiritual home and extended family for many.)

Marie Fortune has found that clergy have great symbolic and personal power in congregations that use the family model. There they are perceived as patriarchs. When relationships in the community are perceived as familial, sex between clergy and congregants is experienced as incestuous. Both the boundaries of family *and* religious institution are broken. In *Is Nothing Sacred?* she points out: "The model raises unrealistic expectations of emotional intimacy for its members. It requires time and energy that would be better used in establishing and nurturing family relationships and friendships. It usually follows a patriarchal model of family, with male roles limited to decision making and control and female roles limited to nurture and childcare. It can sustain the secret of incest to the detriment of its members."

Community, the model we have been using, is more helpful, she suggests: "An alternative model for healthy congregational life would be that of community as distinct from family. Community life is also based on values of respect, mutuality, compassion, and care, but with a lesser degree of intimacy. Using this model, the expectations for emotional or sexual intimacy would be lessened and the opportunity to question authority or unethical behavior of church leaders would be more readily available."[16]

Because *boundaries can easily be blurred in the counseling relationship*, we offer the following recommendations:

- Use your office, not your member's home or an informal place, for counseling sessions.
- Meet at scheduled times when your secretary or a volunteer is in an outer office.
- Use brief counseling or referral methods. Always make a counseling agreement based on the counselee's goals. Stop your work when the goals are met. Do not meet for an unspecified number of sessions in an open-ended way.
- Refer those for whom you have a strong sexual attraction to another counselor.
- Have your counseling work supervised by someone with whom you are comfortable enough to speak about your sexual attraction to a counse-

lee. Speaking about it will defuse the energy and will help you monitor your behavior.
· Pay attention to signs of burnout.
· Have a regular way of getting spiritual and psychological nourishment.

Warning Sign: If while doing counseling you hear yourself say to a vulnerable woman counselee, "I know just how you feel," and then begin to tell her about your personal life, *get help.* You are at risk.

Ministry: A Dangerous Job for Women

The in-depth survey conducted by Lebacqz and Barton showed that women clergy were able to recognize their own subjective "danger" signals; they were able to read sexual signals coming from others; they knew when the other person was crossing over the line; they were able to articulate their professional ethics and moral stance. They did not use the counseling sessions to seduce and meet their sexual needs. However, *an awareness of maintaining appropriate boundaries did not keep them safe.*

Community ministry is dangerous for women clergy and lay ministers. This is true for women rabbis as well as Christian clergywomen. A survey conducted by the American Jewish Congress found that 70 percent of women rabbis have experienced sexual harassment in connection with their work. Among the incidents reported were unsolicited touching, closeness, requests for sexual favors, and receiving letters of a sexual nature. Sixty percent of the harassment came from laypeople, 25 percent came from other rabbis.[17] This parallels a similar study by the United Methodist Church that found that 77 percent of their women clergy had experienced harassment, 41 percent from other ministers.[18] The Lebacqz and Barton study showed that 50 percent of the women clergy they interviewed had experienced aggressive sexual harassment. A study conducted by the Coordinating Center for Women of the United Church of Christ found that 40 percent of their women clergy had been aggressively harassed. Statistics showing *clergymen* being harassed by other clergy or laypeople are negligible.[19]

Even though women ministers or rabbis have the same professional role and the same religious function as male clergy, their power is less because women are not as powerful as men in our culture. Nor do most carry the mantle of *potent* religious investiture. In religious language, God is referred to as "He." Women ministers and rabbis are not seen by their congregants as sharing in the power of a male deity in the same way as their male clergy counterparts. Women clergy do not have power invested in them by our culture; nor are they placed on the same religious pedestal as male clergy.

Because of these perceptions, women clergy are subjected to the same "familiar" behavior as women in the other professions. Since childhood, women are taught to know "where to draw the line because boys can't help themselves." Women clergy have been well trained to set boundaries. However, men in their communities and male clergy also act out of their belief systems: "A woman's 'no' really means 'yes' "; "She's not married; sex will be good for her"; "She denies it, but she's really asking for it." Many men believe that they have the *right* to have "sexual access" to a woman. If they have sex with her, they then have power over her even if she is their minister or rabbi. When men act out of this formulation, sex can overpower the clergywoman's professional power and the power of her religious role; unlike male clergy who increase their power in acting out sexually.

While in most instances women clergy and lay ministers find sexual harassment aggressive and annoying, for the most part they find that they can "handle" it. However, sometimes harassment moves over the line into an abuse of power. Women clergy report being coerced into sleeping with supervisors and clergy who have positions of authority over them; they report sexual assault and rape by congregants. Contrary to much male rationalization, these women are sexually abused.

Religious bodies are setting up ways for members of congregations to register complaints of clergy sexual misconduct. Women clergy are sometimes in a place where it is appropriate to bring charges against members of their own communities. This situation is analogous to the need for protection of family members *in family sexual abuse*. Women clergy need to have systems in place in their congregations and within the larger religious structures that assure them protection from aggressive sexual harassment by members of their religious communities and from their clergy colleagues.

Because a woman is conditioned to believe that if she is sexually violated it *could* be her fault, most women clergy, before calling for help, go through extensive self-examination, looking to see if they should blame themselves. When women clergy reveal the abuse and the abuser, they should be taken seriously. The habit of male professionals protecting each other is strong. It is often hard for clergymen to believe that their male colleagues or male congregants are harassing and sexually exploiting women ministers and rabbis. *Women's experience tells you that they are.*

We recommend Pamela Cooper-White's *The Cry of Tamar: Violence against Women and the Church's Response* for her thoughtful discussion of this issue.

Women clergy have long sustained themselves through women's clergy support groups. In these groups they are free to speak of the stress of their work and of the anxiety they feel because of sexual threats and the annoyance of harassment. Through their networking, women clergy have taught themselves to be prudently protected by:

- Making their work space as safe as possible with well-lighted doorways and parking lots, secure locks and alarm systems. They also avoid going into the church or synagogue late at night unaccompanied, and when they are in the building they try to be covered by support staff, custodians, and volunteers.

- Arranging to have other members accompany them on home visits to newcomers, single men, and families where only the father is likely to be at home.
- Being careful of the messages they send through their own body language.
- Reading the body language of others.
- Women clergy are more comfortable about giving the "good touch" of hugs. They are careful to ask permission before doing so, so as to not be physically intrusive.

Most women clergy and lay ministers are very conscious of their presence as females as it affects their work, and they are also protective of their safety from sexual harassment. However, many are still reluctant to talk about their vulnerability to sexual harassment with members of their congregation. *The silence on this subject needs to be broken.* Your religious community needs to know *why* you need volunteers to be in an outer office while you counsel and *why* you need lay people to accompany you on home visits.

When a woman minister or rabbi speaks of her vulnerability, she opens up the broader topic of sexual violence in religious families. Many of her congregants will deny that she could possibly be in danger in their midst, just as they deny the possibility of sexual abuse in their families. On some level, they know better and so do you. There is a strong possibility that the men who harass you also have trouble maintaining appropriate sexual boundaries with their family members. This denial is to be expected. Denial of the possibility of sexual abuse goes with the territory.

Women clergy and lay ministers who are sexually harassed or abused in the course of their work must take seriously their need for healing. Like all victims of sexual abuse, they will need to be heard, and to be empowered to seek justice. They can only go to work in their church or synagogue if it is a safe place. They need to have an adequate support system around them. Sometimes they will need time off for treatment and reconstitution. They should not be expected to "just carry on." Ministry should not be a "battlefield" where women are wounded in the course of action and must continue to work in a state of acute stress disorder. Women who were either abused as children or had the childhood role of caregiver or rescuer might expect themselves to "handle it" through dissociation. Again, clergy women need other "eyes" to observe them objectively in their work in case they are denying an abusive situation.

Burned-out clergy need time to recuperate and to find themselves. Women clergy and lay ministers who have been aggressively sexually harassed need special care.

Ministry, Change, Stress

Change is everywhere. Nations in the world have collapsed. New alliances are being formed. Domestic social policy is changing. New needs are arising. In the midst of this change, religious institutions, too, are changing. Religious leaders are reeling from changes within and without.

You may be trying try to stay balanced on your feet as you cope with your changing professional identity while trying to lead your community and also respond to the needs of God's people in the world.

No religious group is without its experience of change. Ann O'Hara Graff speaks about the American Roman Catholic church's new vision and new gifts. She notes that the Roman Catholic church is moving from a sacred priesthood to multiple ministries. While the priest is still the ritual maker, the administration of the parish and the carrying out of multiple ministries is done through the leadership of the ministry team in an inclusive church.[20]

Jewish congregations are growing smaller because of the social assimilation of many members. Rabbis must deal with growing numbers of mixed marriages and intermarriages, coping with diversity while also delving deeply into Judaism's spiritual resources. Some rabbis are primarily focusing on the families of their congregation, leading them into a deeper understanding of their traditions; others are encouraging their congregations to engage in conversation with their neighbors of other faiths. Many rabbis feel the threat to Jewish survival while also trusting that God is with them.[21]

Mainline Protestant churches are growing smaller; Evangelical churches are thriving. Some churches that have lost members are nevertheless deepening spiritually because their communities are becoming alive. Team ministries of men and women are driving into rural areas where churches have been dying and these churches are now springing back to life. Nondenominational and some mainline and Roman Catholic megachurches, with their large communities and multiple staffs, understand contemporary mall culture. Through the use of technology and TV/entertainment methods, they reach many who have been alienated from their own religious roots. Some struggling urban churches have become beacons of light, offering comprehensive human services to their neighborhoods. No denomination or faith group is the way it used to be.

As a religious leader you may be experiencing role confusion. Your job description may be changing because your community expects you to meet new needs, to be responsive and to lead flexibly. You may also be expected to be a clear-headed, realistic fiscal manager. Your professional identity may seem fuzzy or conflicted.

At the same time, society wants clergy to know who they are and what they are doing. The place of religious professionals in society has been changing. Although church and state are separate, clergy have increasingly been under public scrutiny. Clergy are not only called by their religious communities and are accountable to them, they are also recognized as professionals with professional responsibilities. They are expected to have professional codes of ethics that they live by. While clergy and religious institutions are given special privileges such as tax exemptions, their clerical status does not give them immunity from legal responsibility.

In recent decades, the subject of clergy misconduct and its consequences has been aired frequently in public. In the past when members of religious communities felt wronged by clergy, the matter was usually dealt with "in-house" by religious officials. Matters were hushed because the officials were often more concerned about the group's public reputation than congregants' injuries. This often meant that aggrieved members did not feel justice was done. Now more and more clergy are being sued and tried for misconduct in civil court. Society is holding clergy and religious institutions more accountable for their actions.

Until recent times, most clergy took their counseling work for granted; they saw it as an extension of their pastoral role. And they expected that their counseling was confidential; they never thought they would have to disclose information or appear in court. You need to understand the limits of confidentiality and with the help of your church's or synagogue's attorneys, establish counseling policies that protect you. Attorney Richard Couser says:

> A pastor can maximize the protection of the privilege against testifying by avoiding counseling situations at which third parties are present. If husbands and wives seek counseling together, the pastor may wish to have each sign an agreement that they will not seek the pastor's testimony. If the counselee insists on the presence of a third person, the pastor should advise the counselee that the third person's presence will probably destroy the privilege of confidentiality.
>
> The church or denomination can support the pastor in maintaining confidentiality by adopting a formal policy that supports the confidentiality of communications made to the pastor on religious grounds and by formally assigning duties, supervising and communicating the expectation of confidentiality with respect to any non-ordained counselors.[22]

Counselors in community must also understand the laws specifying when they must communicate information to others. You need to consult your attorney to find your state's rulings on communicating information to authorities about:

- *Child, elder, and other dependent abuse* that you learn about either through counseling or through other church or synagogue staff. The ruling and its application should be clearly communicated to your entire staff and layworkers.
- *Threat of harm to others.* You and your attorney should decide whether you have some religious reason for withholding information regarding

someone's serious threat of physical violence. In some states, there are statutes that require disclosure. Again, you need legal advice.

- *Information pertaining to minors beyond the child abuse reporting requirement.* If you or a youth worker is counseling a teenager who in confidence tells you of experiences of sexual harassment or assault, or substance abuse, or mental or emotional conditions that would make him dangerous to himself or others, are you obligated to break the confidentiality of counseling to notify parents or other authorities? Know the rules of your state.
- *Confession of a crime.* Under clergy-penitent privilege you would generally not be required to report sincere penitential communication. However, it would be illegal to assist someone who has committed a crime to avoid detection. Again, you must know your state's rules.[23]

Religious institutions have been developing professional standards that encourage clergy to be more reflective about their behavior and to be in more cooperative contact with other professionals. They have observed that often other helping professions have required more disciplined, ethical behavior from their members than have religious institutions. This has challenged religious institutions to hold members to ethical accountability. However, clergy also know that keeping the laws of professional ethics is not enough. Christians and Jews are required to keep the law of love: to love the Lord their God with all their heart, soul, and might, and to love their neighbors as themselves.

Through using the mature ego defense of *anticipation,* you can make your life less stressful by learning how to deal with these issues, should they arise. You can also feel more soothed by gathering a supportive team around you that can give you legal and other supervisory advice to undergird your counseling.

It's Grace That's Brought Me Safe Thus Far

A gardener's life seems relatively safe when compared to that of a counselor in community. Counselors in community, particularly those who are ordained or serve on ministry teams and staffs, are in danger because they are religious professionals. When "religion" is your job it is easy for it to become a habit that loses its freshness and purpose — it can become routine. It is dangerous to pray *for a living.* In keeping religious institutions and programs going, you can lose track of your soul. When counseling others, you can be tempted to live vicariously through them and disconnect from your own life. The work of ministry can become a spiritual liability.

However, you also must know of clergy and lay ministers who seem to *grow* in grace. Over the years, they have blossomed and matured. They have not become cynical and tired out. They are more alive than when they graduated from seminary or graduate school. Although they have had spiritual struggles, they also have been grounded in their love for God. Their ministry to others has grown out of this love.

In order to thrive we need to observe those who have matured in ministry. Think about those whom you know who, in their fifties and sixties, are engaged in their spiritual journey. Connect with them. Ask them to tell you their story. And think about your own spiritual journey. At what places and times in your life has God surprised you?

Those of you who garden know delight when you discover tender green plants beginning to sprout, sometimes in unexpected places. Much of your work as leader in your religious community involves planning and management. Do your part, plan and prepare, but keep your eyes open for *unexpected* growth in another place in the garden.

Those who thrive in ministry stay out of power struggles with themselves and others. They give in to delight. Think of those counselors whom you know who also *find life interesting*. They have a passion for their avocations. They are true *amateurs*, who love and develop their interest in art, photography, music, piloting a plane, or climbing a mountain. They are involved in some way with the world, with creation, with creating. They do not need to live through others for excitement. They live with thanksgiving.

This does not mean that people who give thanks for life do not have troubles. Some live with cancer or other illnesses or social discrimination or with loved ones who have chronic illness. Some struggle with doubts and disappointments. But they have a faith that allows them to say, "The Lord gives, the Lord takes away; blessed be the name of the Lord."

Tending to the gardener — ourselves — requires that we pay attention. That we take pleasure in life. That we allow ourselves to be found.

> *Amazing grace*
> *How sweet the sound*
> *That saved a wretch like me*
> *I once was lost, but now I'm found*
> *Was blind but now I see.*

Chapter Ten
Reading and Resources
Publishing information is found in the Bibliography

• There is a rich literature on understanding the *cause and prevention of professional burnout*. We recommend William Grosch and David Olsen, *When Helping Starts to Hurt*; John Sanford, *Ministry Burnout*; and Margot Hover, *Caring for Yourself While Caring for Others*.

The Alban Institute has developed resources for clergy support and self care. See: Donald R. Hands and Wayne L. Fehr, *Spiritual Wholeness for Clergy: A New Psychology* of *Intimacy with God, Self, and Others*; Gary L. Harbaugh, *Caring for the Caregiver: Growth Models for Professional Leaders and Congregations*; Roy M. Oswald, *Clergy Self-Care: Finding a Balance for Effective Ministry*; and *How to Build a Support System for your Ministry*; Barbara Gilbert, *Who Ministers to Ministers?: A Study of Support Systems for Clergy and Spouses*; and Norman Shawchuck and Roger Heuser, *Leading the Congregation: Caring for Self While Leading Others*.

For a testimony of one who has recovered from burnout, see C. Welton Goode, *A Soul under Siege: Surviving Clergy Depression*.

• For further discussion of *how ministers can hurt and be hurt* by ministry, see Conrad W. Weiser, *Healers — Harmed and Harmful*.

• Discussion of the *complexity of relationship of intimacy and distance to healing* can be found in *Boundary Wars: Intimacy and Distance in Healing Relationships*, edited by Katherine Hancock Ragsdale. These matters are also explored in: Fredrica Harris Thompsett, *Courageous Incarnation: In Intimacy, Work, Childhood and Aging*; Carter Heyward, *When Boundaries Betray Us*; Marie Fortune, *Love Does No Harm*; and Peter Rutter, *Sex in the Forbidden Zone*.

• The role of *touch in healing* is considered by nurse Sara Wuthnow in her article, "Healing Touch Controversies" in the *Journal of Religion and Health*, Fall 1997. Also see T. Harpur, *The Uncommon Touch*, Morton Kelsey, *Healing and Christianity*, Zack Thomas, *Healing Touch: The Church's Forgotten Language*, and Kate Kerman, *A Friendly Touch: Therapeutic Touch Among Quakers*.

* For *coping with the stress caused by changes in religious institutions*, see Michael Jenkins and Deborah Bradshaw Jenkins, *Power and Change in Parish Ministry: Reflections on the Cure of Souls*; Anne Marie Nuechterlein and Celia Allison Hahn *The Male-Female Church Staff: Celebrating the Gifts, Confronting the Challenges*; Anne Marie Nuechterlein, *Improving Your Multiple Staff Ministry*; Donna Schaper, *Common Sense about Men and Women in the Ministry*. Also see *Clergy Ethics in a Changing Society: Mapping the Terrain*, edited by Russell Burck et al.

• *Sexuality is a source of creativity and pleasure* and its energy can enhance community when it is not abused. For thoughtful consideration, see Celia Allison Hahn, *Sexual Paradox: Creative Tensions in Our Lives and Congregations*; Karen Lebacqz and Ronald Barton, *Sex in the Parish*; Ruth Tiffany Barnhouse, *Clergy and the Sexual Revolution*; and *Sexuality and the Sacred: Sources for Theological Reflection*, edited by James B. Nelson and Sandra Longfellow.

• For *ethical concerns about sexuality and ministry* see Marie Fortune, *Is Nothing Sacred?: When Sex Invades the Pastoral Relationship* as well as *Sex and the Parish* cited above. We also recommend Marie Fortune and James Poling's *Sexual Abuse by Clergy* and James Poling's *The Abuse of Power: A Theological Problem*. Also see Katherine M. Clarke's article, "Lessons from Feminist Therapy for Ministerial Ethics," *Journal of Pastoral Care*, Fall 1994.

• For congregations coping with the *aftermath of clergy sexual misconduct*, the Alban Institute has prepared these resources: Anne Underwood, *Considerations for Conducting an Investigation of Alleged Clergy Sexual Misconduct*; Nancy Myer Hopkins, *The Congregation is Also a Victim: Sexual Abuse and Violation of Pastoral Trust*; and *Clergy Sexual Misconduct: A Systems Perspective*, edited by Nancy Myer Hopkins. Also see Anne Underwood, *An Attorney Looks at the Secular Foundation for Clergy Sexual Misconduct Policies*.

• For additional information about *fulfilling professional legal responsibilities* see Seth C. Kalichman, *Mandated Reporting of Suspected Child Abuse: Ethics, Law, and Policy*; Walter Wiest and Elwyn A. Smith, *Ethics in Ministry: A Guide for the Professional.*

• Richard B. Couser's *Ministry and the American Legal System: A Guide for Clergy, Lay Workers and Congregations* is an excellent resource for understanding the *full impact of the law on clergy and religious institutions.* We recommend Ronald K. Bullis and Cynthia S. Mazur's *Legal Issues and Religious Counseling* for its information about *state regulation of religious counselors* and its discussion of the general trends and patterns of religious counseling liability. For another excellent overview of the *law and clergy sexual boundary issues,* see Sally A. Johnson's chapter, "Legal Issues in Clergy Sexual Boundary Violation Matters" in *Boundary Wars: Intimacy and Distance in Healing Relationships,* edited by Katherine Hancock Ragsdale.

We recommend Aaron Liberman and Michael J. Woodruff's *Risk Management* for its thorough treatment of the *legal needs of pastoral counseling centers and pastoral counseling specialists.* The complex matter of *clergy confidentiality* is addressed in W. Rankin's *Confidentiality and Clergy: Churches, Ethics, and the Law.*

Blanton–Peale Institute

In 1937 psychiatrist Smiley Blanton and pastor Norman Vincent Peale founded the American Foundation for Religion and Psychiatry. In 1971 it merged with the Academy of Religion and Mental Health and became the Institutes of Religion and Health. The Blanton-Peale Graduate Institute, chartered by the New York State Board of Regents, is also incorporated. In 1996 the name was changed, unifying all services as the Blanton-Peale Institute.

The organization is accredited by the American Association of Pastoral Counselors and approved by the Commission for Accreditation of Marriage and Family Education. The headquarters' counseling center is certified by the New York State Office of Mental Health.

Today services to relieve emotional suffering and nurture wholeness include:

- Advanced professional training for ministers, rabbis, nuns, priests, and lay caregivers from around the world . . . in pastoral care, psychotherapy, marriage, and family therapy, and the spiritual dimension in therapy.
- Caring, cost-effective counseling for . . . individual adults, teenagers, couples, families, and groups who suffer emotional problems, through the Blanton-Peale Counseling Center and community counseling centers in New York City, Long Island, and New Jersey.
- Initiative to strengthen urban communities . . . African-American, Hispanic, and Asian-American . . . by training in English and Spanish to help church leaders, both clergy and lay, deal with complex human issues.
- Services to congregations and other communities . . . educational programs, consultation on conflict resolutions, crises management, and communal organization.
- A nationwide support service for clergy of all faiths . . . the Clergy Consultation Service . . . that assists with personal and professional problems and provides supervision of pastoral care and counseling. Experienced pastoral clinicians offer this confidential service to members who use an 800 telephone number.

- An employee assistance program (EAP) for companies, social service organizations, and government agencies, providing caring, professional support, confidentially by telephone, plus referrals when more counseling is needed.
- Interdisciplinary communication among theology, psychology, and the social sciences through the *Journal of Religion and Health,* workshops, and conferences.

For additional information, please contact:

> Blanton-Peale Institute
> 3 West 29th Street, New York, NY 10001
> Tel. (212) 725-7850 Fax (212) 689-3212

Forms

Wholeness Network Membership

Member's name _____

Address (home) _____

Address (work) _____

Home Tel. _____ Work Tel. _____

Fax _____ E-Mail _____

PARTICIPATES IN:

(indicate type of participation...member, leader, staff, consultant)

Religious Life of Community

Religious rituals/services _____

Prayer/healing groups; healing services _____

Calling ministry (shut-ins, hospitals, etc.) _____

Youth ministry _____

Religious Education _____

Other _____

Groups

Support:

Grief _____

Critical illness (cancer, AIDS, etc.) _____

Recovery (addiction, abuse, incest, etc.) _____

Education:

Parenting _____

Marriage enrichment _____

Study _____

Personal growth _____

Spiritual discernment _____

Twelve Step _____

Other _____

PARTICIPATES IN (continued):

Consulting

Conflict Resolution Negotiator _____

Divorce Mediator _____

Communication Facilitator _____

Other _____

Natural Counselor (Person to whom other persons are drawn for counseling,

nurture, support), (describe) _____

_____

_____

WORKS OR HAS KNOWLEDGE ABOUT (give specific information)

Alternative medicine practitioner _____

Therapist: movement, art, music _____

Medical (doctor, dentist, nurse, physical therapist, technician, medical secretary, etc.)

_____

Medical or other health related research _____

Mental health worker (psychiatrist, psychologist, psychotherapist, pastoral counselor,

clinical social worker) _____

_____

Massage therapist, body work therapist (Alexander, Rossen, etc.) _____

_____

Nutritionist, dietitian _____

Spiritual director _____

Other _____

Connection to health care facility (name of facility) _____

employee _____

affiliate _____

volunteer _____

(related to anyone in above categories) _____

UNEXPECTED HEALING ACTIVITY/HEALING RESOURCES

(This is a reminder to pay attention to the ways in which we are helped to experience

wholeness...we are often surprised) _____

_____

Care and Counseling Information Log

Time and Date of Call _____ Called you at home, office _____

Person calling _____ Tel. (home) _____

Tel. (work) _____

Address (home) _____

Address (work) _____

Emergency contact _____

Reason for the call (use caller's words for stated need, problem, goal) _____

_____

_____

_____

Crisis Intervention (note nature of the problem, information given by you to address problem, plan for follow-up, names and phone numbers for reaching either the person in crisis or their contact person) _____

_____

_____

_____

_____

_____

Time and date of *next appointment* with you _____

Community resources needed for:

Brief counseling (goal) _____

Community care (specify) _____

Referral (for what? to whom?) _____

_____

Additional follow through by you or members of your wholeness network:

_____

_____

_____

Information for Referral Counseling Form

This information will be kept confidential and will only be shared with other professionals with your written consent.

Name _____ Home Phone _____

Address _____ Work Phone _____

_____ Other Phones _____

Age _____ Date of birth _____ Place of Birth _____

Place/type of work _____

_____

Education (highest grade completed) _____

Lives with (list names) _____

_____

Relationship status (circle): single, married, partnered, divorced, remarried, widowed

Reason for seeking referral _____

_____

Goal for change _____

_____

Resource requested _____

_____

Health Information:

1. Hospitalizations/surgeries _____

2. Serious medical illness _____

3. Chronic medical condition _____

4. Allergies _____

5. Alcohol/drug use (how much? how frequently?) _____

6. Family of origin medical history (serious illness? alcohol, drug use? state of health/cause of death) _____

_____

_____

7. Medications that you are now taking (and for what reason) _____

_____

_____

8. Are you presently in psychotherapy? With whom? _____

9. Religious community affiliation _____

10. Assessment of your present state of well-being _____

_____

_____

If you are asking to be referred to a professional or another resource, information about your problem would be useful in making the best referral.

Problems that you feel apply to you: (check)

___ Depression	___ Fatigue/low energy	___ Health problems
___ Job-related problems	___ Difficulty concentrating	___ Suicidal thoughts
___ Suicidal actions	___ Financial concerns	___ Parent-child conflict
___ Anxiety	___ Parent-child conflict (spouse)	___ Family violence
___ Sleep problems	___ Parent-child conflict (both)	(actual or threatened)
___ Eating disorder	___ Communication problems	___ Panic attacks
___ Physical abuse	___ Marital/relationship problems	___ Sexual problems
___ Sexual abuse	___ Death of loved one	___ Self-esteem
___ Withdrawn behavior	___ Compulsive gambling	___ Alcohol abuse (self)
___ Alcohol abuse (family)	___ Brother/sister problems	___ Blended family problem
___ Legal difficulties	___ Other drug abuse (self)	___ Change of appetite

To be filled out after the referral has been made:
Referred to:
Name (of consultant or other resource) _____

Address _____

Tel. _____ Fax _____ E-Mail _____

Purpose of referral: _____

_____

Counselee seen by person/resource to whom referred on _____

Need for religious community follow-up _____

Community care needed _____

Counselee Permission to Release Information

I, _____ (name), give my permission to

_____ (name of counselor or other professional)

to release information concerning my condition for the purpose of:

        ___ referral   ___ evaluation

        ___ consultation   ___ supervision

To (name of person who will receive the information):

_____

_____

Date _____ Signature: _____

                (self, or parent/guardian for a minor)

Solution-Focused Brief Therapy:
Goal Continuation Worksheet

Name: _____ Date: _____

What's better?

    Elicit:

    Amplify:

    Reinforce:

    What else is better?

    What others would say how client is different?

    No change? if so, review goals, deconstruction, coping questions:

    Change reported (related to goals?):

    What does the client need to do more?

    Compliments/giving credit to the client:

    Task/suggestions:

~ APPENDIX C ~

Life Development Charts

Table 1-1
The Stages of the Family Life Cycle

Family Life Cycle Stage	Emotional Process of Transition: Key Principles	Second Order Changes in Family Required to Proceed Developmentally
1. Between Families: The Unattached Young Adult	Accepting parent-offspring separation	a. Differentiation of self in relation to family of origin b. Development of intimate peer relationships c. Establishment of self in work
2. The Joining of Families through Marriage: The new couple	Commitment to new system	a. Formation of marital system b. Realignment of relationship with extended families and friends to include spouse
3. The Family with Young Children	Accepting new members into the system	a. Adjusting marital system to make space for child(ren) b. Taking on parenting roles c. Realignment of relationships with extended family to include parenting and grandparenting roles
4. The Family with Adolescents	Increasing flexibility of family boundaries to include children's independence	a. Shifting of parent-child relationships to permit adolescent to move in and out of system b. Refocus on midlife marital and career issues c. Beginning shift toward concerns for older generation
5. Launching Children and Moving On	Accepting a multitude of exits from and entries into the family system	a. Renegotiation of marital system as a dyad b. Development of adult-to-adult relationships between grown children and their parents c. Realignment of relationships to include in-laws and grandchildren d. Dealing with disabilities and death of parents (grandparents)
6. The Family in Later Life	Accepting the shifting of generational roles	a. Maintaining own and/or couple functioning and interests in face of physiological decline b. Support for a more central role for middle generation c. Making room in the system for the wisdom and experience of the elderly, supporting the older generation without overfunctioning for them d. Dealing with loss of spouse, siblings and other peers and preparation for own death. Life review and integration

Table 1-1. Betty Carter and Monica McGoldrick, *The Changing Family Life Cycle: A Framework for Family Therapy.* Needham Heights, MA: Allyn and Bacon, 1989, 15. Used by permission of the authors.

Table 1-2

Dislocations of the Family Life Cycle
Requiring Additional Steps to Restabilize
and Proceed Developmentally

Phase	Emotional Process of Transition Prerequisite Attitude	Developmental Issues
Divorce		
1. The decision to divorce	Acceptance of inability to resolve marital tensions	Acceptance of one's own part in the failure of the marriage
2. Planning the breakup of the system	Supporting viable arrangements for all parts of the system	a. Working cooperatively on problems of custody, visitation and finances b. Dealing with extended family about the divorce
3. Separation	a. Willingness to continue cooperative coparental relationship and joint financial support of children b. Work on resolution of attachment to spouse	a. Mourning loss of intact family b. Restructuring marital and parent-child relationships and finances; adaptation to living apart Realignment of relationships with extended family; staying connected with spouse's extended family
4. The divorce	More work on emotional divorce; overcoming hurt, anger, guilt, etc.	a. Mourning loss of intact family; giving up fantasies of reunion b. Retrieval of hopes, dreams, expectations from the marriage c. Staying connected with extended families
Postdivorce Family		
1. Single-parent (custodial household or primary residence)	Willingness to maintain financial responsibilities, continue parental contact with ex-spouse, and support contact of children with ex-spouse and his or her family	a. Making flexible visitation arrangements with ex-spouse and his family b. Rebuilding own financial resources c. Rebuilding own social network
2. Single-parent (noncustodial)	Willingness to maintain parental contact with ex-spouse and support custodial parent's relationship with children	a. Finding ways to continue effective parenting relationship with children b. Maintaining financial responsibilities to ex-spouse and children c. Rebuilding own social network

Table 1-2. Betty Carter and Monica McGoldrick, *The Changing Family Life Cycle.* Needham Heights, MA: Allyn and Bacon, 1989, 22. Used by permission of the authors.

Table 1-3
Remarried Family Formation:
A Developmental Outline*

Steps	Prerequisite Attitude	Developmental Issues
1. Entering the new relationship	Recovery from loss of first marriage (adequate "emotional divorce")	Recommitment to marriage and to forming a family with readiness to deal with the complexity and ambiguity
2. Conceptualizing and planning new marriage and family	Accepting one's own fears and those of new spouse and children about remarriage and forming a stepfamily Accepting need for time and patience for adjustment to complexity and ambiguity of: 1. Multiple new roles 2. Boundaries: space, time, membership, and authority 3. Affective issues: guilt, loyalty conflicts, desire for mutuality, unresolvable past hurts	a. Work on openness in the new relationship to avoid pseudomutuality b. Plan for maintenance of cooperative financial and coparental relationships with ex-spouses c. Plan to help children deal with fears, loyalty conflicts, and membership in two systems d. Realignment of relationships with expended family to include new spouse and children e. Plan maintenance of connections for children with extended family of ex-spouse(s)
3. Remarriage and reconstitution of family	Final resolution of attachment to previous spouse and ideal of "intact" family; Acceptance of different model of family with permeable boundaries	a. Restructuring family boundaries to allow for inclusion of new spouse-stepparent b. Realignment of relationships and financial arrangements throughout subsystems to permit interweaving of several systems c. Making room for relationships of all children with biological (noncustodial) parents, grandparents, and other extended family d. Sharing memories and histories to enhance stepfamily integration

*Variation on a developmental scheme presented by Ransom et al. (1979)

Table 1-3. Betty Carter and Monica McGoldrick, *The Changing Family Life Cycle.* Needham Hwights, MA: Allyn and Bacon, 1989, 24. Used by permission of the authors.

Table ???

Shape of New Forms of Family Life

Nontraditional families may have any arrangement of parents and children as listed below, except two heterosexual parents, never divorced, with children conceived and born by them.

Partners

Two Partners,
heterosexual or homosexual
married and/or committed

Parents

Two Parents,
heterosexual or homosexual
married and/or committed

a. if heterosexual, never divorced
b. one parent, prior divorce
c. both parents, prior divorce
d. one parent, widowed
e. both parents, widowed
f. one parent widowed, one divorced
g. two parents, never married

Single Parent,
heterosexual or homosexual

a. Single parent (mother), never married; pregnancy not planned
b. Single parent (mother), never married; pregnancy planned
c. Single parent (father or mother), divorced
d. Single parent (father or mother), widowed
e. Single parent (father), never married

Grandparent(s) or other relatives

Children

Children—
may have come into family by:

- adoption
- foster care
- from a previous marriage, relationship
- ward of family or of one of the couple
- relative living with family but not adopted
- born to the couple (or surrogate parent) through artificial insemination
- conceived by the couple

Table 4.1
Stages of the Single Adult Life Cycle

Life Cycle Stage	*Emotional Process*
Not yet married	1. Shifting the relationship with the family. Restructuring interaction with family from dependent to an independent orientation. 2. Taking a more autonomous role with regard to the world outside the family in areas of work and friendships.
The Thirties: Entering the "Twilight Zone" of singlehood	1. Facing single status for the first time. 2. Expanding life goals to include other possibilities in addition to marriage.

Midlife (forties to midfifties)	1. Addressing the fantasy of the Ideal American Family.
	   a. accepting the possibility of never marrying.
	   b. accepting the possibility of not having own biological children.
	2. Defining the meaning of work, current and future.
	3. Defining an authentic life for oneself that can be accomplished within single status.
	4. Establishing an adult role for oneself within family of origin.

Later life (fifties to when physical health fails)	1. Consolidating decisions about work life. 2. Enjoying fruits of one's labors and the benefits of singlehood. 3. Acknowledging the future diminishment of physical powers. 4. Facing increasing disability and death of loved ones.
Elderly (between failing health and death)	1. Confronting mortality 2. Accepting one's life as it has been lived.

Lifespan of the Homosexual Single Adult

The markers of the life cycle of single adults apply to homosexuals. However, they must go through additional emotional transitions. A guideline for critical emotional tasks that are accomplished at different points in a person's life may include:

1. The development and the unfolding of a homosexual identity.
2. The development of gender identity in the absence of prescribed roles.
3. The development of a "family of choice."
4. The assertion of a homosexual identity with the family of origin.
5. The development of a fulfilled life when the "prince or princess" does not appear.
6. Realistic planning for old age.

From Natalie Schwartzberg, Kathy Berliner, Demaris Jacob, *Single In a Married World: A Life Cycle Framework for Working with the Unmarried Adult*. New York: W. W. Norton and Company, 1995, pages 56, 132. Used by permission.

On Trying to Change People:
Approaches That Usually Do Not Work

People persist in trying to change others — often with the intention of being helpful. However they discover that it does not work. People resist being changed by others. They make changes when they feel accepted, understood, and supported in their own solutions. In their book *A Brief Guide to Brief Therapy*, William O'Hanlon and Brian Cade have chronicled ineffective interventions people use when attempting to get others to change:

A. The unsolicited lecture

- lectures (especially "for your own good").
- advice.
- nagging.
- hints.
- encouragement; "Why don't you just try to...."
- begging/pleading/trying to justify your position.
- appeals to logic or common sense.
- pamphlets/newspaper articles strategically left lying around, or read aloud.
- the silent, long-suffering "look at how patiently and bravely I am not saying or noticing anything" approach, or an angry version of the same.
- repeated and/or escalating punishments which tend not to work and often result in more of the same, an escalation of, problem behaviors.

B. Taking the high moral ground

Unsolicited lectures given from a position of superiority, or of "unassailable" logic (usually the male position), or of moral outrage, or of righteous indignation

"If you really loved me...."
"Surely you could see that if you...."
"Why can't you realize that...."
"After all I've done...."
"Look how ill/desperate/depressed I've made myself by worrying about...."

"I'll love you and stop being angry/walking out/refusing to speak, if you
   do exactly what I want you to."

Any position, in fact, that implies that the speaker is in possession of the truth
about how things *are* or *should be,* or has superior knowledge, abilities, or a
set of morals in which the other is deficient or lacking.

C. Self-sacrifice/denial

- continually operating in order to keep the peace.
- constantly putting the happiness of the other before your own.
- continually seeking to justify yourself.
- protecting others from the consequences of actions.
- putting your life permanently on hold; hanging on hoping the other will
   change.
- continually trying to please somebody/everybody.

D. Orders to do it spontaneously!

Where one person, through any of the above approaches, tries to make another do something or adopt a different attitude, but demands also that they
should do it because they want to do it:

"You ought to want to please me!"
"I would like you to show more affection, but I'll only accept it if you
   do it because you want to!"
"It's not enough that you help with the washing-up, I would prefer you
   to do it gladly/willingly."

Trying to make somebody more responsible, expressive, reasonable, thoughtful, considerate, sexy, assertive, etc., is an invitation for them to be obedient
to your definitions of how they should be, regardless of your actual intentions. It rarely, if ever, works. The best you will get is obedience; by far the
most likely response will be an increasing inability to respond....It appears
that *most people do not like to be obedient.*

Adapted from Brian Cade and William Hudson O'Hanlon, *A Brief Guide to Brief Therapy*, 1993,
81–83. Used by permission.

A Guide to Suicide Prevention

Common Misconceptions

"People who talk about suicide really won't do it."

> *Not True.* Almost everyone who commits or attempts suicide has given some clues or warning. Statements like "You'll be sorry when I'm dead," or "I can't see any way out" — no matter how casually said — are suicide threats that should be taken seriously.

"Anyone who tries to kill himself must be crazy."

> *Not True.* Most suicidal people are not psychotic or insane. They may be grief-stricken, depressed or despairing, but extreme distress and emotional pain are not necessarily signs of mental illness.

"If a person is determined to kill himself, nothing is going to stop him."

> *Not True.* Most suicidal people do not want death; they want the pain to stop. The impulse to end it all, however overpowering, does not last forever. Even the most severely depressed persons have ambivalent feelings about death, they waver until the very last moment between wanting to live and wanting to die.

"People who commit suicide are unwilling to seek help."

> *Not True.* Studies of suicide victims have shown that more than half had sought medical help within six months before their death.

"Talking about suicide may give someone the idea."

> *Not True.* You don't give a suicidal person morbid ideas by talking about suicide. The opposite is true. Bringing up the subject of suicide and discussing it openly is one of the most helpful things you can do.

Suicide: What You Can Do to Help

1. Recognize signs of depression and suicide risk:

> *Change in personality:* sad, withdrawn, irritable, anxious, tired, indecisive, apathetic.
> *Change in behavior:* cannot concentrate on school, work, routine tasks.
> *Change in sleep patterns:* oversleeping or insomnia, early waking.
> *Change in eating habits:* loss of appetite and weight, or overeating.

Loss of interest: in friends, sex, hobbies, activities previously enjoyed.

Worry: about money or illness (either real or imaginary).

Fear: of losing control, going crazy, harming self or others.

Feeling worthless: "nobody cares," "people will be better off without me."

Feelings: of overwhelming guilt, shame, self-hatred.

Hopelessness: "It will never get better." "I'll always feel this way."

Drug or alcohol abuse.

Recent loss: through death, divorce, separation, broken relationship, or loss of health, job, money, status, self-confidence, self-esteem.

Loss of religious faith.

Isolation.

Suicidal impulse: gestures, statements, plans; self-inflicted cuts or burns; giving away favorite things or making out a will; previous suicide attempts; reckless behavior, inappropriately saying "good-bye."

Depression that disappears and is replaced by a sense of calm — when there is no change of external circumstances. Holidays, anniversaries, and the first month after discharge from a hospital can be difficult periods.

Agitation, hyperactivity, restlessness may indicate masked depression.

Remember: The risk of suicide may be greatest as the depression lifts.

2. Don't be afraid to ask: "Do you sometimes feel so bad that you think of suicide?" Just about everyone has considered suicide, however fleetingly, at one time or another. There is no danger of "giving someone the idea." In fact, it can be a great relief if you bring the question of suicide into the open, and discuss it freely without showing shock or disapproval. Raising the question shows that you are taking the person seriously and responding to the potential of his distress.

3. If the answer is *"Yes, I do think of suicide,"* you must take it seriously and follow through by asking: Have you thought of how you would do it? Do you have the means? Have you decided when you would do it? Have you ever tried suicide before? What happened then? If the person has a definite plan, if the means are easily available, if the method is a lethal one, and the time is set, the risk of suicide is very high. You response will be geared to the urgency of the situation as you see it. Therefore, it is vital not to underestimate the danger by not asking for details.

4. Do not leave a suicidal person alone if you think there is immediate danger. Call a suicide hotline or emergency medical number for help. Stay with the person until help arrives or the crisis passes. In the meantime, your job is to listen. Nearly everyone can be helped to overcome almost any kind of situation if they have someone who will listen, take them seriously and help them feel worthwhile again. What most suicidal people want is not death, but some way out of the terrible pain of feeling *"life is not worth living. I am not fit to live, I am all alone with this. I don't belong and nobody cares."* After the person is allowed to unburden, without interruption, without being judged, or criticized, or rejected, or told what to do, the tension drops, and the pain is relieved, and the suicidal feelings pass — maybe not forever, but for now. Help the person find a counselor so that he or she can deal with the problems that cause the pain.

If you cannot get the person to talk, if the person is hallucinating or influenced by drugs or alcohol, if the danger of the suicide is imminent, *get professional help*. If the means are available, try to get rid of them. Do not try to go it alone. Whenever you deal with a suicidal person, get some help with the situation. List telephone numbers for your *local* suicide hotline and other emergency services.

The Samaritans of New York City have granted readers permission to use this material in their communities.

(Adapted from material prepared by The Samaritans of New York City, P.O. Box 1259 Madison Square Station, New York, NY 10159. Used by permission.)

Notes

I: Support Change: Be a Gardener

1. Julian of Norwich, "Be a Gardener," in *Meditations with Julian of Norwich*, edited by Brendan Doyle.

One: In a Time of Change

1. Chinook Psalter, *Earth Prayers*, 156.
2. Richard Tarnas, *Passion of the Western Mind*, 270–71.
3. Martin Buber, *I and Thou*, 45–46.
4. *Healthcare Leadership Review*, June 1996, 10. Research reported in *Healthplan* 37, no. 2 (March–April 1996), 19–42.
5. *Healthcare Leadership Review*, June 1996, 9. Research cited from *Healthcare Demand Management*, 2, no. 4 (April 1996), 49–54: In light of the knowledge that physical symptoms are related to the whole person, mental and emotional as well, doctors are beginning to use mind/body treatments, in addition to medications or invasive treatments when treating ailments. Empirical studies show that patients who sought medical treatment of symptoms such as palpitations, headaches, and gastrointestinal disturbances had 50 percent fewer outpatient visits after undergoing interventions such as relaxation response training and cognitive restructuring. Behavioral medicine interventions led to a 36 percent reduction in physician visits by chronic pain patients. After undergoing mind/body interventions, 80 percent of hypertensive patients lowered their blood pressure and decreased medications significantly.
   Medical research and epidemiology studies documenting health benefits of religious faith and religious community involvement can also be found in articles by Drs. Lisa Berkman and Thomas Oxman, *Journal of Psychosomatic Medicine* (February 1995); and David Wulff, *Psychology and Religion*.
6. Thomas S. Kuhn, *The Structure of Scientific Revolutions*, 175.
7. Paul Watzlawick, John Weakland, and Richard Fisch, *Change: Principles of Problem Formation and Problem Resolution*, 10.

Two: The Ground of Community

1. Prayer from Singapore Church Missionary Society, edited by George Appleton, *The Oxford Book of Prayer*, 88.
2. Parker J. Palmer, "All the Way Down: A Spirituality of Public Life," in *Caring for the Commonweal: Education for Religious and Public Life*, edited by Parker J. Palmer,

Barbara G. Wheeler, and James Fowler, 149. Cites Annie Dillard, *Teaching a Stone to Talk*, 94–95.

3. *Tao Te Ching*, 15, translated by Stephen Mitchell.

4. Thich Nhat Hanh, *Old Path White Clouds*, adapted from chapter 48, "Covering Mud with Straw," 311–13.

5. Walter Wink, "My Enemy, My Destiny," *Sojourners*, February 1987, 30.

6. Martin Buber, *Hasidim and Modern Man*, 139–40.

7. Pamela Vermes, *Buber*, 76.

8. Martin Buber, *I and Thou*, 115.

Three: Counselor, Caregiver: Yourself as Gardner

1. *Tao Te Ching*, 10, translated by Stephen Mitchell.

2. Anecdote told by Raphael Naomi Remen, M.D., at Mind Body Conference, New York, 1993.

3. Personal communication, Dr. Wilbert Sykes, M.D.

4. See Martin Buber, *I and Thou*.

5. For a discussion of sympathy and empathy from a psychoanalytic perspective see Stanley L. Olinick, M.D., "A Critique of Empathy and Sympathy," *Empathy, Vol. 1*, edited by Joseph Lichtenberg, M.D., Melvin Bornstein, M.D., and Donald Silver, M.D., 137–66.

6. Susan Griffin, *A Chorus of Stone*s, 178. Susan Griffin in her essay, *A Chorus of Stones*, brilliantly grasps the listener's experience when she says:

> The telling and the hearing of a story is not a simple act. The one who tells must reach down into deeper layers of the self, reviving old feelings, reviewing the past. Whatever is retrieved is reworked into a new form, one that narrates events and gives the listener a path through these events that leads to some fragment of wisdom. The one who hears takes the story in, even to a place not visible or conscious to the mind, yet there. In this inner place a story from another life suffers a subtle change. As it enters the memory of the listener it is augmented by reflection by other memories, and even the body hearing and responding in the moment of the telling. By such transmissions, consciousness is woven.

7. A. J. van den Blink, "Empathy Amid Diversity: Problems and Possibilities," *Journal of Pastoral Theology*, Summer 1993, 10.

8. See Margaret Guenther, *Holy Listening*.

9. *Tao Te Ching*, 15, translated by Stephen Mitchell.

II: Facilitating Wholeness

Four: A Guide to Facilitating Change

1. George Appleton, ed., *The Oxford Book of Prayer*, 96

2. Paul Watzlawick et al., *Change: Principles of Problem Formation and Problem Resolution*, 38ff, 40ff, 47ff.

3. The theme of the curative affect of storytelling is developed in James Ashbrook's, *Minding the Soul: Pastoral Care and Counseling*.

4. Ibid., 166–79; also James Ashbrook, "Brain Process and Pastoral Counseling," *Journal of Pastoral Care 50*, no. 2 (Summer 1996), 141–49.

5. Daniel Goleman, *Emotional Intelligence*, description of the processes of emotional memory, 20–22; discussion of trauma and memory, 200–204 and 211–13; See Judith

Herman, *Trauma and Recovery* for an exploration of the process of recovery and its relationship to recovered memories.

6. George Vaillant, *The Wisdom of the Ego*, 285.

7. Ibid., 87.

8. Jeremy Rifkin, *The End of Work*, 110. Cites, "Why Job Growth Has Stalled," *Fortune*, March 8, 1993, 52.

9. James Ashbrook, *Minding the Soul*, 180–97.

10. Wendell Berry, "Song 4," *Collected Poems 1957–82*, 264.

Five: Preparing for Community Care, Counseling, and Referral

1. Rosario Murillo, "I'm Going to Plant a Heart in the Earth," in *Earth Prayers*, edited by Elizabeth Roberts and Elias Amidon, 51.

2. Edward Wimberly, *African-American Pastoral Care*, 31–32.

3. The Church Insurance Company, *Sexual Misconduct Reference Materials*, 1994, 10.

4. Aaron Liberman and Michael Woodruff, *Risk Management*, 9.

5. The Church Insurance Company, *Sexual Misconduct Reference Materials*, 1994, 25.

6. Ibid.

7. Liberman and Woodruff, *Risk Management*, 10.

8. Attorney Michael Woodruff, personal communication:

> When a counselor in community has repeated contact with a counselee, notes can document the counselee's ideational history. This may be very helpful to future treatment by another professional upon referral. It may enable the counselor to arrive at a more accurate assessment of the problem and lead to an appropriate referral. Notes can serve the counselee. Casual notes that avoid documentation of presenting symptoms and concerns, that omit a meaningful review of medical issues or problems, that do not cross reference other treatment by physicians or take into account effects of medication, that provide no responsible axial diagnosis or identify a treatment plan/goal, are dangerous. They may be later used as objective evidence of professional malpractice.
>
> Notes are often understood as the best objective means of assessing the quality of care, or lack of it. The failure to have notes may be tantamount to an admission of negligent practice if the prevailing practice standard is to keep notes. Counselors in community must make clear that when they keep minimal notes of personal use only, that their counseling is limited in duration, that counselees with identifiable mental health needs are referred to others as soon as practicable.

9. R. Scott Sullender and H. Newton Malon, "Should Clergy Counsel Suicidal Persons?" *Journal of Pastoral Care*, Fall 1990, cite Phyliss Hart and Ralph Osborne, *Concurrent Counseling*.

10. Ernest Rossi, "From Mind to Molecule: More Than a Metaphor," in *Brief Therapy: Myths, Methods, and Metaphors*, edited by Jeffrey K. Zeig and Stephen G. Gilligan, 445–72.

Six: Change Supported by the Solution-Focused Method

1. Insoo Kim Berg and Scott D. Miller, *Working with the Problem Drinker*, 94.

2. Ibid., 17. These rules are expanded in Steve de Shazer, *Keys to Solution in Brief Therapy*, chapter 1.

3. Steve de Shazer, *Putting Difference to Work*, 104.

4. Daniel Gallagher, *Solution-Focused Brief Therapy with Problem Drinkers and Drug Abusers,* teaching materials based on materials in Insoo Berg and Scott Miller, *Working with the Problem Drinker,* copyright 1994. (Used by permission.)

5. Steve de Shazer, *Clues: Investigating Solutions in Brief Therapy,* 88.

6. Ibid.

7. Insoo Kim Berg and Scott D. Miller, *Working with the Problem Drinker,* "Setting Goals with a Complainant," 56–61.

8. Steve de Shazer, *Putting Difference to Work,* 161.

9. Discussion of the qualities of well-formed goals can be found in: Steve de Shazer, *Putting Difference to Work,* chapter 10; John Walter and James Peller, "What Does the Solution Solve?" in *Becoming Solution-Focused in Brief Therapy,* chapter 4; Insoo Kim Berg and Scott Miller, "Well-Defined Treatment Goals" in *Working with the Problem Drinker,* chapter 3.

10. Quote cited in Dan Gallagher, *The Five-Step Treatment Model* (Solution-Focused Brief Therapy teaching materials), 4.

11. Ibid., 5.

12. Additional references to interviewing for change through the solution-focused method can be found in: Steve de Shazer, *When Words Were Originally Magic;* Insoo Kim Berg and Scott Miller, *Working with the Problem Drinker,* chapter 5; and William Hudson O'Hanlon and Michele Weiner-Davis, *In Search of Solutions,* chapters 4 and 5.

13. Stephen Mitchell, translator, *A Book of Psalms,* 3.

14. Insoo Kim Berg and Scott Miller, *Working with the Problem Drinker,* 99.

15. Ibid., 100–101.

16. Ibid.

17. Steve de Shazer, *Keys to Solution in Brief Therapy,* 137.

18. William O'Hanlon and Michele Weiner Davis, *In Search of Solutions,* 138.

19. Insoo Kim Berg and Scott D. Miller, *Working with the Problem Drinker,* 101.

20. Daniel Gallagher, *The Five-Step Treatment Model* (based on materials in Berg and Miller, *Working With the Problem Drinker*), 9–10.

21. Steve de Shazer, *Putting Difference to Work,* 118.

22. William O'Hanlon and Michele Weiner-Davis, *In Search of Solutions,* 137.

23. Insoo Kim Berg and Scott Miller, *Working with the Problem Drinker,* 88–91.

24. Ibid., 140–43.

25. Emily Dickinson, *The Complete Poems of Emily Dickinson,* 116.

III: Caring for and Counseling Others in all the Seasons of Life

Seven: Care and Counseling at Life's Many Beginnings

1. Gertrude Stein, *Everybody's Autobiography.*

2. Betty Carter and Monica McGoldrick, "Overview: The Changing Family Life Cycle," in *The Changing Family Life Cycle,* edited by Betty Carter and Monica McGoldrick, 3–10.

3. Susan Marks and Eve F. Roshevsky, eds., *Covenant of the Heart,* 132.

4. U.S. Census, "The Diverse Living Arrangements of Children, Summer 1991," cited in "Census Paints a Picture of Family Life," *New York Times,* August 30, 1994.

5. Betty Carter and Monica McGoldrick, "Overview: The Changing Family Life Cycle," in *The Changing Family Life Cycle,* edited by Betty Carter and Monica McGoldrick, 3–10.

6. U.S. Census, "The Diverse Living Arrangements of Children, Summer 1991," reported in the *New York Times,* August 30, 1994. The 1991 census shows that 50.8 percent

of American children under the age of eighteen lived in nuclear families. Of these, 56.4 percent of white children, 25.9 percent of black children and 37.8 percent of Hispanic children lived in such households.

7. Ibid. In 1991 the Census Bureau reported that nearly one million children lived in blended families. Of these children, 50.6 percent had a half-brother or half-sister.

8. U.S. Census, "The Diverse Living Arrangements of Children, Summer 1991," reported in *The New York Times,* July 30, 1994. In 1991 the Census Bureau reported that 24 percent of all children live in one parent families. Of those families, mothers were the parent in 21.2 percent. Among white children, 19.1 percent lived in one-parent families with mothers accounting for 16.4 percent. Among black children, 49.7 percent lived in one-parent families, 46.7 percent lived with their mothers. In Hispanic families 31.1 percent lived in one-parent homes with 28.5 percent living with their mothers.

9. Jason Deparle, "Rise in Births Outside of Marriage," *New York Times,* July 14, 1993, A1. Of the 23.7 percent of the single parent families where the mother has never married, an increasing number are college educated, professional women who are choosing to be mothers. Of the group of 23.7 percent, 11.3 percent had one or more years of college and 8.3 percent had managerial or professional occupations.

10. Eric F. Jones and Robert F. Stahmann, "Clergy Beliefs, Preparation and Practice in Premarital Counseling," *Journal of Pastoral Care* 48, no. 2 (1994), 181–86.

11. P. C. Glick, "How American Families Are Changing," *American Demographics,* January 1984, cited in *The Changing Family Life Cycle,* edited by Betty Carter and Monica McGoldrick, 235.

12. Betty Carter and Monica McGoldrick, *The Changing Family Life Cycle,* 22.

13. Ibid.

14. Eric F. Jones and Robert F. Stahmann, "Clergy Beliefs, Preparation and Practice in Premarital Counseling," *Journal of Pastoral Counseling,* Summer 1994, 51–86.

15. Ibid.

16. Myers Briggs Types Indicators, Consulting Psychologists, Inc.

17. Schwartzberg et al., *Single in a Married World: A Life Cycle Framework for Working with the Unmarried Adult,* 56.

18. John J. McNeill, *Freedom Glorious Freedom,* 160–94.

19. Schwartzberg et al., 87.

20. Ibid., 90–96.

21. Jason Deparle, "Rise in Births Outside of Marriage," *New York Times,* July 14, 1993, A1. "The 1993 Census found that in an increasingly large number of single-parent families there are mothers who had *never* married (23.7 percent). Of this group, 11.3 percent had one or more years of college and 8.3 percent had managerial or professional occupations."

22. Schwartzberg et al., 115. cite the research of B. L. Simon in *Never Married Women* to support this data.

23. Ibid.

24. Ibid., 119.

25. Ibid., 122.

26. Ibid., 94. In an informal study by Schwartzberg et al., of the Clinical Project on Research, the largest percentage of all, 79 percent, said their deepest need was to connect to community projects.

27. Goleman, *Emotional Intelligence,* 129, cites John Gottman, *What Predicts Divorce: The Relationship between Marital Process and Marital Outcomes* (Hillsdale, NJ: Lawrence Erlbaum Associates, 1993).

28. Nancy Woods, *Many Winters,* 27.

29. Betty Friedan, *Fountain of Age,* 22.

30. Ibid., 102.

31. George Vaillant, *The Wisdom of the Ego*, 326–63.

32. David Moberg in Melvin Kimble, "Pastoral Care of the Elderly," *Journal of Pastoral Care* 41 (September 1987), 270.

33. Erik Erikson, *The Life Cycle Completed*, 139.

34. James Lapsley, "Pastoral Care and Counseling of the Elderly," *Clinical Handbook of Pastoral Counseling Vol. 1*, edited by Robert J. Wicks et al., 245.

35. James Ashbrook, "Soul: Its Meaning and Its Making," *Journal of Pastoral Care*, Summer 1991, 159–68.

36. Richard Bergland, *The Fabric of the Mind*, 139, in James Ashbrook, "Soul: Its Meaning and Its Making," *Journal of Pastoral Care*, Summer 1991, 160.

37. Herbert Benson, *Timeless Medicine*, 208.

38. James Ashbrook, *Journal of Pastoral Care*, Summer 1991, 165.

39. Christie Neuger, "Feminist Pastoral Theology and Pastoral Counseling: A Work in Progress," *Journal of Pastoral Theology*, Summer 1992, 39.

40. Ibid.

Eight: Care and Counseling at Life's Many Endings

1. Chinook Psalter, "O Earthmother from whom we grow," in *Earth Prayers*, edited by Elizabeth Roberts and Elias Amidon, 156.

2. Betty Carter and Monica McGoldrick, *The Changing Family Life Cycle*, 21.

3. Ibid.

4. Pamela Couture, *Blessed are the Poor*, 27–49.

5. Pamela Couture, "The Context of Congregations: Pastoral Care in an Individualistic Society," *Journal of Pastoral Theology*, 12.

6. James Ashbrook, "Soul and Its Meaning and Its Making," *Journal of Pastoral Care*, Summer 1991, 161, cites L. R. Squire, *Memory and Brain*, 179.

7. Gertrude Stein, *Everybody's Autobiography*.

8. Robert Reich, "The Fracturing of the Middle Class," speech to the Center for National Policy, Washington, DC, adapted by the *New York Times*, August 31, 1994, A19.

9. Jeremy Rifkin, *The End of Work*, 19. Speaks of the Protestant work ethic that dominated the American frontier ethos and analyzes the present situation for today's workers.

10. Elisabeth Kübler-Ross, *On Death and Dying*.

11. Al Carmines, "God of Change and Glory." Hymn written for United Methodist Women, 1973. Used by permission.

12. Sherwin B. Nuland, *How We Die*, 255.

13. Nancy Woods, *Many Winters*, 31.

14. Maggie Callahan and Patricia Kelley, *Final Gifts: Understanding the Special Awareness, Needs, and Communications of the Dying*.

15. Ibid., 128.

16. Ibid., 69–128.

17. Ibid., 129–211.

18. Stephen Levine, *Who Dies? An Investigation of Conscious Living and Dying*, 26. Also in Ruth M. Underhill, *Red Man's Religion*, a description of Plains Indian vision quests as preparation for dying, 96.

19. Stephen Levine, *Who Dies?*, 5.

20. *Book of Common Prayer*, 1977 edition, 438.

21. *Tao Te Ching* 16, translated by Stephen Mitchell.

22. Wayne Oates, *Anxiety in Christian Experience*, cited in D. K. Switzer, "Grief and Loss," In *Dictionary of Pastoral Care and Counseling*, edited by Rodney Hunter, 472.

23. Ibid.

24. Kenneth Mitchell and Herbert Anderson, *All Our Losses, All Our Griefs*, 65.

25. Herbert Anderson and Kenneth Mitchell, *Leaving Home*, 132.

26. E. A. Grollman, "Jewish Care in Grief and Mourning," in *Dictionary of Pastoral Care and Counseling*, edited by Rodney Hunter, 477, and Maurice Lamm, *The Jewish Way in Death and Mourning*.

27. Edwin Friedman, "Systems and Ceremonies: A Family View of Rites of Passage," in *The Changing Family Life Cycle*, edited by Betty Carter and Monica McGoldrick, 128–34.

28. Ibid.

29. Fredda Herz Brown, "The Impact of Death and Serious Illness on the Family Life Cycle," in *The Changing Family Life Cycle*, edited by Betty Carter and Monica McGoldrick, 469 ff.

30. Ibid., 467.

31. C. Parkes, *Bereavement*, cited in D. K. Switzer, "Grief and Loss," *Dictionary of Pastoral Care and Counseling*, edited by Rodney Hunter, 473 and Coval MacDonald, "Loss and Bereavement," *Clinical Handbook of Pastor Counseling*, Vol. 1, edited by Robert Wicks et al., 543.

32. American Psychiatric Association, *Diagnosis and Statistical Manual IV* (1994), 684.

33. Ibid., 349.

34. Ibid.

35. Note 35 missing from MS p. 374.*

36. Peter Kramer, *Listening to Prozac.*, 67–108.

37. Wendell Berry, "Song (4)," *Collected Poems 1957–82*, 264.

Nine: Care and Counseling in Life's Daily Round

1. Abraham Heschel, "Just to be is a blessing," in *Earth Prayers*, edited by Elizabeth Roberts and Elias Amidon, 365

2. National Center for Statistics in training material from the Samaritans, New York City.

3. Albert R. Roberts, "Crisis Intervention: A Practical Guide to Immediate Help for Victim Families," in *Abuse and Religion: When Praying Isn't Enough*, edited by Anne L. Horton and Judith A. Williamson, 62–63. *ABC Process of Crisis Management* developed by the Abuse Counseling and Treatment, Inc. in Ft. Myers, Florida.

4. P. J. Peterson, "Stress and Stress Management," in *Dictionary of Pastoral Care and Counseling*, edited by Rodney Hunter, 1227–29.

5. Hans Selye, M.D., *The Stress of Life*, 171 ff.

6. James Gill, S.J., M.D., "Anxiety and Stress," in *Clinical Handbook of Pastoral Care*, Vol. 1, edited by Robert Wicks et al., 459.

7. Peter Kramer, *Listening to Prozac*, 112 ff.

8. Ibid. 123, 136–43.

9. American Psychiatric Association, *Diagnostic and Statistical Manual IV* (1994), 431–32

10. Ibid., 426.

11. Holmes and Rahe, "Social Adjustment Rating Scale," *Journal of Psychosomatic Research* 1967, no. 2, 213–18, cited in Howard Clinebell, *Basic Types of Pastoral Counseling*, 189–90. Researchers Thomas Holmes and R. H. Rahe became interested in whether *negative* stressors were needed in order to elicit anxious responses. They compiled a "Social Readjustment Rating Scale" (1967) and, through this instrument, discovered that out of a list of forty-three life-stress events, of the fourteen most stressful, ten involved families losing or gaining a member. Some events that would presumably be positive — for example, "marital reconciliation" — were experienced as more stressful than some with negative con-

notations, such as "difficulty with sex." A major change in one's financial state— "being a lot worse or a lot better off" —was experienced as equally stressful.

12. P. J. Peterson, "Relaxation, Psychology, and Techniques of," in *The Dictionary of Pastoral Care and Counseling*, edited by Rodney Hunter, 1053.

13. James Ashbrook, "Soul: Its Meaning and Its Making," *Journal of Pastoral Care*, Summer 1991, 64 ff.

14. A. J. Heschel, *The Sabbath: Its Meaning for Modern Man*, cited in P. J. Johnson, "Religious Traditions of Rest and Renewal," *Dictionary of Pastoral Care and Counseling*, edited by Rodney Hunter, 1079.

15. Daniel Goleman, *Emotional Intelligence*, 252–23. Cites statistics on binge drinking from studies of Harvey Wechsler, director of College Alcohol Studies at the Harvard School of Public Health (August 1994); statistics on college women from the report, "More Women Drink to Get Drunk and Risk Rape," Columbia University Center on Addiction and Substance Abuse (May 1993).

16. Ibid., 253, cites Alan Marlatt's report on leading causes of death, American Psychological Association, Annual Meeting, August 1994.

17. Ibid. Statistic from Harvey Wechsler, director of College Alcohol Studies, Columbia University.

18. George Vaillant, *Wisdom of the Ego*, 29 ff.

19. Ibid. Adaptation of: psychotic defenses, 40–45; mature defenses, 66–75; immature defenses, 45–59; neurotic defenses, 59–66.

20. American Psychiatric Association, *Diagnostic and Statistics Manual IV* (1994), 194 ff.

21. Andrew Delbanco and Thomas Delbanco, "Annals of Addiction: A. A. at the Crossroads," *The New Yorker*, May 20, 1995, 61.

22. Daniel Goleman, *New York Times*, August 13, 1996. C1. Report of the unpublished research of Dr. Anna Childress, University of Pennsylvania, Dr. Joseph Wu, University of California, Irvine, Dr. Eric Nestler, Yale University School of Medicine.

23. American Psychiatric Association, *Diagnostic and Statistical Manual IV*, 194 ff.

24. Daniel Goleman, *Emotional Intelligence*, 253.

25. Ibid., 254.

26. Ibid., 255.

27. *Johns Hopkins Medical Letter*, December 1992, 5.

28. *Harvard Mental Health Letter*, May 1993. Research cited: Thomas F. Babor, Michael Hofmann, Frances K. Del Boca et al., "Types of alcoholics, I: evidence for an empirically derived typology based on indicators of vulnerability and severity," *Archives of General Psychiatry* 49 (August 1992): 599–608; and Mark D. Litt, Thomas F. Babor, Frances K. Del Boca et al., "Types of alcoholics, II: application of an empirically derived typology to treatment matching," *Archives of General Psychiatry* 49 (August 1992): 609–14.

29. National Committee to Prevent Child Abuse, "Current Trends In Child Abuse Reporting and Fatalities: NCPCA'S 1995 Annual Fifty-State Survey," 1. In substantiated cases, thirty-four states gave the following breakdown of the types of abuse visited on children: neglect, 54 percent; physical abuse, 25 percent; sexual abuse, 11 percent; emotional maltreatment, 3 percent and "other," 6 percent.

30. Ibid., 4.

31. Daniel Goleman, *Emotional Intelligence*, 98.

32. Ibid., 198 ff.

33. Christie Neuger, "Feminist Pastoral Theology and Pastoral Counseling: A Work in Progress," *Journal of Pastoral Theology*, 1992, 40. (Cites Benokraitis and Feagin 1986 study, 9.)

34. Albert J. Reiss, Jr., and Jeffrey A, Roth, eds., *Understanding and Preventing Violence*, 236.

35. Ibid., 234

36. Christie Neuger, "Feminist Pastoral Theology and Pastoral Counseling: A Work in Progress," *Journal of Pastoral Theology,* 1992, 40. (Cites Benokraitis and Feagin 1986 study, 49.)

37. National Women's Abuse Prevention Project. The National Women's Abuse Prevention Project reports that in the period studied police in the mostly white, upper-class Washington, DC, suburb of Montgomery County, Maryland, received as many domestic disturbance calls as were received in the same period in Harlem, New York City.

38. Albert J. Reiss, Jr., and Jeffrey A. Roth, eds., *Understanding and Preventing Violence,* 231.

39. Missing note?????.

40. The cycle of domestic violence is explored by Lenore Walker, "Spouse Abuse," in *Abuse and Religion: When Praying Isn't Enough,* edited by Anne L. Horton and Judith A. Williamson, 13–20.

41. Adapted from "Signs to Look for in a Battering Personality," Project for Victims of Family Violence, Fayetteville, Ark. Also see Lenore Walker, "Spouse Abuse," in *Abuse and Religion,* ed. Horton and Williamson, 14.

42. Some religious institutions are developing treatment programs that also use the "holding environment" of the religious community. One such program, *Stop Abusive Family Environments* [S.A.F.E.] has been developed by Fuller Theological Seminary and is described by Constance Doran, "A Model Treatment Program That Would Work toward Family Unity and Still Provide Safety," in *Abuse and Religion,* ed. Horton and Williamson.

43. Cited by Giarretto Institute.

44. Ching Tung Lung and Deborah Daro, "Current Trends In Child Abuse Reporting and Fatalities: National Committee on Preventing Child Abuse's 1995 Annual 50 State Survey."

45. Diana Russell, *Sexual Exploitation: Rape, Child Sexual Abuse and Sexual Harassment,* cited in Judith Herman, *Trauma and Recovery,* 30. *Sexual abuse correlates with other social problems:* 80 percent of sexually abusive fathers and physically abusive mothers were abused children; 80 percent of prostitutes were incest victims during childhood (Giarretto Institute); Childhood abuse is in the background of 50 to 60 percent of psychiatric inpatients and 40 to 60 percent of psychiatric outpatients. In one study of psychiatric emergency room patients, 70 percent had abuse histories (Judith Herman, *Trauma and Recovery,* 122); 70 percent of drug and alcohol abusers were sexually molested by family members (Giarretto Institute).

46. Edward O. Loumann et al. *The Social Organization of Sexuality,* 343.

47. Heidi Vanderbilt, "Incest: A Chilling Report," *Lears,* February 1992, 69. Defining incest as only occurring between blood relatives are California, the District of Columbia, Florida, Hawaii, Indiana, Kansas, Louisiana, Maryland, Minnesota, Nevada, New Mexico, New York, and North Dakota.

48. David Finkelhor and Linda Meyer Williams, *Toward a Typology of Incestuous Fathers* (Research Abstract 1994), 11–20: Type One: *Sexually preoccupied* (26 percent) — These fathers have a clear and often obsessive sexual interest in their daughters; some think of them as sex objects almost from birth. Many of these offenders have been sexually abused as children and are so sexualized that they project their sexual needs everywhere; their children are available. Type Two: *Adolescent Regressives* (33 percent). They become sexually interested in their daughters when their daughters entered puberty. The men sound and act like adolescents. They see their daughters as "dates" whom they have to "make." Type Three: *Instrumental self-gratifier* (20 percent). When these fathers abuse their daughters they do not think about them. They use their daughters as "receptacles" as they engage in sexual activity but think of their wife, or another woman, or even their daughter grown up. They use-abuse their daughters sporadically and sometimes are preoccupied by guilt.

To alleviate the guilt, they convince themselves that their daughters are aroused. Type Four: *Emotionally Dependent* (10 percent). They are emotionally needy, lonely, and depressed, and look to their daughters for close, exclusive, emotionally dependent relationships that include sexual gratification. The average age of the daughter when the incest begins is six to seven years. When it happens with older daughters the fathers describe them as if they were lovers. Type Five: *Angry Retaliators* (10 percent). These fathers often have a history of violent rape and assault. They have little sexual feeling for the daughter and abuse her out of anger. The anger is displaced; they are angry at the child's mother, whom they feel gave the child too much attention. Some angry retaliators tie up, gag, beat, and rape their daughters and are aroused by the violence.

49. Linda Meyer Williams and David Finkelhor, "Characteristics of Incestuous Fathers: A Review of Recent Studies," in W. L. Marshall, D. R. Laws, and H. E. Barbaree, eds., *Handbook of Sexual Assault: Issues, Theories, and Treatment*, 252.

50. Heidi Vanderbilt, "Incest: A Chilling Report," *Lears*, 58. *Teacher-lover:* older women who have sex with young adolescents; *Experimenter-exploiters:* women who usually come from rigid families where sex education is forbidden; they use baby-sitting opportunities to explore small children; *Predisposed:* women who, because of their own physical and sexual abuse, are predisposed to abuse their own children or siblings; *Male-coerced:* women who abuse children because they are forced to by men. Many have their own sex abuse history and are married to sex offenders who also abuse their children. Some, once forced to abuse their children, may continue to do it on their own.

51. Ibid., 62.

52. Anne L. Horton and Doran Williams, "What Incest Perpetrators Need (But Are Not Getting) from the Clergy and Treatment Community," in *Abuse and Religion*, ed. Horton and Williamson, 264. Refers to the California-based Giarretto Institutes treatment programs as an example of the effectiveness of a combined approach. Their treatment programs are made up of the combined efforts of professionals in counseling, law enforcement, criminal justice, and human services; self-help groups for incested families (Parents United), led by professionals, for parents, children, and adults molested as children, as well as individual and family counseling for everyone in the abused family. This comprehensive treatment program, which has the child's well-being in view, is being replicated across the country. They also provide training for professionals, including seminarians and clergy. (See Hank Giarretto, *Integrated Treatment of Child Sexual Abuse*).

53. Linda Meyer Williams, *Journal of Consulting and Clinical Psychology*, February 1995, 1167–76.

54. Barbara Snow and Geraldine G. Hanni, "Counseling the Adult Survivor of Child Sexual Abuse," in *Abuse and Religion*, ed. Horton and Williamson, 158.

55. Edward O. Laumann et al., *The Social Organization of Sexuality*, 343.

56. Ibid., 336.

57. Kersti Yllo and Donna LeClerc, "Marital Rape," in *Abuse and Religion*, ed. Horton and Williamson, 53.

58. Edward O. Laumann et al., *The Social Organization of Sexuality*, 337. Being active in their religious group was a characteristic of one half of the sexually abused women in another study reported by Anne L. Horton, Melany M. Wilkins, Wendy Wright, "Women Who Ended Abuse: What Religious Leaders and Religion Did for These Victims," in *Abuse and Religion*, ed. Horton and Williamson, 241.

59. S. Amelia Stinson Wesley, "Daughters of Tamar: Pastoral Care for Survivors of Rape," in *Through the Eyes of Women*, edited by Jeanne Stevenson Moessner, 235.

IV: Our Changing Ways

1. Ojibway Prayer, "Grandfather look at our brokenness," in *Earth Prayers*, edited by Elizabeth Roberts and Elizabeth Amidon, 95.

Ten: Tending Yourself

1. American Psychiatric Association, *Diagnostic and Statistical Manual IV* (1994), 429.
2. In conversation with Paul Goodman and Larry Kornfeld.
3. Karen Lebacqz and Ronald Barton, *Sex in the Parish*, 65. Subjective signals used by clergy to tell them when they might be getting into intimacy trouble: the "publicity" test: what would others think?; physical arousal — one's own or the other's; inordinate sexual fantasy; sexual gestures or body language; sexual innuendo in verbal exchange; intuition, instinct, or not feeling right;wanting to share intimacies that are not called for; a parishioner wanting too much time or attention; wanting to shift the focus to sexual subjects.
4. Ibid., 113–25.
5. Ibid., 103.
6. Ibid., 126–31.
7. Ibid., 55–57.
8. Donald Capps, "Sex in the Parish: Social-Scientific Explanations for Why it Occurs," *Journal of Pastoral Care* 47, no. 4 (Winter 1993), 356–57.
9. Cited in *Sexual Exploitation in the Church: Guidelines for the Diocesan Response Team*, Episcopal Diocese of Western New York. Based on data provided by Gary Schoener, Ph.D., director of the Walk-In Counseling Center, Minneapolis.
10. From the *Ethics Code* of the American Association of Pastoral Counselors: All forms of sexual behavior or harassment with clients are unethical, even when a client invites or consents to such behavior or involvement. Sexual behavior is defined as, but not limited to, all forms of overt and covert seductive speech, gestures, and behavior as well as physical contact of a sexual nature; harassment is defined as, but not limited to, repeated comments, gestures or physical contacts of a sexual nature. We recognize that the therapist/client relationship involves a power imbalance, the residual effects of which are operative following the termination of the therapy relationship. Therefore, all sexual behavior or harassment as defined in Principle III, G with former clients is unethical. (*Principle III, Client Relationships, G and H*).
11. Marie Fortune, *Is Nothing Sacred?*, 156.
12. Karen Lebacqz and Ronald Barton, *Sex and the Parish*, 45. Cite statistics reported by Richard Exlely in "A Support System: Your Way of Escape," *Ministries Today*, May/June 1988, 36.
13. Data obtained from Dr. Roy Woodruff, Executive Director, AAPC.
14. Marie Fortune, *Is Nothing Sacred?* 47.
15. Gary Schoener, "Assessment, Rehabilitation and Supervision of Clergy Who Have Engaged in Sexual Boundary Violations." Paper presented at Instruments of Thy Peace Conference sponsored by the House of Bishops of the Episcopal Church, St. Paul, MN, November 12, 1996. Among the great variety of situations seen in consultation, some are clear-cut exploitation, others less so: "1. Cases involving romantic and/or erotic talk of a type not appropriately part of counseling that creates a great deal of fantasy about involvement, but no improper physical contact. In some of these cases we have seen more client harm than with overt sexual touch; 2. Cases involving a single episode of erotic contact, followed by an acknowledgment, an apology, and often the seeking of help from a consultant; 3. Cases involving the revelation that a professional and spouse were formerly in a professional counseling relationship many years earlier, but where the client/spouse has no grievance or complaint; 4. Cases involving same-sex contact that became erotic (e.g.,

during a hug) in which the counselor (or clergy) was not gay or lesbian-identified, and in fact was shocked and confused about what happened and sought immediate consultation; 5. Cases involving 'old' complaints that involved conduct before the offender was professionally trained, licensed or ordained (e.g., at a time when he/she was a paraprofessional). These are not technically offenses, but require careful review in terms of risks of future misconduct exist; 6. Cases involving use of touch that had been taught to the practitioner or trainee as part of a counseling approach, but that was high-risk and led to eroticized contact. The practitioner sought consultation after quickly realizing the inappropriateness of the behavior."

Schoener cites Pope's (1994, 86) description of "10 of the most common scenarios" of therapist-client sex; these are also seen in clergy/congregant sexual exploitation 1. *Role Trading* (therapist becomes the patient); 2. *Sex Therapy* (sex fraudulently presented as "sex therapy"); 3. *As if*, wherein the therapist ignores that feelings are likely to be transference; 4. *Svengali* (therapist exploits dependent client); 5. *Drugs and/or alcohol* used in seduction; 6. *Rape* (force or threats); 7. *True love* (therapist rationalizes that it is "true love"); 8. *It just got out of hand* (loss of control in context of the emotional closeness of therapy); 9. *Time out* (therapist rationalizes that contact outside of session, or office, is legitimate); and 10. *Hold me,* in which therapist exploits client's need to be held or touched.

16. Marie Fortune, *Is Nothing Sacred?*, 105–6.

17. "Poll of Female Rabbis," *New York Times*, August 28, 1993, 5.

18. Karen Lebacqz and Ronald Barton, *Sex and the Parish*, 69.

19. Ibid., 135.

20. Ann O'Hara Graff, "Women in the Roman Catholic Ministry: New Vision, New Gifts," in *Clergy Ethics in a Changing Society*, edited by James P. Wind, Russell Burck, Paul Camenisch, Dennis McCann, 215–30.

21. Joseph Edelheit, "An Ethics for the Interpretation of the Contemporary Jewish Experience," in *Clergy Ethics in a Changing Society,* edited by James P. Wind et al., 251–72.

22. Richard Couser, *Ministry and the American Legal System*, 267–68.

23. Ibid.

Selected Bibliography

Books and articles are arranged by the subject matter of chapters. Subjects are also cross-referenced within the bibliography.

I: Support Change: Be a Gardner

Chapter One: In a Time of Change

Theories of Change
Referenced in chapter 4.

Sources of Paradigmatic Shift toward Holism
Ashbrook, James, ed. *Brain, Culture and the Human Spirit.* Lanham, MD: University Press of America, 1993.
Capra, Fritjof. *The Turning Point.* New York: Simon and Schuster, 1982.
Childs, Brian H., and David W. Waanders, eds. *The Treasure of Earthen Vessels: Explorations in Theological Anthropology.* Louisville: Westminster/John Knox Press, 1994.
Covey, Stephen R. *The Seven Habits of Highly Effective People.* New York: Simon and Schuster, 1989.
Craige, Betty Jean. *Laying the Ladder Down: The Emergence of Cultural Holism.* Amherst: University of Massachusetts Press, 1992.
Kuhn, Thomas S. *The Structure of Scientific Revolutions.* Chicago: University of Chicago Press, 1962.
Küng, Hans. *Judaism: Between Yesterday and Tomorrow.* New York: Crossroad, 1992.
Pagels, Heinz R. *The Cosmic Code.* New York: Simon and Schuster, 1982.
Tarnas, Richard. *The Passion of the Western Mind.* New York: Ballantine Books, 1991.
Teilhard de Chardin, Pierre. *The Phenomenon of Man.* New York: Harper Torchbooks, 1948.
———. *The Divine Milieu.* New York: Harper Torchbooks, 1960.
———. *Human Energy.* New York: Harcourt Brace Jovanovich, 1962.

The Mind/Brain, Body, and Holism
Ashbrook, James. *The Human Mind and the Mind of God: Theological Promise in Brain Research.* Lanham, MD: University Press of America, 1984.
———. *Brain and Belief.* Bristol, IN: Wyndam Hall Press, 1988.
———. *Faith and Ministry in the Light of the Double Brain.* Bristol, IN: Wyndham Hall Press, 1989.

——. *Brain, Culture and the Human Spirit: Essays from an Emergent Evolutionary Perspective*. Lanham, MD: University Press of America, 1993.

Bergland, Richard. *The Fabric of the Mind*. New York: Penguin, 1988.

Borysenko, Joan. *Minding the Body, Mending the Mind*. New York: Simon and Schuster, 1988.

Dossey, Larry. *Space, Time, and Medicine*. Boulder, CO: Shambhala Publications, 1982.

Edelman, Gerald M. *The Remembered Present: A Biological Theory of Consciousness*. New York: Basic Books, 1990.

Goleman, Daniel and Joel Gurin. *Mind Body Medicine*. New York: Consumer Reports Books/St. Martin's Press, 1993.

Goleman, Daniel. *Emotional Intelligence: Why It Can Matter More than I.Q.* New York: Bantam Books, 1995.

Moyers, Bill. *Healing and the Mind*. New York: Doubleday, 1993.

Squire, L. R. *Memory and Brain*. New York: Oxford University Press, 1987.

Weil, Andrew. *Spontaneous Healing*. New York: Fawcett Group, 1996.

ARTICLES

Ashbrook, James. "Brain Process and Pastoral Counseling." *Journal of Pastoral Care* 50, no. 2 (Summer 1996): 141–49.

——. "Soul: Its Meaning and Its Making." *Journal of Pastoral Care* 45, no. 2 (1991:) 159–68.

Healthcare Review, June 1996, 9, in *Healthcare Demand Management* 2, no. 4 (April 1996): 49–54.

Spiritual Practice, Spiritual Direction, Spirituality and Psychotherapy
Referenced in chapter 4.

Religion, Spirituality, and Healing

Ashbrook, James. *Minding the Soul: Pastoral Counseling as Remembering Who We Are*. Minneapolis: Fortress Press, 1997.

Ackerman, John. *Spiritual Awakening: A Guide to Congregations*. Bethesda, MD: Alban Institute.

Benson, Herbert. *Timeless Healing: The Power of Biology and Belief*. New York: Scribners, 1996.

Calvi, John. *The Dance between Hope and Fear*. Southeast Yearly Meeting. Philadelphia: Friends General Conference, 1992.

Dossey, Larry. *Prayer Is Good Medicine*. San Francisco: HarperSanFrancisco, 1996.

Duniho, Terence. *Wholeness Lies Within: 16 Natural Paths of Spirituality*. Bethesda, MD: Alban Institute.

Feldman, David. *Health and Medicine in the Jewish Tradition*. New York: Crossroad, 1986.

Harpur, T. *The Uncommon Touch*. Toronto: McClelland and Stewart, 1994.

Kelsey, Morton. *Healing and Christianity*. New York: Harper and Row, 1973.

Kerman, Kate. *A Friendly Touch: Therapeutic Touch among Quakers*. Philadelphia: Friends General Conference, 1994.

Pargament, Kenneth J., Kenneth I. Maton, and Robert E. Hess. *Religion and Prevention in Mental Health: Research, Vision and Action*. Binghamton, NY: Haworth Press, 1992.

McCormick, Richard. *Health and Medicine in the Catholic Tradition*. New York: Crossroad, 1987.

Mitchell, Hobart. *Prayer for Healing*. New England Yearly Meeting. Philadelphia:Friends General Conference, 1991.

Siegel, Bernie. *Love, Medicine and Miracles*. New York: HarperCollins, 1986.

——. *Peace, Love and Healing*. New York: HarperCollins, 1993.

Thomas, Zack. *Healing Touch: The Church's Forgotten Language.* Louisville: Westminster/John Knox Press, 1994.

ARTICLE
Wuthnow, Sara. "Healing Touch Controversies." *Journal of Religion and Health* 36, no. 3 (Fall 1997): 221.

Community Care and Counseling (Pastoral): Influence of Anton Boisen
Aden, Leroy and J. Harold Ellen. *Turning Points in Pastoral Care: The Legacy of Anton Boisen and Seward Hiltner.* Grand Rapids, MI: Baker Book House, 1990.
Asquith, Glenn, ed. *Vision from a Little Known Country.* Journal of Pastoral Care Publications, 1992.
Boisen, Anton. *Out of the Depths: An Autobiographical Study of Mental Disorder and Religious Experience.* New York: Harper and Brothers, 1960.
———. *The Exploration of the Inner World.* New York: Harper and Brothers, 1961.

Faith Community Care and Counseling Reference Books
Hunter, Rodney J., ed. *Dictionary of Pastoral Care and Counseling.* Nashville: Abingdon Press, 1990.
Stone, Howard W. and William M. Clements. *Handbook for Basic Types of Pastoral Care and Counseling.* Nashville: Abingdon Press, 1991.
Wicks, Robert, Richard D. Parsons, and Donald Capps, eds. *Clinical Handbook of Pastoral Counseling Volume I.* Expanded edition. Mahwah, NJ: Paulist Press, 1993.
Wicks, Robert and Richard D. Parsons, eds. *Clinical Handbook of Pastoral Counseling Vol. II.* Mahwah, NJ: Paulist Press, 1993.

Chapter Two: The Ground of Community

Caring for and Building Community
Bellah, Robert N., Richard Madsen, William M. Sullivan, Ann Swidler, and Steven M. Tipton. *Habits of the Heart: Individualism and Commitment in American Life.* New York: Harper & Row, 1985.
Bellah, Robert N., Richard Madsen, William M. Sullivan, Ann Swidler, and Steven M. Tipton. *The Good Society.* New York: Vintage Books, 1992.
Buber, Martin. *Between Man and Man.* Translated by R. Gregor Smith. London: Fontana, 1961.
———. *Hasidim and Modern Man.* Translated by M. Friedman. New York: Horizon Press, 1958.
———. *I and Thou.* Translated by R. Gregor Smith. New York: Charles Scribners Sons, 1958.
Buchanan, John M. *Becoming Church, Becoming Community.* Louisville: Westminster/John Knox Press, 1996.
Detwiler-Zapp, Diane, and William Dixon. *Lay Caregiving.* Philadelphia: Fortress Press, 1982.
Dudley, Carl S. *Basic Steps toward Community Ministry: Guidelines and Models in Action.* Bethesda, MD: Alban Institute.
Gunderson, Gary. *Deeply Woven Roots.* Minneapolis: Fortress Press, 1997.
Parsons, George, and Speed B. Leas. *Understanding Your Congregation as a System.* Bethesda, MD: Alban Institute.
Palmer, Parker. *The Company of Strangers: Christians and the Renewal of America's Public Life.* New York: Crossroad, 1981.

———. *The Active Life: A Spirituality of Work, Creativity, and Caring.* San Francisco: Harper & Row, 1990.

———, Barbara G. Wheeler, and James Fowler, eds. *Caring for the Commonweal: Education for Religion and Public Life.* Macon, GA: Mercer University Press, 1990.

Peck, M. Scott. *A World Waiting to be Born: Civility Rediscovered.* New York: Bantam Books, 1993.

———. *The Different Drum: Community Making and Peace.* New York: Touchstone Book, 1987.

Rademache, William J. *Lay Ministry: A Theological, Spiritual and Pastoral Handbook.* New York: Crossroad, 1992.

Richardson, Ronald. *Creating a Healthier Church: Family Systems Theory, Leadership and Congregational Life.* Minneapolis: Fortress Press, 1995.

Saarinen, Martin. *The Life Cycle of a Congregation.* Bethesda, MD: Alban Institute.

Stone, Howard. *The Caring Church: A Guide for Lay Pastoral Care.* Minneapolis: Augsburg Fortress Press, 1991.

Thomas, Leo. *The Healing Team.* Mahwah, NJ: Paulist Press, 1987.

Vermes, Pamela. *Buber.* New York: Grove Press, 1988.

Faith Community: Conflict Resolution/Creative Listening

Claremont Meeting. *Quaker Dialogue "Creative Listening."* Philadelphia: Friends General Conference, 1991.

Couture, Pamela D., and Rodney Hunter, eds. *Pastoral Care and Social Conflict.* Nashville: Abingdon Press, 1995.

Furniss, George M. *The Social Context of Pastoral Care.* Louisville: Westminster/John Knox Press, 1994.

Gendlin, Eugene. *Focusing.* New York: Bantam Books, 1978.

Green, Tova, Fran Peavy, and Peter Woodrow. *Insight and Action.* East Haven, CN: New Society Publishers, 1994.

Harris, John C. *Stress, Power, and Ministry.* Bethesda, MD: Alban Institute, rev. 1982.

Leas, Speed. *Discover Your Conflict Management Style.* Bethesda, MD: Alban Institute.

———. *Leadership and Conflict.* Nashville: Abingdon Press, 1982.

———. *Moving Your Church through Conflict.* Bethesda, MD: Alban Institute.

———. *How to Deal Constructively with Clergy-Lay Conflict.* Bethesda, MD: Alban Institute.

———. *A Lay Person's Guide to Conflict Management.* Bethesda, MD: Alban Institute.

Loring, Patricia. *Spiritual Discernment: The Context and Goal of Clearness Committees.* Pendle Hill Pamphlet. Philadelphia: Friends General Conference, 1992.

Sheeran, Michael J. *Beyond Majority Rule: Voteless Decision Making in the Religious Society of Friends.* Philadelphia: Philadelphia Yearly Meeting, 1983.

Thich Nhat Hanh. *Old Path White Clouds.* Gardinia, CA: Parallax Press, 1991.

Faith Community and Diversity

Augsburger, David. W. *Conflict Mediation across Cultures: Pathways and Patterns.* Louisville: Westminster/John Knox Press, 1992.

Edelheit, Joseph. "An Ethics for the Interpretation of the Contemporary Jewish Experience," in *Clergy Ethics in a Changing Society,* ed. James Wind, Russell Burck, Paul Camenisch, and Dennis McCann. Louisville: Westminster/John Knox Press, 1991.

Kliewer, Stephen. *How to Live with Diversity in the Local Church.* Bethesda, MD: Alban Institute.

Trickett, Edison J., Roderick J. Watts, Dina Birman, eds. *Human Diversity: Perspectives on People in Context.* San Francisco: Jossey-Bass, 1995.

Graff, Ann O'Hara. "Women in the Roman Catholic Ministry: New Vision, New Gifts," in *Church Ethics in a Changing Society*, ed. James Wind, Russell Burck, Paul Camenisch, and Dennis McCann. Louisville: Westminster/John Knox Press, 1991.

ARTICLE AND UNPUBLISHED ADDRESS

Couture, Pamela. "The Context of Congregations: Pastoral Care in an Individualistic Society." *Journal of Pastoral Theology*. 2 (Summer 1992): 1–13.

Van den Blink, A. J. "Pastoral Psychotherapy: The Impact of Social Change and Social Difference." Plenary Address, Centers and Training Conference American Association of Pastor Counselor, January 11, 1994.

Ministering to Angry People

Amanecida Collective. *Revolutionary Forgiveness*, ed. Anne Gilson and Carter Heyward. Maryknoll, NY: Orbis Books, 1987.

Goleman, Daniel. *Emotional Intelligence*. New York: Bantam Books, 1995.

Saussy, Carroll. *The Gift of Anger: A Call to Faithful Action*. Louisville: Westminster/John Knox Press, 1995.

Tavris, Carol. *Anger: The Misunderstood Emotion*. New York: Touchstone, 1989.

Williams, Redford. *The Trusting Heart*. New York: Times Books/Random House, 1989.

Chapter Three: Caregiver, Counselor: Yourself as Gardner

Feminist Perspective on Faith Community Care and Counseling
Referenced in chapter 4.

Internalizing the God of Love or the God of Fear

McNeill, John J. *Taking a Chance on God: Liberating Theology for Gays, Lesbians and Their Lovers, Families and Friends*. Boston: Beacon Press, 1988.

Rizzuto, Ana-Marie. *The Birth of the Living God*. Chicago: University of Chicago Press, 1979.

Saussy, Carroll. *God Images and Self-Esteem: Empowering Women in a Patriarchal Society*. Louisville: Westminster/John Knox Press, 1991.

ARTICLE

Wink, Walter. "My Enemy, My Destiny." *Sojourners*, February 1987: 30.

Empathy

Gilligan, Carol. *In a Different Voice: Women's Conception of Self and Morality*. Cambridge, MA: Harvard University Press, 1982.

Lichtenberg, Joseph, Melvin Bornstein, Donald Silver, eds. *Empathy, Vols. 1 and 2*. Hillsdale, NJ: Analytic Press, 1984.

Marguilies, Alfred. *The Empathic Imagination*. New York and London: W. W. Norton, 1989.

Ulanov, Ann, and Barry. *The Healing Imagination: The Meeting of Psyche and Soul*. Mahwah, NJ: Paulist Press, 1991.

ARTICLES

Davis, Patricia H. "Women and the Burden of Empathy." *Journal of Pastoral Theology*, Summer 1993: 29–38.

McCarthy, Marie. "Empathy Amid Diversity: Problems and Possibilities." *Journal of Pastoral Theology*, Summer 1993: 15–28.

——. "Empathy: A Bridge Between." *Journal of Pastoral Care*, Summer 1992: 119–30.

Schlaugh,* Chris. "Defining Pastoral Psychotherapy." *Journal of Pastoral Care*, December 1987.

Van den Blink, A. J., "Empathy Amid Diversity: Problems and Possibilities." *Journal of Pastoral Theology*, Summer 1993: 1–14.

Religion, Spirituality, and Healing
Referenced in chapter 1.

Spiritual Practice
Cox, Michael. *Handbook of Christian Spirituality.* San Francisco: Harper & Row, 1983.

Edwards, Tilden. *Living in the Presence: Disciplines for the Spiritual Heart.* San Francisco: Harper and Row, 1987.

Faber, Heije. *Above the Treeline: Towards a Contemporary Spirituality,* trans. John Bowden, Nashville: Abingdon Press, 1989.

Johnston, William. *The Mirror Mind: Spirituality and Transformation.* New York: Harper and Row, 1981.

McMakin, Jacqueline and Rhoda Nary. *Journeying with the Spirit.* San Francisco: Harper-SanFrancisco, 1993.

Moore, Thomas. *Care of the Soul: A Guide for Cultivating Depth and Sacredness in Everyday Life.* New York: HarperCollins Publishers, 1992.

Steere, Douglas V. *Gleanings: A Random Harvest.* Nashville: The Upper Room, 1986.

Thich Nhat Hanh. *The Miracle of Mindfulness.* Gardinia, CA: Parallax, 1987.

Wicks, Robert J. *Handbook of Spirituality for Ministers.* New York and Mahwah, NJ: Paulist Press, 1995.

ARTICLE
James Ashbrook. "Soul: Its Meaning and Its Making." *Journal of Pastoral Care* 45 (Summer 1991): 159–68.

Spiritual Direction/Spirituality and Psychotherapy
Barry, William, and William Connolly. *The Practice of Spiritual Direction.* San Francisco: Harper and Row, 1982.

Edwards, Tilden. *Spiritual Friend: Reclaiming the Gift of Spiritual Direction.* Mahwah, NJ: Paulist Press, 1980.

Guenther, Margaret. *Holy Listening: The Art of Spiritual Direction.* Cambridge, MA: Cowley Press, 1992.

Johanson, Greg, and Ron Kurtz. *Grace Unfolding: Psychotherapy in the Spirit of the Tao-te Ching.* New York: Bell Tower, 1991.

Jones, Alan. *Exploring Spiritual Direction: An Essay on Christian Friendship.* New York: Harper, 1982.

May, Gerald G., M.D. *Care of Mind/Care of Spirit: A Psychiatrist Explores Spiritual Direction.* New York: HarperCollins, 1982, revised, 1992.

——. *Will and Spirit: A Contemplative Psychology.* San Francisco: HarperSanFrancisco, 1987.

——. *Simply Sane: The Spirituality of Mental Health.* New York: Crossroad, 1993.

II: Facilitating Wholeness

Chapter Four: A Guide to Facilitating Change

Religion, Spirituality, and Healing
Referenced in chapter 1.

Prayer and Preaching: Bridge to Counseling
Biersdorf, John E. *How Prayer Shapes Ministry*. Bethesda, MD: Alban Institute.
Capps, Donald. *Pastoral Counseling and Preaching: A Quest for an Integrated Ministry*. Philadelphia: Westminster Press, 1980.
Hulme, William E. *Pastoral Care and Counseling: Using the Unique Resources of the Christian Tradition*. Minneapolis: Augsburg Press, 1981.
Oglesby, William. *Biblical Themes for Pastoral Care*. Nashville: Abingdon Press, 1980.
Ramshaw, Elaine. *Ritual and Pastoral Care*. Philadelphia: Fortress Press, 1987.
Wimberly, Edward P. *Prayer in Pastoral Counseling: Suffering, Healing, and Discernment*. Louisville: Westminster/John Knox Press.

Faith Community Ministry: Care and Counseling
Ashbrook, James B., and John E. Hinkle, Jr., eds. *At the Point of Need: Living Human Experience* (Essays in Honor of Carroll A. Wise). Lanham, MD: University Press of America, 1988.
Ashbrook, James. *Minding the Soul: Pastoral Counseling as Remembering Who We Are*. Minneapolis: Fortress Press, 1997.
Campbell, Alistar. *Rediscovering Pastoral Care*. Philadelphia: Westminster Press, 1981.
Capps, Donald. *Reframing: A New Method of Pastoral Care*. Minneapolis: Fortress Press, 1990.
Clinebell, Howard. *Basic Types of Pastoral Care and Counseling: Resources for the Ministry of Healing and Growth*. (Rev. ed.) Nashville: Abingdon Press, 1984.
Faber, Heije. *Psychology of Religion*. trans. Margaret Kohn. Philadelphia: Westminster Press, 1975.
Ferris, Margaret. *Compassioning: Basic Counseling Skills for Christian Care-Givers*. Kansas City, MO: Sheed & Ward. 1993.
Gerkin, Charles V. *The Living Human Document: Revisioning Pastoral Counseling in a Hermeneutical Mode*. Nashville: Abingdon Press, 1984.
Graham, Larry Kent. *Care of Persons, Care of Worlds: A Psychosystems Approach to Pastoral Care and Counseling*. Nashville: Abingdon Press, 1992.
Hiltner, Seward. *Pastoral Counseling*. New York (Nashville): Abingdon Press, 1949.
———. *Preface to Pastoral Theology*. New York (Nashville): Abingdon Press, 1958.
———. *The Christian Shepherd*. New York (Nashville): Abingdon Press, 1959.
Nouwen, Henri. *The Wounded Healer*. Garden City, NY: Doubleday, 1972.
Oates, E. Wayne. *Pastoral Counseling*. Philadelphia: Westminster Press, 1974.
Patton, John. *Pastoral Counseling: A Ministry of the Church*. Nashville: Abingdon Press, 1983.
———. *Pastoral Care in Context: An Introduction to Pastoral Care*. Louisville: Westminster/John Knox Press, 1993.
Poling, James, and Donald E. Miller. *Foundations for a Practical Theology of Ministry*. Nashville: Abingdon Press, 1985.
Sipe, A. W. Richard and Clarence J. Rowe, eds. *Psychiatry, Ministry, and Pastoral Counseling*. Collegeville, MN: Liturgical Press, 1984.
Taylor, Charles. *The Skilled Pastor*. Minneapolis: Fortress Press, 1991.

Underwood, Ralph. *Pastoral Care and the Means of Grace*. Minneapolis: Fortress Press, 1993.

Wise, Carroll A. *Pastoral Counseling: Its Theory and Practice*. New York: Harper and Brothers, 1951

Smith, Archie. *The Relational Self: Ethics and Therapy from a Black Church Perspective*. Nashville: Abingdon Press, 1982.

Wimberly, Edward P. *African-American Pastoral Care*. Nashville: Abingdon Press, 1991.

Feminist Perspective on Faith Community Care and Counseling

Belenky, Mary Field, Blythe Clinchy, Nancy Goldberger, Jill Tarule. *Women's Ways of Knowing: The Development of Self, Voice, and Mind*. New York: Basic Books, 1986.

Brown, Joanne Carlson, and Carole R. Bohn, eds. *Christianity, Patriarchy, and Abuse: A Feminist Critique*. Cleveland: Pilgrim Press, 1989.

Couture, Pamela D. *Blessed Are the Poor?: Women's Poverty, Family Policy, and Practical Theology*. Nashville: Abingdon Press, 1991.

DeMarinis, Valerie. *Critical Caring: A Feminist Model for Pastoral Psychology*. Louisville: Westminster/John Knox Press, 1993.

Gilligan, Carol. *In a Different Voice: Psychological Theory and Women's Development*. Cambridge, MA: Harvard University Press, 1982.

Glaz, Maxine, and Jeanne Stevenson Moessner, eds. *Women in Travail and Transition: A New Pastoral Care*. Minneapolis: Fortress Press, 1991.

Harrison, Beverly Wildung, with Carol Robb. *Making the Connections: Essays in Feminist Social Ethics*. Boston: Beacon Press, 1985.

Luepnitz, Deborah Anna. *The Family Interpreted: Psychoanalysis, Feminism, and Family Therapy*. New York: Basic Books, 1988.

Moessner, Jeanne Stevenson, ed. *The Handbook of Womencare: Through the Eyes of Women*. Minneapolis: Fortress Press, 1996.

Neuger, Christie Cozad, ed. *The Arts of Ministry: Feminist-Womanist Approaches*. Louisville: Westminster/John Knox Press, 1996.

Rhodes, Lynn. *Co-Creating a Feminist Vision of Ministry*. Philadelphia: Westminster Press, 1987.

Russell, Letty. *Human Liberation in a Feminist Perspective — A Theology*. Philadelphia: Westminster Press, 1974.

Thistlethwaite, Susan. *Sex, Race, and God: Christian Feminism in Black and White*. New York: Crossroad, 1989.

ARTICLES

Clarke, Katherine M. "Lessons from Feminist Therapy for Ministerial Ethics." *Journal of Pastoral Care* 48 (Fall 1994): 233–44.

Neuger, Christie Cozad. "Feminist Pastoral Theology and Pastoral Counseling: A Work in Progress." *Journal of Pastoral Theology* 2 (Summer 1992): 40–41.

Gifts to Ministry from the African-American Church

Cone, James. *A Black Theology for Liberation*. Philadelphia: Lippincott, 1970.

Harris, James H. *Pastoral Theology: A Black-Church Perspective*. Minneapolis: Fortress Press, 1991.

Lincoln, C. Eric, and Lawrence H. Mamlya. *The Black Church in the African-American Experience*. Bethesda, MD: Alban Institute.

Mitchell, Henry H., and Nicholas Cooper Lewter. *Soul Theology: The Heart of American Black Culture*. San Francisco: Harper and Row, 1986.

Smith, Archie. *The Relational Self: Ethics and Therapy from a Black Church Perspective*. Nashville: Abingdon Press, 1982.

Wimberly, Edward P. *African-American Pastoral Care*. Nashville: Abingdon Press, 1991.

Theories of Change
Watzlawick, Paul, and John Weakland, Richard Fisch. *Change: Principles of Problem Formation and Problem Resolution*. New York: W.W. Norton, 1974.
———. *The Language of Change: Elements of Therapeutic Communication*. New York: W.W. Norton, 1978.
———, ed. *The Invented Reality: How Do We Know What We Believe We Know?* New York: W.W. Norton, 1984.
———. *The Situation Is Hopeless, But Not Serious*. New York: W. W. Norton, 1983.
———. *Ultra-Solutions: How to Fail Most Successfully*. New York: W. W. Norton, 1988.

Chapter Five: Preparing for Community Care, Counseling, and Referral

Faith Community Ministry: Care and Counseling
Referenced in chapter 4.

Feminist Perspective on Faith Community Care and Counseling
Referenced in chapter 4.

Brief Counseling/Brief Pastoral Counseling
Baur, Gregory P., and Joseph C. Kobos. *Brief Therapy: Short-Term Psychodynamic Intervention*. New York: Jason Aronson, 1987.
Cade, Brian, and William Hudson O'Hanlon. *A Brief Guide to Brief Therapy*. New York: W. W. Norton, 1993.
Childs, Brian. *Short-Term Pastoral Counseling: A Guide*. Nashville: Abingdon Press, 1990.
Haley, Jay. *Problem Solving Therapy*. San Francisco: Jossey-Bass, 1976.
Stone, Howard W. *Brief Pastoral Counseling: Short-Term Approaches and Strategies*. Minneapolis: Fortress Press, 1994.
Zeig, Jeffrey K., and Stephen G. Gilligan, eds. *Brief Therapy: Myths, Methods, and Metaphors*. New York: Brunner/Mazel, 1990.

Counseling Skills (General)
Egan, Gerard. *The Skilled Helper: A Systemic Approach to Effective Helping* (4th Ed.). Pacific Grove, CA: Brooks/Cole Publishing Co., 1990.
Hart, Phyliss, and Ralph Osborne. *Concurrent Counseling*. Pasadena, CA: Integration Press, 1987.
Kennedy, Eugene. *On Becoming a Counselor: A Basic Guide for Non-professional Counselors*. New York: Continuum, 1977.

Referral and Diagnosis in Community Counseling
American Psychiatric Association. *Diagnostic and Statistical Manual of Mental Disorders, Fourth Edition*. Washington, DC: American Psychiatric Association, 1994.
Charry, Dana. *Mental Health Skills for Clergy*. Valley Forge, PA: Judson Press, 1981.
Hollinger, Paul C. *Pastoral Care of Severe Emotional Disorders*. New York: Irvington Publishers, 1985.
Oglesby, William B. *Referral in Pastoral Counseling*. Nashville: Abingdon Press, 1978.
Pruyser, Paul. *Personal Problems in Pastoral Perspective: The Minister as Diagnostician*. Philadelphia: Westminster Press, 1976.

Community Care of Emotionally and Mentally Disturbed People and the Chronically Ill

Anderson, Herbert, Laurence E. Hoist, and Robert H. Sunderland. *Ministry to Outpatients: A New Challenge in Pastoral Care.* Minneapolis: Fortress Press, 1995.

Bynum, Edward Bruce. *Pastoral Approaches in Psychospirituality and Personality Development.* Binghamton, NY: Haworth Press, 1995.

Ciarocchi, Joseph W. *A Minister's Handbook of Mental Disorders.* Mahwah, NJ: Paulist Press, 1993.

Fitchett, George. *Assessing Spiritual Needs: A Guide to Caregivers.* Minneapolis: Fortress Press, 1995.

Govig, Stewart. *Souls Are Made of Endurance: Surviving Mental Illness in the Family.* Louisville: Westminster/John Knox Press, 1994.

Hollinger, Paul. *Pastoral Care of Severe Emotional Disorders.* New York: Irvington Publishers, 1985.

Larson, Dale G. *The Helper's Journey: Working with People Facing Grief, Loss, and Life-Threatening Illness.* Champaign, IL: Research Press, 1993.

LeShan, Lawrence. *Cancer As a Turning Point: A Handbook for People with Cancer, Their Families, and Health Professionals.* New York: A Plume Book, Penguin Books, 1990.

Oates, Wayne. *The Care of Troublesome People.* Bethesda, MD: Alban Institute.

———. *Behind the Masks: Personality Disorders in Religious Behavior.* Louisville: Westminster/John Knox Press, 1987.

Severino, Sally K., and Richard Liew. *Pastoral Care of the Mentally Disabled.* Binghamton, NY: Haworth Press, 1995.

Vanderzee, John T. *Ministry to Persons with Chronic Illness.* Minneapolis: Fortress Press, 1995.

ARTICLE

Aist, Clark S. "Pastoral Care of the Mentally Ill: A Congregational Perspective." *Journal of Pastoral Care* 41 (December 1987): 299–310.

AIDS/AIDS Ministry

Hallman, David G., ed. *AIDS Issues: Confronting the Challenge.* New York: Pilgrim Press, 1989.

Perelli, Robert J. *Ministry to Persons with AIDS: A Family Systems Approach.* Minneapolis: Augsburg Press, 1991.

Russell, Letty. *The Church with AIDS: Renewal in the Midst of Crisis.* Louisville: Westminster/John Knox Press, 1990.

Smith, Walter J. *AIDS: Living and Dying with Hope — Issues in Pastoral Care.* New York: Paulist Press, 1988.

Sontag, Susan. *AIDS and Its Metaphors.* New York: Farrar, Straus, and Giroux, 1988.

Sunderland, Ronald, and Earl Shelp. *AIDS, A Manual for Pastoral Care.* Louisville: Westminster/John Knox Press, 1988.

Ministry: Professional Ethics and Responsible Practice
Referenced in chapter 10.

Chapter Six: Change Supported by the Solution-Focused Method

Solution-Focused Therapy Method
Berg, Insoo Kim. *Family-Based Services.* New York: W. W. Norton., 1994.

Berg, Insoo Kim and Scott D. Miller. *Working with the Problem Drinker.* New York: W. W. Norton, 1992.

Berg, Insoo Kim, and Steve de Shazer. "Making Numbers Talk: Language in Therapy," in *The New Language of Change: Constructive Collaboration in Psychotherapy,* ed. Steven Friedman. New York: Guilford Press, 1993, 5–24.

de Shazer, Steve. *Words Were Originally Magic.* New York: W. W. Norton, 1994.

———. *Putting Difference to Work.* New York: W. W. Norton, 1991.

———. *Clues: Investigating Solutions in Brief Therapy.* New York: W. W. Norton, 1988.

———. *Keys to Solution in Brief Therapy.* New York: W. W. Norton, 1985.

———. *Patterns of Brief Family Therapy.* New York: Guilford Press, 1982.

Kral, Ron. *Techniques for Solutions in Schools.* Milwaukee: Brief Family Therapy Center Press, 1995.

Miller, Scott D., and Insoo Kim Berg. *The Miracle Method: A Radically New Approach to Problem Drinking.* New York: W. W. Norton, 1995.

O'Hanlon, William Hudson, and Michele Weiner-Davis. *In Search of Solutions: A New Direction in Psychotherapy.* New York: W. W. Norton, 1989.

Walter, John, and James Peller. *Becoming Solution Focused in Brief Therapy.* New York: Brunner/Mazel, 1992.

Unpublished Materials

Gallagher, Daniel. *Solution-Focused Brief Therapy with Problem Drinkers and Drug Abusers* (Teaching materials based on materials in Insoo Berg and Scott Miller's *Working with the Problem Drinker*), 1994.

III: Caring for and Counseling Others in all the Seasons of Life

Chapter Seven: Care and Counseling at Life's Many Beginnings

Many books in this chapter are also referenced in chapter 8.

Human Life Cycle Theories

Erikson, Erik. *Childhood and Society.* New York: W. W. Norton, 1963.

Kegan, Robert. *The Evolving Self.* Cambridge, MA: Harvard University Press, 1982.

———. *In over Our Heads.* Cambridge, MA: Harvard University Press, 1994.

Fuller, Robert. *Religion and the Life Cycle.* Minneapolis: Fortress Press, 1988.

Tennant, Mark C., and Philip Pogson. *Learning and Change in Adult Years: A Developmental Perspective.* San Francisco: Jossey-Bass, 1995.

Resources for Ministering to Children and Young People

Anderson, Herbert, and Kenneth R. Mitchell. *Leaving Home.* Louisville: Westminster/John Knox Press, 1993

Anderson, Herbert, and Susan B. S. Johnson. *Regarding Children: A New Respect for Childhood and Families.* Louisville: Westminster/John Knox Press, 1994.

Hammer, Margaret. *Giving Birth: Reclaiming Biblical Metaphor for Pastoral Practice.* Louisville: Westminster/John Knox Press, 1994.

Resources for Ministering to Single People

Collier-Stone, Kay. *Singles in the Church: New Ways to Minister with 52% of God's People.* Bethesda, MD: Alban Institute.

Langraf, John R. *Singling: Creative Singlehood and Pastoral Care.* Philadelphia: Fortress Press, 1982.

Schwartzberg, Natalie, Kathy Berliner, and Demaris Jacob. *Single in a Married World: A Life Cycle Framework for Working with the Unmarried Adult.* New York: W. W. Norton, and Co., 1994.

Resources for Ministering to Adults
Liebert, Elizabeth, SNJM. *Changing Life Patterns: Adult Development in Spiritual Direction.* Mahwah, NJ: Paulist Press, 1992.

Theories on Aging and Resources for Ministering to Older People
Benson, C. Z. "Aging." *Dictionary of Pastoral Care and Counseling,* ed. Rodney Hunter. Nashville: Abingdon Press, 1990, 16.
Butler, Robert N. *Why Survive? Being Old in America.* New York: Harper and Row, 1977.
Erikson, Erik H. *The Life Cycle Completed.* New York: W. W. Norton, 1982.
Clements, William M., ed. *Ministry with the Aging.* Binghamton, NY: Haworth Press, 1989.
Faber, Heije. *Striking Sails: A Pastoral Psychological View of Growing Older,* trans. Kenneth Mitchell. Nashville: Abingdon Press. 1984.
Fowler, Margaret, and Priscilla McCutcheon, eds. *Songs of Experience: An Anthology of Literature on Growing Old.* New York: Ballantine Books, 1991.
Friedan, Betty. *The Fountain of Age.* New York: Simon and Schuster, 1993.
Lapsley, James. "Pastoral Care and Counseling of the Aging," in the Clinical *Handbook of Pastoral Counseling, Vol. I,* ed. Robert J. Wicks, Richard D. Parsons, Donald Capps. New York: Paulist Press, 1993, 245–66.
Koenig, Harold G. *Aging and God: Spiritual Pathways to Mental Health in Midlife and Later Years.* Binghamton, NY: Haworth Press, 1994.
Lapsley, James N. *Renewal in Late Life through Pastoral Counseling.* New York: Paulist Press, 1992.
LeFever, Carol, and Perry LeFevre, eds. *Aging and the Human Spirit.* Chicago: Exploration Press, 1981.
Robb, Thomas B. *Growing Up: Pastoral Nurture for the Later Years.* Binghamton, NY: Haworth Press, 1991.
Schacter-*Shalomi, Zalman, and Ronald S. Miller. *From Age-ing to Sage-ing.* New York: Warner Books, 1995.
Seeber, James J., ed. *Spiritual Maturity in Later Years.* Binghamton, NY: Haworth Press, 1991.

ARTICLES
Ashbrook, James. "Soul: Its Meaning and Its Making," *Journal of Pastoral Care,* Summer 1991: 159–68.
Kimble, Melvin. "Pastoral Care of the Elderly," *Journal of Pastoral Care* 41 (September 1987): 270.

Family Theory and Therapy
Carter, Betty, and Monica McGoldrick. *The Changing Family Life Cycle: A Framework for Family Therapy.* 2nd ed. Needham Heights, MA: Allyn and Bacon, 1989.
Lewis, Jerry M. *How's Your Family?: A guide to identifying your family's strengths and weaknesses.* New York: Brunner/Mazel, 1989.
McGoldrick, Monica, and Randy Gerson. *Genograms in Family Assessment.* New York: W. W. Norton, 1985.
McGoldrick, Monica, John K. Pearce, Joseph Giordano, eds. *Ethnicity and Family Therapy.* New York: Guilford Press, 1982.
Minuchin, Salvador. *Families and Family Therapy.* Cambridge, MA: Harvard University Press, 1974.

———. *Family Kaleidoscope*. Cambridge, MA: Harvard University Press, 1984.

Olsen, David. *Integrative Family Therapy*. Minneapolis: Fortress Press, 1993.

Satir, Virginia. *Peoplemaking*. Palo Alto, CA: Science and Behavior Books, 1972.

Resources for Ministering to Families

Anderson, Herbert. *The Family in Pastoral Care*. Minneapolis: Fortress Press, 1984.

Burton, Laurel Arthur. *Religion and the Family: When God Helps*. Binghamton, NY: Haworth Press, 1992.

Friedman, Edwin. *Generation to Generation: Family Process in Church and Synagogue*. New York: The Guilford Press, 1985.

Goodman-Malamuth, Leslie, and Robin Margolis. *Between Two Worlds: Choices for Grown Children of Jewish-Christian Parents*. New York: Pocket Books, 1992.

Kramer, Sheldon Z. *Transforming the Inner and Outer Family: Humanistic and Spiritual Approaches to Mind-Body Systems* Theory. Binghamton, NY: Haworth Press, 1995.

Wynn, J. C. *Family Therapy in Pastoral Ministry: Revised and Expanded Edition*. San Francisco: HarperCollins, 1991.

Marriage and Remarriage

Anderson, Herbert, and R. Cotton Fite. *Becoming Married*. Louisville: Westminster/John Knox Press, 1994.

Anderson, Herbert, David Hogue, and Marie McCarthy. *Promising Again*. Louisville: Westminster/John Knox Press, 1995.

Cavanagh, Michael E. *Before the Wedding: Look before You Leap*. Louisville: Westminster/John Knox Press, 1994.

Lauer, Jeanette C., and Robert C. Lauer. *'Til Death Do Us Part*. Binghamton, NY: Haworth Press, 1995.

Mace, David, and Vera Mace. *How to Have a Happy Marriage: A Step-by-Step Guide to an Enriched Relationship*. Nashville: Abingdon Press, 1992.

Rassieur, Charles L. *Pastor, Our Marriage Is in Trouble: A Guide to Short-Term Counseling*. Binghamton, NY: Haworth Press, 1988.

Scarf, Maggie. *Intimate Partners: Patterns in Love and Marriage*. New York: Random House, 1987.

Schwartz, Pepper. *Peer Marriage: How Love between Equals Really Works*. New York: Free Press, 1994.

Tournier, Paul. *To Understand Each Other*. Richmond, Va.: John Knox Press, 1973.

Divorce

Ahrons, Constance. *The Good Divorce: Keeping Your Family Together When Your Marriage Comes Apart*. New York: HarperCollins, 1994.

Emerick-Cayton, Tim. *Divorcing with Dignity (Mediation: The Sensible Alternative)*. Louisville: Westminster/John Knox Press, 1993.

Everett, Craig A. *Minority and Ethnic Issues in the Divorce Process*. Binghamton, NY: Haworth Press, 1988.

Nichols, Randall. *Ending Marriage, Keeping Faith*. New York: Crossroad, 1993.

Volgy, Sandra S., ed. *Women and Divorce/Men and Divorce: Gender Differences in Separation, Divorce and Remarriage*. Binghamton, NY: Haworth Press, 1991.

Wallerstein, Judith S., and Joan Berlin Kelly. *Surviving the Breakup: How Children and Parents Cope with Divorce*. New York: HarperCollins, 1980.

The Family: In All Its New Forms

Caron, Ann F. *Strong Mothers, Strong Sons: Raising the Next Generation of Men*. San Francisco: HarperCollins, 1994.

Hall, C. Margaret. *New Families: Reviving and Creating Meaningful Bonds*. Binghamton, NY: Haworth Press, 1995.

Hanson, Shirley, Marsha L. Heims, Doris J. Julian, and Marvin B. Sussman. *Single Parent Families: Diversity, Myths and Realities*. Binghamton, NY: Haworth Press, 1995.

Kelley, Patricia. *Developing Healthy Stepfamilies*. Binghamton, NY: Haworth Press, 1995.

Lewis, Robert A., and Marvin B. Sussman, eds. *Men's Changing Roles in the Family*. Binghamton, NY: Haworth Press, 1986.

Marciano, Teresa D., and Marvin Sussman. *Wider Families: New Traditional Family Forms*. Binghamton, NY: Haworth Press, 1992.

McGoldrick, Monica, Carol Anderson, and Froma Walsh, eds. *Women and Families: A Framework for Family Therapy*. New York: W. W. Norton, 1989.

Pittman, Frank. *Man Enough: Fathers and Sons in Search for Masculinity*. New York: Putnam and Sons, 1993.

Sager, Clifford J., Hollis Steer Brown, Helen Crohn, Tamara Engel, Evelyn Rodstein, and Libby Walker. *Treating the Remarried Family*. New York: Brunner/Mazel, 1983.

Settles, Barbara, Daniel E. Hanks, and Marvin Sussman, eds. *Families on the Move: Immigration, Migration, and Mobility*. Binghamton, NY: Haworth Press, 1993.

Somerville, Charles. *Stepfathers: Struggles and Solutions*. Louisville: Westminster/John Knox Press, 1989.

ARTICLES

Close, Henry. "An Adoption Ceremony." *Journal of Pastoral Care* 47, no. 4 (Winter 1993): 382.

De Parle, Jason. "Big Rise in Births outside Wedlock," *New York Times*, 7.14.93: A1.

Couture, Pamela. "The Context of Congregations: Pastoral Care in an Individualistic Society." *Journal of Pastoral Theology* 2 (Summer 1991): 12.

Jones, Eric F., and Robert F. Stahmann. "Clergy Beliefs, Preparation and Practice in Premarital Counseling." *Journal of Pastoral Care* 48, no. 2 (1994): 81–86.

Reich, Robert. Speech to the Center for National Policy, Washington, DC. "The Fracturing of the Middle Class," adapted by *New York Times*, 8.31.94: A 19.

U.S. Census. "The Diverse Living Arrangements of Children, Summer 1991" cited in "Census Paints a Picture of Family Life," *New York Times*, 8.30.94.

Ministering to Gays and Lesbians

Cherry, Kittredge, and Zalmon Sherwood, eds. *Equal Rites: Lesbian and Gay Worship, Ceremonies and Celebrations*. Louisville: Westminster/John Knox Press, 1995.

Glaser, Chris. *Coming Out to God: Prayers for Lesbians and Gay Men, Their Families and Friends*. Louisville: Westminster/John Knox Press, 1991.

Graham, Larry Kent. *Discovering Images of God: Narratives of Care among Lesbians and Gays*. Louisville: Westminster/John Knox Press, 1997.

Marshall, Joretta. *Counseling Lesbian Partners*. Louisville: Westminster/John Knox Press, 1997.

McNeill, John J. *The Church and the Homosexual*. Boston: Beacon Press (revised and expanded), 1988.

———. *Taking a Chance on God: Liberation Theology for Gays, Lesbians, and Their Lovers, Families and Friends*. Boston: Beacon Press, 1988.

———. *Freedom Glorious Freedom*. Boston: Beacon Press, 1995.

O'Neill, Craig, and Kathleen Ritter. *Coming Out Within: Stages of Spiritual Awakening for Lesbians and Gay Men*. San Francisco: Harper, 1992.

ARTICLE
Marshall, Joretta L. "Pastoral Theology and Lesbian/Gay/Bisexual Experiences." *Journal of Pastoral Theology,* Summer 1994.

Chapter Eight: Care and Counseling at Life's Many Endings

(*Human Development, Family Theory and Resources for Ministry within the Life Cycle are referenced in chapter 7.*)

Resources for Thinking about Death and Ministering to the Dying
Aries, Phillipe. *The Hour of Our Death.* New York: Alfred A. Knopf, 1981.
Becker, Ernest. *The Denial of Death.* New York: Free Press, 1973.
Bertman, Sandra L. *Facing Death: Images, Insights, and Interventions.* Bristol, PA: Taylor and Francis, 1991.
Blackmore, Susan. *Dying to Live: Near Death Experience.* Buffalo, NY: Prometheus Books, 1993.
Bowker, John. *The Meaning of Death.* New York and Cambridge: Cambridge University Press, 1991.
Bregman, Lucy. *Death in the Midst of Life: Perspectives on Death from Christianity and Depth Psychology.* Grand Rapids, MI: Baker Book House, 1992.
Callahan, Maggie, and Patricia Kelley. *Final Gifts: Understanding the Special Awareness, Needs, and Communications of the Dying.* New York: Poseidon Press, 1992.
Cobb, John. *Matters of Life and Death.* Louisville: Westminster/John Knox Press, 1991.
Counts, David, and Dorothy A. Counts. *Coping with the Final Tragedy: Cultural Variations in Dying and Grieving.* Amityville, NY: Baywood Publishing, 1991.
Duda, Deborah. *Coming Home: A Guide to Dying at Home with Dignity.* New York: Aurora Press, 1987
Irish, Donald P. *Ethnic Variations in Dying, Death, and Grief: Diversity in Universality.* Bristol, PA: Taylor and Francis, 1993.
Johnson, Christopher Jay, and Marsha G. McGee, eds. *How Different Religions View Death and Afterlife.* Philadelphia: Charles Press, 1991.
Kübler-Ross, Elisabeth. On *Death and Dying,* New York: Macmillan, 1969.
———, ed. *Death: The Final Stage of Growth.* Englewood Cliffs, NJ: Prentice-Hall, 1975.
———. *To Live Until We Say Good-bye.* Englewood Cliffs, NJ: Prentice-Hall, 1978.
Lamm, Maurice. *The Jewish Way in Death and Mourning.* New York: Jonathan David Publishers, 1969.
Levine, Stephen. *Who Dies?: An Investigation of Conscious Living and Conscious Dying.* New York: Anchor Books, Doubleday, 1982.
Morgan, Ernest. *Dealing Creatively with Death: A Manual of Death Education and Simple Burial.* Barclay House, 1990.
Morrissey, Paul. *Let Someone Hold You.* New York: Crossroad, 1994.
Nouwen, Henri J. M. *Our Greatest Gift: Meditation on Dying and Caring.* New York: HarperCollins, 1994.
Nuland, Sherwin. *How We Die: Reflections on Life's Final Chapter.* New York: Alfred Knopf, 1994.
Oates, Wayne. *Anxiety and the Christian Experience.* Philadelphia: Westminster Press, 1955.
Ring, Kenneth. *Heading toward Omega.* New York: William Morrow, 1984.
Southard, Samuel, Compiler. *Death and Dying: A Bibliographical Survey.* New York: Greenwood Press, 1991.

Walsh, Froma, and Monica McGoldrick, eds. *Living beyond Loss: Death in the Family*. New York: W. W. Norton, 1991.

Webb, Marilyn. *The Good Death: The New American Search to Reshape the End of Life*. New York: Bantam Books, 1997.

Resources for Ministering to Those Who Mourn

Anthony, Nancy. *Mourning Thoughts: Facing a New Day after the Death of a Spouse*. Mystic, CT: Twenty-Third Publications, 1991. (Poetry)

Arnold, William, and Margaret Anne Fohg. *When You Are Alone*. Louisville: Westminster/John Knox Press, 1990.

Cook, Alicia Skinner, and Daniel Dworkin. *Helping the Bereaved: Therapeutic Interventions for Children, Adolescents, and Adults*. New York: HarperCollins, 1992.

Holden, Sue. *My Daddy Died and It's All God's Fault*. Dallas: Word Publishing, 1991. (Autobiographic story of a nine year old boy whose father died.)

Jones, Mary. *Love after Death: Counseling in Bereavement*. Bristol, PA: Taylor and Francis, 1995.

Kushner, Harold. *When Bad Things Happen to Good People*. New York: Avon Books, 1983.

Lindemann, Erich. *Beyond Grief: Studies in Crisis Intervention*. New York: Jason Aronson, 1979.

Maes, John. *Suffering: A Caregiver's Guide*. Nashville: Abingdon Press, 1990.

Meyer, Charles. *Surviving Death: A Practical Guide to Caring for the Dying and Bereaved*. Mystic, CT: Twenty-Third Publications, 1991.

Mitchell, Kenneth, and Herbert Anderson. *All Our Losses, All Our Griefs*. Philadelphia: Westminster Press, 1983.

Oates, Wayne. *Anxiety and the Christian Experience*. Philadelphia: Westminster Press, 1955.

———. *Pastoral Care and Counseling in Grief and Separation*. Philadelphia: Fortress Press, 1976.

———. *Your Particular Grief*. Louisville: Westminster/John Knox Press, 1981.

Parkes, C. *Bereavement*. Madison, CT: International University Press, 1972.

Rando, Therese. *Treatment of Complicated Mourning*. Champaign, IL: Research Press, 1993.

Robbins, Martha. *Mid-Life Women and Death of Mother: A Study of Psychohistorical and Spiritual Transformation*. New York: Peter Lang, 1990.

Schwiebert, Pat, and Paul Kirk. *When Hello Means Good-bye*. Portland, OR: Prenatal Loss, 1985

Sherokee, Lise. *Empty Arms: Coping after Miscarriage, Stillbirth and Infant Death*. Long Lake, MN: Wintergreen Press, 1982.

Sullender, Scott. "Loss and Grief," in *Handbook for Basic Types of Pastoral Care and Counseling*, ed. Howard Stone and William Clements. Nashville: Abingdon Press, 1991.

Switzer, David K. "Unresolved Grief," in *Handbook for Basic Types of Pastoral Care and Counseling*, ed. Howard Stone, and William Clements. Nashville: Abingdon Press, 1991.

Viorst, Judith. *Necessary Losses*. New York: Ballantine Books, 1986.

Watson, Jeffrey A. *The Courage to Care: Helping the Aging, Grieving, Dying*. Grand Rapids: Baker Book House, 1992.

Williams, Donna Reilly, and JoAnn Sturzl. *Grief Ministry: Helping Others Mourn with Facilitator's Guide*. San Jose, CA: Resource Publications, 1992. (Ten session course to train lay volunteers for grief ministry.)

Worden, William. *Grief Counseling and Grief Therapy*. New York: Springer, 1982.

JOURNAL ARTICLES ON DYING, GRIEF, AND MOURNING

Fickling, Karl F. "Stillborn Studies: Minister to Bereaved Parents." *Journal of Pastoral Care* 47, no. 3 (Fall 1993): 217–29.

Hart, Curtis W. "Our Minister Died of AIDS: Pastoral Care of a Congregation in Crisis." *Journal of Pastoral Care* 47, no. 3 (Summer 1993): 109–16.

Maxwell, Travis, and Jann Aldredge-Clanton. "Survivor Guilt in Cancer Patients: A Pastoral Perspective." *Journal of Pastoral Care* 48 (Spring 1994): 25–32.

VanKatwyk, Peter L. "A Family Observed: Theological and Family Systems Perspectives on the Grief Experience." *Journal of Pastoral Care* 47, no. 2 (Summer 1993): 141–48.

Loss and Change in the Workplace

Bohm, Katja, Giovanni Sgritta, and Marvin B. Sussman, eds. *Cross-Cultural Perspectives on Families, Work and Change.* Binghamton, NY: Haworth Press, 1990.

Lewis, Roy. "Pastoral Care to the Unemployed," in *Clinical Handbook of Pastoral Counseling,* Vol. 2, ed. Robert Wicks et al. Mahwah, NJ: Paulist Press, 1993.

Rifkin, Jeremy. *The End of Work.* New York: G. P. Putnam, 1995.

Depression

Anderson, Carol M., and Diane P. Holder. "Women and Serious Mental Disorders," in *Women and Families: A Framework for Family Therapy,* ed. Monica McGoldrick, Carol Anderson, and Froma Walsh. New York: W. W. Norton, 1989.

Badal, Daniel W. *Treatment of Depression and Related Moods: A Manual for Psychotherapists.* New York: Jason Aronson, 1988.

Neuger, Christie Cozad. "Women's Depression: Lives at Risk," in *Women in Travail and Transition: A New Pastoral Care,* ed. Maxine Glaz and Jeanne Stevenson Moessner. Minneapolis: Fortress Press, 1990: 146–61.

McGrath, Ellen, Gwendolyn Puryear Keita, Bonnie R. Strickland, and Nancy Felipe Russo, eds. *Women and Depression: Risk Factors and Treatment Issues.* Hyattsville, MD: American Psychological Association, 1990.

Real, Terrance. *"I Don't Want to Talk About It:" Overcoming the Secret Legacy of Male Depression.* New York: Scribner Publishers, 1997.

Styron, William. *Darkness Visible.* New York: Random House, 1990.

Wetzel, Janice Wood. *The Clinical Handbook of Depression.* New York: Gardner Press, 1984.

Whybrow, Peter C. *A Mood Apart: Depression, Mania, and Other Afflictions of the Self.* New York: Basic Books, HarperCollins, 1997.

Faith Community Response to Depression

Capps, Donald. *Agents of Hope: A Pastoral Theology.* Minneapolis: Fortress Press, 1994.

Dayringer, Richard, ed. *Dealing with Depression: Five Pastoral Interventions.* Binghamton, NY: Haworth Press, 1995.

Lester, Andrew. *Hope in Pastoral Care and Counseling.* Louisville: Westminster/John Knox Press, 1995.

Chapter Nine: Care and Counseling in Life's Daily Round

Resources for Crisis Intervention

Gerkin, Charles V. *Crisis Experience in Modern Life: Theory and Theology for Pastoral Care.* Nashville: Abingdon Press, 1979

Kennedy, Eugene. *Crisis Counseling: A Guide for Non-Professional Counselors.* New York: Continuum, 1981.

Leaver, Wayne. *Clergy and Victims of Violent Crimes: Preparing for Crisis Counseling.* Lima, OH: C.S.C. Publishing Co., 1990.

Switzer, David. *The Minister as a Crisis Counselor.* Nashville: Abingdon Press, 1986.

———. *Pastoral Care Emergencies.* Mahwah, NJ: Paulist Press. 1988.

Stone, Howard. *Crisis Counseling: An Introduction to the Theory and Practice of Crisis Counseling.* Philadelphia (Minneapolis): Fortress Press, 1976.

Suicide

Berman, Alan. *Suicide Prevention.* New York: Springer, 1990.

Colt, George Howe. *The Enigma of Suicide.* New York: Simon and Schuster (Touchstone), 1991.

Durkheim, Emile. *Suicide: A Study In Sociology.* New York: Free Press, 1951

Kunklin, Susan. *After Suicide: Young People Speak Up.* New York: G. P. Putnam and Sons, 1994.

ARTICLE

Ross, Alan. "Preventing Teenage Suicide—The Samaritans 'Befriending' Model" *New York Health Sciences Journal* 1 [2], 1994:137–46.

Requests for reprints should be addressed to: Alan Ross, Executive Director, Samaritans of New York, P.O. Box 1259, Madison Square Station, New York, NY 10154.

Stress and Stress Disorders

Benson, Herbert. *The Relaxation Response.* New York: William Morrow, 1975.

Foy, David, Kent D. Drescher, Allan G. Fitz, and Kevin R. Kennedy, "Posttraumatic Stress Disorder," in *Clinical Handbook of Pastoral Counseling, Vol. 2,* ed. Robert Wicks et al. (Mahwah, NJ: Paulist Press, 1993: 621–37.

Gill, James J., S.J., M.D. "Anxiety and Stress" in *Clinical Handbook of Pastoral Counseling, Vol. 1, 2nd ed.,* ed. Robert Wicks et al. Mahwah, NJ: Paulist Press, 1993: 452–65.

Harris, John C. *Stress, Power, and Ministry.* Washington, DC: Alban Institute, 1977.

Kramer, Peter. *Listening to Prozac.* New York: Penguin Books, 1993.

Peterson, P. J. "Stress and Stress Management," *Dictionary of Pastoral Care and Counseling,* ed. Rodney Hunter. 1990:1227–29.

Selye, Hans. *The Stress of Life.* New York: McGraw Hill, 1956; revised, 1978.

———. *Stress without Distress.* Philadelphia: Lippincott, 1974.

———. *Stress in Health and Disease.* Reading, PA: Buttersworth's, 1976.

Stress: A Pastoral Response

Rodgerson, Thomas E. *Spirituality, Stress, and You.* New York: Paulist Press, 1994.

Parsons, Richard. *Adolescents in Turmoil, Parents under Stress: A Pastoral Ministry Primer.* Mahwah, NJ: Paulist Press, 1987.

Sinclair, N. Duncan. *Horrific Traumata: A Pastoral Response to the Posttraumatic Stress Disorder.* Binghamton, NY: Haworth Press, 1993.

Human Sexuality and Spirituality

Arnold, William V. *Pastoral Responses to Sexual Issues.* Louisville: Westminster/John Knox Press, 1994.

Laumann, Edward O., John H. Gognon, Robert T. Michael, and Stuart Michaels. *The Social Organization of Sexuality: Sexual Practices in the United States.* Chicago and London: University of Chicago Press, 1994.

Mollenkott, Virginia Ramey. *Sensuous Spirituality.* New York: Crossroad, 1992.

Nelson, James B. *The Intimate Connection: Male Sexuality, Masculine Spirituality*. Philadelphia: Westminster Press, 1988.

————. *Embodiment: An Approach to Sexuality and Christian Theology*. Minneapolis: Fortress Press, 1979.

Nelson, James B., and Sandra Longfellow, eds. *Sexuality and the Sacred: Sources for Theological Reflection*. Louisville: Westminster/John Knox Press, 1995.

Rediger, G. Lloyd. *Ministry and Sexuality: Cases, Counseling, and Care*. Minneapolis: Fortress Press, 1990.

Ulanov, Ann. *Transforming Sexuality*. Boston: Shambhala Publications, 1994.

Alcohol Abuse and Dependency

Apthorp, Stephen. *Alcohol and Substance Abuse — A Clergy Handbook*. Connecticut: Morehouse-Barlow, 1985.

Clinebell, Howard. "Alcohol Abuse, Addiction, and Therapy," *Dictionary of Pastoral Care and Counseling*, ed. Rodney Hunter, ed. Nashville: Abingdon Press, 1990: 18–21.

Krestoan, JoAnn, and Claudia Bebko. "Alcohol Problems and the Family Life Cycle," in *The Changing Family Life Cycle*, ed. Betty Carter and Monica McGoldrick. Needham Heights, MA: Allyn and Bacon, 1989.

Lininger, Paul D. "Pastoral Counseling and Psychoactive Substance Use Disorders," in *Clinical Handbook of Pastoral Counseling, Vol. 2*, ed. Robert Wicks et al. Mahwah, NJ: Paulist Press, 1993: 543–76.

Peele, Stanton, and Archie Brodsky. *The Truth about Addiction and Recovery*. New York: Simon and Schuster, 1991.

Royce, James E., S.J. "Alcohol and Other Drug Dependencies," in *Clinical Handbook of Pastoral Counseling, Vol. 1*, ed. Robert Wicks et al. Mahwah, NJ: Paulist Press, 1993: 502–19.

ARTICLES

The Johns Hopkins Medical Letter. "Alcoholism," Dec. 1992: 5.

Harvard Mental Health Letter. "Typing Alcoholics," May 1993: 7. Research cited: Thomas F. Babor, Michael Hofmann, Frances K. Del Boca et al. Types of Alcoholics, I: evidence for an empirically derived topology based on indicators of vulnerability and severity. *Archives of General Psychiatry* 49: 599–608 (August 1992) and Mark D. Litt, Thomas F. Babor, Frances K. Del Boca et al. Types of alcoholics, II: application of an empirically derived typology to treatment matching. *Archives of General Psychiatry* 49: 609–14 (August 1992).

Delbanco, Andrew, and Thomas Delbanco. "Annals of Addiction: A.A. at the Crossroad," *The New Yorker*, March 20, 1995.

Goleman, Daniel, *New York Times*, August 13, 1996. C1. Report of the unpublished research (about the addictive substance in brain circuitry itself that causes craving)of Dr. Anna Childress, University of Pennsylvania, Dr. Joseph Wu, University of California, Irvine, Dr. Eric Nestler, Yale University School of Medicine.

Addiction and Healing

Albers, Robert H. *Shame: A Faith Perspective*. Binghamton, NY: Haworth Press, 1995.

Burns, John. *The Answer to Addiction — The Path to Recovery from Alcohol, Drug, Food, and Sexual Dependencies*. New York: Crossroad, 1990.

Fossum, Merle A., and Marilyn J. Mason. *Facing Shame: Families in Recovery*. New York: W. W. Norton, 1986.

Keller, John E. *Ministering to Alcoholics*. Minneapolis: Augsburg Press, 1991.

May, Gerald, M.D. *Will and Spirit*. San Francisco: HarperSanFrancisco, 1982.

———. Addiction and Grace: Love and Spirituality in the Healing of Addictions. San Francisco: HarperSanFrancisco, 1988.

Seixas, Judith S., and Geraldine Youcha. Children of Alcoholism. A Survivors Manua 1. New York: Harper and Row, 1985.

Yoder, Barbara. The Recovery Resource Book. (The Best Available Information on Addictions and Codependence). New York: Fireside, Simon and Schuster, 1990.

Sexual Addiction

Carnes, Patrick. Contrary to Love: Helping the Sexual Addict. Minneapolis: Compare Publishers, 1989. (Includes Sexual Addiction Screening Test.)

———. Don't Call It Love: Recovering from Sexual Addiction. New York: Bantam Press, 1991.

Schaef, Ann Wilson. Escape from Intimacy: Untangling the "Love" Addictions. San Francisco: Harper & Row, 1989.

Sexual Abuse: Overviews

Bass, E., and L. Thornton, eds. I Never Told Anyone: Writings by Women Survivors of Child Sexual Abuse. New York: Harper and Row, 1983.

Blume, E. Sue. Secret Survivors: Uncovering Incest and Its Aftereffects in Women. New York: Ballantine Books, 1990.

Crewdon, John. By Silence Betrayed: Sexual Abuse of Children in America. New York: Little, Brown & Co., 1988.

Faller, Kathleen Coulborn. Child Sexual Abuse: An Interdisciplinary Manual for Diagnosis, Case Management and Treatment. New York: Columbia University Press, 1988.

Finkelhor, David. A Source Book on Child Sexual Abuse. Beverly Hills: Sage Publications, 1986.

Giarretto, Hank. Integrated Treatment of Child Sexual Abuse. Giarretto Institute. 232 E. Gish Road, San Jose, CA 55112.

Giarretto Institutes. An Outline of Bibliographies on Child Sexual Abuse Topics. Giarretto Institutes. 232 Gish Road, San Jose, CA 55112.

Herman, Judith Lewis. Father-Daughter Incest. Cambridge: Harvard University Press, 1981.

———. Trauma and Recovery: The Aftermath of Violence — From Domestic Abuse to Political Terror. New York: Basic Books, HarperCollins, 1992.

Marshall, W. L., D. R. Laws, and H. E. Barbaree, eds. Handbook of Sexual Assault: Issues, Theories, and Treatment. New York: Plenum Press, 1990.

Russell, Diana. Sexual Exploitation: Rape, Child Sexual Abuse, and Workplace Harassment. Beverly Hills, CA: Sage, 1984.

———. The Secret Trauma: Incest in the Lives of Girls and Women. New York: Basic Books, 1986.

Sgroi, Suzanne M., ed. Handbook of Clinical Intervention in Child Sexual Abuse. Lexington, MA: Lexington Books, 1982.

Trepper, Terry S. Systemic Treatment of Incest: A Therapeutic Handbook. New York: Brunner/Mazel, 1989.

Veltkam, Lane J., and Thomas W. Miller. Clinical Handbook of Child Abuse and Neglect. Madison, CT: International Universities Press, 1994.

Wiehe, Vernon. Sibling Abuse: Hidden Physical, Emotional, and Sexual Trauma. New York: Lexington Books, 1990.

JOURNAL ARTICLES

Williams, Linda Meyer. "Recall of Childhood Trauma: A Prospective Study of Women's Memories of Child Sexual Abuse." *Journal of Counseling and Clinical Psychology* 62, no. 6 (December 1994): 1167–76.

———. "What Does It Mean to Forget Child Sexual Abuse? A Reply to Loftus, Gary and Feldman." *Journal of Counseling and Clinical Psychology* 62, no. 6 (December 1994): 1182–86.

Incest Offenders

Scully, Diana. *Understanding Sexual Violence: A Study of Convicted Rapists.* Boston: Unwin Hyman, 1990.

ARTICLES AND RESEARCH ABSTRACT

Finkelhor, David, and Linda Meyer Williams. "Characteristics of Incestuous Fathers." Report given to the National Center of Child Abuse and Neglect. Tucson, AZ, 1992.

Finkelhor, David, and Linda Meyer Williams. *Toward A Typology of Incestuous Fathers.* Research Abstract, 1994.

Finkelhor, David, and Linda Meyer Williams. "Paternal Caregiving and Incest: Test of a Biosocial Model." *American Journal of Orthopsychiatry* 65, no. 1 (January 1995): 101–13.

Rape

Beneke, Timothy. *Men on Rape: What They Have to Say about Sexual Violence.* New York: St. Martin's Press, 1982.

Brownmiller, Susan. *Against Our Wills: Men, Women, and Rape.* New York: Simon & Schuster, 1975.

Russell, Diana. *Rape in Marriage.* New York: Macmillan, 1982.

ARTICLES

Browne, A., and D. Finkelhor, "Impact of Childhood Sexual Abuse: A Review of the Research." *Psychological Bulletin* 99 (1), 1986: 66–77.

Vanderbilt, Heidi. "Incest: A Four-Part Chilling Report." *Lear's,* February 1992: 49–77.

Male Sexual Abuse

Lew, Mike. *Victims No Longer: Men Recovering from Incest and Other Sexual Child Abuse.* New York: Harper and Row, 1990.

Grubman-Black, Stephen D. *Broken Boys, Mending Men: Recovery from Childhood Sexual Abuse.* TAB: 1990.

Thomas, T. *Men Surviving Incest: A Male Survivor Shares on the Process of Recovery.* Launch Press, 1989.

Abusive Religion

Booth, L. *Breaking the Chains: Understanding Religious Addiction and Religious Abuse.* Long Beach: Emmaus Publications, 1989.

Capps, Donald. *The Child's Song. The Religious Abuse of Children.* Louisville: Westminster/John Knox Press. 1995.

Enroth, Ronald. *Recovering from Churches that Abuse.* Grand Rapids, MI: Zondervan Publishing House, 1994.

Healing the Wounds of Incest and Sexual Abuse

Bass, Ellen, and Laura Davis. *The Courage to Heal: A Guide for Women Survivors of Child Sexual Abuse.* New York: Perennial Press, 1988.

Bear, Evan, with Peter Dimock. *Adults Molested as Children: A Survivor's Manual for Women and Men*. Orwell, VT: The Safer Society Press, 1988.

Bradshaw, John. *Healing the Shame That Binds You*. Deerfield Beach, Fla.: Health Communications, 1988.

Courtois, Christine. *Healing the Incest Wound: Adult Survivors in Therapy*. New York: W. W. Norton, 1988.

Cage, Richard, and S. Sgroi, eds. *Vulnerable Populations: Evaluation and Treatment of Sexually Abused Children and Adult Survivors*. New York: Free Press, 1989.

Bass, Ellen, and Laura Davis. *The Courage to Heal: A Guide for Women Survivors of Child Sexual Abuse*. New York, Harper and Row, 1988.

———. *Allies in Healing*. San Francisco: HarperCollins, 1991.

Dolan, Yvonne M. *Resolving Sexual Abuse: Solution-Focused Therapy and Eriksonian Hypnosis for Adult Survivors*. New York: W. W. Norton, 1991.

Flanigan, Beverly. *Forgiving the Unforgivable: Overcoming the Bitter Legacy of Intimate Wounds*. New York: Macmillian, 1992.

Love, Patricia. *The Emotional Incest Syndrome*. New York: Bantam Books, 1991.

Maltz, Wendy, and Beverly Holman. *Incest and Sexuality: A Guide to Understanding and Healing*. Lexington, MA: Lexington Books, 1987.

Meiselman, Karin C. *Incest: A Psychological Study of Causes and Effects with Treatment Recommendations*. San Francisco: Jossey-Bass, 1978.

Miller, Alice. *Banished Knowledge: Facing Childhood Injuries*. Garden City, NY: Anchor Press, Doubleday, 1991.

———. *Thou Shalt Not Be Aware: Society's Betrayal of the Child*. New York: Farrar, Straus & Giroux, 1984.

Wisechild, Louise. *The Obsidian Mirror: An Adult Healing from Incest*. Seattle: Seal Press, 1988.

Abuse and Religion: Resources for the Ministry of Healing

Allender, Dan. *The Wounded Heart: Hope for Adult Victims of Childhood Sexual Abuse*. Colorado Springs, CO: Navpress, 1990.

Clark, Ave. *Lights in The Darkness: For Survivors and Healers of Sexual Abuse*. Mineola, NY: Resurrection Press, 1993.

Foote, Catherine. *Survivor Prayers: Talking with God about Childhood Sexual Abuse*. Louisville: Westminster/John Knox Press, 1994.

Kimble, Dorothy Wilson. *Ministering to Adult Survivors of Child Sexual Abuse*. Bethesda, MD: Alban Institute.

New England Yearly Meeting. *Addressing Sexual Abuse in Friends Meetings*. Philadelphia: Friends General Conference, 1994.

Norberg, Tilda. *Threadbear: A Story of Christian Healing for Adult Survivors of Sexual Abuse*. New York: Penn House Press, 1997.

Patton, John. *Is Human Forgiveness Possible? A Pastoral Care Perspective*. Nashville: Abingdon, 1985.

Pellauer, Mary D., Barbara Chester, and Jane Boyajian. *Sexual Assault and Abuse: A Handbook for Clergy and Religious Professionals*. San Francisco: HarperSanFrancisco, 1991.

Seldmeth, Joan, and M. W. Finley. *We Weep for Ourselves and Our Children*. San Francisco: Harper, 1990. (A book for survivors who are struggling for their faith.)

Sexual Abuse: Religion Bearing Responsibility

Brown Carlson, Joanne, and Carole R. Bohn, eds. *Christianity, Patriarchy and Abuse*. Cleveland: Pilgrim Press, 1989.

Cooper-White, Pamela, *The Cry of Tamar*. Minneapolis: Fortress Press, 1995.

Fortune, Marie. *Sexual Violence: The Unmentionable Sin.* Cleveland: Pilgrim Press, 1983.

Heggen, Carolyn Holderread. Abuse *in Christian Homes and Churches.* Scottdale, PA: Herald Press, 1993.

Horton, Anne L., and Judith A. Williamson. *Abuse and Religion: When Praying Isn't Enough.* Lexington, MA: D. C. Heath, 1988.

Imbens, Annie, and Ineke Jonker. *Christianity and Incest.* Trans. Patricia McVay. Minneapolis: Fortress Press, 1991.

Poling, James Newton. *The Abuse of Power: A Theological Problem.* Nashville: Abingdon Press, 1991.

Violence in Society

Comstock, Gary David. *Violence against Lesbians and Gay Men.* New York: Columbia University Press. 1991.

Eron, Leonard D., Jacquelyn Gentry, and Peggy Schlegel, eds. *Reason to Hope: A Psychosocial Perspective on Violence and Youth.* Hyattsville, MD: American Psychological Association, 1994.

Finkelhor, David. *Stopping Family Violence.* Beverly Hills: Sage Publications, 1988.

Fortune, Marie. *Violence in the Family.* Cleveland: Pilgrim Press.

Levinson, David. *Family Violence in Cross-Cultural Perspective.* Beverly Hills, CA: Sage Publications, 1989.

Pagelow, Mildred Daley. *Family Violence.* New York: Prager Publishers, 1984.

Reiss, Albert J., Jr., and Jeffrey A. Roth, eds., *Understanding and Preventing Violence.* Washington, DC: National Academy Press, 1993.

Winters, Mary. *Laws against Sexual and Domestic Violence.* Cleveland: Pilgrim Press, 1988.

Violence against Women

Adams, Carol J. *Woman-Battering.* Minneapolis: Fortress Press, 1994.

Celani, David. The *Illusion of Love: Why the Battered Woman Returns to Her Abuser.* New York: Columbia University Press, 1994.

Koss, Mary, Lisa Goodman, Louise Fitzgerald, Nancy Felipe Russo, Gwendolyn Puryear Keita, and Angela Browne. *No Safe Haven: Male Violence against Women at Home, at Work, and in the Community.* Hyattsville, MD: American Psychological Association, 1994.

Schechter, Susan. *Women and Male Violence: The Visions and Struggles of the Battered Women's Movement.* Boston: South End Press, 1982.

Walker, Lenore. *The Battered Woman.* New York: Harper & Row, 1979.

———. *Abused Women and Survivor Therapy: A Practical Guide for the Psychotherapist.* Hyattsville, MD: American Psychological Association, 1994.

White, Evelyn C. *Chain, Chain Change: For Black Women Dealing with Physical and Emotional Abuse.* Seattle: Seal Press, 1985.

Treating Men Who Batter

Bathrick, Dick, Kathleen Carlin, Gus Kaufman, and Rich Vodde. *Men Stopping Violence: A Program for Change.* Men Stopping Violence. 1020 DeKalb Ave., Atlanta, GA 30307.

Caesar, P. Lynn, and L. Kevin Hamberger, eds. *Treating Men Who Batter: Theory, Practice, and Programs.* New York: Springer, 1989.

JOURNAL ARTICLES AND UNPUBLISHED MATERIAL

"Signs to Look for in a Battering Personality," Project for Victims of Family Violence, P.O. Box 2915, Fayetteville, Arkansas.

Violence against Children

Boswell, John. *The Kindness of Strangers: The Abandonment of Children in Western Europe from Late Antiquity to the Renaissance.* New York: Pantheon Books, 1988.

Greven, Philip. *Spare the Child: The Religious Roots of Punishment and Psychological Impact of Physical Abuse.* New York: Vintage Books, 1990.

Miller, Alice. *Breaking Down the Wall of Silence.* New York: Dutton, 1991.

Resources for Ministry to Violent Families and Survivors of Physical Abuse

Angelico, Jack C. *A Moral Emergency: Breaking the Cycle of Child Sexual Abuse.* New York: Sheed and Ward, 1993.

Bussert, J. M. K. *Battered Women: From a Theology of Suffering to an Ethic of Empowerment.* New York: Division for Mission in North America, Lutheran Church in America, 1986.

Clarke, R. L. *Pastoral Care of Battered Women.* Philadelphia: Westminster Press, 1986.

Fortune, Marie, and Denise Hormann. *Family Violence: A Workshop Manual for Rural Communities.* Seattle: Center for the Prevention of Sexual and Domestic Violence, 1980.

Fortune, Marie. *Violence in Families: A Workshop Curriculum for Clergy and Other Helpers.* New York: Pilgrim Press, 1991.

Grayson, Curt, and Jan Johnson. *Creating A Safe Place: Christians Healing from the Hurt of Dysfunctional Families.* San Francisco: HarperSanFrancisco, 1991.

Halsey, Peggy. *Abuse in the Family: Breaking the Church's Silence.* New York: United Methodist Church Office of Women in Crisis, 1984.

Leehan, James. *Pastoral Care for Survivors of Family Abuse.* Louisville: Westminster/John Knox Press, 1989.

———. *Defiant Hope: Spirituality for Survivors of Family Abuse.* Louisville: Westminster/John Knox Press, 1994.

Lester, Andrew. *Pastoral Care with Children in Crisis.* Louisville: Westminster/John Knox Press, 1985.

Miller, Melissa. *Family Violence: The Compassionate Church Response.* Waterloo, Ontario: Herald Press, 1994.

NiCarthy, Ginny, and Sue Davidson. *You Can Be Free: An Easy-to-Read Handbook for Abused Women.* Seattle: Seal Press, 1989.

ARTICLE

Bowker, L. H. "Battered Women and the Clergy: An Evaluation," *Journal of Pastoral Care* 34 (April 1982): 226–35.

Resiliency of Some Abused People

Higgins, Gina O'Connell. Resilient Adults: Overcoming a Cruel Past. San Francisco, CA: Jossey-Bass, 1994.

Wollin, Steven J., M.D., and Sybil Wollin, Ph.D. *The Resilient Self: How Survivors of Troubled Families Rise above Adversity.* New York: Villard Books, 1994.

Vaillant, George. *The Wisdom of the Ego.* Cambridge: Harvard University Press, 1993.

IV: Our Changing Ways

Chapter Ten: Tending Yourself

Stress and the Caregiver: Help for Professional Burnout
Freudenberger, H. J. *Burnout: The High Cost of Achievement*. Garden City, NY: Anchor Press, 1980.
Gilbert, Barbara. *Who Ministers to Ministers?: A Study of Support Systems for Clergy and Spouses*. Bethesda, MD: Alban Institute.
Goode, C. Welton. *A Soul under Siege: Surviving Clergy Depression*. Louisville: Westminster/John Knox Press, 1991.
Grosch, William, and David Olsen. *When Helping Starts to Hurt*. New York: W. W. Norton, 1993.
Hahn, Celia A. *Especially for Women: The Best of Action Information* (for women in ministry). Bethesda, MD: Alban Institute.
Hands, Donald R., and Wayne Fehr. *Spiritual Wholeness for Clergy: A New Psychology of Intimacy with God, Self, and Others*. Bethesda, MD: Alban Institute.
Harbaugh, Gary L. *Caring for the Caregiver: Growth Models for Professional Leaders and Congregations*. Bethesda, MD: Alban Institute.
Hover, Margot. *Caring for Yourself While Caring for Others*. Mystic, CT: Twenty-Third Publications, 1993.
Maslach, C. *Burnout: The High Cost of Caring*. Englewood Cliffs, NJ: Anchor Press, 1982.
Oswald, Roy. *How to Build a Support System for Your Ministry*. Bethesda, MD: Alban Institute.
————. *Clergy Self-Care: Finding a Balance for Effective Ministry*. Bethesda, MD: Alban Institute.
Sanford, John. *Ministry Burnout*. Louisville: Westminster/John Knox Press, 1992 (reissue).
Shawchuck, Norman, and Roger Heuser. *Leading the Congregation: Caring for Self While Leading Others*. Nashville: Abingdon Press. 1993.
Weiser, Conrad. *Healers — Harmed and Harmful*. Minneapolis: Fortress Press, 1994.

Stress: A Response to Change in Religious Institutions
Jenkins, Michael, and Deborah Bradshaw Jenkins. *Power and Change in Parish Ministry: Reflections on the Cure of Souls*. Bethesda, MD: Alban Institute.
Nuechtertein, Anne Marie, and Celia Allison Hahn. *The Male-Female Church Staff: Celebrating the Gifts, Confronting the Challenges*. Bethesda, MD: Alban Institute.
Nuechtertein, Anne Marie. *Improving Your Multiple Staff Ministry*. Minneapolis: Augsburg Fortress, 1989.
Pohly, Kenneth. *Transforming the Rough Places: The Ministry of Supervision*. Dayton: Whaleprings, 1993.
Randall, Robert. *The Eternal Triangle: Pastor, Spouse, and Congregation*. Minneapolis: Fortress Press, 1992.
Schaper, Donna. *Common Sense about Men and Women in Ministry*. Bethesda, MD: Alban Institute.

Ministry: Professional Ethics and Responsible Practice
Code of Ethics. American Association of Pastoral Counselors, 950A Lee Highway, Fairfax VA 22031-2303.
Bullis, Ronald K., and Cynthia S. Mazur. *Legal Issues and Religious Counseling*. Louisville: Westminster/John Knox Press, 1993.
Calfee, Barbara, J. D. *Lawsuit, Prevention Techniques for Mental Health Professionals, Chemical Dependency Specialists, Clergy*. Cleveland: ARC Publishing Co., 1992.

Couser, Richard B. *Ministry and the American Legal System: A Guide for Clergy, Lay Workers, and Congregations*. Minneapolis: Fortress Press, 1993.

Fortune, Marie. *Love Does No Harm*. New York: Continuum, 1995.

Kalichman, Seth. *Mandated Reporting of Suspected Child Abuse: Ethics, Law, and Policy*. Hyattsville, MD: American Psychological Association, 1995.

Heyward, Carter. *When Boundaries Betray Us*. San Francisco: HarperCollins, 1993.

Lebacqz, Karen. *Professional Ethics: Power and Paradox*. Nashville: Abingdon, 1985.

Liberman, Aaron, and Michael J. Woodruff. *Risk Management*. Minneapolis: Fortress Press, 1993.

Noyce, Gaylord. *Professional Responsibilities of the Clergy: Pastoral Ethics*. Nashville: Abingdon, 1988.

Ragsdale, Katherine Hancock, ed. *Boundary Wars: Intimacy and Distance in Healing Relationships*. Cleveland: Pilgrim Press, 1996.

Rankin, W. W. *Confidentiality and Clergy: Churches, Ethics and the Law*. Harrisburg: Morehouse Publishers, 1990.

Thompsett, Fredrica Harris. *Courageous Incarnation: In Intimacy, Work, Childhood, and Aging*. Cambridge, MA: Cowley Publications, 1993.

Wiest, Walter, and Elwyn A. Smith. *Ethics in Ministry: A Guide for the Professional*. Minneapolis: Fortress Press, 1990.

Ministry: Sexual Ethics and the Sexual Revolution

Barnhouse, Ruth Tiffany. *Clergy and the Sexual Revolution*. Bethesda, MD: Alban Institute.

Edelwich, J., and A. Brodsky. *Sexual Dilemmas for the Helping Professional*. New York: Brunner/Mazel, 1991.

Hahn, Celia Allison. *Sexual Paradox: Creative Tensions in Our Lives and Congregations*. Cleveland: Pilgrim Press, 1991.

Nelson, James, and Sandra Longfellow, eds. *Sexuality and the Sacred: Sources for Theological Reflection*. Louisville: Westminster/John Knox Press, 1994.

Clergy Sexual Misconduct, Its Ramifications, and Prevention

Fortune, Marie. *Is Nothing Sacred? When Sex Invades the Pastoral Relationship*. San Francisco: Harper & Row, 1989.

Fortune, Marie, and James Poling. *Sexual Abuse by Clergy*. Journal of Pastoral Care Publications.

Hopkins, Nancy Meyer, ed. *Clergy Sexual Misconduct: A Systems Perspective*. Bethesda, MD: Alban Institute.

———. *The Congregation Is Also a Victim: Sexual Abuse and Violation of Personal Trust*. Bethesda, MD: Alban Institute.

Lebacqz, Karen, and Ronald G. Barton. *Sex in the Parish*. Louisville: Westminster/John Knox Press, 1991.

Poling, James. *The Abuse of Power: A Theological Problem*. Nashville: Abingdon Press, 1991.

Rutter, Peter. *Sex in the Forbidden Zone: When Men in Power — Therapists, Doctors, Clergy, Teachers, and Others — Betray Women's Trust*. Los Angeles: Jeremy P. Tarcher, 1989.

Underwood, Anne. *Considerations for Conducting an Investigation of Alleged Clergy Sexual Misconduct*. Bethesda, MD: Alban Institute.

———. *An Attorney Looks at the Secular Foundation for Clergy Sexual Misconduct Policies*. Bethesda, MD: Alban Institute.

UNPUBLISHED PAPER AND REFERENCE MATERIALS

The Church Insurance Company. *Sexual Misconduct Reference Materials*, 1994.

Schoener, Gary R. "Assessment, Rehabilitation and Supervision of Clergy Who Have Engaged in Sexual Boundary Violations." Paper presented at the Instruments of Thy Peace Conference sponsored by the House of Bishops of the Episcopal Church, St. Paul, Minnesota, November 12, 1996.

ARTICLE
Capps, Donald. "Sex in the Parish: Social-Scientific Explanations for Why It Occurs," *Journal of Pastoral Care* 47, no. 4 (Winter 1993): 356.

Ministry and Social Ethics
Browning, Donald. The *Moral Context of Pastoral Counseling*. Philadelphia: Westminster Press, 1976.
Lebacqz, Karen. *Justice in an Unjust World*. Minneapolis: Augsburg Press, 1987.
James P. Wind, Russell Burck, Paul F. Camenisch, and Dennis P. McCann, eds. *Clergy Ethics in a Changing Society*. Louisville: Westminster/John Knox Press, 1991.
Task Force on Gay/Lesbian Issues. *Homosexuality and Social Justice*. San Francisco: The Consultation on Homosexuality, Social Justice, and Roman Catholic Theology, 1986.

ARTICLE
Clarke, Katherine M. "Lessons from Feminist Therapy for Ministerial Ethics," *Journal of Pastoral Care* (Fall 1994): 233–44.

Scriptures, Poetry, Literature
Appleton, George, ed. *The Oxford Book of Prayer*. Oxford, New York: Oxford University Press, 1985.
Book of Common Prayer, According to the Use of The Episcopal Church. Church Hymnal Corporation and Seabury Press. Kingsport, TN: Kingsport Press, 1977.
Berry, Wendell. *Collected Poems 1957–82*. New York: North Point Press, Farrar, Straus and Giroux, 1984.
Brussat, Frederic and Mary Ann Brussat. *Spiritual Literacy: Reading the Sacred in Everyday Life*. New York: Scribner, 1996.
Carmines, Alvin A. "God of Change and Glory." Hymn written for United Methodist Women, 1973.
Dickinson, Emily. *The Complete Poems of Emily Dickinson*. Boston: Little, Brown and Co., 1960.
Dillard, Annie. *Teaching a Stone to Talk*. New York: Harper & Row, 1982.
Doyle, Brendan. *Meditations with Julian of Norwich*. Santa Fe: Bear and Co., 1983.
Griffin, Susan. *A Chorus of Stones*. New York: Anchor Books, 1992.
Marks, Susan, and Eve F. Roshevsky. *Covenant of the Heart*. Women of Reform Judaism, 838 Fifth Avenue, New York, NY 10021.
Mitchell, Stephen. *A Book of Psalms*. New York: HarperCollins, 1993.
Murillo, Rosario. "I'm going to plant my heart in the earth" in *Vulcan Poems from Central America*, ed. Alejandro Muguia and Barbara Paschce. San Francisco: City Lights Books, 1983.
Roberts, Elizabeth, and Elias Amidon, eds. *Earth Prayers*. San Francisco: HarperSanFrancisco, 1991.
Stein, Gertrude. *Everybody's Autobiography*. New York: Vintage Books, Random House, 1937.
Tao Te Ching. Stephen Mitchell, Trans. New York: Harper Perennial, 1991. (Hardcover, Harper Row, 1988.)
Woods, Nancy. *Many Winters*. New York: Doubleday for Young Readers, 1974.

Index

To come.